Renegotiating Patriarchy
Gender, Agency
and the Bangladesh Paradox

Naila Kabeer

LSE Press

Published by
LSE Press
10 Portugal Street
London WC2A 2HD
press.lse.ac.uk

Text © Naila Kabeer 2024

First published 2024

Cover design by Diana Jarvis

Cover image: Women in Subarnachar, Noakhali, Bangladesh, 2024.
Photograph by Jannatul Mawa

Print and digital versions typeset by Siliconchips Services Ltd.

ISBN (Paperback): 978-1-911712-22-0
ISBN (PDF): 978-1-911712-23-7
ISBN (EPUB): 978-1-911712-24-4
ISBN (Mobi): 978-1-911712-25-1

DOI: https://doi.org/10.31389/lsepress.rpg

The full text of this book has been peer-reviewed to ensure high academic
standards. For our full publishing ethics policies, see https://press.lse.ac.uk

Suggested citation:
Kabeer, Naila (2024) *Renegotiating Patriarchy: Gender, Agency
and the Bangladesh Paradox*, London: LSE Press.
https://doi.org/10.31389/lsepress.rpg. License: CC BY-NC 4.0

To read the free, open access version of this book online, visit
https://doi.org/10.31389/lsepress.rpg or scan this QR code with your mobile
device:

This book is dedicated to the memory of Simeen Mahmud (1950–2018): friend, collaborator and a very special human being.

Renegotiating Patriarchy is a major contribution to the literature on gender inequality. Kabeer shows how and why a deeply entrenched form of 'classic patriarchy' has been radically transformed through the interplay between women's agency and structural opportunities in recent Bangladeshi history. The book is cogently argued and lucidly written. It is also an inspiration to women and all others who need to see that large-scale structural transformation is possible.

Sherry B. Ortner, Distinguished Research Professor
of Anthropology, University of California, Los Angeles (UCLA)

In *Renegotiating Patriarchy*, Naila Kabeer offers optimism to the sometimes discouraging field of development studies. She draws on years of creative thought, systematic analysis and careful fieldwork in Bangladesh to show that positive social change can outpace economic growth, overcome bad government, and address cultural resistance. This happens when women have agency to change their lives, their families, their communities, and the everyday practices of their work and livelihoods. This is a book I will recommend to students for years to come and that colleagues should celebrate.

Craig Calhoun, University Professor of Social Sciences
at Arizona State University, Former President
of the Social Science Research Council, US

A brilliant and powerful book that gives voice to ordinary Bangladeshi women, a welcome antidote to 'top-down' theories of development that shines a light on the crucial role that women play in how social change actually happens.

Monica Ali CBE, author of *Brick Lane* and *Love Marriage*

In the decades after independence in 1971, Bangladesh was widely dubbed 'a basket case' in terms of its development prospects. Its adverse geographical conditions, desperate poverty, corrupt state apparatus, political instability, and apparent drift away from democracy gave rise to the gloomiest predictions. Yet since this inauspicious start and despite ongoing problems, including the steady rise of a particularly orthodox version of Islam in public life, which might be thought likely to hold back women's contribution, Bangladesh has made impressive progress in many areas of the Millennium Development Goals. Achievement in the teeth of so many odds, the Bangladesh Paradox, is the topic of Naila Kabeer's scholarly but accessible monograph. An expert on Bangladesh, Kabeer uses her own extensive ethnographic research, along with other quantitative and qualitative evidence to document not only

Bangladesh's surprising performance but the even more astonishing fact that growth has been both pro-poor and pro-women. While acknowledging the importance of structural and institutional factors in this astonishing story, Kabeer's emphasis is on the ways in which ordinary men and (particularly) women negotiated social and cultural constraints to respond to new opportunities for themselves and their children, thus remaking their world and their lives. Any researcher interested in the interaction between structure and agency and the ways in which individuals can and do effect change will benefit from reading this fine book.

Jane Humphries, Centennial Professor
at the London School of Economics and Political Science

Bangladesh was once seen as the textbook case study of a country that was impoverished, over-populated and highly patriarchal, with very little hope of improvement in the foreseeable future. It has now become the textbook case study of a country that defied the odds, making progress on what matters most: the health, wellbeing and education of its people. There have been various attempts to explain what has been termed the Bangladesh paradox. They touch mainly on the significant contributions of various institutional actors – the state, Grameen Bank, NGOs, donors, the private sector and so on. Naila Kabeer, in this well-researched book, takes a different tack. Drawing on her own work and on ethnographic studies, life histories and personal narratives carried out by others, she argues that it was the aspirations and actions of ordinary people responding to the changing circumstances of their lives that was the driving force behind the Bangladesh paradox. Furthermore, she uses these narratives to tease out the important role that women played in bringing about these changes, how their experiences of discrimination in their own lives gave them the courage to seek to carve out a better life for their daughters.

Professor Muhammad Yunus,
recipient of the Nobel Peace Prize 2006

In contrast to recent attempts to explain the 'Bangladesh paradox' that have relied on top-down perspectives and have attributed this remarkable accomplishment to NGOs, foreign donors, or the Bangladeshi government, Naila Kabeer draws our attention to the voices and activities of the impoverished village women who have been the target of much national and international policymaking. Drawing on her considerable body of research in the villages and factories of Bangladesh and the scholarship of colleagues on related topics, Kabeer is able to highlight changes over a span of several decades in rural Bangladeshi women's own ideas of acceptable and necessary behaviour. She draws important conclusions about the relationship between such ideas and the material world that shapes these ideas and is at the same time shaped by them.

Elora Shehabuddin, Professor, Gender & Women's Studies and Global Studies; Director, Chowdhury Center for Bangladesh Studies, University of California, Berkeley

Anyone wanting to understand the surprising 'Bangladesh paradox' must read Naila Kabeer's elegant, nuanced, and convincing analysis of its multiple roots and uncertain future. Kabeer's study is based on critical scrutiny of an impressive body of varied evidence. It shows why a weak economy, poor governance, and the rise of religious orthodoxy formed no obstacle to felicitous changes in fertility behaviour, girls' education, women's paid employment, and gender and generational kinship relations. Donor, government and NGO interventions were important prerequisites, but Naila Kabeer argues compellingly that it was ordinary women across the country who were the primary architects of these key habitus changes.

Willem van Schendel, University of Amsterdam and International Institute of Social History

In this fascinating account, Naila Kabeer tells the story of how Bangladesh scored impressive social and economic gains in the half century since independence, defying predictions that the country would be an 'international basket case'. She makes a persuasive case that the resourcefulness of ordinary people was crucial in this result, and that profound changes in women's lives and livelihoods played a central role in the process. This book is a must-read for anyone who wants to learn more about how 'development' really happens.

James K. Boyce, Political Economy Research Institute, University of Massachusetts Amherst

Bangladesh has puzzled many for a long time with its rapid strides in human development against heavy odds. Naila Kabeer hits the nail on the head with an account of the story that puts gender relations and women's agency at the centre of the stage.

Jean Drèze, Honorary Professor, Delhi School of Economics

This is a mature work that combines analytical rigour with empirical wealth, meticulously unpicking the complex array of influences explaining the 'Bangladesh paradox'. It complements the more conventional 'big picture' approaches with a uniquely powerful 'bottom-up' account of ordinary people's changing experiences, placing women's agency at the centre of the narrative. This is a must read for anyone interested in development theory and policy, and in gender relations in South Asia.

Deniz Kandiyoti, Emeritus Professor of Development Studies, School of Oriental and African Studies

Kabeer's volume is a most welcome and significant addition to a long-standing debate on Bangladesh's development and processes of social and cultural change. Offering a long temporal lens and rich evidentiary material from multiple researchers, she calls for a critical reading of the Bangladesh paradox. More broadly, her critical reading of this paradox invites a rethinking of the processes of change, one that is grounded in people's actual lived experience. While acknowledging the structural and institutional reorganization of the country's economy and culture, she advances an innovative analysis of the formation of new social relations and subjectivities. Such a focus exposes the rich terrain of agency, experience, and, importantly, the power of women's negotiation with patriarchy, not only as a critical basis for increasing gender equality, but, also, as a challenge to popular explanations of the Bangladesh paradox rooted in the western imagination.

Shelley Feldman, International Professor (1987–2016), Cornell University

Bangladesh provides a fascinating story of achieving rapid progress in many social development indicators, defying formidable odds and gloomy predictions of early years. The phenomenon is yet to be fully understood despite a growing literature on what is now often called a development puzzle or a paradox. While some analysts have pointed to the role of female agency as a dominant contributing factor, this begs the question as to why such agency has worked so well particularly in a patriarchal society that represses women. This book fills this gap in our understanding of the so-called Bangladesh paradox as well as being an important addition to gender and poverty studies generally.

Wahiduddin Mahmud, Former Professor of Economics, University of Dhaka

Contents

About the author

Naila Kabeer (FAcSS) is Professor of Gender and Development in the Department of International Development at the London School of Economics and Political Science (LSE) and on the faculty of the International Inequalities Institute at LSE. She has carried out several years of interdisciplinary research on gendered inequalities in relation to labour markets, livelihoods, social protection and collective action. Her publications include *Reversed Realities: Gender Hierarchies in Development Thought* (Verso), *The Power to Choose: Bangladeshi Women and Labour Market Decision-Making in London and Dhaka* (Verso) and *Mainstreaming Gender and Social Protection in the Informal Economy* (Commonwealth Secretariat). She has worked in an advisory capacity with a number of international and bilateral agencies as well as national and international non-governmental organisations. She is on the editorial boards of *Feminist Economics* and *Gender and Development* and on the international advisory boards of *Development and Change* and the *Canadian Journal of Development Studies*. She is also on the advisory boards of the United Nations Research on Social Development (UNRISD) and the United Nations University – Institute for Global Health and has recently joined the UN Women's Leaders Network.

Acknowledgements

The idea for this book had been gestating for a while but I was only able to make a proper start on it in September 2019, when I was given a sabbatical by the two departments at the London School of Economics and Political Science to which I was jointly affiliated: Gender Studies and International Development. I was very grateful for it but in March 2020 the whole world came to a halt as we went into the extraordinary two years of the COVID-19 lockdown. Many people I know used that period to write memoirs of various kinds – their own or those of their families or someone they admired. This book too can be seen as a kind of memoir – about a country that has been, and continues to be, an important part of my personal life and about the research I have undertaken in it over my professional life, starting with my PhD in the late 1970s.

There are therefore far too many people whose help I have benefited from over these years to include in these acknowledgements. I am confining myself to those who I have collaborated with in the more recent research projects that feature in this book and to those who have given helpful comments on various chapters of the book.

First, I would like to acknowledge how much I have benefited from my association with the BRAC Institute of Governance and Development (BIGD), Bangladesh, which provided me with an academic home from home whenever I worked in Bangladesh. Particularly special to me was my long-standing collaboration with Simeen Mahmud, lead scholar at the Institute, till she died far too early in April 2018. We had many years of thinking ideas through together, agreeing on many things, disagreeing on a few, conceptualising and implementing projects together and co-authoring several articles together. This book is dedicated to her memory.

I want to thank Dr Imran Matin, Director of Research at BIGD, who made it an extremely hospitable environment for the kind of collaborative research that I wanted to pursue. I have benefited from the support of various kinds, intellectual, technical and logistic, provided by BIGD's team of researchers. There has been a solid core of people who have been part of the research and ideas that have gone into this book. I owe a great deal to Lopita Huq, who builds the kind of rapport in the field that makes for very rich qualitative research and who I have worked and written with a great deal over the years. I have also benefited from my collaborations with Dr Munshi Sulaiman, a skilled quantitative researcher with an appreciation of the contributions of qualitative research.

Other longer-term associates include Maheen Sultan, Sohela Nazneen and Kabita Chowdhury. I also want to thank Sakiba Tasneem, Mahbubur Rahaman, Sufia Khatun, Sanjida Parvin, Saklain Al Mamun, Hossen Khan, Md. Kamruz-zaman, Sadia Mustafa, A.I. Sudin and the late Saiful Islam.

Beyond the orbit of the BIGD are various people who were involved in many different ways in the research that has gone into this book, discussing ideas, pointing me towards useful material, and offering insights that sharpened what I wanted to say: Deniz Kandiyoti (a major influence on this work), Wahid Mahmud, Sajeda Amin, Naomi Hossain (whose take on the Bangladesh paradox I found extremely helpful), Sara Hossain, Rani YanYan, Tahera Yasmin Huq, Samia Khatun, Alaka Basu, Sarah Ashwin, Jo Beall, Ashwini Deshpande, Meghna Guhathakurta, Navsharan Singh, Rajni Palriwala, Mary John, Binayak Sen, Hossain Zillur Rahman, Tasneem Azim, Sarah White, and my life-long friends and interlocutors, Khushi Kabir, Shireen Huq and Ameerah Haq.

I owe a huge debt of gratitude to those who read and gave comments on earlier chapters – Wendy Forrest and Ayesha Khan – and even more to those who read the full draft – David Lewis, Hilary Standing, Olivia Marchant and of course the external reviewers whose comments were invaluable. I owe special thanks to the wonderful team at LSE Press for their support and particular thanks to Alice Park, whose careful and sympathetic reading of an unwieldy earlier draft helped me to shape the book into a more manageable form.

This book draws on a number of research projects that were carried out while I was at the Institute of Development Studies, Sussex, and I benefited from my interactions with various colleagues who were involved with them – Dzodzi Tsikata, Hania Sholkamy, Andrea Cornwall, John Gaventa, Sarah Cook and Anne Marie Goetz. The projects that inform the analysis in this book benefited from different donors but, most prominently, the Department for International Development, UK. DFID funded the Development Research Centre on Citizenship (2000–2010) and the Research Partners Consortium on Pathways of Women's Empowerment (2006–10). The most recent research project I have drawn on is 'Choice, Constraint and the Gender Dynamics of Labour Markets in Bangladesh', jointly funded by the Economic and Social Research Council and the FCDO (Grant ES/L005484/1). I want to also thank the International Development Research Centre, Canada, which provided additional support to the Bangladesh component of the Pathways of Women's Empowerment. This allowed me to return to Amarpur, the village where I had done my fieldwork for my PhD in 1979 and where I first became interested in the questions of son preference and daughter devaluation, key underlying themes of this book.

I want to extend very special thanks to the Rockefeller Foundation, which funded me for a month's residence in 2017 at the magical Bellagio Center in Italy, where I was able to make a start on thinking through the key themes of the book with my wonderful fellow residents. And, finally, I owe a great deal to Chris Leaf, my long-suffering partner, whose heart sinks when I say I am going to write a book because he knows that I will be completely immersed in the process till it is over. But his support is always unwavering.

Glossary and acronyms

Glossary

abhab	scarcity
Ahmadi	a modern Muslim sect
akhirat	afterlife
anchal	edge of sari
ashraf	of noble birth
ajlaf	low-born
apa	older sister
atoor ghar	outside hut where women gave birth
Baidya	an upper Bengali Hindu caste
Baniya	merchant caste
bari	homestead
baul	devotional community
bazaar	fixed marketplace
bhadrolok	respectable people
bigha	0.14 hectare
birangona	war heroine
boodhi	intelligence
burqa	tent-like garment with head covering worn by Muslim women
Chakri	formal job
char	land thrown up by movement of rivers
chotolok	lower class of people
daabi	dowry
ghar	house, household
gram	village
gushti	lineage group
haat	weekly or bi-weekly village market

Hadith	teachings of the Prophet
haram	sinful
hijab	head covering worn by Muslim women
jal	fishing net
jat/jati	caste
imam	mosque leader
kabin nikah	marriage contract
kazi	Islamic scholar
khas land	unused state-owned land
jihad	praiseworthy struggle
jotedar	rich tenant farmer/medium-sized landowner
joutuk	dowry
lakh	one hundred thousand
lathi	cudgel
lungi	men's sarong
madrassa	Islamic school
marfat	Islam doctrine that emphases inner knowledge
mastaans	gangster, muscle men
matabor	village leader or elder
mehr or *mohrana*	sum of money promised to bride by groom's family in Muslim marriage contract
milad	thanksgiving ceremony
muhajirs	immigrant
nawab	title given to ruler or noble
Orna	long scarf
palki	palanquin
para	neighbourhood or hamlet
paribar	family
parishad	council
pati	woven mat
pir	spiritual guide (male)
piranis	spiritual guide (female)
purdah	norm of female seclusion
raiyat	tenant farmer
samaj	local community

samity	association, most often linked with NGO activity in Bangladesh
sardar	village chief or headman
shakti shali	physical strength
shalish	informal council for arbitrating village-level disputes
shalwar kameez	tunic and loose trousers worn by women
sharia/shariat	Islamic scriptural law
sharkar	government
sher	weight measure
sindur	spot on forehead worn by women for religious/cosmetic purposes
taka	Bengali currency
taleem classes	Quranic reading classes
taluk	tax collecting unit
tariqat	Islamic doctrine devoted to pursuit of inner vision
teep	same as *sindur*
thana	old subdistrict, literally police station
tom-tom gari	horse-drawn carriage
umma	Islamic moral community
upazila	new administrative unit since Ershad period: subdistrict level
waz mahfil	lectures by religious scholars
zakat	Islamic duty to pay one-fortieth of income to the poor
zamindar	originally tax collectors, later referred to landlord

Acronyms

AL	Awami League
ASA	Association for Social Advancement
BGMEA	Bangladesh Garments Manufacturers and Exporters Association
BIGD	BRAC Institute of Governance and Development
BRAC	used to be Bangladesh Rural Advancement Committee. Now just BRAC
DFID	Department for International Development, UK government

EPI	Expanded Programme on Immunization
EPZ	export-processing zone
GDP	gross domestic product
ICDDR,B	International Centre for Diarrhoeal Diseases Research, Bangladesh
MDGs	Millennium Development Goals
MFA	Multi Fibre Arrangement
NGO	non-governmental organisation
ORT	oral rehydration therapy (treatment for diarrhoea)
ORW	oral replacement workers – staff of BRAC ORT programme
RMG	ready-made garments
SDGs	Sustainable Development Goals
UNDP	United Nations Development Programme
UNFPA	United Nations Population Fund
UNICEF	United Nations Children's Fund
WHO	World Health Organization
USAID	United States Agency for International Development
VGD	Vulnerable Group Development
VGF	Vulnerable Group Feeding
WFP	World Food Programme

1. Unravelling the paradox: meaning, motivation and methodology

A paradox is 'a person or thing conflicting with preconceived notions of what is reasonable or possible … contrary to accepted opinion'.
(Concise Oxford Dictionary 1983)

A paradox, as the definition above suggests, refers to something that runs contrary to expectations or preconceived ideas. Recurring references to the 'Bangladesh paradox' in the development studies literature are shorthand for the unexpectedness of certain aspects of the country's development experience. Bangladesh has progressed on the social dimensions of development in ways that have not only run contrary to received wisdom in this field but have also confounded the gloomy predictions that accompanied its independence in 1971. Here is one attempt to convey this:

> Would you say that a country was likely to reach any of the Millennium Development Goals if it is affected by adverse geographical conditions, has a state apparatus perceived as chronically corrupt, is subject to substantive political instability and is also perceived as moving away from democracy? No, we would not. Yet, Bangladesh, once famously dubbed a test case for development, has made impressive progress in many areas of the MDGs. This is good news. But the really interesting bit is that progress was achieved against the odds, because many would have predicted otherwise. (Asadullah and Savoia 2018)

In fact, the *really* interesting bit is not only that this progress has been achieved against the odds but that it has been both pro-poor and gender-equitable. In a country that had been described as among the very poorest in the world, with a particularly extreme form of patriarchy, this was another aspect of the paradox: 'Bangladesh stands out as the shining new example in South Asia of a poor country achieving impressive gains in gender equality' (World Bank 2008, p.3).

We can distinguish three dimensions to the Bangladesh paradox. There is an economic dimension, the view that a country needs to accumulate a minimum level of wealth before it sees an improvement in the health and wellbeing of its population. Indeed, some scholars adhere to what Sen (1999) describes as a 'growth-mediated' model of social progress, the idea that economic growth is a *necessary* condition for countries to progress on the social front. Yet Bangladesh has performed better on its social development indicators – and on the gender equality of these indicators – than other countries at similar, and even higher levels, of per capita GDP. It is regarded a 'positive outlier' on the international stage (Asadullah, Savoia and Mahmud 2014).

There is a political dimension, reflecting the argument that the quality of governance in a country can make a difference, that responsive states can steer 'policy-supported' pathways to social progress – sometimes regardless of levels of GDP (Sen 1999). But here, too, Bangladesh has defied expectations. Its state has been widely depicted as corrupt and inefficient, with the politics of clientelism and rent-seeking permeating all levels of government. This has not prevented the country from achieving a pro-poor development trajectory.

Similarly paradoxical, but largely absent from the paradox literature, is that improvements in gender equality began and gathered momentum during a period that saw the steady rise of a particularly orthodox version of Islam in political and public life. The cultural dimension of the paradox derives from the widespread view in the modernisation literature that Islam itself is antithetical to women's emancipation: it is seen as the 'other' of modernity (White 2012). Inglehart and Norris (2003) conclude on the basis of their cross-country analysis of World Values surveys that the 'true clash of civilizations' between Islam and the West was not, as suggested by Huntingdon (1993), over conflicting attitudes to democracy but over conflicting attitudes to gender equality: it was, in other words, a 'sexual clash of civilizations' (p.65).

The country's status as a 'positive outlier' in cross-country comparisons of social progress, its reputation as one of the success stories of the Millennium Development Goals, has clearly attracted a great deal of interest within the international development community. But, for longer-standing scholars of Bangladesh, the unexpectedness of the country's achievements lies less in the comparison with other countries and more in the comparison with its not-so-distant past. They look back to the decade or so following the country's independence in 1971, when it was ranked as one of the poorest countries in the world, when its uncontrolled population growth rates combined with recurring natural and man-made disasters to wipe out any gains it managed to make, appearing to condemn it to be caught forever in a 'below poverty level equilibrium trap'.[1] And they want to know: what went right? How did the country manage to pull itself out of these catastrophic conditions and set itself on the road to a moderate degree of success?

In response to these questions, the literature provides elements of a plausible answer. It explains why a dysfunctional state could still promote equitable policies; it refers to the vibrancy of the country's development NGOs; it notes the role of the donor community that provided generous assistance over the years in exchange for compliance with its advice; it points to the emergence of a dynamic private sector – and it commends the collaboration between these different institutional actors.

But it has largely been a 'big picture' story, the 'view from above'. It tells us a great deal about the beliefs and actions of powerful groups in the society but very little about the role of ordinary people, those who were absent from the established centres of decision-making and largely nameless in the literature. Yet it was the responses of these ordinary people to their changing environment that was the ultimate driving force behind the country's unexpected progress. It is this missing piece of the story that is related in this book.

This book is therefore about a subject that is of perennial interest in the social sciences: how social change happens. But, more than that, it is a story about how change happens in the face of apparently insurmountable barriers. It retells this story as it has been told so far but it takes the 'view from below'. And, for reasons that I explain next, it places women's agency in the processes of change at the heart of the story.

1.1 Women's agency and the Bangladesh paradox

The origins of my interest in this story go back to the late 1970s, when I was doing my PhD at the London School of Economics and Political Science (LSE). I was trying to explain the high rates of fertility that prevailed in the country at the time and that were widely attributed to cultural irrationality on the part of peasants. As someone trained in economics and registered in the Economics Department, I wanted to find out if an economic rationale revolving around the contributions of children to the household economy compared to their costs might have a role to play. It was not, however, the formal rational choice models of neoclassical economics that I found most persuasive but the approaches taken in economic anthropology, suggesting that culture, institutions and social relationships mediated the costs and benefits of children in different contexts. In South Asia, for instance, anthropologists had pointed out that a strong patriarchal culture that marginalised women in the economy had led to forms of gender discrimination so extreme that they were described as the 'endangered sex' (Miller 1983): unlike the rest of the world, female mortality exceeded male almost from birth. In a culture where boys were far more valued than girls, families ended up having more children than they wanted to ensure the survival of a minimum number of sons (Cain, Khanam and Nahar 1979).

Influenced by their approach, I decided I wanted to carry out my own fieldwork and explore these questions for myself. The Economics Department did not encourage primary fieldwork so I shifted to Population Studies and went off to live for 18 months in the village of Amarpur (pseudonym) in Faridpur district. Unfortunately, my training in economics left me with very little idea about how to do ethnographic research. Instead I ended up designing my own surveys to reflect the ideas I had absorbed,[2] although I believe that my time living in the village for over a year gave me a feel for the rhythm of rural life that I would not have otherwise had and a greater appreciation for hands-on research.

Amarpur was similar to many villages in Bangladesh at the time, not as rich as some, not as poor as many. Women had around seven children by the time they had completed childbearing, the same high rates of fertility that prevailed elsewhere in Bangladesh. My survey data confirmed that sons made a greater economic contribution to their families than daughters for reasons discussed in Chapter 5; daughters appeared to be a net liability. In addition, my survey of married women included a series of questions that allowed me to construct 'preference scales' that separated out their desire for large numbers of children from their preference for sons[3] (Kabeer 1986). I will discuss the findings from this early Amarpur research in greater detail in Chapter 9. What is relevant to report at this stage is that they suggested that the high rates of fertility I found in the village were motivated by the desire for sons rather than for large families per se. In other words, they echoed the wider literature on the topic.

After my PhD, I joined the Institute of Development Studies, Sussex. I retained my commitment to field-based research in South Asia, honed my qualitative research skills, and undertook various projects that took me back to the region on a regular basis. I was therefore aware of studies documenting the emergence of what became known as the Bangladesh paradox. An illustration of the paradox was provided by Drèze and Sen (2013) through a comparison of Bangladesh, India and Pakistan, three neighbouring countries in South Asia, using data from 1990 and 2011.[4] These are presented in Table 1 in Appendix 5, supplemented with information from other sources. Drèze and Sen noted India's near-uninterrupted record on democracy since its independence in 1947, in contrast to extended periods of military rule in both Bangladesh and Pakistan. They also noted that Bangladesh lagged behind both India and Pakistan on the economic front: its per capita GDP was lower throughout this period and its levels of poverty higher.[5]

However, in terms of social indicators, Bangladesh began out behind the other two, but at some point after 1990 it had caught up with them and forged ahead:

- Fertility rates declined in all three countries but, while Bangladesh started out with higher rates than the other countries in 1950, they were 2.2 in 2011 compared to 2.6 in India and 3.4 in Pakistan (Bloom, Canning and Rosenberg 2011; Drèze and Sen 2013).
- Broad-based progress in health services and living standards across the region had led to an increase in overall life expectancy in all three countries. Again, Bangladesh had started out with the lowest life expectancy of the three in 1950 but reported a dramatic increase, overtaking India in 2000 and catching up with Pakistan in 2010 (Bloom, Canning and Rosenberg 2011).
- All three countries had reported higher male life expectancy than female in the 1960s. By 2016, female life expectancy had exceeded

male in all three countries, converging with the pattern that prevailed in most countries. The shift began earlier in Bangladesh and went further. By 2011, life expectancy in Bangladesh was 70 for women and 68 for men; it was 67 and 64, respectively, for India and 66 and 64 in Pakistan.[6]

– The story was similar for infant mortality rates. Countries in the South Asia region reported average rates of 168 per 1000 live births in the early 1950s. They had fallen to 53 by 2010 (Bloom, Canning and Rosenberg 2011) but of the three countries, they fell furthest in Bangladesh (Drèze and Sen 2013). By 2011, its infant mortality rates were 37 per 1000 live births compared to 47 in India and 59 in Pakistan.

The picture on gender differentials in child mortality diverged from what was a pattern of progress, albeit an uneven one, in all three countries. Gender differentials remained high in India, leading to some of the highest levels of excess female mortality in the world and a persisting female deficit in the under-five age group (Alkema et al. 2014; Guilmoto et al. 2018, p.e657).[7] In addition, evidence began to emerge of a growing resort to female-selective abortion in India, made possible by the introduction of prenatal diagnostic technologies that could detect the sex of the foetus. By ensuring that more sons were born than daughters, parents were able to combine their desire for fewer children with their continued preference for sons. As a result, not only did excess levels of female mortality persist among children but sex ratios at birth began to rise from what were considered 'normal' levels of 105 male to 100 female births (which prevailed in much of the world) to levels of 111 by 2011, reflecting the malign new strategy of 'death before birth' (Das Gupta and Bhatt 1997; Tong 2022).[8] We will return to possible explanations for this in the concluding chapter.

There seemed to have been some rise in sex ratios at birth in Pakistan after the 1990s, but by no means as dramatic as that in India (Ritchie and Roser 2019; Zaidi and Morgan 2016). In Bangladesh, on the other hand, gender differentials in infant and child mortality had largely disappeared by 2000, while sex ratios at birth remained remarkably constant at the international norm of 105 males to every 100 females.[9]

This decline in older forms of discrimination against girls in Bangladesh, unaccompanied by a rise in the lethal new forms observed in neighbouring India, strongly suggested that a shift had taken place at some fundamental level in its structures of patriarchy, one that had led to a revaluation of daughters in a culture long characterised by strong son preference.

Intrigued by this possibility, I decided to investigate it as part of a larger research project on gender, work and social change in Bangladesh, a collaboration between IDS and the BRAC Institute of Governance and Development (BIGD) in Bangladesh. The project included Amarpur in a survey of women from different districts that we carried out in 2008. The project team returned to Amarpur in 2010 to collect life history narratives from men and women from different generations in order to explore their views about sons and daughters. Once again, I will discuss the findings from the later research in Amarpur in greater detail in Chapter 9 but here I highlight some key ones that helped to shape the analysis in this book.

The first key finding, which was reported by both the survey data and qualitative interviews, was that there had been a decline in fertility rates in Amarpur, mirroring the decline that had taken place in the rest of Bangladesh. There had also been a decline in the preference for large families and an even greater decline in the preference for sons. Most men and women now wanted both sons and daughters, with some even expressing a preference for daughters. The life history narratives confirmed the near-universal shift to the norm of small families documented by the survey data. Also echoing the survey data, they confirmed that there had been a marked shift in favour of balanced sex composition of children.

In addition, their narratives provided an account of how life had been in the past and how it was today. The older generation recalled the immense poverty of the early years of independence and the precarious nature of their lives. Men and women across the generations believed that positive social changes had taken place since that period and clearly saw their own actions as part of this change ('keeping up with the changing times'). They did not describe their role in terms of a purely individual cost–benefit analysis, although costs and benefits did enter into their decisions. Instead, changes at the individual level appeared to be bound up with the changes that were taking place at the societal level, changes that were affecting relationships between men and women, parents and children, individuals and communities.

Finally, interspersed throughout the narratives were direct and indirect references to women's agency as one of the forces behind these changes. There seemed to be a widespread belief that women were taking greater control of their lives (almost *too much* control, in the view of some), that they were using their agency to carve out a better deal for themselves and for their children, and that daughters featured prominently in their aspirations in a way that they had not done in the past. Given that those we were speaking to had been brought up to think and behave in ways that were rooted in the long-standing structures of female subordination that characterised Bangladesh, their accounts offered important insights into how women in Amarpur were being able to renegotiate the terms of what had been described as 'among the least negotiable patriarchies in the world' (Goetz 1992, p.12).

These narratives explain the central role given to women's agency in my account of the Bangladesh paradox. In the rest of this chapter, I discuss the wider literature that provides the theoretical rationale for this focus as well as the broader context of my research. I sketch out a conceptual framework that helps to pull together different pieces of this account and draw out their interconnections. I conclude with a discussion of my methodological approach and a roadmap of the book.

1.2 Gender, economy and demography in the belt of 'classic patriarchy'

Comparative research on the structures of patriarchy since the 1970s has documented systematic regional variations in the organisation of family, kinship and gender relations across the world, a 'geography of gender' (Townsend and Momsen 1987). Of specific relevance to this book is what this research has said about a range of countries stretching from North Africa across the Middle East to the northern plains of South Asia, termed the belt of 'strong' or 'classic' patriarchy (Cain 1984; Kandiyoti 1988). While the countries in question varied considerably in terms of their religions, political regimes and development trajectories, their family and kinship systems had certain features broadly in common, summarised by Caldwell (1978) as 'extended, patrilineal, patrilocal, patriarchal, endogamous and occasionally polygynous' (p.558).

These features gave rise to the forms of gender discrimination that I noted earlier, discrimination so extreme that women in these countries died in larger numbers than men in almost every age group – in marked contrast to the rest of the world, where women generally lived longer than men in different age groups and in the overall population. The results were highly 'masculine' sex ratios in the populations of these countries, ranging anywhere between 106 to 110 or more men to every 100 women compared to the ratios of 100 or fewer men that prevailed elsewhere. Sen (1990a) coined the phrase 'missing women' to refer to the deficit in the number of women that resulted from these lethal forms of discrimination. Estimating it at more than 100 million women globally, he described it as one of the worst human catastrophes of the 20th century.[10]

Family and kinship structures in the belt of classic patriarchy stood in contrast with those prevailing in other regions. For instance, the predominant pattern of kinship and descent in South East Asia was bilateral, with rights of inheritance extended to both men and women; there was relative flexibility in post-marital residence; and women retained ties with their natal kin after marriage. There were also far fewer restrictions on their mobility: they were more likely to be active in the labour force, primarily in agriculture and trade, and hence contributed directly to household production. In sub-Saharan Africa as well, while systems of inheritance and marital practice varied across the region, it was possible for women to either inherit or enjoy use rights to land, while high rates of female labour force participation were common.

These studies provided a broad-brush sketch of geographical variations in patriarchal regimes across developing countries. Detailed research from South Asia offered a more disaggregated picture (Dyson and Moore 1983; Miller 1981; Sopher 1980; Visaria 1961; Visaria 1967). It suggested that the region did not constitute a homogenous bloc, that there were variations in patriarchal regimes within it. In particular, it suggested a north–south pattern to kinship regimes within the Indian context, a pattern so clear that it allowed the country to be divided into two by an east–west diagonal line that followed the contours of the Vindhya hills and the Narmada river valley (Sopher 1980).

Kinship systems north of this divide, referred to as the Indo-Aryan model, displayed many of the features of classic patriarchy, but inflected through the Hindu caste system. The patrilineal system of kinship, which traced descent and inheritance practices through the male child, meant that the gender and paternity of the child were paramount to the reproduction of the patrilineage. Male honour, and the honour of the family, required strict controls over women's sexuality and reproductive behaviour, secluding them within the domestic domain and restricting their participation in the economy.

Caste endogamy, or marriage within the same *jati* (sub-caste) group, ensured the reproduction of the caste hierarchy.[11] At the same time, patrilocal marriage together with strict enforcement of kin and village exogamy meant that spouses were unrelated in terms of kinship and that brides left their natal village after marriage to join their husbands' families, often travelling considerable distances to do so. Marriage among caste Hindus was also hypergamous: women married 'upwards' into a socially and ritually superior status family within their caste hierarchy. The inferiority of 'wife-givers' was signified by the payment of dowry, the transfer of wealth from the bride's family to the groom's, at the time of marriage.[12]

These interlocking practices provided powerful incentives in favour of sons, who were central to the transmission of property, the continuation of the patrilineage and the perpetuation of the caste system. They were active in the economy, brought in dowry when they married, lived with or close to their parents, provided support as they grew older and performed the obligatory funeral rites when they died. Daughters were denied property rights and had to be married off at considerable cost, only to move away from their natal village after marriage, with the result that their productive and reproductive labour was lost to parents.

The limited contribution by daughters, the premium placed on female chastity, and the fact that dowry costs tended to rise with age of marriage put pressure on parents to marry them off at an early age. For the husband's family, young brides were advantageous because they could start bearing children from an early age, increasing the probability of producing male heirs. But, from the bride's perspective, the pressure for early and frequent childbearing to produce the sons on which their status within the family so crucially depended led to high levels of fertility accompanied by high levels of maternal mortality.

Kinship systems to the south of this divide, the Indo-Dravidian model, were more flexible with greater diversity of practice. They allowed for bilateral rules of inheritance so that women could also inherit property, and they were characterised by preferred rather than prescribed forms of marriage, with close-kin marriage the ideal form. Marriage could take place close to the natal home and post-marital residence patterns varied considerably. Women generally married into families that were socially and ritually equal; bridewealth was more common than dowry and marriage expenses were shared between the kin groups of bride and groom. There was less stress on female chastity and fewer controls over women's sexuality and freedom of movement. They were more likely to be active in production outside the home and daughters were as likely as sons to render support to parents as they got older.

As Dyson and Moore (1983) note, these north–south differences gave rise to distinct regional patterns in economic, social and demographic outcomes (Appendix 5, Table 2).[13] Women's literacy and labour force participation rates were lower in the northern states than in the south; they were more likely to be secluded within the home, were married at younger ages, were less likely to use contraception and reported higher rates of fertility. In addition, female mortality rates exceeded male in most age groups so that sex ratios in their overall population were highly masculine, ranging from 106 to 114 males to every 100 females, compared to ratios ranging from 107 to 97 in the southern states. Using an index to measure son preference, where a value of zero would imply equal preference for sons and daughters, Dyson and Moore (1983) found much stronger son preference in the north, where the value of the index ranged from 20.7 to 31.3, than in the south, where values ranged between 8.9 and 18.4.

While their study focused mainly on empirical material from India, they also attempted to locate their kinship typology within the larger Asia region. They suggested that the north Indian system belonged within the 'West Asian' system, what we described as the belt of classic patriarchy, while the south Indian one overlapped with the South East Asian constellation. In other words, the Vindhya–Narmada divide also represented the 'great divide' between two larger sociocultural systems (Miller 1981, p.24).

Dyson and Moore located Sri Lanka within the south Indian kinship system because there was very little evidence of excess female mortality, while Pakistan, with its high fertility rates and excess female mortality, appeared closer to the north Indian system. The eastern regions presented more of a challenge. The smaller states of India's north-eastern promontory were largely populated by indigenous ethnic minorities, 'tribal' peoples, with very different kinship practices to either of the two main paradigms. They clearly represented a distinctive cultural and demographic regime.

The eastern states of Orissa, Bihar and West Bengal, on the other hand, appeared to represent intermediate regimes. They had some elements in common with both the main systems but differed considerably from each other, despite geographical proximity. The prevalence of cross-cousin marriage in Bihar seemed to place it in the south Indian system, although its strong son preference and excess female mortality among children was more characteristic of classic patriarchy. There was greater consistency between kinship and demographic patterns within Orissa and West Bengal. Their marital patterns (cross-cousin marriage in the former case and village endogamy in the latter), lower levels of fertility, weak or absent levels of excess female mortality and lower son preference together suggested closer affinity to the south Indian model.

Bangladesh proved even harder to place. Though Bangladesh and West Bengal had made up the united province of Bengal in pre-partition India, shared a common ethno-linguistic identity, and might be expected to display strong similarities, Dyson and Moore believed that Bangladesh had stronger affinities with the northern kinship and demographic regime. They based this on the rareness of cross-cousin marriage (associated with the south Indian model), early age of marriage among women, their isolated and vulnerable position after joining their husbands' kinship group and high rates of fertility and child mortality (all associated with the north Indian model). They also noted that there had been a shift some time in the second half of the 20th century from the practice of bridewealth at marriage, common among Muslims in the subcontinent, to the practice of dowry, which characterised the north Indian model, suggesting a strengthening of the association with this model. They did, however, notice some uncertainty in the existing literature about whether there was excess female mortality among children in Bangladesh, a hallmark of the north Indian demographic regime. This led them to conclude that the 'situation [was] complicated and by no means analogous in all respects' (p.52).

As Dyson and Moore point out, differences in aspects of kinship and demography between Hindu-majority West Bengal and Muslim-majority Bangladesh appeared to foreground religious differences as part of the explanation. However, they note that the consensus among scholars was that regional variations in kinship systems, demographic regimes and sex ratios across the South Asian subcontinent were of longer historical standing, predating the arrival of Islam on the subcontinent. This suggested that regional differences between the northern Aryan and the southern Dravidian cultural formations were more plausible explanations of the variations in demographic outcomes than religious differences. The practice of Islam varied considerably across the regional divide and appeared to reflect localised social practices (Mandelbaum 1970).

This view was borne out by Miller (1983), who found that juvenile sex ratios differed considerably between Bangladesh and Pakistan, the two Muslim-majority countries on either side of the north Indian plains – but closely resembled the Hindu-majority states in India that neighboured them. The preponderantly male child sex ratios in Pakistan were similar to those of the neighbouring north-western Indian states of Rajasthan and Punjab, while the more egalitarian sex ratios reported in Bangladesh resembled those of the neighbouring state of West Bengal.[14] So, while the influence of religion may have played some role in explaining the differences between West Bengal and Bangladesh noted by Dyson and Moore, these differences were more likely to reflect their different histories of migration and settlement than their religion (discussed in the next chapter).

1.3 Gender, agency and patriarchal regimes

Differences in gender and kinship regimes were clearly relevant to explanations of regional variations in patterns of gender discrimination, but these explanations also contained some interesting propositions about the implications of different regimes for women's agency and its role in mediating demographic outcomes. For instance, Dyson and Moore suggest that, within south Indian kinship systems, women's greater mobility and freedom to participate in the labour force meant that daughters constituted less of a dependency burden on their parents and wives on their husbands. This, they suggest, was an important factor in explaining the more equal treatment meted out to female members of the family.

Sen (1990b) discusses the issue of women's agency in his work on 'missing women'. He points to the positive correlation between women's economic activity rates and their survival chances relative to men across Africa and Asia. He suggests two pathways through which the correlation might reflect causality. One pathway worked at the societal level. In regions where women customarily worked outside the household, their contributions to the household were more socially visible, more likely to be recognised by family and society and hence more likely to entitle them to a fairer share of household resources. By contrast, in societies where women were confined to domestic activities, where their contributions were less visible and less valued, gender discrimination from an early age was likely to be the norm.

A second causal pathway operated at household level, with women's contributions to household livelihoods differentiating the degree of voice and influence they were able to exercise within their households. Women's engagement in paid activity, their contribution to household finances, was likely to increase their ability to negotiate a more egalitarian distribution of its resources. Important to note here is the assumption that mothers would be less likely than fathers to discriminate against daughters.[15]

Drèze and Sen (1995) explored these ideas in greater detail in the context of India. Controlling for the regional divide in patriarchal regimes, they found that districts with higher levels of female economic activity and literacy reported lower fertility rates and lower female disadvantage in child survival. Female literacy also reduced overall child mortality. Male literacy rates reduced the female disadvantage in child survival but the effect was much smaller and they had no effect on under-five mortality or fertility rates. In other words, while variations in patriarchal structures contributed to variations in the pattern of demographic outcomes, a societal effect indicated by the significant effect of regional variables, variations in women's individual agency also had an impact on these outcomes, independent of structures.

A somewhat different approach to the analysis of women's agency and its implications for reproductive behaviour can be found in Kandiyoti (1988). She suggests that different regimes could be seen as embodying distinct 'rules of the game' or 'patriarchal bargains', which spelt out the structure of constraints and opportunities within which women and men could exercise agency. While most women in most contexts had an interest in securing their place in their societies, and minimising threats to it, the agency permitted to them and the strategies they could pursue reflected the possibilities embodied in these context-specific gendered constraints. They were consequently likely to deal with the implications of patriarchal power in their lives, to 'bargain with patriarchy', very differently within the belt of classic patriarchy compared to the strategies pursued by women in less tightly controlled patriarchal regimes.

For instance, studies from the African context testified to the considerable degree of autonomy displayed by women in their efforts to safeguard their own interests. Their access to property of their own and their ability to engage in independent economic activities seemed to have given rise to a greater willingness to engage in open forms of conflict with those in authority. Within families, they prioritised their own farms and trading enterprises to reduce their dependence on, and obligations to, husbands and they deserted their marriages when conditions became intolerable. In the public domain, they were willing to resist government policies that went against their interest. This degree of independence meant that they had no reason to favour sons over daughters.

This presented a stark contrast to women's behaviour within classic patriarchy. Here women strove to adhere as far as possible to the restrictive societal norms defining their behaviour: they avoided mobility in the public domain, deferred to male authority within the household and sought to produce as many sons as possible to assure their place within their husband's patrilineage. The risks and uncertainties associated with women's dependence on men within classic patriarchy created powerful incentives for son preference and high levels of fertility.

These studies provide the outlines of the hypothesis about women's agency and reproductive outcomes that underpins the analysis in this book. Its starting premise is that the overarching structures of patriarchy in a society determine the value given to its women as evidenced by the degree of equality they enjoy. Those that embody greater freedom for women are also more likely to give them greater value because they are able to participate in a wide range of roles within the economy and make substantial contributions to household production.

Within the restrictive context of classic patriarchy, such as the one that characterises Bangladesh, the hypothesis suggests two different, though mutually compatible, routes through which greater gender equality might emerge:[16]

- Through shifts in patriarchal structures which allow an expansion of the range of productive roles that women are able to play, reduce their dependency status and promote their revaluation at societal level – and the revaluation of daughters within the family.
- Through the increased bargaining power that accrues to individual women within their households as a result of expanded economic opportunities, which they are able to use to achieve a more gender-egalitarian distribution of household resources.

1.4 Conceptualising continuity and change

The narratives I heard in Amarpur persuaded me that there was a story to be told about the Bangladesh paradox from a different standpoint to that taken in the literature so far. It would focus on how the larger drivers of change identified in this literature were experienced and acted on as they unfolded in the lives of ordinary people and how their experience and agency helped to shape the course of change. And it would focus on women's experience and agency as the central core of the story. But it was clear that individual responses could not be understood independently of the context in which they took place. There was a path dependence to the change narratives we heard in Amarpur: they bore strong traces of the past because past constraints had set the parameters within which subsequent change evolved.

There was thus a twofold analytical challenge to unravelling the Bangladesh paradox. It required an explanation for the conditions that prevailed at the start of the paradox and why they had appeared to scholars of that period to be so intransigent. And it required an explanation of the pathways through which change *did* take place in subsequent years.

This dual challenge in turn needed a conceptual framework that could bring its two strands together in a coherent way. Theories of practice in the fields of anthropology and sociology provide a promising way forward, starting with Giddens's structuration theory, which sought to integrate the two dominant social science traditions of structural determinism and methodological individualism (1979). Structuralist traditions focus primarily on the larger social forces in a society that are considered to govern human behaviour. One strand of these traditions highlights the cultural systems that prevail in particular contexts. Some of the early literature on gender discrimination in Bangladesh, for instance, explained it in terms of customs, beliefs and role expectations rooted in Bengali Muslim culture (Aziz 1979; Aziz and Maloney 1985). The other strand is concerned with the material arrangements of a society and their impact on identities and interests. In the Bangladesh context, for instance, this tradition focused on its agrarian power structure, on the 'intermediate' character of its governance regime and on its patriarchal kinship system.

A diametrically opposite view is to be found within voluntarist traditions, which portray human behaviour as the expression of individuals' tastes and preferences, subject to the resources they have at their disposal. This is, of course, the dominant view within mainstream neoclassical economics. An early example of this in the Bangladesh literature can be found in Khandker (1987), who sought to demonstrate that women's labour force participation was not 'inflexibly fixed by local custom' (p.24) as claimed by cultural explanations but could be explained by standard economic variables such as education, land and livestock.

Structuration theory brings these traditions together in a mutually interdependent relationship: structures constrain human agency but are simultaneously produced by human agency. The actions of individuals are seen to be guided by, and operating within, the range of possibilities generated by the cultural beliefs and material arrangements of their society. Because their conduct is constrained in this way, it generally serves to reproduce these beliefs and arrangement – but not invariably. There is scope for human conduct to modify, destabilise and even transform aspects of structure. In the rest of this section, I bring together the key building blocks of structuration theory – structure, practice and agency – to sketch out a conceptual framework that will help to make sense of the different processes of continuity and change that feature in this book.

Conceptualising continuity

Structure

The concept of structure refers to those aspects of the social world that impose patterns on, or 'structure', other aspects of this world, including the behaviour of human actors. As Sewell (1992) points out, it has both virtual and real dimensions. The virtual dimension refers to the systems of norms, beliefs and conventions, or cultural schemas, which provide a pattern to social life. Structures in this sense do not exist concretely in time and space but are lodged in the human brain and the collective consciousness of social groups.

These cultural schemas become 'real' through the concrete arrangements that they give rise to. They demarcate society into different institutional domains that are organised around their own internal logic – familial reproduction, the production of subsistence and surplus, the governance of communities. They classify people into different groups on the basis of differentially valued identities. And they distribute valued resources between these groups. The unequal nature of these classifications and distributions gives rise to a social order in which privileged groups have both a stake in the existing order and the resources to ensure its reproduction.

Resources are conceptualised in ways that capture what makes them valuable in different societies. Bourdieu (1977) distinguishes between 'resources' as latent possibilities of different kinds and 'capital' as the mobilisation of these possibilities in purposeful activities: the pursuit of needs, interests and goals. What is valued about resources, in other words, is what they enable people to achieve, their implications for agency. Material resources are, of course, the most familiar within the literature – I have cited land and livestock as examples from the early Bangladesh literature. Today, as Bangladesh strives to become a modern, market-oriented society, new kinds of material resources, such as institutional finance and digital technology, have taken on greater significance.

Human resources refer to the physical and mental capabilities embodied in human being, their bodily capacity, skills, education and knowledge. Also widely recognised in the literature is the importance of social resources, networks of relationships, which spell out claims and obligations between people and can be mobilised in the pursuit of objectives. Later chapters will discuss the importance of social relationships in Bangladesh for the kinds of agency people were able to exercise: horizontal ones based on family and kinship, as well as vertical ones based on power and patronage. Poverty and helplessness in Bangladesh, it has been observed, was as much about being 'poor in people', having no one to turn to in times of trouble, as it was about being poor in property (McCarthy 1967).

Finally, practice theory gives central role to symbolic capital, the status, prestige and respect associated with position in the social order. While resources more generally determine the courses of action available to groups of people, symbolic resources bestow certain groups with the authority to interpret cultural norms, to determine which courses of action are considered acceptable and which transgress normative boundaries. They have the power, in other words, to constrain and enable the actions of others in ways that reproduce the social order and their own privileged position within it.

Practice

The norms, beliefs and conventions of a society operate at the everyday level through the various bundles of activities that define and differentiate the domains of social life. They are embedded within these activities through the generalised, taken-for-granted procedures that are routinely invoked by people as they go about their daily business without much reflection and thought. While the concept of practice could refer, in principle, to anything that people do, practice theory is concerned with issues of power and domination. It tends to focus on actions that are bound up, intentionally or otherwise, with the processes of structuration through which the inequalities of the social order are produced and reproduced (Ortner 1984). For instance, while the social conventions of Bengali culture that prescribe the most auspicious time of day to cut one's hair and nails (see Chapter 3) may be intriguing phenomena, they are far less consequential for processes of structuration than conventions about how food is distributed within the family and who is given priority.

Shove, Pantzer and Watson (2012) suggest that we can conceptualise social practices as constituted by specific combinations of elements – material elements, relevant knowledge and the social meanings attributed to the practice. It is the extent to which these constituent elements remain fused in repeated enactments over time that gives continuity to social practice. Equally, it is the loosening of one or more of these elements, their incorporation into other kinds of activities, that brings about change.

Social practices do not exist in isolation but are interwoven with each other over time to create the systemic character of everyday life. For instance, the patriarchal norms that assign primary responsibility for domestic work to women in Bangladesh and shape how they carry it out within their households also govern the market-based activities of men. Unequal access to market-based activities, in turn, feeds into domestic practices, determining whose claim on household food and other resources will be given priority.

Agency

Agency, the capacity for thought and action embodied in social actors, is the third central concept within structuration theory, linking the routinised performance of social practice with the subjectivity of the actor. Social actors enact social practices, rather than simply pursuing their own random and idiosyncratic preferences, because they do not, and cannot, exist as isolated individuals; they are always persons enmeshed in social relations that require them to behave in certain ways. Bourdieu's concept of habitus has been very influential in practice theory as a way of capturing how structural principles take root in individual subjectivities so that people adhere routinely and largely unconsciously to the social conventions that govern the conduct of daily life. Habitus describes how actors internalise the culturally defined and materially organised structures of their external world in the form of 'durable dispositions', propensities to think, feel and act in ways that accord with the structures that produced them and thus reproduce them over time.

The concept of habitus goes beyond mental schemas that shape individual subjectivities to also encompass embodied ways of being in the world, influencing how people occupy spaces, through their gestures, posture and deportment in the different domains of their lives. Bourdieu talks about the 'hauteur of the aristocrat' and 'the stance of the peasant' by way of examples, but anyone who has done fieldwork in the sexually segregated context of Bangladesh will be only too aware of the embodied nature of habitus in the ease with which men inhabit public space and the contrasting discomfort that characterises women, their efforts to dress and conduct themselves in public so as to deflect attention from themselves as far as possible.

Habitus becomes part of individual subjectivities through experiences over the life course, with the early formative years having a particularly powerful effect. People who share a given social position and face similar objective conditions of existence are likely to share certain similarities in their habitus, in how they think and feel about the social world, what they expect of others and what is expected of them. So, while individual history is an important element in the formation of habitus, so too is the collective history of the family and social groups of which the individual is member. And inasmuch as individuals simultaneously belong to different social groups – in the Bangladesh context, groups are organised by gender, class, religion and ethnicity – these intersecting identities and experiences are likely to be internalised as core aspects of their habitus.

Conceptualising change

As Sewell points out, the conceptualisation of structures within practice theory shares the reproductive bias of structuralist theories more generally since the point of the concept is to explain the durability of certain aspects of social life. This does not necessarily rule out scope for agency to be incorporated into the performance of practice. So, while habitus structures the range of possibilities perceived to be available in relation to certain structures, demarcating a realm of unquestioned routine, habit and tradition, the realm of what Bourdieu refers to as doxa, social actors are still able to engage in purposive forms of agency within its limits, to interpret custom and convention rather than mechanically following it.

However, many do not think that this formulation goes far enough to overcome reproductive bias since the change envisaged is limited to ways of acting, thinking and feeling that are consistent with customs and conventions. This has led Ortner to pose a more general version of the research question that informs this book: 'the question of how actors who are so much the product of their own social and cultural contexts can ever come to transform the conditions of their own existence – except by accident?' (1989, p.14, my italics).

McLeod (2005) suggests that space for more intentional forms of change can be opened up by allowing for a less tightly presumed relationship between external realities and internalised constraint, thereby allowing scope for improvisation, creativity, reflectiveness and emotions, particularly in the face of unanticipated events of life. Periods of social instability, for instance, are likely to see gaps emerge between internalised dispositions and the social world in which they evolved; patterns of behaviour are likely to become more irregular, to depart from previous social practice. At lower levels of analysis, there are likely to be events that are exceptional, crises, 'blips' in the system, when circumstances require more reflective and intentional forms of agency than is customary (Elder-Vass 2007, p.329).

In addition, the habitus that people acquire in their childhood may be attenuated or modified through changes that occur in the course of their lives, as they grow up and deal with events and experiences their childhood did not prepare them for (McNay 1999). And, as societies become more differentiated, as more ways of earning a living become available, as more ways of learning become possible, the habitus also becomes more open to crosscutting influences.

Returning to Ortner's question about how change can come about other than accidentally, I want to focus in the rest of this section on what the literature tells us about the different kinds of agency that women who are indeed 'very much the product of their own social and cultural context' might exercise to transform the conditions of their existence and what might motivate them to do so. This provides a useful springboard for a book that is interested in the possibilities for agency available to women in the face of an oppressive patriarchy.

Ortner (2006, p.6) suggests that we can place different manifestations of agency along a spectrum conceptualised in terms of psychological depth of power, its 'pervasiveness or invasiveness' and the scope for intentionality and consciousness – locating unquestioning conformity to social norms at one end of the spectrum and more intentional forms of action along the rest of it. We can also distinguish between different kinds of intentionality.

For instance, Huang (2020) cites a woman in her Bangladesh study who spoke of the different kinds of dreams that women had: 'small dreams' that did little to change their situation, a woman's dream that her husband would bring her back a cooker when he returned from the city, and the 'big dreams' of those who sought to transform the conditions of their existence, women who cultivated a strong sense of self, a directed sense of agency.

Conceptualisations of habitus that stress the deeply 'invasive' nature of power belong at the structurally driven end of the spectrum. For instance, Sen's idea of adaptively formed preferences describes compliance with social norms as the behaviour of those who are 'habituated to inequality, may be unaware of the possibilities of social change, may be hopeless about upliftment of objective circumstances of misery, may be resigned to fate' (1990b, p.127).

Alternatively, women may conform unquestioningly to patriarchal cultures because they do not consider them unjust. They grew up within these cultures, acquired their gendered sense of self through their practices, and they have dreams that can be realised within the limits imposed by them. As Abu-Lughod (2002) argues, Western feminist critiques of patriarchal norms that privilege women's freedom and liberation may have relevance in particular historical or cultural situations but it is possible that different desires, aspirations and capacities shape the subjectivities of women with other histories and cultures. The values of their own culture, such as closeness of family or the cultivation of piety, may have greater meaning for these women: 'We must consider that they might be called to personhood, so to speak, in a different language' (p.788).

Habitus may also ensure conformity by structuring women's interests to give them a stake in upholding the status quo. As Kandiyoti (1988) notes, young brides within the belt of classic patriarchy have a stake in producing and valuing sons at the expense of daughters since their status in their husband's family is dependent on this. Whatever hardships and deprivation they might experience as subservient daughters-in-law will be eventually be superseded when their sons get married and they are able to exercise the control and authority that inheres in the position of mothers-in-law:

> The cyclical nature of women's power in the household and their anticipation of inheriting the authority of senior women encourages a thorough internalization of this form of patriarchy by women themselves. (p.279)

A less mentally invasive understanding of power in social life can be found in the work of theorists like Scott (1990). This suggests that women may be aware of the injustice of their situations, perhaps even of the existence of alternative possibilities, but their ability to bring about change is constrained by the sanctions that such efforts will bring in their wake: dissent is costly. But, like most oppressed groups, they may have their own strategies, the 'weapons of the weak', to win tacit gains or simply to allow the expression of discontent in ways that are relatively safe.

The feminist literature provides many examples of these hidden expressions of rebellion: folk tales, provocative or mocking songs, intrusive noise, disapproving silence, sexually irreverent discourse and taunts (Abu-Lughod 1990; Agarwal 1994; Jackson 2012). As Abu-Lughod points out, when women live in the sexually segregated worlds of classic patriarchy, they are able to use 'secrets and silences to their advantage' (p.43), to cover for each other, colluding to hide knowledge from male authority.

Feminist theories of bargaining and negotiation spell out a third form of agency. This is not 'bargaining' in the structural sense used by Kandiyoti but the more individual forms that come into play when women are sufficiently dissatisfied with the prevailing order that they seek ways of influencing social practices but do so within normative boundaries that do not jeopardise relationships they need or value (Agarwal 1997; Kabeer 2000). This is a conceptualisation that acknowledges greater scope for reflexivity on the part of individual women, but also the need for continued caution. It is exemplified in the strategies of 'wielding and yielding' that Villareal talks about in her study of women in rural Mexico, of making concessions in order to gain concessions in return (1994, p.28).

Where women have few material resources of their own to bargain with, they must draw on the less tangible resources at their disposal to bring about desired changes. Most often we find that they deploy a cultural resourcefulness that seeks to reinterpret and modify discursive boundaries between acceptable and unacceptable behaviour in ways that expand the forms of agency permitted to them. There are limits to the change that can be brought about through discursive strategies alone, given the resilience of material constraints (Bourdieu 1998) but, when these reinterpretations are reflective of, and made possible by, openings and cracks in the 'harder' structures of material and political life, they can serve to 'derail' practice, to become one way in which change becomes embedded in new discourses and new sets of meanings (Nicolini 2012).

The different kinds of agency discussed so far all seek to avoid any form of confrontation that might jeopardise women's claims within the family and their place in the social order. But agency can also take the form of overt departures from accepted practice, the open defiance of those in authority. Such resistance is likely to carry very high costs, particularly in regimes of classic patriarchy in which women are likely to be outcasted for attempts to do so. So what might lead women in these contexts to take such risks?

At the level of consciousness, it is most likely to be motivated by circumstances that open up a gap between what they had been led to expect in exchange for their compliance with social expectations and the reality they are confronted with, by the heightened sense of injustice that this brings. But such awakening of consciousness is not always sufficient on its own to give them the courage or desperation to act if their actions plunge them into even more desperate circumstances.

I will be exploring examples of open resistance to the patriarchal order in the course of this book but I will note here that it was most often made possible by women's access to new kinds of resources that helped to break how far they would fall. Individual women were able to access new material resources through the external agency of government, markets and civil society that allowed them to contemplate actions that would have been previously inconceivable. Groups of women were able to engage in more organised forms of collective action when it became possible for them to build 'chosen' social networks that acknowledged their grievances and supported their actions, acknowledgement and support that they rarely found within the 'given' social relationships they were born or had married into.

1.5 Road map and methodology

This book sets out to address the twofold analytical challenge of unravelling the Bangladesh paradox that I laid out earlier: to explain both the apparently immutable structural conditions that defined the early stages of the paradox and the unexpected processes of change that took place subsequently. If the first part of the story is concerned with the structural aspects of structuration theory, their reproduction through social practice, the latter part focuses on the agency aspect, the transformation of structures through the medium of changing practice.

Strictly speaking, I am defining the start of the paradox as the period following the country's independence in 1971. It was the grim conditions that prevailed at that time that provided the base line against which later progress was measured. But, in order to analyse how these conditions came into existence and to explain the immutability ascribed to them, I needed to examine what had happened before, to go back into the country's history.

In his book on the history of Bangladesh, Van Schendel (2009) distinguishes between three types of historical process that overlap with each other and continue to play a significant role in contemporary Bangladesh. The first type relates to the very-long-term processes that explain how, over millennia, the forces of history and geography helped to shape the delta region that later became Bangladesh. The second type focuses on the last few centuries, when these longer-term processes interacted with middle-range ones, particularly those associated with foreign rule. And, finally, there are the contemporary historical processes that deal with the decades preceding and following Bangladesh's emergence as an independent nation.

Chapter 2 of this book uses a compressed account of Van Schendel's first two phases to narrate the early history of the region, the particularities of its history and geography that shaped the contours of the country that became Bangladesh. It discusses the waves of rulers who came in search of wealth and sought to impose their beliefs on the delta's indigenous population. Thanks to the extraordinary geography of the delta, its inhospitality to outsiders, they were only partially successful. They left behind a hybrid cultural formation and a syncretic belief system, a collective habitus that gave the delta's population a pragmatic worldview that stood them in good stead in dealing with the frequent crises that marked their lives. The chapter thus provides an account of how the economic, political and cultural structures that prevailed at the time of the country's independence had been consolidated over time, but it also teases out the potentiality for change contained within these apparently durable structures.

Chapter 3 focuses on the period that constitutes the start of the story of the Bangladesh paradox, the early decades of independence. The party that had led the struggle for independence had defined its vision in idealistic terms: a just economic order, a tolerant and democratic political culture, and a strong sense of Bengali national identity. The donor community, on the other hand, regarded it as an 'international basket case': poor, overpopulated, unable to feed itself, testing to the utmost the ability of foreign assistance to rescue it from impending Malthusian disaster. The chapter examines how these competing discourses played out in the policy debates of that time and why the epithet of 'international basket case' won out as the defining image of the newly independent country.

Chapter 4 turns to the academic research carried out during that period. This focused on the resilience of the structures that kept Bangladesh trapped in poverty, including an agrarian power structure that led to stagnating agricultural productivity, blocking the possibility of technological change and giving rise to the high and apparently intransigent fertility rates in a country already among the most densely populated in the world. This was also a period when more systematic research began to be carried out into the nature of patriarchy in the country and the extreme forms of discrimination against women and girls that it generated.

The studies of this period were generally characterised by an 'etic' perspective, the standpoint of external observers, rather than attempting to draw on the 'emic' knowledge that came from seeking an insider understanding of the world.[17] This research mirrored the pessimism that characterised the prevailing policy discourse. But it also contributed insights that made some of the subsequent change easier to understand. In particular, it pointed out that Bangladesh was characterised by a stratified but essentially unstable social structure. Privilege was not inherited; it had to be fought for. There was scope for mobility and gains to risk-taking.

Chapter 5 describes the emerging contours of the paradox and draws together the broad-based explanations that were put forward for it in the literature. Along with the actors that were considered to have played a leading role – the state, donors and the NGO sector, as well as private enterprise – these explanations emphasised the importance of the collaboration between them. The question of women's agency was touched on in these explanations but in a general way that offered little concrete insight into why and how it was exercised.

This then provides the point of departure for the main contribution that I want to make in this book. The subsequent four chapters focus on the micro-level manifestations of the changes under way at the macro-level, how they reshaped the local environments in which ordinary men and women went about their daily lives, how their responses in turn gave rise to the progress that was documented by the paradox literature – and on the role that women played in making this progress happen. **Chapter 6** focuses on changing practices in the reproductive domain in response to the new technologies, new forms of knowledge and the new meanings about bearing and caring for children that were put into circulation by policymakers, donors and NGOs. In all these aspects of reproductive practice, I trace how the actions of different actors converged to bring about change, some more controversial than others.

Chapter 7 examines the rise in women's labour force participation. The high costs, symbolic and practical, that they had to bear when they took up forms of work that fell outside the boundaries of gender propriety meant that the entry of many into such work was very often the product of desperation. Less predictably, however, was that for many others it was motivated by their dreams, both small and large, for themselves and for their families. These dreams fuelled some of the changes associated with the Bangladesh paradox.

Chapter 8 explores the under-researched dimension of the Bangladesh paradox that we noted earlier: the achievement of progress in gender equality in an era that saw the spread of a form of Islamic orthodoxy that was fundamentally opposed to many aspects of this progress. The chapter argues that it was precisely because the orthodoxy threatened to wipe out these gains, particularly those that had been made by poorer women and their families, that it was resisted.

Chapter 9 returns to the question that motivated the book in the first place: the steady disappearance of earlier forms of gender discrimination that had characterised the country – and the absence of new forms of prenatal discrimination. The chapter draws on detailed life history narratives that were collected in 2010 from different generations of men and women in the village of Amarpur, where I had carried out fieldwork back in 1979. It explores what they tell us about the shifts in reproductive preferences and practices observed in the literature and about the reconfiguration of gender relations that helped to explain them.

Finally, **Chapter 10** steps back from the paradox story to draw out a number of themes raised by the book. First, it reflects on the popularity of the concept of the paradox in development studies more generally, and its frequent use to describe a variety of phenomena in a variety of places, and asks whether the Bangladesh paradox was ever indeed a paradox. Rather than using the predetermined model of social change that gave rise to the idea of the Bangladesh paradox, it considers how insights from the theories of practice that underpinned this book help to provide a more empirically grounded analysis of changes in question. Second, it briefly revisits the reverse paradox that appeared to have occurred in India – the intensified forms of gender discrimination evident in its deteriorating sex ratios despite its rapid rates of growth and commitment to democratic governance – and considers what a practice-theoretical approach might contribute to its explanation. And finally, returning to the Bangladesh story, it asks whether the social progress the country has experienced can be sustained in the foreseeable future.

In terms of methodology, I have tried to capture the processes of structuration that form the analytic core of the book by moving between detailed historical and contemporary descriptions of the evolution of structural constraints, on the one hand, and, on the other, a ground-level analysis of how these constraints were reproduced, modified, and transformed by the practices of 'real' actors. A great deal of the material used in the book comes from secondary sources, but, as the bibliography shows, I have drawn heavily on findings from my own studies over the years, many of which have a direct bearing on the concerns of this book. Much of the material in the book is qualitative: policy analysis, life histories, anecdotes, in-depth interviews, focus group discussions and participant observation. But I have also woven statistics and quantitative findings into the analysis where these add depth or increase confidence in the interpretations I offer.

I distinguished earlier between 'etic' and 'emic' approaches to analysis. I combine these perspectives in the book because they offer different kinds of standpoints and information on the same phenomena and hence a more holistic understanding of these phenomena. The ground-level stories of different generations of men and women tell us how they viewed the larger forces of structural change as they played out in their lives. They provide a 'people's history' of change, allowing us to pick up on the existence of what Ortner (2005) calls 'subjective counter currents', feelings, emotions and perceptions that go against dominant practices. These often proved to contain the early seeds of change that evolved over time into new forms of practice. Such change is evident in my analysis in the shift in narratives from the realm of doxa, a realm characterised by views that conformed to prevailing norms, to a more diverse, often contradictory, set of attitudes and opinions as hitherto hidden counter-currents come to the surface. At the same time, I do not rely solely on the explanations offered by these men and women because these are bounded, on the one hand, by their habitus, by what they do not question, and, on the other, by their incomplete knowledge and what they do not know. 'Etic' analysis and statistical data allowed me to address the limits to individual knowledgeability.

No story about the Bangladesh paradox can hope to provide a complete account and there are clearly important gaps in the version narrated in this book. For instance, while there is some discussion of urban change, the book is mainly concerned with change in rural areas because that is where the majority of the country has lived and continues to live, despite rapid urbanisation. Also missing is any discussion of climate change even though Bangladesh is regarded as the world's most vulnerable country in this respect: 'climate change is increasingly the lens through which the nation represents itself abroad; and, in turn, it is the primary means through which the world recognizes Bangladesh' (Paprocki 2021, p.14). There is a reason for this omission. For much of the period I am writing about, climate change has been remarkably absent from national and local politics, from civil society agendas and from local activism. Although the natural environment, in all its unpredictability and its frequent destructiveness, has never been far from the concerns of policymakers and the consciousness of ordinary people, it is only in recent years that the links between the two have been being made.

Most of the analysis in the book deals with Muslims, who make up around 90% of the overall population. There is some attention to Hindu experiences and some of the voices in the book are Hindu, although I have not identified them by religion except where it seemed relevant. But there is very little about the indigenous people of Bangladesh. I myself have done very little research on these groups and the secondary research that exists tends to focus on their political struggles for indigenous rights and recognition. As a result, we have estimates of their exclusion from the social progress associated with the Bangladesh paradox but little qualitative research into their experiences of this exclusion or their efforts to counter it.

There is another form of bias in the book but it is more deliberate. Jackson and Rao (2004) once pointed to what they describe as 'the habitus' of those doing research in the field of gender and development, their unquestioned disposition 'to read social change negatively (bad and getting worse) so that nothing ever seems to improve' (p.8). This, they suggest, is grounded in the need to focus on the legion of problems that women continue to face across the world, despite real improvements. This book suffers from a bias in the opposition direction. Because it is seeking to explain improvements in the lives of women and girls in Bangladesh, it may give too short a shrift to the very real problems that they continue to face. It is not always easy to find the right balance. But, if I have erred towards the positive, it is because stories of Bangladesh in its early post-independence were so relentlessly negative that some bias in the opposite direction seemed necessary to correct the balance.

Notes

[1] The phrase comes from Alamgir (1978).

[2] The methodology for this research and for the two other later research projects that are particularly drawn on in this book are described in Appendix 1.

[3] See explanation of these preference scales in Appendix 2.

[4] See also *The Economist* (2012) for similar comparisons ('The path through the fields', https://www.economist.com/briefing/2012/11/03/the-path -through-the-fields)

[5] Bangladesh's per capita GDP in 1990 was $741, rising to $1,569 in 2011. In India, it rose from $1,193 to $3,203 and in Pakistan from $1,624 to $2,424. Poverty rates also declined in all three countries but remained higher in Bangladesh: 76.5% in 2011 compared to 68.7% for India and 60.2% for Pakistan.

[6] http://www.worldlifeexpectancy.com

[7] In 2019, it was one of the few countries in the world where girls continued to die in larger numbers than boys (Ritchie and Roser 2019).

[8] See Appendix 3 for an explanation of how sex ratios in mortality rates, life expectancy and population groups are used as indicators of gender discrimination/gender equity.

[9] According to digital maps produced by Ritchie and Roser (2019), sex ratios at birth had started to diverge from the global norm around the 1970s in India and around the 1990s in Pakistan as the new technology became available but the ratio for Bangladesh had remained unchanged at 105.

[10] The number of 'missing women' in the early 1990s was larger than the combined casualties of all famines in the 20th century. It also exceeded the combined death toll of both world wars and the casualties of major epidemics such as the 1918–20 global influenza epidemic and the AIDS pandemic (Klasen and Wink 2003).

[11] The caste system in India is organised at two levels, *varna* and *jati*. The *varna* system stratifies caste Hindus into four ranked groups, the Brahmins, the priestly group at the top, followed by the Kshatriyas (warrior group), then the merchants, traders and artisans (Vaishya) and finally the labourers (Shudras) at the bottom. The Dalits are those considered so low as to be 'untouchable' and outside the caste system. The *jati* system is made up of numerous endogamous groups within these castes. They are assigned a particular rank in the *varna* system and complicated rules of endogamy prevent people from marrying outside their *jati* even to someone of the same *varna* level (Reich 2019, p.141).

[12] As Mason (1986) points out, dowry is commonly used in the demographic literature on women's status as an indicator of devalued status.

[13] Dyson and Moore classify states in the Hindi-speaking belt of the north Indian plains as constituting the northern kinship system: Gujerat, Rajasthan, Uttar Pradesh, Madhya Pradesh, Punjab and Haryana. The Dravidian-language states of Kerala, Tamil Nadu, Andhra Pradesh and Karnataka are generally taken as 'the south', although Dyson and Moore also include Maharashtra. Their eastern states consist of West Bengal, Orissa and Bihar.

[14] In line with the general pessimism expressed about Bangladesh in the literature of that period, Miller predicted that its child sex ratios would deteriorate in the future to become more 'north Indian'. As I show later in the chapter, this prediction was not borne out. Indeed, it was south Indian sex ratios that became more 'northern' (Chapter 10).

[15] This assumption was supported by international evidence compiled by Mason and Taj (1987) suggesting that the tendency of men to prefer sons over daughters to a greater extent than women might explain their preference for larger families. It was contested by Cleland and Van Ginneken (1988) on the basis of studies of women's behaviour in cultures of son preference. For instance, a study by Das Gupta (1987) in rural Punjab found that higher levels of education among women, believed to increase their bargaining power, was associated with stronger discrimination against daughters.

[16] See Mason (1988) for another version of these routes.

[17] While the distinction between etic and emic originated in linguistic theory, it has been adopted by a range of disciplines (Harris 1976). I use it here to describe differences in how analysis is conducted, whether it is describing relationships and behaviour from the standpoint of the researcher, their understanding of a context, or from the standpoint of the researched, their understanding of their own lives.

2. Frontiers and crossroads: economy, politics and culture in the Bengal delta

Bangladesh is an old land but a new nation. (Nurul Islam 1974, p.1)

You cannot make sense of contemporary Bangladesh unless you understand its history long before [the] last few decades ... How have long-term processes shaped the society that we know as Bangladesh today? (Van Schendel 2009, p.xxv)

The history of Bangladesh, a new nation but an old land, is a 'complicated and spectacular tale' (Van Schendel 2009, p.xxv), fascinating in its own right but also essential background to my account of the Bangladesh paradox. At the time of its independence in 1971, Bangladesh was the second-poorest country in the world (after Rwanda), the most densely populated and characterised by a particularly extreme form of patriarchy (Cain 1984; Faaland and Parkinson 1976). The forces that gave rise to these conditions had deep roots in its past. Indeed, the historical durability of these forces accounted for the pessimism about the country's future that formed the policy consensus at the time.

This chapter offers a selective account of the past, focusing primarily on what is relevant to understanding the aspects of the present we are interested in: the economic structure that characterised the country at the time of its independence, the nature of its politics and its cultural formation. Of particular relevance to this formation is the history of Islam in the Bengal delta. That it was the religion of the majority of its people only came to light when the British colonial administration carried out the first census of the region in 1872. The administration was based in the city of Kolkata in the predominantly Hindu south-west of Bengal Province. It knew very little about Bengal's eastern districts, which it perceived as a vast and remote hinterland whose inhabitants they presumed to be Hindu, the majority religion of the rest of the province as well as the rest of India.

The 1872 census revealed that there were more than 16 million Muslims in the Bengal province, making up 50% of its total population, rising to over 70% in a number of eastern districts (Khan 1996). While some Muslim presence within India's population was to be expected, given that it had been under Muslim rule for nearly five centuries, it was difficult to explain why, of all of India's interior provinces, it was only in Bengal that the majority of the local population had embraced Islam, making it 'an island of Muslim majority in the sea of Hinduism' (Khan 1996, p.18).

Bengal also represented an outlier in the domain of Islam itself. It was physically and culturally distant from the Middle East, where Islam had originated. It was also physically and culturally distant from the heartland of the faithful, the contiguous landmass that stretched across the globe 'from Mauritania to Pakistan and from Turkey to Somalia' (Khan 1996, p.83). These were largely arid and semi-arid zones in which Islam was the religion of town dwellers and merchants who scorned those who worked on the land.

Bengal, on the other hand, was wet delta country on the eastern margins of India, populated by peasant farmers, woodcutters, fishermen and boatmen who relied on the land and the rivers to make a living. How was it, Khan asked, that Hinduism, the long-established religion of the majority of the subcontinent, had defended itself so successfully against conversion to the religion of its rulers across much of the subcontinent, but had failed to do so in Bengal?

Explanations for this puzzle vary, but the way in which Islam took root in the delta region gave it a particular character that shaped a great deal of its subsequent history – and remains relevant today. Eaton's description of Bengal as a society constituted by multiple frontiers that moved generally from the west of the subcontinent to the east provides a useful framework for thinking about the aspects of Bengal's history in which we are interested: its economy, politics and culture (Eaton 1994). One was the agrarian frontier, whose eastward movement across the northern plains of India into the Bengal delta represented the movement of a settled plough-based agriculture into an economy that had been based on hunting, fishing and shifting cultivation.

The second was the political frontier that defined the boundaries between state and other forms of rule. Its movement in the Bengal region was marked by a series of 'amazing twists and turns' (Van Schendel 2009, p.xxv) as a series of rulers, most often from outside the region, sought with varying degrees of success to govern the delta and extract its wealth. It started with early Hindu and Buddhist monarchies, was followed by an extended period of Muslim rule that gave way to the British empire, a brief period as the eastern wing of Pakistan and finally the emergence of the independent state of Bangladesh.

Finally, and of particular interest to the concerns of this book, is the cultural frontier, the frontier between different systems of norms, beliefs and customs. Here the metaphor of the moving frontier does not work too well. Rather than a linear eastward movement of the 'great traditions' of the subcontinent,[1] the Sanskritic traditions of Hinduism and Buddhism and the Abrahamic tradition of Islam, the Bengal delta is better represented as a kind of cultural crossroads 'where Sanskritic and non-Sanskritic worldviews met, clashed and intermingled' (Van Schendel 2009, p.20). The Islam that finally became the religion of the majority was syncretic in nature, a fusion of the 'great traditions' with the pre-existing 'little traditions' of its indigenous population.

2.1 Shifting frontiers in land, livelihoods and culture

Van Schendel begins his history of Bangladesh with an account of its extraordinary geography, tracing the huge natural forces that influenced the course of its history and cultural beliefs and that still exert an enormous influence on its daily life today. At the heart of these forces was the continuously shifting frontier between land and water, the earliest phase of which brought the delta into existence. This fertile alluvial landmass was at the confluence of three of the largest rivers of the subcontinent. The Ganges originated in the western Himalayas; once it reached the plains, it split into the Hooghly, which flowed into the sea through the western part of the delta, and the Padma, which flowed through its eastern part. The Brahmaputra originated in the northern Himalayas and was called the Jamuna in East Bengal, while the Meghna entered the delta from the hilly regions of the east. There were, in addition, around 50 other rivers that criss-crossed the country in an immense system of tributaries and distributaries, streams and canals.

The constant movements of these rivers led to regular shifts in the boundaries between land and water. Flooding submerged a significant portion of the country under water during every summer. The rich silt deposited replenished the soil, but siltation also steadily raised the beds of rivers, rendering their courses unstable. Each monsoon, some banks were eaten away, while new land was built up elsewhere, only for some of it to disappear again at some future season. This annual flooding introduced considerable instability in the local economy.

In addition, over the longer term, tectonic movements far below the earth's surface changed the topography of the region, leading to the gradual tilting of the entire Bengal Basin eastward and to the long-drawn-out eastward movement of its river system. By the late 16th century, the Ganges river system had abandoned its former channels in the south-western Bengal and linked up with the Padma, so that the main river system flowed through the eastern delta into the sea. Consequently, the active stage of delta formation migrated eastwards, leaving decaying rivers and moribund land in the western region.

The geography of the delta was bound up with one of the defining aspects of the region's history: an extended period of isolation from the northern Indo-Gangetic plains. For many thousands of years, the region was covered by dense rainforests and marshlands, inhospitable to human habitation. Very little is known about when humans first made their appearance in the region and who they were. It is likely that the earliest inhabitants were aboriginal, possibly Dravidian-speaking, hunter-gatherer communities. They were joined by tribal groups speaking Tibeto-Burman languages who entered the delta from the north-east, crossing the mountains from China and via South East Asia (Heintzman and Worden 1989; Maloney 1977; Maloney, Ashraful and Sarker 1981; Rashid 1965; Van Schendel 2009). These migrants introduced shifting rice cultivation into the region along with their cultural-religious beliefs and way of life. A relatively low division of labour and unstable communications appeared to have given rise to decentralised and undifferentiated communities (Addy and Azad 1975; Nicholas 1962).

The rest of the Indian subcontinent was inhabited by Dravidian hunter-gatherer communities who had a very different historical trajectory. Between 1800 and 1500 BCE, waves of Indo-Aryan groups – Steppe pastoralists and Iranian agriculturalists – migrated through the Hindu Kush into northern India. They initially settled in the Indus Valley and the Ganges Plain, conquering most of the Dravidian hunter-gatherer communities that inhabited the region and pushing others to the southern part of the Indian peninsula. It was during this period that we find the early origins of the north–south distinction in kinship regimes discussed in Chapter 1 and the emergence of a priestly caste and culture.[2]

By the 5th century BCE, a broad social system had evolved that integrated the kinship systems of Aryan and non-Aryan groups into a single, hierarchically structured social system, the Brahmin-based Vedic religion that later evolved into Hinduism (Eaton 1994). Men and women of the subjugated tribes, despised for their dark skin and ascribed racial inferiority, were relegated to labouring in the fields. The upper classes of non-Aryan groups were absorbed into the higher ranks of a caste hierarchy headed by a hereditary priesthood, the Brahmins, and sustained by a Sanskritic ideology of ritual purity and pollution. This conferred a pure status on Indo-Aryan groups who hailed from the west, while stigmatising the non-Aryans as impure 'barbarians' (*mleccha*) who inhabited ritually polluted lands considered unfit for the performance of Vedic sacrifices.

The historian Uma Chakravarti (1993) has pieced together evidence from various historical manuscripts and religious texts to show how these changes in social organisation of the Indo-Gangetic plains also encompassed changes in the organisation of gender. She notes that the early hunter-gatherer societies in the subcontinent did not appear to be characterised by rigid gender division of labour, that both men and women played a role in the productive activities of their groups. The subjugation of these groups was accompanied by the establishment of the basic institutions of classic patriarchy embedded within a rigid caste-based hierarchy dominated by preoccupations with pollution and purity. The fundamental organising principles of this hierarchy were the inter-linked imperatives to protect land, women and purity of caste. These were achieved through strict controls over women's sexual and reproductive behaviour: 'The purity of women has a centrality in brahmanical patriarchy … because the purity of caste is contingent upon it' (p.579). The controls included rules of caste endogamy that only permitted marriage within the same caste, pre-puberty marriage to ensure chasteness of the bride, the exclusion of higher-caste women from productive work and their seclusion within the shelter of the home.

The practice of *jati* (sub-caste) hypergamy, the requirement that women marry men ranked higher than them within their caste group, ensured the inferiority of the 'wife-giver' to the 'wife-taker' and was accompanied by the payment of dowry. It served to guard against the form of union that attracted the greatest horror in the caste system and received the harshest punishment: that between women from higher castes and men of lower castes.

Patriarchal authority within the kinship system was backed by the right to physically chastise women who violated established norms. However, Chakravarti notes, the Brahminical texts recognised that social control was most effective when upper-caste women not only accepted their condition but considered it a mark of distinction: 'no man can completely guard a woman by force and therefore it is women who of their own accord keep guard over themselves that are well guarded' (p.583). Idealised notions of womanhood, spelt out by all the major Brahmanical codes, held chastity and wifely fidelity as the highest expression of womanhood and women's surest pathway to salvation. These ideological principles shaped the structures and practices of the patriarchal caste system in India and continue to influence its contemporary forms.

The evolution of the Brahminical social order went hand in hand with the expansion of settled agriculture. Brahmins were granted land and other privileges by state authorities and began to move from the Gangetic valley into other regions of India, carrying with them advanced agricultural knowledge and technology as well as their caste-based social order. As Eaton (1994) notes,

> Indo-Aryan groups gradually settled the upper, the middle and finally the lower Ganges region, retroactively justifying each movement by pushing further eastward the cultural frontier that they believed separated themselves from tribes they considered ritually unclean. (p.7)

Sometime in the 5th century BCE, they reached the edges of the Bengal delta and began the process of absorbing its indigenous cultivators into a socially stratified agrarian society based on settled rice production.

However, the expansion of the early Indo-Aryan agrarian civilisation, and its later Hindu offshoot, did not occur evenly across the delta. The indigenous tribes of eastern Bengal remained secluded from Sanskritic influences and the accompanying advances in agriculture. As Miller points out, the mere fact of distance probably contributed to the slowness with which the 'Aryans and their Vedic ways' (Miller 1981, p.73) penetrated the eastern delta, but it was rendered even more inaccessible by its much heavier monsoon rainfall and greater density of vegetation. According to the early literature of the subcontinent, the eastern delta continued to be perceived as a 'distant land of barbarians, beyond the pale of Sanskritic culture' (Van Schendel 2009, p.19).

2.2 'Twist and turns' in the political frontier

The advances and setbacks in the movement of the political frontier into the Bengal delta reflected the difficulties of establishing centralised control over its inhospitable terrain by rulers usually from outside the region. Consequently, as Lewis (2011) points out, the delta's socio-economic and political development rarely conformed to an all-South Asia or even a north Indian model. When integration of the delta with the larger political realm began to take place, it was initially confined to the western delta. The eastern region remained a backwater, largely isolated from its nominal rulers in the north. The historical evidence suggests periods of strong dynastic rulers who brought to bear a range of religious influences, including Hinduism, Jainism and Buddhism, on the local population, interspersed with periods of political fragmentation when 'small principalities bloomed and withered like wild flowers in this region' (Khan 1996, p.73). It was not until quite late into Muslim rule in India that the 'little Bengals' of the earlier period were finally welded into 'Greater Bengal'.

Islam appears to have entered Bengal in two separate waves. The first wave came as part of a seaborne trade between the 8th and 12th centuries, bringing Arab and Persian traders and travellers to the Bengal coast. Many settled in coastal towns and engaged in proselytising but made no attempt at political control (Rashid 1965). The most influential were the Sufis, who represented the mystical branch of Islam that had achieved prominence in Persia since the 10th century.

The second wave brought Muslims as invaders into the Indian subcontinent, marking the beginning of an extended period of Muslim rule. Major geopolitical convulsions wrought by Mongol armies in Central Asia had led large numbers of newly Islamised Turkic tribes to migrate into the Iranian plateau. Some of these groups began a series of invasions into the subcontinent from the 11th century onwards, bringing successive incursions by Afghan, Turkish and Persian armies into the region (Bose and Jalal 1998). The Delhi Sultanate was established in the early 13th century and saw the expansion of Muslim rule across the north-west of India.

A succession of rulers from different Turk and Afghan dynasties sought to integrate Bengal into their larger political entities but encountered once again the problems of geographical distance and challenging terrain as well as regular bids for independence by governors placed in charge of different parts of Bengal. The Mughals took control of Delhi in the early 16th century. They too sought to expand into Bengal but it was not till the late 16th century that they were able to annex Bengal to their vast Indian empire, ending the delta's long isolation from northern India.

It was during Mughal rule that the continuing eastward movement of the delta's river system led the Ganges to finally merge with the Padma so that the main course of the combined Ganges–Padma River system began to flow directly through the heart of the eastern delta. This opened up new river-based communications with the northern heartlands of India, dramatically reducing costs of transporting textiles and food from the frontier to the imperial metropolis, making greater economic integration possible along with political integration.

In addition, as the main body of Ganges silt was now deposited over ever greater areas of the eastern delta during the annual floods, the agricultural potential of the eastern delta greatly increased. The systematic efforts of the Mughal rulers to extend settled cultivation into the newly formed lands finally led to the movement of the agrarian frontier into the eastern delta, this time in tandem with the Islamic frontier. Land fertility, rice cultivation and population density grew at a fast pace in the east, leading to levels of agricultural and demographic growth no longer possible in the now moribund western delta.

The Mughal conquest of Bengal was accomplished with considerable brutality but, as Van Schendel notes, it eventually helped to unify the delta politically, to set up a more regulated system of surplus extraction and to increase industrial and agrarian prosperity. The Mughal rulers incorporated the upper class of learned and landed Hindu castes as privileged functionaries in their administrative structure to mediate their rule with the local population. They also formed alliances with wealthy north Indian Baniya caste in order to invest in commerce and luxury craft industries, including Bengal's famed muslin textiles. The production of cash crops, particularly cotton and silk, flourished throughout the region. The eastern delta was also now producing so much surplus grain that rice joined silk and cotton textiles as its principal export to regions as far west as Goa and as far east as the Moluccas in South East Asia.

This was a period of considerable prosperity. In the concluding years of the 17th century, the Venetian chief physician to the Moghul emperor Aurangzeb wrote:

> Bengal is of all the kingdoms of the Mogul best known in France. The prodigious riches transported thence to Europe are proof of its greater fertility. All things are in plenty here, fruits, pulse, muslins, cloths of gold and silk. (Addy and Azad 1975, p.81)

At the same time, a great deal of Bengal's wealth was drained away to finance the wars of the Delhi court in the rest of India. It was estimated that the tax-to-GDP ratio at the height of Mughal rule in Bengal was around 44%, with the locally converted Muslims and lower-caste Hindus bearing the brunt of this extractive system (Addy and Azad 1975).

Stories of Islam in the Bengal delta: the elites and the masses

Bengal had been under Muslim rule from the 13th century onwards and a significant proportion of its population were Muslim. However, the Islam of the ruling elites in Bengal, the high-born *ashraf*, was very different from the Islam of the low-born *ajlaf* majority. The Islam of the elites had its source in the Islam of the Mughal ruling class. This had initially been made up of ethnic Iranians and Turks who had migrated directly from Iran and Central Asia. Its composition changed over time so that by the 17th century only a third of the nobility were of known Iranian or Turkish ancestry and less than a quarter were foreign-born immigrants. A growing section of Muslims in the imperial corps who claimed paternal ancestry beyond the Khyber had in fact been born in northern India of Indian mothers and spoke vernacular Hindi and Urdu as their mother tongue.

The need of the *ashraf* to distinguish themselves from low-born converts to their faith and from people of other faiths in India, and to claim membership of a wider Islamic *umma* extending beyond the frontiers of India, meant they continued to draw their political and cultural referents from the distant lands from which their ancestors had originated:

> When it came to the question of genealogy, nothing short of a pure Arab origin, especially proximity to the Prophet, or his tribe seemed acceptable ... appropriation of Arab or Persian cultural symbols, including language, dress and social customs, and claims especially to an Arab ancestry, became integral to an authentic Islamic identity in the Indian subcontinent. (Ahmed 2001, pp.9–10)

The attitudes of Mughal officials posted in Bengal towards its indigenous population exacerbated these feelings of cultural distance. Accustomed to north Indian ways, the *ashraf* classes regarded far-off Bengal as distinctly alien, a 'hell full of bread' (Van Schendel 2009, p.60), peopled by 'mere fishermen' whose culture, diet and way of life were far inferior to their own. A student of *ashraf* culture in Bengal noted the constant harking back to the land of its origins:

> Urdu poetry exuded the nostalgia for lands that had been left behind long ago, but never forgotten. It sang of the cooler lands where roses bloomed and nightingales sang, where lilies made the air fragrant and tulips carpeted the forests, where the plane trees brightened the autumn with their red leaves and cypresses stood sentinel on the running springs. (Qureshi 1965, pp.12–13, cited in Khan 1996, p.123)

The *ashraf* classes had little inclination to convert the local population to Islam, despite pressure from local mullahs and Sufi preachers. Even the Indian-born Muslim officials from Punjab shared the beliefs of the Mughals that Islam was by definition foreign to Bengal and its natives could not be Muslims. Their own adherence to Islam, their family origins and their political connections to north India all served to distinguish them from the delta's indigenous peoples.

These attitudes make the mass conversion of the peasant masses of the eastern delta to Islam even less explicable. While the scale of the conversion did not become known to the rulers of Bengal till the 1882 census, it was too large to have occurred overnight. Various theories were put forward to explain the 'incongruity of masses of Muslims turning up in regions far from the ancient centres of Muslim domination' (Eaton 1994, p.120). However, as Khan points out, few of the early theories were able to explain why it was only in the eastern region of Bengal among all of India's interior provinces that this mass conversion occurred.

Two explanations in the recent literature do attempt to come to grips with the geographical specificity of conversion. Both revolve around the dynamic relationship between the geography of the delta and the organisation of its social life but interpret this relationship somewhat differently. According to Eaton (1994), the main process of conversion took place in the late 16th century during Mughal rule, the period when the changing course of the river system opened up the eastern delta to the possibility of settled rice cultivation. Although ownership of land was ultimately vested in the Mughal emperor, a distinctive land tenure system was established in Bengal in order to encourage the spread of settled cultivation while extracting as much wealth as possible from the land. Imperial officials were appointed to work with the help of local Hindu administrators who were familiar with the land and people to ensure a steady flow of tax revenues to the imperial courts in Delhi.

Revenue was collected by a system of intermediaries or *zamindars*, who generally resided in the provincial capital and had access to the office of the chief provincial revenue officer. High-caste Hindus, typically Brahmins or Baidyas, predominated the upper reaches of the administrative system. Social taboos prevented them from undertaking the cultivation themselves, but they acquired *zamindari* rights from the Mughal governor, which permitted them to extract as much profit as they could from a given *taluk* (estate) as long as they remitted the stipulated amount of land revenue to the government. They advanced capital to enterprising colonists, largely 'charismatic' holy men or *pirs* drawn from the lower Muslim religious establishment, but also Hindus from the middle ranks.

Their reputation for religious power and piety gave these pioneers the capacity to enlist followers, usually immigrants from the western and northern districts of Bengal, to clear the forests, plant rice fields and build mosques and shrines, a requirement under the state grant. The hundreds of tiny mosques and shrines dedicated to holy Muslim men that sprang up across the interior of eastern Bengal were intended to create stable communities loyal to the Mughal state. These institutions facilitated the diffusion of uniquely Islamic conceptions of divine and human authority among peasant communities who had been 'only lightly touched, if touched at all, by Hindu civilization' (Eaton 1994, p.309).

The other explanation comes from Khan (1996), who suggests that the conversion to Islam was a more drawn-out process than suggested by Eaton.[3] Sufi preachers had been active in Bengal some time before the Mughal conquest. There was intensive missionary activity from the 13th century, although a major surge occurred in the period discussed by Eaton. These preachers had been active in other parts of the subcontinent for some time before they began their activities in Bengal. Yet nowhere had the conversion to Islam occurred on the scale it did in Bengal. Khan argues that it was unlikely that Sufi preachers were somehow more powerful, more persuasive or more persistent in Bengal than elsewhere. Instead, he suggests that the challenges faced by the inhabitants of the delta who sought to make a living in an uncertain and hazardous environment had given rise to a social environment that proved particularly conducive to efforts at proselytisation. He uses the pattern of settlements in the eastern delta to make his point.

British officials had noted that rural settlements in northern India were organised along corporate lines – a nucleus of households belonging to cultivators and labourers who worked on the land alongside households belonging to various service providers such as the village watchman and money lenders, a common meeting place, a place of worship and some basic form of municipal government. This corporate pattern reflected the governance of rural communities along caste lines: powerful and intensely conservative Hindu communities such as Jats and Rajputs were governed by a strong Brahmin hierarchy independently of the state. These communities resisted all attempts at religious proselytisation by Muslim rulers, using the ultimate sanction of social ostracism to discourage anyone who might wish to convert.

Nor was it in the interests of the Muslim state to challenge the social structure of Brahmanism as long as its overriding goal of wealth extraction was not hindered. Instead, as Bose and Jalal (1998) note, the Mughals sought to preserve law and order by creating a parallel system of courts alongside specifically Islamic ones. Muslim law officers were given some degree of flexibility in interpreting *sharia* law, while other religious communities were allowed to consult their own local customs and religious laws in personal matters such as marriage and inheritance. The strength of the caste hierarchy in the northern plains of India where Muslim rule was at its most concentrated and caste oppression at its harshest was precisely the reason for the failure of Islamic missionary efforts in this region.

Patterns of settlement were far less corporate in the province of Bengal than elsewhere in India and the degree of corporateness of rural institutions within Bengal itself diminished gradually from west to east. Better communications meant that West Bengal were more securely integrated into the Hindu culture of the northern Gangetic plains. Its villages were more nucleated than those in the east, its settlements older and characterised by a more elaborate division of labour and a more established caste system. The strength of its caste-based organisation and the unchallenged authority of Brahmins in social life explained the resilience of traditional mechanisms of social control in the face of Muslim rulers.

This was less the case in the active eastern delta. The geography here had given rise to very diffuse patterns of settlement, dictated by the location of elevated land desirable for homestead construction in the face of regular seasonal flooding. Settlements had to be flexible and were often transient: the lay of the land changed frequently in the active delta and villagers were frequently forced to relocate and rebuild their houses elsewhere. Few rural dwellings were built to last. The result was amorphous patterns of settlement throughout the East Bengal countryside, where houses were dispersed with little or no physical demarcation where one village ended or another began (Mandelbaum 1970, p.337).

Social organisation was consequently much weaker in the villages of the eastern delta. As one official noted, 'the more east and north the country lay from the centre of Brahmanical orthodoxy the lesser was and even today is, its grip on the social organization' (Roy 1945, p.44, cited in Khan 1996, p.114). While patrilineal descent groups existed in East Bengal, they did not have the social cohesiveness or cultural significance of the endogamous patrilineal kinship groups of Muslims in northern India or of the endogamous *jati* groups of fully developed Hindu caste society.

Village organisation was also undermined by other particularities of geography. The abundant availability of fertile cultivable land in the active delta meant that it continued to receive immigration from neighbouring provinces so that the settlement of new land continued. The threat of social ostracism had little power since families could always find land elsewhere to clear for cultivation and to build homes. In addition, given the unpredictability of the environment and constant changes in the boundaries between land and water, the people of the lower delta were accustomed to resorting to physical violence, to their skills with the *lathi* (cudgel), to establish their claims after a flood had changed the location of cultivable land.

These conditions did not lend themselves to tightly organised village communities with centralised administrative power. Reports of the period noted that, while men of influential position commanded a certain account of respect, there appeared to be a near-total absence of the 'germs of corporate life' and very little semblance of civic unity (Martin 1923; Thompson 1921). Khan suggests that it was this weakness in social organisation, the absence of effective restrictions on the individual's choice of belief and practices, which allowed 'unbridled individualism' in much of East Bengal, promoting a 'congenial environment for heresy, heterodoxy and esoteric practices' (p.114). In the face of a Brahminical hierarchy that reduced the 'semi-amphibious aborigines of Bengal' into 'hewers of wood and drawers of water' for masters who regarded them as 'unclean beasts and altogether abominable' (Beverley 1872, p.95), the peasant cultivators, fishermen, woodcutters and boatmen of the Bengal delta responded with enthusiastic support for every major anti-Brahminical movement throughout its history – Buddhism, Vaishnavism and then finally Islam (Addi and Azad 1975).

Conversion to Islam did not happen overnight but as a slow and imperceptible process of mutual accommodation made possible by prolonged cultural contact between exogenous Islamic practices and the pre-existing Hindu-Buddhist and non-Sanskritic belief systems of pre-modern Bengal. The Sufi mystics who had been trickling into the region for centuries had made Islamic ideas and practices easy for its peasant cultivators and fishermen to understand

and accept. These ideas and practices gradually merged with locally existing religious ideas and worldviews and came to dominate them over time.

Examples of this fusion can be found in the rich tradition of folk ballads that were passed orally by generations of professional bards and in the romances, epics, narratives and devotional poems that featured in Bengali literature. They showed not only the efforts of writers to translate Perso-Islamic romantic literature into the Bengali language but also to adapt the whole range of Perso-Islamic civilisation to the Bengali cultural universe. As Eaton writes,

> Thus the Nile was identified with the Ganges and a story set in biblical Egypt alludes to dark forests filled with tigers and elephants ... The countryside in such stories abounds with banana and mango trees, peacocks and chirping parrots; people eat fish, curried rice, ghee and sweet yogurt, and chew betel; women adorn themselves with sandal paste and glitter in silk saris and glass and gold bangles. Everywhere one smells the sweet aroma of fresh rice plants. (1994, p.277)

He comments also on the efforts of a Sufi poet from late 16th-century Chittagong region who 'spared no detail' in endowing Eve with the unmistakeable attributes of a Bengali beauty.

> She uses sandal powder and wraps her hair in a bun adorned with a string of pearls and flowers. She wears black eye paste, and a pearl necklace is draped around her neck. Adam is struck by the beauty of the spot (*sindur*) on her forehead 'because it reminded him of the sun in the sky'. (p.278)[4]

The eastern delta's long history of isolation also meant that the social practices of classic patriarchy came later to the region than it did elsewhere and took a form that was mediated by local practices. Eaton points out that in Bengal, both before and during the rise of Islam, outsiders had commented on the visibility of women in the society. In 1415, the Chinese ambassador to Bengal noted the absence of a rigid division of labour in productive activities, with both men and women engaged in the fields and in weaving, depending on the season. In 1595, another observer commented that men and women for the most part went naked, wearing only a cloth (*lungi*) around the loins and that the main public transactions fell to women (Van Schendel 2009).

By 1700, the process of Islamisation had proceeded to the point that romantic literature set in the Bengali countryside included Muslim peasants as central characters, but the rigid gender division of labour and the practice of secluding women within the domestic domain had not yet made an appearance. A ballad composed in 1700 described both men and women working alongside each other in the fields, harvesting rice, spreading it for drying and transplanting it.

The gradual evolution of a Muslim culture in the delta could be seen in the changing status of women in rural society. The scriptural norms that gave men authority over women were gradually translated into social reality. At some stage in its history, women began to withdraw from field-based operations and confine themselves to post-harvest operations within the home: winnowing, soaking, parboiling, husking. The primary drive behind the domestication of female labour appeared to be the gradual dissemination of norms associating proper Islamic behaviour with the observance of *purdah*. There was, in other words, quite a time lag between the appearance of a normative vision of Islamic propriety in gender relations among the communities in the delta and its realisation in the practices that were seen as established norm in the studies of patriarchy in the post-independence period.

By the time the British conquered the delta, most of its rural masses thought of themselves as Muslims, but the line separating Islam and non-Islam was porous and shifting. This can be seen in the renaming practices observed among Muslim peasants in the early 20th century. The syncretic processes through which they converted to Islam meant that many had retained their Hindu caste names. The 1872 census recorded that, of the total of around 17 million Muslims in Bengal, just 1.5% claimed foreign extraction as Shaikhs, Pathans, Saiyads and Mughals, the four highest-status social groups among Indian Muslims. By the 1901 census, around 90% of the 21.5 million Muslims in the delta had dropped their caste names and claimed to be Shaikhs.

Eaton interprets this adoption of Arabic surnames as evidence of a deepening attachment to Islam. Roy (1983) suggests a more pragmatic interpretation, noting the social importance attached to foreign extraction and a tendency to claim fictitious foreign ancestry by those aspiring to social position. 'People began to *discover* for themselves as far as possible a foreign ancestry' (p.62). In the fluid 'frontier' context of the eastern delta, it was possible for Muslims other than those in the most menial occupations to call themselves Shaikhs (Sopher 1980). It was a strategy that spoke to the optimism of the low-born Muslim, escaping his fate as a low-caste Hindu, about the prospect of upward mobility, captured in a saying popular across the region: 'Last year I was a Jolaha, this year I am a Shaikh, next year if prices rise I shall be a Syed' (Ahmed 1981, p.21).[5]

2.3 British rule in India: from company to empire

The power of the Mughal empire had begun to decline by the mid-18th century and Bengal came once again under local rule, this time Muslim *nawabs* of non-Bengali origin who had been governing in the name of the Mughal emperor. This was also a period of rising European influence in the subcontinent, with Portuguese, Dutch and English companies competing for trade.

In the end, it was the British East India Company, which had been granted a trading monopoly in India by the British Parliament, which gained ascendance and grew into a vast military and administrative organisation able to secure British colonial interests across the subcontinent.

There were some important advances under British rule – better transport, institutions of higher education, an administrative structure – but, as with other rulers, much of its energy was channelled into efforts to intensify surplus extraction. Its success in this endeavour can be seen from estimates provided by the British economic historian Angus Maddison (2006), according to whom India's share of the world economy was 27% in the last years of the Mughal empire – as large as all of Europe put together. By the time the British departed, it had dropped to 3%. British rule led to the steady impoverishment of much of the population and to the creation of lethal religious divisions, the effects of which endured beyond the end of empire.

Transforming the economy

The East India Company wrested political control from the ruling *nawab* in 1757 and ruled it thereafter through a series of puppets. In 1765, it signed a contract with the last of the Mughal emperors, by now only a nominal power, to become the primary revenue collector in Bengal and hence its de facto ruler. The apparently inexhaustible wealth of Bengal encouraged the steady intensification of efforts by the company to increase tax revenue.[6] Within a few years of its rule in Bengal, the company's efforts at extraction and unchecked profiteering turned the drought and floods of 1769–70 into an epic famine in which a third of Bengal's population was estimated to have died.

Efforts were subsequently made to regularise the taxation system through a new system of land ownership. The Permanent Settlement Act (1793) assigned de facto ownership of land to the *zamindars* of Bengal by giving them private property rights in revenue collection (Bose and Jalal 1998, p.69). It brought about momentous changes in the rural structure. The old system recognised the right of peasants to till the soil and the right of *zamindars* to collect taxes. The new system recognised only the rights of the new landlords: to sell, mortgage or gift their land; to set the rent at their discretion, while the amount they remitted as tax to the state was settled in perpetuity; and to exercise formidable powers of extra-economic coercion over peasants. Cultivators became *raiyats*, tenants who had the right to work the land only if they paid their rent regularly and who could transfer this right only through inheritance, not sale.

The Act had assumed that *zamindars* would invest in agriculture to make it more productive since the fixed amount of tax they were required to pay meant any increased surplus would remain in their hands. But there were easier ways for them to make money. They became an absentee rentier class, extracting ever higher rents from the tenants who cultivated their land. They appointed their own intermediaries, leading to a multi-tiered system of leisured tenure-holders, all living off the wealth created by the tillers of the soil.

Meanwhile, company rule remained a reign of terror for Bengal's weavers as it used 'every conceivable roguery', including fines, imprisonments, floggings and forced bonds, to acquire their cloth at a fraction of its value (Hartmann and Boyce 1983, p.11). Its excesses sparked the rebellion of 1857 and the British government stepped in to take over control and to extract economic advantage from its colonial possession in a more orderly way. Using Bengal as its base, the British undertook a steady expansion of their control across large swathes of land in the Ganges valley. The profits from its trade in Bengal's textiles were used to finance colonial conquest of other parts of India, but also to finance its own industrial revolution, including the mechanised production of textiles (Bose and Jalal 1998). Britain used an elaborate system of protection to eliminate competition from Bengal's textiles in British markets so that its own textile industry could grow while it used taxes within India to discriminate against the market in local textiles. The local industry was systematically destroyed, commercial centres declined and thousands of artisans were forced to turn to the land for a living.

Deindustrialisation meant that agriculture became the main source of surplus. The colonial period saw the introduction of large-scale export-oriented cash cropping and Bengal emerged as a supplier of agricultural raw materials to the world. The earliest of these export crops was indigo, based on a contract labour system close to slavery till a major peasant revolt pushed the indigo planters to other states. Jute then became the major cash crop, grown by smallholders across the delta. By the end of the 19th century, East Bengal produced half of the world's jute, although the manufacture of jute fibre and products took place in mills in Calcutta and Dundee.

By the end of the Raj, the delta had been transformed from a balanced agrarian economy into the classic colonial pattern, importing manufactured goods from the metropolis and exporting a variety of agricultural raw materials. With the age-old agrarian frontier closing, the expansion of cultivation was no longer possible while the *zamindari* system blocked investment in raising agricultural productivity: 'rural living standards had been low at the beginning of British rule; they were lower still at its end' (Van Schendel 2009, p.74).

The politics of empire: dividing and ruling

As in other parts of its empire, the British adopted a conscious divide and rule policy in order to govern their subjects. These divisions were along a number of fault lines, but the religious divide had the most far-reaching consequences. Censuses from 1872 onwards required the population to identify itself by religion and caste, a recurring exercise with profound implications. It was the first step in carving out an ideological space within which geographically scattered and culturally differentiated groups were now encouraged to reconstitute themselves as coherent supra-local social categories based on shared religious or caste identity.

Divide and rule policies were advanced through efforts to codify what had been informal norms and practices of different religious groups. While the colonial rulers established a standardised legal system for their subjects in the domains of civil and criminal law, the 1857 uprising persuaded them to refrain from interfering in the personal laws that sustained the social order of traditional Indian society. They passed legislation on a number of practices they found particularly abhorrent (such as child marriage, female infanticide and widow immolation) but invoked the 'inviolability of the home' (Miller 1981, p.52) to adopt an overall policy of non-interference with regard to personal law. This governed relationships within the private sphere of the family, including those relating to marriage, divorce, maintenance, guardianship of children, adoption, succession and inheritance, all of which had direct implications for the status of men, women and children within the family. Such matters would continue to be regulated by the religious laws of each community but these would be codified after consultations with learned authorities within each religion, its priests, scholars and clerics.

The interpretations given by these authorities bore little relationship to the more fluid and syncretic practices that prevailed in local communities (Bose and Jalal 1998; Menon 1998). Codification effectively subsumed the diversity of religious customs and practices of different social groups, the 'little' traditions of ordinary people, within the rubric of the 'great' traditions, as defined by those with interpretive power within each religion. It reconstituted the meaning of community along primarily religious lines, in effect sharpening the hitherto fuzzy boundaries of overlapping community identities and reinforcing politically demarcated ones. The religious basis of personal law, and its treatment of women as unequal citizens, remains in operation to the present day across much of the subcontinent.

Divide and rule also worked along political lines. The British had originally favoured their Hindu subjects, distrusting the Muslim elites from whom they had seized power. Their own policies had served to create a new Hindu elite in West Bengal. One of the effects of the Permanent Settlement Act was the changing religious composition of the *zamindari* gentry in the eastern delta. Whereas Muslims had dominated in the reclamation of the eastern delta during the Mughal period, the British colonial period saw the advance of Hindu landlords, high-caste Hindus who worked for the company and understood the system (Bose and Jalal 1998). By the 1920s, the *zamindar* class in Bengal was predominantly Hindu. In the western regions of Bengal, where the majority of cultivators were also Hindu, class tensions between landlord and tenant did not take on a religious slant. But, in East Bengal, religious and class divisions began to overlap, with high-caste Hindus at the upper end of the tenure chain and mainly Muslim cultivators at the lowest end.

The new Hindu rentier class lived as urban-based absentee landlords. Their ability to take advantage of Western education and administrative jobs led to urban professionals, Westernised intelligentsia, clerics and others emerging from the ranks of the *zamindars* and *taluqdars*. They styled themselves as the *bhadrolok* (the 'respectable' folk), in antithesis to the *chotolok* (the 'small' people) who laboured in the fields. They also began to draw on various strands of Hindu tradition and mythology, harking back to the greatness of Hindu rulers in the pre-Mughal era, to argue for a greater role for Indians in their own government. The Indian National Congress had been founded in 1885 to promote the principle that the privileges of British subjects be extended to obedient Indians. It now began to coalesce around a nationalist politics that claimed the right to self-rule.

Their alarmed rulers began extending patronage to sections of the Muslim community to serve as a counterweight to this Hindu nationalism. In 1905, the government decided to partition Bengal, ostensibly for reasons of administrative efficiency but with a clear political agenda, spelt out by Herbert Risley, secretary to the viceroy: 'Bengal united is a power … Bengal divided would pull in different directions' (Bose and Jalal 1998, p.117). Educated Muslims supported the partition because it offered opportunities in the colonial administrative structure they did not enjoy in united Bengal. In addition, the cultural politics espoused by the Hindu upper castes, its appeal to Hindu revivalism, alienated many Muslims. The All-India Muslim League was formed in Dhaka by a group of *ashraf* politicians in 1906 with the objective of protecting the interests of Muslims in British India. But there was vocal opposition to partition from Hindu middle and upper classes in Bengal, who feared loss of economic power and administrative privilege. Their opposition was picked up at the national level and became an all-India cause, sparking anti-colonial organising across India. The British gave in to the opposition and annulled the partition in 1911.

Within Bengal itself, partition exposed the division between religious communities. Opposing views on the partition of Bengal gave rise to mob violence between religious groups and strengthened religious solidarities. It heralded the 'communalization' of politics in that 'Muslims' and 'Hindus' became clear-cut *political* categories (Van Schendel 2009, p.80). In 1909, in response to the request of the Muslim League, separate electorates were created for Muslims so that they voted separately for reserved seats.[7]

Political unrest in the countryside

The process by which Muslims began to define themselves self-consciously as a community was not an easy one. They continued to be characterised by traditional hierarchies of birth and status. The small but powerful urban-based *ashraf* elite, aristocratic by birth, considered themselves the guardians of 'authentic' Islamic culture and resisted assimilation into indigenous Bengali culture, speaking only Persian, Arabic and, later, Urdu. The vast majority of Bengali Muslims, on the other hand, the *ajlaf*, saw themselves as part of the larger Bengali community comprising Hindus, Muslims, Buddhists and animists with deep roots in the region's rural culture.

But, as agriculture became increasingly commercialised by the introduction of railways, a mainly Muslim class of rich tenant farmers, the *jotedars*, producing jute and other cash crops, began to emerge in the countryside by the second half of the 19th century. The spread of education among these families led to the formation of a new 'vernacular' elite among the Muslims, one that originated in the small towns and rural areas of East Bengal and had agriculture as its main source of income.

There were tensions within this expanding middle class. The *ashraf* elite supported the status quo and an extra-territorial vision of Islam and north Indian culture. The vernacular elite favoured agrarian reform to curb exploitation of peasant cultivators from whose ranks they had emerged, and they were attached to their indigenous cultural heritage and its understanding of Islam. But British rule had deprived the Muslim aristocracy of its political and economic privileges, narrowing their distance from their vernacular co-religionists. As conditions of Muslim Bengali peasantry worsened under British rule, various movements materialised in the countryside, pitting cultivators and the rising Muslim middle class against Hindu *zamindars*, European entrepreneurs and the colonial state.

Religion played a role in these movements. Developments in the transportation system, the rising incidence of pilgrimage to Arabia and the spread of literacy brought ordinary Muslims in Bengal closer to the wider world of Islam, making them more aware of the difference in beliefs and practices current in the Arab heartland. The 19th and early 20th centuries saw waves of Islamic reform movements such as the Faraizi and the Tariqah-i-Muhammadiyah emerge in the Bengal countryside. They were led by Bengali preachers who had spent years in Mecca and returned home with ideas derived from its austere Wahhabi Islamic movement,[8] determined to strip Bengali Islam of the indigenous beliefs and practices of its folk culture. By propagating strict Islamic observances, these movements had the potential to rend the syncretic cultural fabric that tied Hindu and Muslim cultivators together in a common social life. But in reality they were hardly ever frontal assaults on popular religion; over time they evolved into peasant struggles, broadening along class lines, and ending up in violent confrontation with their Hindu *zamindars* and the colonial state. As a result, it was not always simple to distinguish between movements that were ostensibly communitarian, class or communal in character (Addy and Azad 1975; Bose and Jalal 1998).

The road to partition: 'Two peoples fanatically at odds'[9]

The last decades of colonial rule were marked by nationalist civil disobedience campaigns to demand that the British quit India. But resistance to British rule was fractured along communal lines, which sharpened over time, leading to the widespread violence and killing that led up to and accompanied the partition of India. Communist-inspired strikes and peasant movements against agrarian oppression in Bengal presented a strong challenge to the privileges of upper-caste Hindu landlord and professional classes. Their response was to interpret nationalism through an increasingly communal lens and the Bengal

Congress Party renewed its attempts to build its base among Hindus, seeking support from the lower castes.

At the same time, the two-nation theory, the idea that Muslims were not merely a separate community within the Indian nation but a separate nation with the right to self-determination, was beginning to take shape. In 1940, the Muslim League adopted a resolution that geographically contiguous units be demarcated into regions in which Muslims were in the majority, namely the north-western and eastern zones of India, and grouped together to form independent states within a Muslim Free National Homeland.

The disruptions associated with the Second World War hit the rural poor badly. The devastating Bengal famine of 1943–44, which resulted in the loss of around 3 million lives, mostly in the eastern delta, provided a dramatic illustration of colonial priorities to ensure food supplies for its own troops and for the urban industrial classes who were deemed essential for war production. Any legitimacy that the Raj may have enjoyed in Bengal faded after the famine.

Rising nationalist demands, the financial debts incurred by the British as a result of the war, and the installation of a new Labour government all brought the question of British withdrawal from India to the forefront of the political agenda. The increasingly unmanageable state of affairs in the country added to the haste with which they did so. The decision was taken to partition India and, just six weeks before their departure, two boundary commissions, both headed by Sir Cyril Radcliffe, were appointed to decide how Bengal and Punjab would be divided. The violence that accompanied partition is estimated to have killed one million people and displaced 12 million. There was a swift, bloody and almost complete exchange of Muslim and non-Muslim inhabitants across the Punjab border. According to the 1951 census, religious minorities, mainly Christian, made up less than 2% of the population in West Pakistan. The bloodshed in Bengal was also massive but the exchange was a more long-drawn-out one. The Hindu minority made up 22% of the population in East Pakistan at the time of partition.

2.4 The Pakistan interlude

The new state of Pakistan was a geographical anomaly, consisting of two wings on the eastern and north-western borders of the subcontinent, separated by over 1,000 miles of hostile Indian territory. Aside from religion, the two wings had very little in common. West Pakistan was made up of four geographically contiguous provinces with distinct cultural and ethnic identities but with a shared interpretation of Islam. Carved out of the eastern delta of the province of Bengal, East Pakistan was more homogenous. The vast majority of the population shared a common language and ethnic identity, diet, dress and religious tradition. It also contained 55% of the country's population. The country's first constitution, put in place in 1956, declared it to be an Islamic

Republic, making it the first theocratic state of the modern world (Israel followed two years later). It also allowed selected political parties to function within restricted parameters and a number of provincial elections were held.

The country was characterised from the outset by a high level of administrative and political centralisation. Political power was concentrated in the hands of a national elite drawn mainly from the landed aristocracy of West Pakistan, wealthy *muhajirs* (migrant trading communities) from India, most of whom had settled in the West, and some *ashraf* politicians from the eastern wing. They were supported by a highly centralised civil service based in the country's capital in West Pakistan. They also monopolised key positions in banking, administration, business and the armed forces.

The eastern wing was marginalised within this political set up. At the time of partition, only one of the 133 Muslims from the Indian Civil Service who opted for Pakistan was a Bengali Muslim. Most trained civil servants who had worked for the British administration in Bengal had been Hindus and opted for India. There was very little Bengali participation in the military services or in higher ranks of the civil service. Few Bengalis made it to the top of the service and those who did were from the Urdu-speaking *ashraf* elite.

In the face of their marginalisation, the vernacular elite that had begun to emerge from the Bengali-speaking lower middle classes founded their own political party, the Awami Muslim League, in 1949, based on a distinct linguistic nationalism (Jahan 1972). Worth noting here is that Sheikh Mujibur Rahman, who later became the first prime minister of independent Bangladesh, was the assistant secretary general of the party. The party's support came from the faction within the Muslim League that had been anti-landlord in its politics. It also drew support from other groups opposed to the policies of the ruling elite, including the Communist Party and various student organisations.

Pakistan's political class was swept aside by a military coup in 1958 led by Ayub Khan. The new regime introduced a system of local government designed to both restrict democratic participation and neutralise East Pakistan's majority in the electoral system. Around seven to 15 individuals were elected by direct franchise to union *parishads* (local councils), the lowest administrative unit, and given limited local powers for revenue collection and management of rural development projects. The state thus appeared at local level as a dispenser of valued resources. These 'basic democrats' were responsible for electing the provincial and national assemblies, with equal numbers selected by each wing. This system deprived the population of direct voting rights, instead allowing selected local groups from their ranks to enjoy patronage of the regime in exchange for their loyalty. It did, however, put in place some of the infrastructure of local government that still exists in Bangladesh today (Lewis 2011).

Women made some limited progress during the Pakistan years. While there were a number of local voluntary organisations, the first and most prominent was the All-Pakistan Women's Association (APWA), set up in 1947 by the wife of its first prime minister (Khan 2018). Though composed of elite women, and largely active in the urban centres, the association lobbied on a number of issues that had cross-class relevance. It struggled, but without success, to include a Charter of Women's Rights in the 1956 constitution. While 10 seats were reserved for women, this fell far short of their demands.

Their efforts to promote family planning met with some success under the Ayub Khan regime as part of its efforts to project a modern style of leadership. A government family planning programme was established under the Third Five Year Plan (1965–70). The programme operated independently of the Health Ministry under the National Family Planning Council. It was target-driven, largely supply-oriented, with the main focus on IUDs and vasectomies, and implemented through hospitals, dispensaries, health centres and individual doctors. It spread information about modern contraceptives but did little to change practice. Contraceptive prevalence was only 3.8% in in 1968–69 (Larson and Mitra 1992).

The APWA also organised around the reform of Muslim personal law to protect the rights of women in relation to marriage, polygamy, divorce, maintenance, inheritance and child custody. The Muslim Family Laws Ordinance (1961), passed under the Ayub regime, was a product of their activism. The ordinance is considered a landmark for women's progress because, despite embodying a narrow interpretation of Islamic law, it modified some key discriminatory practices (Khan 2018).

Economic exploitation

The bulk of resources and industry had gone to India after partition. Pakistan inherited raw material producing regions, mainly in the eastern wing. The administrative integration of the two discrete territories allowed the central government to frame policies to promote the interests and priorities of the ruling classes of the western wing. Pakistan benefited considerably from external funding, particularly from the US as part of its Cold War strategy. Between 1959 and 1969, when the flow of external aid grew sixfold, West Pakistan was allocated five times more aid than the east. Between 1949–50 and 1969–70, economic disparity in per capita income between East and West Pakistan increased from 21.9% to 61%.

More than half of the country's central expenditure was invested in the military. A third of the remaining budget went on a rapid industrialisation drive through support to private enterprise, based primarily in the western wing. Industrial development in the eastern wing was led by state-sponsored entrepreneurs from the western wing, mainly in the processing of raw materials – sugar, tea, paper mills. A mere tenth of the budget went on agriculture, which was the main source of income and livelihoods in East Pakistan and whose jute provided two-thirds of country's foreign exchange.

There had been an opportunity to bring about a more equal distribution of land at the time of partition when a large number of Hindu landlords, who had owned nearly 75% of the land, migrated to India. The East Bengal State

Acquisition and Tenancy Act 1950 eliminated the rights of *zamindars* and their intermediaries, made peasant cultivators the direct tenants of the state and imposed a ceiling on landholdings of 32 acres per family. However, powerful *jotedar* families were able to grab the property of Hindu landlords who had left, using various means to circumvent the land ceiling. The reform eradicated the old tax-harvesting elite but reinforced unequal ownership of land and left sharecroppers without rights.

There was a great deal of investment around this time in the new high-yielding seed technology of the Green Revolution, which promised to increase agricultural productivity, but it mainly made headway in West Pakistan, where the large size of land holdings and the well-developed irrigation system inherited from the British provided favourable conditions. One initiative in the eastern wing that does stand out from that period was the experiment with rural co-operatives. Community development through the US-funded Village Agricultural and Industrial Development (V-AID) programme had been introduced in 1953. In 1958, the Academy for Rural Development was established in the Comilla district of East Pakistan to train V-AID officials. The top-down character of the V-AID approach led to its abandonment in 1961. Instead the academy began to experiment with the co-operative approach. Villagers were formed into co-operative societies through which training, research and extension activities were provided in order to modernise agriculture.

When the military came into power, the co-operatives became the lynch-pin of its efforts to win local-level legitimacy. It added family planning programmes, irrigation and electrification schemes, credit facilities, women's training, and the storage and marketing of agricultural produce. The co-operatives, linked by a *thana*-level federation,[10] served as channels for the infusion of subsidised resources: credit, irrigation pumps, fertiliser, improved seeds, pesticides and extension services. The Comilla experiment was held up for a while as a model for developing countries, an alternative to the compulsory communes of China. Problems became evident by the late 1960s. Large farmers were initially slow to join because they got quicker returns from moneylending but began to monopolise the co-operatives as their advantages became apparent (Blair 1978). In 1970, the government decided to use the Comilla model as the basis of a new nationwide Integrated Rural Development Program (IRDP) but did not get very far in East Pakistan because of its deteriorating political situation.

Cultural antagonisms

The imbalances in the political and economic systems that became evident soon after the inception of the new state were mirrored very visibly in the cultural arena. In fact, the first cracks took a cultural form and reflected divisions over the question of a national language. Jinnah, who led the movement for Pakistan and was the country's first governor-general, declared in a visit to East Pakistan in 1948:

Make no mistake about it. There can be only one state language if the component parts of this state are to march forward in unison and that language, in my opinion can only be Urdu.[11]

It was, he said, the language that had been nurtured by a hundred million Muslims on the subcontinent, a language that more than any other embodied all that was best in Islamic culture and Muslim tradition and was nearest to the languages used in other Islamic countries (Jinnah 2004, p.150). In fact, in Pakistan itself, Urdu was spoken by just 3% of the population, mainly the wealthy migrants from India.

The language issue stood for a more general cultural and political divide within the new nation. The new rulers used their version of Islam as a political idiom to legitimate their actions, portraying all opposition as un-Islamic. Their ability to do so reflected the long-standing view among Muslims of the north Indian heartlands that Bengali Muslims were lesser Muslims. The decision to adopt Urdu as the national language was part of the mission of Islamising Bengal.

But they had underestimated the political, cultural and emotional significance that the Bengali language held for the people of East Pakistan. In 1952, student-led protests at attempts to impose Urdu as the national language were suppressed by the army and led to the death of six students. The Muslim League suffered an overwhelming defeat in the 1954 provincial elections to the United Front led by the Awami Muslim League. The latter renamed itself the Awami League (AL) to emphasise its non-communal character and henceforth became the voice of the disenfranchised middle classes of East Pakistan. The 1956 constitution, which declared Pakistan an Islamic Republic, gave Bengali equal status with Urdu as state language.

Cultural issues came to the forefront again under the military regime. A Bureau for National Reconstruction was set up to purge the Bengali language of Sanskrit/Hindu elements and to introduce the Arabic script. The songs of Tagore, the Hindu Nobel-prize winning laureate from West Bengal, were banned from the state-controlled radio and television. The regime's attempts to appropriate the mantle of Islamic authenticity for its cultural traditions were met by counterefforts on the part of Bengalis that crystallised what was particular to *their* community: its common history and distinct way of life, reaffirmed continuously through shared cultural references, rituals and modes of communication. The dress and deportment of Bengali women took on increasing symbolic value in this struggle over cultural identity (Kabeer 1991a). It led to the politicisation of normally uncontroversial aspects of everyday middle-class life. The right to sing the songs of Tagore and to wear the *teep*, the practice of the Bengali middle classes of training their daughters in the arts – singing, dancing and drama – and allowing them to perform in public: 'all these activities which seemed so commonplace, now in the 50s and 60s became acts of dissent given the Pakistan government's branding of them as Hindu aberrations' (Ahmed 1985, p.47).

These cultural assertions were extended to the countryside through the close relationships that most urban-based people still had with their villages and through the broadcasting of folk music, poetry and stories on the radio. It was through its appeal to shared cultural symbols that the vernacular elite was able to stay connected with the rural population as they became more urban and more prosperous. It was also through these connections that it was able to mobilise the rural population. Although initially the province of the middle classes, Bengali nationalism had, by 1971, become a mass movement under the leadership of the AL.

The end of the interlude

The period of military rule saw political movements in East Pakistan shift from movements for equal participation in the national system to an increasingly radical movement for provincial autonomy. It came at a delicate time in Pakistan's foreign relations. It was acting as intermediary in US efforts to build a rapprochement with China. This had led to a schism between the pro-Moscow and pro-Peking factions of Pakistan's left-wing National Awami Party. It also meant that there was very little sympathy from the US for East Pakistan's demands for autonomy.

A brief war with India in 1965 made it clear to the politicians and people in East Pakistan that the priorities of the military establishment were the defence of its western wing. The east was left isolated. In 1966 the AL put forward a six-point programme, demanding a greater degree of autonomy by restructuring Pakistan as a confederation of two separate units. The programme's launch was supported by street-level demonstrations that went beyond students and intellectuals, its main supporters in the past, to include organised workers as well as a more unorganised constituency of small shopkeepers, rickshaw pullers, day labourers, and bus and taxi drivers (Jahan 1972). The regime responded with heavy-handed repression, arresting the movement's political leaders and closing down its main newspaper.

But Ayub Khan's days in power were numbered. A popular movement against the regime swept across Pakistan in 1968–69, bringing together parties in both wings. In the face of this united opposition, he resigned. The movement subsided in West Pakistan but maintained its momentum in the East as a movement for regional autonomy. There was reimposition of martial law in 1969 under General Yahya Khan but he opened up a dialogue with Bengali politicians and agreed to national elections in December 1970. In November of that year, one of the deadliest tropical cyclones ever recorded hit the delta region, killing around 500,000 people, destroying homes, crops and livestock. The callous response of the central government angered Bengalis: accounts circulated that Yahya Khan, who was returning from a successful trip to China that he had not cut short following news of the cyclone, surveyed the damage from the air while nursing a hangover with a few beers, and pronounced that 'it did not look so bad' (Hossain 2017, p.29).

The elections were held a few weeks later and saw the AL win an overwhelming victory, gaining 160 of the 162 seats allotted to East Pakistan and an absolute majority in the whole country. Bhutto's People's Party came second but won only 81 seats, confined to West Pakistan. The AL, under the leadership of Sheikh Mujibur Rahman ('Mujib'), assumed that it would take control of national government. But this was not a prospect that either the military or the People's Party was prepared to countenance. There followed a period of negotiations, apparently to find some sort of compromise. They were accompanied by mass demonstrations in East Pakistan, with activists demanding independence and carrying the flag of Bangladesh.

Faced with this mass protest, the military intervened. Its troops were secretly flown into the east wing and, on the night of 25 March 1971, began a brutal crackdown, killing all those considered in any way associated with the independence movement. The occupation of East Pakistan lasted longer than the military had anticipated. Volunteers from all over the country joined the *Mukti Bahini*, the country's freedom fighters, led by Bengalis who had served in the Pakistan army. They were able to maintain a guerrilla resistance, with training from the Indian army and support from the civilian population. They were eventually joined by the Indian army and the struggle moved into more conventional warfare. On 16 December 1971, the Pakistan army formally surrendered to the chief of the Indian army.

The war dealt a severe blow to the country's economy, destroying physical infrastructure and assets and leading to substantial declines in agricultural output and food stocks. Estimates of the human costs of the war were also enormous. Between 500,000 and 1 million were believed to have been killed. Around 10 million people crossed the borders to refugee camps in India. In addition, between 200,000 and 400,000 women were raped by Pakistani soldiers, purportedly in their mission to 'improve the genes of the Bengali people' and thus populate Bangladesh with 'pure' Muslims (Ali 1983, p.91).[12]

2.5 The legacies of the past

This chapter set out to provide the history and context that gave rise to the conditions that characterised Bangladesh at the time of its independence, the 'initial conditions' of the Bangladesh paradox. As the chapter has made clear, while its abysmal poverty at its independence partly reflected its years as quasi-colony of Pakistan, the causes went further back in its history – as did the causes of its overpopulation. The delta had been subjected to several centuries of rule by mainly foreign powers whose primary objective was to transfer wealth out of the region in order to finance the administration and expansion of their empires. The diet of the ordinary man had been poor at the end of the Mughal era; it had become poorer by the time that the British colonial rulers left (Maddison 1970). And over the Pakistan period it fell from already-low levels in the early 1960s to even lower levels by the time of Bangladesh's independence (Arthur and McNicoll 1978).

The fertility of the delta and the expansion of settled rice cultivation in the region explain the pattern of population growth. While fertility rates were extremely high, high rates of mortality had kept population growth in check at moderate rates of 1% a year at the start of the 20th century. Much of the expansion in the population during these years took the form of migration from other parts of the region as people came to settle new land.

Certain trends came together to make the high levels of fertility increasingly problematic. Improvements in transport, communications and public health measures during British rule led to a decline in mortality, gradually in the first half of the century and more rapidly after that (Cleland et al. 1994): average life expectancy rose from just 20 years at the start of the 20th century to around 40 years by the 1950s.[13] However, fertility did not adjust downward and migrants once settled tended to stay. As a result, population growth rates began to rise. The early period of population growth was accommodated by the extension of the agrarian frontier, but its natural limits were reached by the middle of the 20th century. New settlers increasingly pushed to the ecological margins, reclaiming remaining forests, coastal and river islands and much of the mangrove swamplands in the south of the delta. As the agrarian frontier closed, rural crowding in the absence of rising agricultural productivity meant that per capita output began to decline, poverty increased noticeably and life became increasingly fragile.

The chapter has also sought to explain the puzzle posed by the mass conversion to Islam in a part of the subcontinent very distant from the Muslim heartland. It has suggested that the processes by which Islam was absorbed into the pre-existing culture of the delta, and the kind of Islam that resulted, played a significant role in its subsequent history. It has explained, for instance, why the population of East Bengal joined the demand for a separate homeland for the Muslims of India at the end of British rule and why it then broke away just 24 years later to set up an independent state based on its ethno-linguistic identity.[14]

Bengali Islam has been characterised in the historical literature as 'syncretic', the willingness to accommodate as well as to co-exist with local non-Islamic folk practices. Its ballads and literature suggest communities of people who were remarkably open to accepting any sort of agency, human or super-human, that might assist them in coping with life's everyday problems. The incorporation of the practices associated with Islam into their belief systems was not seen as challenging their existing beliefs and practices or requiring their abandonment, merely as new ways to deal with existing problems (Eaton 1994). This pragmatism went hand in hand with the belief that individuals were not fated to the position they had been born into, that it was possible to improve their situation through their own efforts, to become Shaikhs and even Syeds.

So, while the chapter has provided a broad-brush account of the history of the delta and the processes that led to the abject state of the country at the time of its independence, it has also offered glimpses into the potentiality for change contained within its apparently durable structures. It has suggested some of the reasons why, while the Bengal delta may have shared many features in common with the classic form of patriarchy that characterised the northern plains of the Indian subcontinent, attempts to classify it as such were indeed, as Dyson and Moore put it, 'complicated'. Its history, as Van Schendel points out, gave rise to traditions that ran counter to later efforts to enforce more rigid versions of gender roles in the delta region. Powerful goddesses featured in its religions from early times and some remain as part of folklore. Its literature produced female characters, such as Behula and Lalmon, not known for their docility: they donned armour to fight off bandits, slayed raging rhinos, harnessed flying horses to rescue lovers, transformed ignorant men into billy goats to serve as breeding stock and instructed kings and princes of the world in the art of statecraft.

And, while there is widespread recognition in the contemporary literature of the importance of Islamic spiritual guides, *pirs* who were often connected with Sufism, they are almost always male. Indeed, recent scholarship in Bangladesh states very clearly that the *pir* role is explicitly masculine:

> in many ways *pir* serves as masculine emblems of a spiritual order which is reproduced by transmission between men. The power granted by initiation passes through perfected souls in male bodies … Women do not have the capacity to become Pir. (Landell-Mills 1992, p.315)

Yet *piranis*, women recognised to have spiritual powers, have also existed. Callan (2008) writes about saintly female healers who used their recognised spiritual powers to heal the men and women from the communities they lived in. In her ongoing research into the cultural and political economies of cotton in 18th-century East Bengal, the historian Samia Khatun came across a remarkable number of shrines devoted to *piranis*.[15] They were invisible in the official histories of the areas she visited but very alive in the memories of local communities, as present in their ballads as female goddesses. She also found evidence of hidden economies that centred on elite landed women in these areas who extended patronage to communities who looked after the shrines of *piranis*, along with small land grants to the retinue of service providers who revolved around their families, wet-nurses, dancers, musicians and midwives. These unofficial traditions and hidden histories all suggest the existence of barely acknowledged counter-currents to the dominant culture of classic patriarchy and of a collective habitus that was not as seamlessly reflective of it as was generally assumed. They may explain why classic patriarchy proved easier to negotiate in the face of the challenging conditions of later years than had been generally assumed.

Notes

1 The concepts of 'great' and 'little' traditions distinguished between formal customs and rituals observed in peasant societies that emanated from their dominant social categories, their priests and rulers, and the informal and localised practices of 'folk religion' (Redfield 1955). In reality, the two generally merged to form the lived reality of peasant life.

2 Reich (2019) has synthesised a vast array of studies that use genetic tools to provide new insights into the human past. Some of these have examined the ancestry of the ancient inhabitants of the Indian subcontinent. They suggest that there were two separate groups in ancient India: 'Ancestral North Indians' and 'Ancestral South Indians' 'as different from each other as Europeans and East Asians are today' (p.135). It was among the Ancestral North Indians that they found the emergence of a priestly caste and culture. While there has been considerable mixture of people in terms of their ancestry so that no group in India can claim genetic purity, there are different proportions of mix, with some having a stronger proportion of ancestry related to West Eurasians and some more closely related to diverse East Asian and South Asian populations. Out of curiosity after reading this literature, I took a Living DNA test and found that 48% my DNA is unspecified 'South Asian', some of it presumably my indigenous heritage, 16.8% Pashtun, 14.3% Sindhi, 4.1% Burusho, 10.6% South East Asian, 4.1% South West China and 1.8% East Asian (Japan/Korea).

3 His interpretation echoes of that Bose and Jalal (1998), who pointed out that early conversions to Islam were gradual rather than sudden and went furthest in regions where a weak Brahmanical superstructure overlaid a much stronger Buddhistic substratum, as was case in Sindh in the 8th century and Bengal after the 11th. While few religions can be regarded as completely 'pure', references to religious syncretism in the subcontinent occur particularly frequently in relation to Bengal and Sindh.

4 Eaton is relying on translation by Mannan (1966).

5 The Sayyids claimed descent from the Prophet, the Sheiks from the Prophet's Arab followers, while the Mughals and Pathans were reputed to be descended from Turkic and Afghan conquerors. The rest were lowborn *ajlaf* who were identified by Hindu caste names.

6 It was, according to sources cited in Tharoor (2018), set at a minimum of 50% of their income.

7 These were extended in 1932 to other religious minorities and the 'depressed' castes.

8 Wahhabism, a movement that rose in Saudi Arabia in the 18th century as a movement within its dominant Sunni tradition, claimed that anything

not mentioned in the Qur'an or the authentic Hadith was a *bid'ah* (innovation) and that the adoption of any innovation was a departure from Islam (Bayram 2014).

[9] These lines come from W.H. Auden's caustic 1966 poem 'Partition', which dealt with the haste with which the British drew up the boundaries that separated independent India from the newly created Pakistan (https://www.poeticous.com/w-h-auden/partition).

[10] For administrative purposes, East Pakistan/Bangladesh was divided into divisions, districts, subdivisions, *thanas/upazilas*, which were the most important unit for extending government services, and unions, the lowest administrative unit.

[11] Hindi and Urdu have their origins in the same medieval language but the two draw their formal vocabulary from different sources, Sanskrit and Persian, respectively, and Urdu is written in the Persian script. The identification of Urdu with Islam is, according to Rahman (2011), a product of the British creation of monolithic religious communities and the emergence of claims about distinctive languages to distinguish Hindus from Muslims.

[12] There is, of course, considerable debate about these numbers but, as Hossain (2017) points out, there is agreement that sexual violence during the war was 'unusually extreme' (p.80).

[13] https://en.wikipedia.org/wiki/Demographics_of_Bangladesh#Life _expectancy_at_birth

[14] Chatterji (2023) describes it as 'an astonishing occasion in modern history in which the majority seceded from a nation' (p.83).

[15] Personal communication with Dr Khatun.

3. 'The test case for development': policy debates in the aftermath of independence

For many people Bangladesh is a catalogue of woes: constant food shortage and recurrent famine, devastating floods and cyclones, disorder, violence and corruption, an uncontrollable population explosion, failure of government and administration, a malfunctioning economy beset with financial crisis and bankruptcy – a begging bowl to the rest of the world. (Faaland and Parkinson 1976, p.192)

The population is poor (per capita income of $50-$70, a figure which has not risen over the past 20 years), overcrowded (population density is nearly 1400 per square mile) and becoming more so (population is growing at 3 percent per annum), short-lived (life expectancy at birth was well under 50 years), in many cases unemployed (perhaps 25–30 percent), and largely illiterate (under 20 percent literacy rate). (World Bank 1972, p.i)

This chapter lays out the policy challenges that the country faced in the difficult years after its independence. The policy debates of this period provide an interesting reminder that, difficult as it is to imagine today, there was a period in Bangladesh's history when its leaders were seriously discussing how to go about implementing a socialist vision for the country's future. The chapter examines the practical steps they sought to take, but also failed to take, in that direction and the grim challenges they faced as an abjectly poor, overpopulated and highly patriarchal country emerging from a catastrophic war. In terms of its contribution to the aims of this book, the chapter provides a policy perspective on the dire 'initial conditions' that characterised the Bangladesh paradox and that made later progress all the more astonishing.

A memorable, and much-cited, description of the challenge facing the new nation of Bangladesh came out of a conversation between Henry Kissinger, then the US President's National Security Advisor, and officials in US Department of State on 6 December 1971.[1] For Kissinger, Bangladesh's war for independence was hampering efforts to build US relations with China with Pakistan as useful intermediary. He was now being warned that there was likely to be a famine in Bangladesh the following March and the country would need all kinds of help: 'They'll be an international basket case.' To which Kissinger responded, 'But not necessarily our basket case.'

It was a contemptuous exchange, indicative of the US's hostility to Bangladesh throughout its efforts to secede from Pakistan, but the epithet of 'basket case' haunted the literature of the period and continues to surface in contemporary discussions of those years. Its use in this exchange implied that Bangladesh would not be able to survive on its own, that it would remain permanently dependent on international aid. And indeed, as the quote from Faaland and Parkinson opening this chapter illustrates, as far as the international community was concerned, the country had all the makings of a 'basket case'. Various 'litanies of grim statistics'[2] such as that of the World Bank cited above, were compiled to summarise the enormity of the challenge.

But, for the people of the country, liberation marked the beginning of a new phase in their history. The independent People's Republic of Bangladesh would be ruled for the first time by a prime minister, Sheikh Mujibur Rahman, and a party, the Awami League, who shared the majority culture. The optimism of the time and the vision that inspired the national imaginary of those who had led the struggle were encapsulated in the four basic principles enshrined in its new constitution: nationalism, democracy, secularism and socialism.

The rationale for nationalism was self-evident. It represented the sense of national pride and belonging that had fuelled the struggle for self-governance and provided the foundations of the newly imagined national community. The principle of democracy, while a standard one for most newly independent nations, also provided a sharp contrast to the military rule that dominated the Pakistan era.

The commitment to secularism was an explicit response to the country's recent history. It signified a spirit of religious tolerance, born out of the bitter experience of the use of religion as a political weapon to devalue the country's culture and divide its citizens. It was defined as opposition to communalism in all forms, to state promotion of any religion at the expense of others and to all forms of religious discrimination. It was not intended to signal the rejection of religion by the state but the equality of all religions in the eyes of the state. One of its effects was a ban on religious political parties, which had actively supported Pakistan during the liberation war.

The adoption of socialist principles was less predictable. It was not clear whether Mujib was himself a socialist[3] but the struggle for independence had received much support from leftist groups in the country, particularly the left associated with the India–Soviet axis. Moreover, this was still the era of the dirigiste state, and socialism still held out the promise of planned development as the road to a more just society.

3.1 A turbulent beginning

In the early years of independence, the country was not in any position to embark on the aspirational agenda adopted by its leaders. The fact that different branches of the central government had been dominated by officials drawn from West Pakistan meant that there was a serious dearth of administrative expertise to manage the economy. A small group of economists with little practical experience of government was charged with crafting its development trajectory while simultaneously required to manage the daily problems confronting a country emerging from a devastating war: a serious shortage of food grains, a badly damaged transport system, inadequate financial reserves, and a breakdown in foreign trade arrangements.

The government found itself politically isolated. Its socialist rhetoric did not find favour with Western donors. At the same time, its commitment to secularism alienated the Middle Eastern bloc who had not in any case been supportive of its efforts to break away from the world's first Islamic state. But Bangladesh was a Muslim-majority country and needed to be recognised as such – at the very least to ensure its pious citizens could go on pilgrimage to Mecca. After several diplomatic overtures and efforts to establish its Islamic credentials, it gained admission into the Organisation of the Islamic Conference in 1974.

The commitment to democracy proved difficult to uphold in the face of the challenges the country faced. In addition to dealing with post-war destruction, the government faced a deterioration in the world economic situation linked to the rise in oil prices in 1973.

Bangladesh had attracted a great deal of humanitarian aid in its first three years, a product of international sympathy for 'the underdog'. This aid was ending and donors were reluctant to renew it in the face of the government's failure to take control of the economic situation. With growing evidence of corruption and nepotism in the ruling party, disillusionment set in as it became clear that the party was elevating its own interests and those of its clientele above those of the nation.

But the government had yet to face its biggest challenge. Bad harvests in 1972–73 were followed by unusually destructive floods in the summer of 1974. Later that year, the country suffered a famine of catastrophic proportions (Sobhan 1979). The situation was worsened because that year the US government decided to cancel its food aid to Bangladesh on the grounds that it was exporting jute sacks to Cuba in violation of US rules that banned food aid recipients from trade with communist countries. The deaths from the famine were estimated at 1.5 million. The suffering was widespread and visible:

> Streams of hungry people (men, women and children), who were nothing but skeletons, trekked into towns in search of food. Most of them were half-naked. Abandonment of family dependents, parents trying to sell children, mothers killing babies, man and dog fighting for a piece of bone, women and young girls turning to prostitution became very commonplace. (Alamgir 1980, pp.128–29)

Blame for the devastating effects of the famine were laid squarely at the door of the government. Mainstream and radical left groups had already begun challenging the AL's leadership. Their efforts coalesced as the human tragedy of the famine unfolded. In response to the growing unrest, Mujib declared a national emergency in early 1975 and amended the constitution to allow him to declare himself president and the Bangladesh Peasant and Workers' League (a merger of the AL and a number of left-wing parties) the sole political party. The country was now under one-party rule and a period of repression of opposition followed.

In August 1975, Mujib – and all members of his family who were in his residence at the time – were assassinated by a group of junior military officers. There followed a short period of intense political turbulence, during which many of the leading members of the AL were murdered. The military assumed power under General Ziaur Rahman, first as chief martial administrator in late 1975 and then as president in 1977. He was in turn assassinated in an army coup in 1981. Once again, martial law was declared, constitutional rights suspended and, in 1982, General Ershad declared himself president. In 1990, a popular movement saw the overthrow of Ershad and the establishment of a multi-party democracy.

3.2 Policy aspirations for a newly imagined nation

The policy discussions that took place in the years following independence provide us with a valuable record of how policymakers in a highly aid-dependent new nation that declared its commitment to socialism engaged with an international development community that was largely hostile to its aspirations. Some of these discussions were captured in the proceedings of a high-level conference convened by the International Economic Association (IEA) in Dhaka in 1973 and published under the title *The Economic Development of Bangladesh within a Socialist Framework* (Robinson and Griffin 1974).

The conference brought together eminent economists from the international community and Bangladeshi planners responsible for drafting the First Five Year Plan due later in the year. The Bangladesh members of the IEA imposed one condition on conference deliberations: they had to respect the fact that the country had chosen a socialist framework as its pathway to development. This was in order to avoid endless arguments as to whether Bangladesh would be better off with socialist or capitalist policies.

This precondition explained the composition of conference participants. The Bangladeshi participants were drawn from the Planning Commission and the Bangladesh Institute of Development Studies, which conducted policy research for the government. The international participants were made up of economists from both capitalist (mainly US and UK) and socialist (mainly East European) countries, all selected on the basis of their sympathy for the country's aspirations. According to Anisur Rahman, one of the Bangladeshi participants, there were two groups of people at the conference: those who were ignorant of Bangladesh (presumably the Eastern European economists) and those who were ignorant of socialism (presumably those from the World Bank). While participants agreed to locate their contributions within a broadly socialist framework, the discussions during the conference revealed tensions between those who described themselves as favouring pragmatism and those who espoused idealism.

Rahman (1974a) put himself squarely in the idealist camp, stating that the purpose of his contribution to the conference was 'to dream and try out ideas' (p.66). He expressed his impatience with the preoccupations of mainstream economists with mundane matters like material balances and GDP projections (Rahman 1974b). He drew instead on Marxist–Leninist theory to call for the redistribution of land, property and wealth, for shared austerity to put the country on the path to long-run self-sufficiency, for fast yielding emergency programmes that would increase output in agriculture and for the full utilisation of labour resources.[4] However, he acknowledged that 'socialism was in the air but had yet to land on the ground' (Rahman 1974a, p.66). The average elected representative was unlikely to have a clear understanding of what it meant. The first step therefore would have to be to educate and create the socialist cadres needed to carry out the necessary reforms.[5]

His analysis was strongly supported by Vanek (1974), an East European economist, who confessed he had never been to Bangladesh before but pronounced himself convinced that Rahman's prognosis demonstrated a 'considerable – and in my view entirely correct – understanding of the real situation in Bangladesh' (p.59). He commended the fact that Rahman's agenda went beyond planning to the demand for 'fundamental change of attitude – perhaps change of heart is a better term' on the part of the authorities and the people of Bangladesh.

Horvat, another East European economist, also confessed to never having visited Bangladesh and admitted his ignorance of the country was considerable: 'I ought to keep quiet and listen' (1974, p.62). He nevertheless expressed his belief that the war had opened the possibility for institutional change; society was in flux, and there was an opportunity to build a socialist society for peasants before institutions had time to harden.

Dumont (1974a), who had written extensively about socialist countries, drew on the experiences of China, North Korea and North Vietnam to suggest that the new Bangladesh recognise the dignity of manual labour and embrace a life of austerity: 'the private automobile should be banned; only bicycles should be permitted' (p.65). Thorner (1974) cautioned that too much doomsday Malthusian thinking about population growth ruled out the possibility of thinking about food production creatively, and there was nutritional value in plants that grew wild in Bangladesh – water lettuce, water lilies, hyacinths, banana leaves and ordinary weeds.

Austin Robinson, the Cambridge economist who helped organise the conference, spoke for the pragmatists. He expressed his exasperation at the failure of certain participants to engage with the urgency of the practical problems that Bangladesh was facing: 'there is danger of being too brave, too inspiring and too ambitious' (Robinson 1974a, p.65). He was concerned that those who were visiting Bangladesh for the first time had been deceived by the 'lovely, green, apparently fertile' appearance of the country in January into forgetting that it was 'unquestionably ... low in the lowest decile of world incomes per head' (Robinson 1974b, p.xv). He pointed out that it was supporting some 1,400 persons per square mile, which was 25 times the average of the United States, nearly twice as many as Belgium or the Netherlands, two and a half times as many as the United Kingdom and more than three times the average of India:

> It is too easy to forget it is an almost wholly agricultural country which, through population growth, has slipped into the position of importing year by year one-eight of its food needs. (p.xv)

He regretted that the conference did not have before it a paper that 'rubbed its nose in these problems and constraints' (1974a, p.xv) and forced it to address the key challenges that lay ahead:

> How to escape from poverty, how to maximize the growth rate of the economy consistently with doing what is possible to mitigate the effects of inequitable distribution of income, inadequate social services, maldistribution of land and institutions which tend to per-petuate these things. (p.xv)

Ranis (1974a) from Yale University also spoke in favour of a 'pragmatic social-ism' for the country: 'Can one really do away with automobiles in Bangladesh? The effort put into development will respond to the discipline of ideology but the quality of the effort also matters' (p.65). Ghosh (Jadavpur University) said that Thorner might be right, 'there is no end to the things that people could eat – slugs, rats etc.' (Ghosh 1974, p.286), but added that the goal of develop-ment was not merely to enable people to survive but to improve their diets.

3.3 Beyond aspirations: policy challenges in the 'real' world

Challenges in the economic domain

Beyond these debates about the country's aspirations to socialism, there were also concrete discussions about the policy agenda, both at the conference and in wider policy circles. These crystallised around an agreed set of pri-orities. There was widespread consensus that agriculture was the country's most urgent priority. Ninety per cent of the population of the country lived in rural areas, 80% of employment was in agriculture, 90% of exports were either agricultural products or manufactures of them and finally services were either based on agriculture or directed towards it (Faaland and Parkinson 1976).

For a number of policymakers, national planners and World Bank economists, the key to raising agricultural productivity lay in the Green Revolution package of improved seeds, fertiliser and pesticide combined with irrigation technology. World Bank economists believed that the private sector could be relied on for the immediate distribution of most inputs, while large-scale irrigation and flood protection arrangements could be left to longer run and undertaken by some combination of private initiative and state intervention.

But there were fears on the part of others that the adoption of the new technology would be concentrated in the larger farms because of the 'lumpy' nature of the investments required. Irrigation, in particular, was crucial for increasing agricultural productivity but even small-scale irrigation, such as low-lift pumps and tubewells, required large outlays and could only be adopted by farmers owning at least seven acres of land, whereas the average farm size in 1960 was just 3.5 acres (Bose 1974).

Various solutions were considered: the collectivisation of agriculture, land redistribution, the imposition of a land ceiling or the co-operative route, which could allow smaller farmers to achieve economies of scale. The argument for land redistribution chimed with the country's socialist aspirations but there were pragmatic arguments as well: widespread evidence, from Bangladesh and elsewhere, suggested that small farms were more productive than larger ones (Lipton 1974). But it encountered strong political resistance. While the post-partition departure of large numbers of Hindus had meant that the region's traditional landlords and money lenders had gone, powerful *jotedar* farmers had stepped into the gap, taking on the role of landlords, traders and moneylenders. They strongly resisted efforts to either redistribute or tax land.

In the end, the government reactivated the IRDP, the nationwide adaptation of the Comilla co-operative model, as the most practical option and one in keeping with the country's socialist ideology (Bose 1974). Because the Planning Commission had found that the co-operatives during the Pakistan era had turned into 'closed clubs of kulaks',[6] it was decided that the benefits of the programme would be more broadly distributed if small farmers and landless labourers who had not previously participated were now also included within the co-operatives (Bose 1974).

The other priorities were industry and trade. There was general agreement that, in view of the country's endowments, it needed a labour-intensive industrialisation strategy to absorb its vast reservoir of potential workers. There was also convergence of opinion about the importance of diversifying the country's export capacity. The world market for jute had been shrinking steadily in the 1970s in the face of competition from synthetic fibres leading to a decline in the country's foreign exchange earnings. Various possibilities were considered for diversifying export production including textile goods, light engineering, fish, tea and natural gas but none seemed promising. But, in the light of Bangladesh's later success in the export-oriented manufacture of garments (see Chapter 5), a prescient suggestion came from Ranis (1974b). He noted that the 1960s had seen the rapid growth of the East Asian economies through their adoption of export-oriented, labour-intensive industries such as textiles and garments but that this growth was slowing down with the tightening of their labour markets:

> It is by no means unrealistic to expect Bangladesh to ultimately become an important competitor in this area, a field vacated by Taiwan, Korea, Singapore, Hong Kong etc. whose wages are rising as a consequence of the exhaustion of their labour surpluses. (p.855)

This was greeted with scepticism by Arthur and McNicoll (1978): 'Gustav Ranis is more hopeful than we on the prospects for export-processing zones, leading in turn to decentralized, labour-intensive industrial production for export.' Even if assembly plants for re-exports on the South Korea–Taiwan model were developed, they believed it was unlikely to occur on a scale large enough to have 'more than a minor impact' (p.34).

Meanwhile, while debates about Bangladesh's transition to a modern socialist economy continued within policy circles, the realities on the ground were very different. This period has been described as one of 'primitive accumulation on an unprecedented scale' (Khan 2013, p.101), the grabbing of assets using political affiliations and organisational power. A committee set up by the Planning Commission in 1972 had recommended a reduction of the maximum landholding from 33 acres to 10 acres. The report was endorsed by the commission and sent to the cabinet for approval in 1973 but was never discussed (Sobhan and Ahmed 1980). The AL was a middle-class party drawing its support from 'surplus' farmers, those owning more than 10 acres of land, traders and small industrialists. 'Surplus' farmers made up the absolute majority in Parliament in 1970 and 1973 (Hasnath 1987). The party could not afford to alienate them. Aside from some modest changes, land was not redistributed. 'Surplus' farmer MPs built their private fortunes on state subsidies, grants and loans, all augmented by inflows of foreign aid. They also controlled the rural co-operatives, using them as a means of distributing patronage towards their personal and political ends.

While large industrial establishments along with banks, insurance, shipping companies, trade in imports and the export of jute had been nationalised after independence, most had been abandoned by former Pakistani owners and fallen into public hands by default. Ceilings were imposed on private investments, both domestic and foreign. Trade was heavily protectionist, with rigid controls on exports and imports along with high tariffs. These all played into the hands of powerful groups linked to the party in power. They took control of the nationalised industries, surpluses accumulated in private hands through profitable import and trading activities, including illegal trade in contraband goods and smuggled jute and other goods across the border (Nurul Islam 1979). The result was a new moneyed class who began to press the government to commit itself to a more substantial and permanent role for private enterprise in the economy of Bangladesh.

Challenges in the social domain

Attention in both national and donor policy circles was concentrated on the economic sectors. As Husain (1974) pointed out in his presentation to the IEA conference (tellingly the last paper at the conference), the importance attached to social objectives in the country's new constitution was not reflected in its policies. He argued that there was a strong case for greater investment in education, health, family planning, social welfare and expanded public works programmes, both as a matter of human rights and to provide long-term social protection against hunger, disease and unemployment. By way of response, Robinson (1974c) put forward a version of the received wisdom at the time (and touched on in the introduction). Poor countries like Bangladesh faced a harsh trade-off between economic growth and social development; they had to prioritise economic growth through investments in agriculture, industry and infrastructure before they could afford to invest in their human capital.

However, there were certain areas of social policy on which the government did take action. Education had been recognised by the 1972 constitution as one of the fundamental principles of state policy. That year the government set up the Qudrat-e-Khuda Education Commission to help it develop an education system in keeping with its goal of building a socialist society. It also set up the Madrassah Education Commission to advise it on how to proceed in relation to religious education and the Islamic Foundation to promote Islamic studies more generally.

The Khuda Commission recommended a mass-oriented, universal, modern and secular education, with the emphasis on Bengali as the primary language for instruction along with provision for second languages which could include English or Arabic. As a first step towards this, the government nationalised the country's 26,000 community-run primary schools.

Community schooling at the time included secular schools as well as two streams of religious education.[7] The *aleya madrassas*, which taught other subjects along with religion, were nationalised, along with non-religious community schools, and targeted for reform. The *qawami madrassas*, which followed a purely religious curriculum, remained outside government control. They were seen as the *madrassas* of the poor: they provided their students with free room and board and prepared them for religious forms of employment, such as *imams, kazis*, religious tutors and so on (Bhuiyan 2010). It was not considered advisable to interfere with them.

Education at the time was focused on boys, but the Qudrat-e-Khuda Commission strongly recommended that more girls be sent to school and more female teachers appointed to make this possible. Its main emphasis was on preparing girls for their future role in domestic life, but it also urged that female students be given vocational education to equip them for employment considered suitable for them[8] so that they would be able to 'lead an independent economic life and raise national income'.

A second social policy area in which the government was active was its response to the 1974 famine. With donor assistance, the government set up Food for Work projects across the country to provide a certain number of days of work to those in need in exchange for food rations. It also set up the Vulnerable Group Feeding (VGF) Programme, which provided rations of wheat to participants selected by local government representatives. This included a quota for poor women.

But, in terms of gender equality per se, the government's preoccupation with the consequences of war and famine meant that the issue was very low down on its agenda. The 1972 constitution did guarantee formal political equality and encouraged the participation of women in all spheres of national life. Mujib introduced the reservation of 15 seats for women in the parliament in 1972. They were to be nominated by the ruling party and added to the existing 300 general seats. He also introduced a 10% quota for women in public sector employment.

It is likely that Mujib will best be remembered on the issue of women for his attempt to honour the suffering of women who had been raped during the 1971 war by officially labelling them *birangona* (war heroines). The term was an attempt to disguise the sexual violence of the crime so as to make social ostracism of its victims less severe. However, it did little to counter the social hypocrisy and unease surrounding the issue of female sexuality in Bangladesh and many of the women were rejected by their families. A 5% quota of government employment reserved for rape victims was, needless to say, never filled, since it merely served to mark them out.

Parallel to the efforts of the government to address the country's social problems were the efforts of an emerging development NGO sector. Founded by idealistic individuals who responded to the challenges facing the new nation, it can be seen as part of Bangladesh's 'liberation dividend'.[9] Some of these founders went on to become household names. Gonoshastya Kendra (GK), or the People's Health Centre, was set up during the war by a medical doctor, Zafrullah Chowdhury, who joined the freedom fighters and set up a mobile unit just across the border in India to treat wounded freedom fighters. It grew into its name over the years, becoming an organisation that advocated and acted on the principle of basic healthcare for all. The Bangladesh Rehabilitation Action Committee (BRAC) was set up in 1971 by Fazle Hasan Abed, who resigned from his job with Shell Pakistan to raise funds for the war effort. Its initial mission, spelt out in its name, was relief and rehabilitation of the war-affected, but over time, as it took on broader development activities, it was renamed the Bangladesh Rural Advancement Committee. It grew into one of the largest NGOs in the world. Professor Yunus began experimenting with lending small amounts of money to the poor, an experiment that later formed the basis of Grameen Bank, a model of banking that was adopted around the world.

Organisations such as these were regarded as indigenous in the sense they were founded by citizens of the new nation who responded to Bangladesh's problems in ways they considered most appropriate to local conditions rather than to the demands of external funders. They defined their mission in radical terms, to address the structural causes of poverty rather than seeking to alleviate its symptoms. Where external funding was taken, it was taken on a solidarity basis from international NGOs with similar missions, such as Oxfam and War on Want, rather than on the conditions imposed by donors. The Canadian University Students' Organisation (CUSO), which had been active after the war, withdrew in 1976 after the youth groups associated with it founded a new local NGO, Proshika, committed to a radical development agenda.

The population question: donor priorities

As far as the donor community was concerned, one issue dominated all others, both economic and social: the country's high rate of population growth. No progress was considered possible without bringing it under control. Family planning had become a central plank of aid policies more generally, a response to Malthusian predictions about the disastrous consequences of population growth outstripping the world's capacity to feed itself and the social unrest triggered by the resulting worldwide famine.

There were many in developing countries who asserted that donor preoccupation with overpopulation sidestepped the real problems of structural inequality between wealthy industrialised countries and the developing world. It was the Indian representative to the UN Population Conference in 1974 who coined the phrase 'development is the best contraceptive', the view that a more balanced developmental approach would, on its own, lead to fertility decline.

For the population establishment, such views were beside the point, particularly in the context of Bangladesh. The urgency of the problem was spelt out in stark terms. Crude deaths had fallen from around 50 per thousand in the early 20th century to less than 20 by 1968. This fall, combined with the absence of any appreciable change in birth rates, had led to the doubling of the population, from 36 million in 1931 to 77 million in 1974. As Robinson put it,

> A country as poor as Bangladesh, with population growth somewhere between 2.8 and 3.0 per cent a year, comes nearer to one's nightmares of Malthusia than almost any other country in the world – an agricultural country that cannot feed itself. (1974b, p.vxiii)

The alarm over the rate of population growth was coupled with despair that it would decline in the foreseeable future (Faaland and Parkinson 1976). There was no evidence of any interest in birth control on the part of the population. Religion encouraged widespread fatalism, the belief that human beings had no control over their destiny, that it lay in the hands of God. There was the additional problem of culture: 'History has given Bangladesh a very marked system of social norms which have changed little over time in response to the accumulation of knowledge' (p.103). They noted the customs and rituals that governed almost every aspect of daily life, prescribing when farmers could sow their seeds, plant their saplings or cut their trees, and what time of day it was auspicious to cut nails and hair. 'It is a pity,' they observed dryly, 'that such inhibitions cannot be extended to abstention from intercourse outside of the safe period!' (p.105).

There was also the low status assigned to women. They did not go to school, they were married off at a young age, they began childbearing early and they lived most of their lives in seclusion within the home, with no access to mass media of any kind. Not surprisingly, they subscribed to the pro-natalism of the country's culture: a study from Comilla district had reported that women with no living children desired four children and those with four wanted seven, while those with more than four children desired eight or nine (Stoeckel and Choudhury 1973).

Donors believed that the situation called for drastic measures on the part of the state, regardless of the rights of the individual:

> Intervention in the affairs of individuals is a thing to be avoided whenever possible, but it simply cannot be avoided as far as population is concerned, if Bangladesh is to survive. (pp.113–14)

What they saw instead was a state that fell far short of the effort required. There was a significant omission of population concerns in the First Five Year Plan. Planned expenditures amounted to just 1.5% of the total budget and focused primarily on the delivery of family planning. There was little evidence of policy efforts to bring about the massive behavioural change necessary to create a demand for these services.

The overall message from the donor community was simple and brutal. If population growth were allowed to continue unchecked in Bangladesh, it would reduce the economy to a Malthusian state. That this had not happened so far was because of the availability of international aid to pay for food imports. The country's manifest vulnerability in the face of rising prices, floods and famine made it clear that a massive and continuing injection of aid would be necessary if the government was going to meet the basic needs of its people and achieve a self-sustaining pathway to growth. It was not easy to see how the donor community could be persuaded to provide aid on this scale to a country whose socialist aspirations it did not approve of and who had little strategic importance, except to its neighbours.

However, Faaland and Parkinson suggested that there was an alternative path that Bangladesh could follow that might have appeal. For all its rhetoric about socialism, Bangladesh was in reality a mixed economy – but it needed to get the mix right. It needed to rein in government intervention in economic affairs which were best left to the private sector. And it needed to increase its role where it was most needed. Not surprisingly, population control was singled out as the obvious case for government intervention. The social engineering efforts of the Chinese state to enforce population control was held up as a model but only a state was capable of mounting the scale of effort that was required. They suggested that aid to Bangladesh could be treated as an experiment to see how a mixed economy tackled one of the most intractable development challenges in the world:

> If development can be made to succeed in Bangladesh, there can be little doubt that it can be made to succeed anywhere else. It is in this sense that Bangladesh is the test case for development. (p.197)

3.4 Gender: the other significant omission

I have dwelt on the policy debates of this period in some detail because it allows us to see the world as it was seen by policymakers who were looking for solutions to the enormous challenges that faced Bangladesh at the time. It reminds us that there was a short period in Bangladesh's history when its leaders were seriously thinking about the possibility of building a socialist future for the country. That this was considered as a serious possibility at the time reflected the substantial left-wing presence in politics, both in the form of parties but also as part of larger movements. But the chapter also draws attention to the power of donors to make or break the policy agenda of a country as desperately in need of external assistance as Bangladesh was at the time. The country had been treated with 'unparalleled generosity' in the immediate aftermath of liberation but aid dried up in the light of Bangladesh's socialist aspirations. It was only restored after the assassination of Mujib when the country shifted its course in the direction recommended by the donor community (see Chapter 5).

As donors repeatedly pointed out, attention to the issue of population control was a significant omission in the country's policy discourse. But there was another significant omission in both government and donor discourse that went largely unremarked. This was an era when much of policy discourse was formulated in abstract categories or categories that took male actors as the norm. If women entered the discussion at all, it was in relation to population issues and their role in producing babies – and not always then. Thorner's comment on the paper on population policy at the IEA conference is telling:

> To my knowledge, the words 'woman' or 'women' do not appear once in the paper. Nothing is said at all about women's liberation. It is a pity that the paper was not co-authored by a woman. (p.285)

While this is true, Thorner could have added the fact that the words 'woman' or 'women' did not appear in any other paper, with the exception of Husain's paper to the conference on the social sector. Here women featured either in their role as midwives and family planning workers or as recipients of social services to rehabilitate those who had been left 'dishonoured and destitute' by the war and various other misfortunes (p.321). Women made a fleeting appearance in the later publication by Faaland and Robinson on the policy challenge for Bangladesh but were confined to the discussion about population where their illiteracy and isolation were identified as key factors in maintaining high fertility rates. And, predictably, the only reference to women in the country's First Five Year Plan was in relation to family planning objectives. The broader issue of gender inequality was beginning to make its way into the academic research of the period – I discuss this in the next chapter – but had yet to make its way into the policy debates.

Notes

[1] US Department of State (1971) cited in Hossain (2017, p.34).

[2] The phrase comes from Arthur and McNicoll (1978).

[3] Robinson (1974b) reports that, when asked at a conference of the International Economic Association held in Dhaka in 1972 (discussed later in the chapter) what was meant by 'Bangladeshi socialism', Mujib's response was 'socialism as we shall practice it in Bangladesh' (p.xiii). According to Robinson, this was not 'a quick and clever repartee to a troublesome question' but a 'perfectly accurate reflection of the practical and pragmatic attitude of the Bangladesh government to its problems' (p.xiii).

[4] While these ideas were dismissed impatiently by the 'pragmatists' at the conference, they can in fact be seen as a reasonable agenda for a desperately poor country seeking to develop in a way that expressed its aspirations for a just society.

[5] In fact, the First Five Year Plan did indeed contain the suggestion that the ruling party should set about organising 'cadres' of young, dedicated workers who believed in an evolutionary transition of socialism, who would mobilise the rural masses and suppress the dominant interest group (Hasnath 1987, p.67).

[6] Cited in Hartmann and Boyce (1983, p.205).

[7] The *aleya madrassas* had been established in Bengal under British rule to provide a broad-based religious education. The *qawami madrassas* followed the purely religious curriculum of the Deoband school established in Uttar Pradesh in 1857.

[8] Examples offered were primary school teaching, nursing and para medical work, office, and bank assistance, typing and stenography, telephone operators and receptionist.

[9] I owe the idea of a 'liberation dividend' to David Lewis.

4. Behind the grim litany: researching a development impasse

> *What is interesting about this litany of grim statistics is not that life in Bangladesh is at a bare subsistence level but that economic and demographic behaviour worsening these conditions can persist in the face of such circumstances and may indeed be fostered by them ... Growth of population numbers must be expected to show the usual demographic inertia.* (Arthur and McNicoll 1978, p.59)

> *The systematic nature of patriarchy suggests that the solutions to the problem of women's vulnerability and lack of income-earning opportunity will not be easily reached ... resistance can be expected from women as well as men if policy initiatives imply violating the norms of purdah and thus threaten an important component of women's social status.* (Cain, Khanam and Nahar 1979, p.434)

This chapter moves from the generalised policy analysis of the previous chapter to the research that was carried out during this period and the insights it offered into the country's problems. Given the dominance of agriculture in the economy of the country and in the livelihoods of its people, it is not surprising that much of this research centred on rural production systems and the low productivity of agriculture. But, as the country's population growth rates began to occupy centre stage in the policy domain, there were growing efforts to understand the micro-level determinants of the fertility behaviour that gave rise to these rates. And, with the rising interest in women and development at the international level, we also see the beginnings of academic interest in women's roles and status.

These studies sought to shed light on how structures operated in everyday life to block the country's ability to progress and people's ability to escape poverty. They suggested that class inequalities embedded in the rural power structure constituted the fundamental cause for the low productivity of agriculture. They analysed the 'patriarchal bargain' as it was constructed in Bangladesh, the gender asymmetries it embodied and why women failed to protest, or even perceive, the injustice of its terms. And, finally, they traced the country's high fertility rates to these overarching structures of class and patriarchy, to the cultural beliefs underpinning them, and to the powerful incentives these generated for individual families to continue to value large numbers of children, despite adverse effects at the collective level.

While a great deal of the research discussed in this chapter was based on fieldwork carried out by the authors, it tended to adopt an 'etic' perspective, seeking to understand social behaviour from an outsider's analysis of structural constraints. It was generally conducted within a political economy framework, very different from the instrumentalism that characterised policy analysis, but it shared the same pessimism. As the opening quotes to this chapter suggest, it painted a picture of a country trapped in a development impasse: the forces that contributed to Bangladesh's abject state in the post-independence period gave rise to a structural dynamic that blocked the possibility of progressive change in the foreseeable future.

4.1 The agrarian structure: land, kinship and community

The intertwined relations of class and status appear in this literature as central principles of the agrarian power structure. Land had always been at the heart of power relations in the countryside, the material capital most likely to generate other forms of valued capital, but it took on ever greater importance as the land frontier was reached and the delta went from a region of land abundance to one of extreme land scarcity.

The amount of land owned, the surplus or deficit returns it yielded and the activities associated with it defined class relations. While the departure of the large Hindu landowners after partition had left behind a rural economy made up of small landholdings, it did not rule out the existence of some large landowners, particularly among families who appropriated or purchased at low prices the land left behind by the departing Hindus. According to figures from the late 1970s, 10% of farm households owned 50% of cultivable land, while 33% had no cultivable land at all. The average farm size had fallen from 3.5 acres in the late 1960s to 2.3 acres by the late 1970s (Januzzi and Peach 1980).

Dominating the rural class structure were those who had enough land to generate a sizeable investible surplus. They did not cultivate their own land but relied on sharecroppers and wage labourers. Below them were middle peasants, who had enough land to enjoy some surplus in good years but faced the likelihood of deficits in bad years. At the bottom of the rural order were those with little or no cultivable land, who relied mainly on hiring out their labour as sharecroppers, tenant farmers or wage labourers. They often suffered extended periods of hunger during the year.

Caste, as we saw, had not taken deep roots in the social hierarchy of the eastern delta, while the old distinction between *ashraf* and *ajlaf* had faded over time. Instead, families were ranked by the perceived status of their lineages, the symbolic capital they had either inherited *or* accumulated through their achievements (Aziz 1979). Lineage titles acted as indicators of status (Bertocci 1972). High-status lineage titles, which could be religious (Khondokar, Haji, Maulana) or secular (Bhuiya, Kaji, Choudhuri), frequently functioned as patronymics. Most villagers were alert to the status of different lineages in their community, based on their titles or lack of it. While those with high-status titles were not necessarily wealthy, partly because considerable differences in landholdings could co-exist within the same patrilineage, there was an overall association: in the long run, property and status coincided with 'extraordinary regularity' (Bertocci 1972, p.41).

Family, kinship and community

Social relations in the countryside were characterised as concentric circles of affiliation, claims, and obligations: 'A man's duties are, in order, to his own family ... then towards his *paribar* [natal family], then to his *gushti* [patrilineage] and then to his village' (A.K.M. Aminul Islam 1974, p.75). The greatest density of ties was found within the individual household (*ghar*), made up of immediate family members who cooked and ate together and constituted the centre of the circle. Households from the extended patrilineal family generally lived in the same homestead (*bari*), grouped around a shared courtyard. Membership of the *bari* constituted a key source of identity through a person's life course, although it was more central to male identity since women were absorbed into their husbands' patrilineage after marriage.

Clusters of homesteads belonging to the same patrilineage group made up different hamlets (*para*) within the village. Kinship ties and proximity of residence bound members together in a range of mutual claims and obligations, operating as a form of 'moral economy'. Wealthier families gave preference to poorer kin to work on their fields or in their homes and provided support in times of crisis. Poorer families placed themselves at the beck and call of wealthy relatives and deferred to them for advice and guidance.

Kinship ties merged with the more diffuse relations of *samaj* (community), which co-ordinated relationships between households who were not necessarily related to each other, although the language of 'fictive kinship' was often used to bind them together in loose relationships of reciprocal obligations, particularly during the critical lifecycle rituals of birth, marriage and death (Aziz 1979). Patrilineage groups higher up in the class and status hierarchy occupied positions of authority, setting standards of proper behaviour for the rest of the community. Their senior male members were regarded as *samaj* leaders or *matabors* and played a prominent role in community activities, such as the Friday prayers and the distribution of *zakat*. They also made up the *shalish*, an informal village council whose function was to mediate disputes, uphold approved codes of behaviour and sanction those who violated them by denying them employment, ostracising or expelling them from the village. The fact that men from dominant lineages sat in the *shalish* meant that economic, social and juridical positions of power were concentrated in more or less the same set of individuals (Adnan 1990).

But, despite this concentration of power within a small number of families, the social structure was not a stable one. The geography of the delta reproduced many of the instabilities that had defined rural settlements throughout its history. The constant movement of rivers meant that old village boundaries were frequently wiped out, families lost their land and were often forced to migrate, while the emergence of new land elsewhere triggered fresh disputes between rival claimants. One further consequence of the steady but uneven growth of population pressure was that it frequently forced families to move out of the more densely populated villages and settle in areas where land was available. These constant movements meant that the boundaries of rural settlements remained in flux, making them 'elusive entities',[1] as did the relationships between those who lived in them (Arthur and McNicoll 1978). A man could reside in one village, attend the mosque in another, patronise a market in a third and cultivate plots of land in any or all of them. For adjudication of minor disputes, he might call on the head of his *gushti* or the leader of the *samaj* to which he belonged. For assistance in ploughing or harvesting he might turn to other members of his *paribar* or to local wage labour.[2]

Prevailing inheritance practices exacerbated the effects of population growth in undermining the stability of the social order. The growing pressure of population pushed increasing numbers of farms below the size necessary to support family subsistence. Partible inheritance stressed the equal division of land between male (and to a lesser extent female) heirs and entitled the heirs to both higher- and lower-lying land. As a result, the land held by individual cultivators were fragmented into scattered plots of increasingly small sizes, the main reason why families that belonged to the same high-status patrilineage group might own very different-sized landholdings.

New sources of instability in the social order had also emerged, particularly since the Pakistan era, as national politics became an increasingly important factor in village life. Political affiliations gradually displaced the *samaj* from its pre-eminence in regulating village life because they promised access to state munificence and possibilities of 'brokerage' between government programmes and the local population. Leading families formed their own informal factions made up of clusters of households brought together by a combination of proximity, patronage, and political allegiance (BRAC 1983). Factions were frequently pitted against each other as their leaders sought to gain ascendancy within the community and access to government resources and political power. Rural factions rose and fell as fierce rivalries were fought out through tactics of violence, intimidation, and trickery: *mastaans* (petty hoodlums) in the pay of faction leaders became familiar figures in factional politics and muscle power a key means of settling disputes.[3]

These intertwined relationships meant that vertical hierarchies based on the unequal ownership of land, status and other valued assets were cut across by horizontal relationships embodying ties of kinship, patronage and faction. The continuous interaction between conflicting factions and their changing position within local hierarchies resulted in shifting patterns of mobility within a community, with different sets of households affected at different times. Leading families sought to promote not only their own interests but also those of their client-followers so that the fortunes of the leadership of a given network had repercussions for those who belonged to it. Its upward mobility could result in the upward mobility for the whole range of their followers, irrespective of their initial class position. The reverse process could also occur so that a landless family might earn enough to purchase land as a result of the ascendance of the faction it had attached itself to, while an upper middle peasant who was affiliated to a declining faction and subject to harassment by the dominant faction would be forced to sell some of his land in order to sustain his family (Adnan and Rahman 1978).

In short, while land, status, power and authority might have been concentrated in a small number of families within a village, these resources were not necessarily passed down through generations within the same family. Rather, they had to be fought for and gains constantly defended from the predatory strategies of others. Neither economic inequality nor class stratification was institutionalised in the deep structures of the country in the way that feudal relationships and caste hierarchies were embedded in the social structures elsewhere in South Asia. Very few people could claim power through inherited social legitimacy while prevailing social hierarchies remained constantly exposed to challenge because their legitimacy was not automatically accepted (Sobhan 2000). The result was that Bangladesh society remained more fluid than elsewhere in South Asia, with considerable scope for upward mobility; even poor households did not regard this as an impossible dream (Boyce 1983).

Rural inequality and agricultural inefficiency

The rural class structure was identified as a major factor in blocking growth in agricultural productivity (Boyce 1987). The concentrations of social, political and economic power in the hands of the rural elite served to reproduce a version of the disjuncture between property and production noted in colonial times. While this elite were not 'absentee landlords' in the colonial sense, since most lived in villages, they were 'absent' from the direct cultivation of their land, relying instead on tenants and wage labourers.

They rarely used the resulting surpluses to raise agricultural productivity, preferring less risky ways of getting rich: investments in patron–client relations as a platform for gaining access to political resources, off-farm intermediary activities, such as trade, speculation and moneylending, and luxury forms of consumption that enhanced individual prestige and their family's standing. One of the landlords in Katni village, studied by Hartmann and Boyce in 1974, purchased a Japanese motorcycle, an item apparently in great demand at the time and the very first in the village. Its cost exceeded what a wage labourer in that village could have earnt in 20 years and naturally added considerably to his social prestige.

The story was very different for owner-cultivators with small landholdings and unreliable surpluses. Their optimal strategy was to invest whatever resources they had at their disposal, particularly their family labour, into their land to maximise crop yields. Cropping intensity (crop yields per acre) on their farms generally exceeded that of large landowners: the additional returns to each extra hour of labour might be low, but the alternative was unemployment and hunger (Boyce 1987). This explained the inverse relationship noted in the previous chapter between farm size and productivity and was a major source of inefficiency in agriculture.

Other groups with little or no land had to rely on the use of their labour through sharecropping or wage labour. Sharecropping was generally preferred because it was closer to the status of *malik* (master), with connotations of working for oneself rather than for others, but it could only be taken up by those who had necessary resources, such as draft animals and farm implements, and the ability to ride out failing harvests. Sharecropping was an important means through which patronage relations were established, with sharecroppers providing political support and clientelist loyalty to landlords in return for continued access to land, preferential employment, seasonal credit and support in times of crisis. Marginal farmers and landless labourers who had few resources to fall back on took up wage work whenever they could find it.

Inequalities within the agrarian structure also blocked prospects for technological innovation (Boyce 1987). Despite the stated objective of the post-independence IRDP programme to benefit small farmers and landless peasants, it was the larger landowners, those with political clout and cultural capital, who inevitably monopolised government-subsidised benefits for themselves and their supporters:

> Their land serves as collateral, and they know how to deal with government officials: how to fill out the necessary forms, and when to propose a snack at the nearest tea stall. (Hartmann and Boyce 1983, p.194)

There was an additional factor blocking the growth of agricultural productivity. A leading constraint to the spread of the Green Revolution technology was the lack of water management through irrigation and flood control. This would have rendered agriculture less dependent on local conditions, leading to major production gains in the dry winter season.

Although Bangladesh had vast surface area and ground water resources, British colonial investment in irrigation had been insignificant in the delta. This was in sharp contrast to Punjab, where investments in major irrigation and canal systems since the 1880s meant that Pakistan inherited one of the largest gravity irrigation systems in the world at the time of its independence (Stevens 1976). State promotion of the Green Revolution technology in the 1960s had taken off in West Pakistan, particularly Punjab and Sindh, where the large size of land-holdings[4] and higher levels of investment in irrigation favoured the rapid spread of large-scale mechanisation. Efforts to promote similar technologies were far less successful in rural East Pakistan, with its 'postage-stamp' farm sizes of around three acres and highly fragmented landholdings (Bertocci 1976, p.3). By the time of independence in 1971, only 12% of farmland was under irrigation, less than one-eighth of gross cropped area.

The Bangladesh Agricultural Development Corporation continued with the pre-independence efforts. It offered a rental service programme for the distribution of irrigation equipment and the supply of diesel and mechanic services, but dissemination remained limited and agricultural productivity stagnated. Studies pointed out that both modern irrigation and flood control infrastructure required investment in capital-intensive and 'lumpy' technologies along with some minimum level of organisation and co-operation (Boyce 1987). This was missing in the Bangladesh countryside thanks to the general diffuseness of its traditional social arrangements and the historical absence of a strong local administrative system. Given bitter competition for the control of land, and the fragmentation of land ownership into small, multiple and scattered individual holdings, there was little incentive for those with land to sacrifice any of it for the construction of canals and irrigation channels that would benefit others. It was the larger landowners who were able to appropriate a disproportionate share of canal water for cultivation purposes, maximising output and profit on their own lands but reducing efficiency of irrigation in the economy as a whole.

Fragmented landownership patterns and control by the more powerful landowners further undermined efforts to provide irrigation by means of smaller-scale technologies.[5] The same power dynamics ensured that local elites commandeered the benefits of other government efforts to promote rural development. They subverted efforts to lease unused government land to landless co-operatives; funds for rural works projects were distributed based on political affiliations rather than productivity potential; and a great deal of the wheat allocated for the Food for Work programmes was appropriated by government officials and locally elected bodies. The net effect of the injection of external resources through these programmes was to strengthen the rural elite vis-à-vis the poor.

The large landlords who benefited from the new technologies started to renegotiate their sharecropping contracts to retain a larger share of crops and to shorten the duration of the contracts. Many began to abandon sharecropping arrangements altogether in favour of pure tenancy contracts or wage labour, eroding one of the few sources of security available to those with little or no land.

Landlessness rose as small farmers who got into debt had to sell off their land: from around 15–20% of the rural population in the early 1960s to 30–35% a decade later (Arthur and McNicoll 1978). They joined the large number of wage labourers competing for work and added to a steady decline in already abysmally low wages.[6] In another memorable phrase from this period, they were caught in a 'below poverty equilibrium trap', oscillating between the poverty line and the famine line (Alamgir 1978).

There was also a growing trend towards the nuclearisation of families among these households (Adnan 1990; Jansen 1987; Khuda 1985). With little or no land to bind them together, patrilineages began to split into 'atomistic' units. In fact, the extreme poverty of the 1970s forced partition within the nuclear unit itself. Adult sons opted to separate from parents soon after or even before marriage so that they did not have to share their earnings. Landless labourers became more geographically mobile, responding to seasonal labour demands and migrating to urban areas in search of employment: the urban population grew from around 5% of the total population in 1961 to 15% in 1981 (Rahman 2014).

4.2 A non-negotiable patriarchy

Very little attention was paid to the patriarchal dimensions of structural constraints in the pre-independence period. In his review of village studies carried out since the 1940s, Adnan (1990) describes the changing dynamics of agriculture, demography, labour relations and the social structure, but women are largely absent from the analysis. However, a glance at his bibliography reveals references to publications that clearly focused on women's role in village life. These dated from the 1970s, attesting to the beginning of interest in gender issues among feminist academics and sections of the development community. These studies inaugurated a more systematic attention to the topic. Much of the research during this period was devoted to carrying out a 'structural inventory' of classic patriarchy as it was manifested in Bangladesh.

Although Islam was identified as part of this inventory, it was clear that many elements cut across religious lines. Bengali Muslims and Hindus shared a common ethno-linguistic identity and many aspects of culture. Their family and kinship systems were also organised along the patriarchal, patrilineal and patrilocal lines typical of classic patriarchy. However, there were some differences. For instance, both religious and personal law for Muslims recognised the right of daughters to half of sons' share of inherited property (and of widows to an eighth of their husbands' property), although this right was rarely claimed: to have done so would have been likely to rupture relations with their natal family, particularly their brothers, relationships they valued as a source of support after their marriage (Kabeer 1985; Westergaard 1983). There was no provision for Hindu women to inherit land within either religious or personal law. Both groups in turn differed significantly from indigenous groups, who were often animists or Buddhists but whose way of life, governed by custom rather than religion,[7] was less marked by the rigid gender division of labour and restrictions on women's freedom of movement that characterised the cultural mainstream.

As in patrilineal kinship systems more generally, strict controls were exercised over women's sexuality and reproductive behaviour to enforce their pre-marital chastity and post-marital fidelity. Key in these controls was the institution of *purdah*, or female seclusion, which incorporated the dominant notions of female virtue and propriety, governing how women were meant to think and act and minimising their contact with any man who did not belong to their kin group. *Purdah* required women to remain within the shelter of the homestead for much of their lives, restricting their movement in the public domain. It also prescribed their dress and conduct in the public domain. They were to cover themselves properly to signal their modesty and to conduct themselves with decorum, moving through the public domain with downcast eyes. The enforcement of *purdah* was the responsibility of male family members, crucial to their honour and to the status of the family. Any violation of *purdah* on the part of women reflected the failure of these men to exercise due control of female members and a source of shame for the entire family.

Gender and family

The generalised rules, norms and practices that defined patriarchal arrangements and the collective habitus in Bangladesh served to explain the remarkably similar life course trajectories reported for women in studies carried out during this time (Aziz 1979; Cain 1978; Ellickson 1972). There were some variations in these trajectories, reflecting the social position of households or the circumstances of individual women, but clear limits in the extent to which they deviated from normative expectations.

Gender discrimination began early. A study by Chen (1982) used data from the Health and Demographic Surveillance System in Matlab *thana*[8] for the period 1974–77 to provide a detailed account of how the mechanisms underlying excess female mortality among children operated. It showed that boys were more likely to die than girls in the first month of life, the neo-natal period, a reflection of their weaker immune systems and a pattern typically observed in all populations, rich and poor.[9] After the first month, however, the pattern was reversed, and female deaths began to exceed male; by then, the influence of gender-discriminatory practices was strong enough to offset the greater biological vulnerability of the male infant. Discrimination magnified mortality differentials during childhood (one to four years), with female mortality exceeding that of males by 53%. Excess female mortality persisted across much of the life course, leading to the lower life expectancy for women than men that was noted in Chapter 1.

Boys were more likely to be sent to school by households who could afford it and kept in school for as long as households could pay the fees and deemed it worth the investment. Girls were generally kept back at home, not only on financial grounds but also because there did not seem any point in educating them. They were socialised instead in the dispositions and attributes they would need for their future roles:

> The female voice should not reach male ears outside the household. She must therefore speak in a low voice. Girls are admonished by their mother 'you are female and should speak in a soft voice'.
> (Mahmuda Islam 1979, p.227)

Purdah norms were enforced more strictly once girls reached puberty – any girl sent to school was likely to be withdrawn at this stage. Parents had strong incentives to marry their daughters off as soon as possible to ensure their chastity and to pass responsibility for them to their husbands' family. Marriages were arranged – for both sons and daughters – by their guardians, often with the help of intermediaries, an arrangement between families that did not require the consent of groom or bride. Marriage could take place within the natal village or outside it, within the lineage group as well as out-side – different locations report different practices depending on whether there is concern about keeping property within the family or expanding networks and social standing (Amin and Huq 2008; Aziz 1979; McCarthy 1967). While marriages were typically between families with similar status positions, marrying into families of higher or lower status was not unknown as the economic situation of a family became increasingly more important than their social status, as villagers told Bertocci during his fieldwork in the late 1960s: 'Nowadays if one's economic position is good, one's lineage status is also good' (1972, p.45). Polygamy was permitted under Islamic law. The right to divorce was also permitted, but it was more easily exercised by men than women.

A radical change occurred in marital practices sometime in the second half of the 20th century. It had been customary among Muslims for the groom's family to provide an obligatory payment (*mehr* or *mohrana*) in cash or kind or both. While it symbolised her worth to the groom and his family, the value of these gifts would depend on whether the bride's family was considered to come from a superior, similar or inferior status to the groom's (Aziz 1979; Lindenbaum 1981). The practice of dowry (*joutuk*), in which the net transfer of wealth at marriage was from the bride's family to the groom's, had previ-ously been confined to higher-caste Hindus. A generalised shift to the dowry system began to take place so that it was now the bride's family that bore the bulk of expenses associated with marriage.

The fact that the shift to dowry occurred not only among Muslims but also lower-caste Hindus as well as Christians suggested that it reflected the political economy of the region rather than religious factors (Ahmed and Naher 1987; Bleie 1990; Lindenbaum 1981; Westergaard 1983). In particu-lar, while the spread of the market relations and rural mechanisation was eroding the significance of subsistence production and the basis of women's productive role within the household, it was evident that cultural constraints excluded them from paid formal and informal opportunities in the emerg-ing cash economy to which men had easier access (Lindenbaum 1981). These opportunities often required education but offered more secure income and greater social prestige: 'the income potential of the groom now [surpassed] the previously valued attributes of the bride' (Lindenbaum 1981, p.399; Aziz 1979).[10] Parents of grooms started first to request and then to demand dowry (referred to as *daabi* or, very often, the English word 'demand') as reimburse-ment for their investment in their sons.

The shift to dowry began in urban areas and among wealthier families but it spread across social groups to the poorest households and to other parts of the country, acquiring the status of a taken-for-granted norm, with the earlier 'gift-giving' aspect hardening into increasing levels of demand: for money, for consumer goods such as TVs and motorbikes, for property, for jobs for the prospective son-in-law or for finance for his migration over- seas, with demands often continuing after marriage (Ahmed and Naher 1987). It became a source of financial crisis for poorer parents of daughters, leading to the sale of land and other assets and frequently plunging them into greater impoverishment (Alam 1985; Kabeer 1989; Simmons, Mita and Koenig 1992). If daughters had been regarded as a burden on their parents before, dowry turned them into a major liability. According to a 27-year-old woman in rural Comilla, 'Girls have become a rope around their parents' neck' (Simmons 1996, p.258), while a mother in Rangpur district declared, 'It is better not to have daughters' (Alam 1985, p.370).

Regardless of who bore the main costs of marriage, the practice of patri- local residence meant that the daughter left her natal home and village after marriage to join her husband's family as a 'stranger bride', to be absorbed into his patrilineage. After marriage, she could only visit her natal family with the permission of her in-laws. The early years of marriage were usually hard for the new bride. She was placed under the authority of her mother-in-law and took on most of the burden of housework under her supervision. Any infrac- tion risked her honour and jeopardised the status of her husband's family.

Her status within the marital home began to change with the birth of children, but it was the birth of sons that assured her place within the family. The cycle was completed when the first daughter-in-law entered the house- hold and was placed under her authority. The gender hierarchy within the household therefore intersected with age and life course: older women were in positions of authority over younger women, mothers-in-law dominated their daughters-in-law and wives of older brothers dominated the wives of younger brothers.

There were, of course, power dynamics within marriage itself. A great deal of it operated through taken-for granted assumptions, a shared habitus about the legitimacy of husbands' authority and unquestioning submission by wives: a saying repeated in numerous studies, very often by women themselves, was that a wife's heaven lay beneath her husband's feet. Marriage tended to be to men considerably older than them, usually more educated, reinforcing their subordinate position from the outset.

There were also more naked manifestations of power. Domestic violence against women appeared an almost routine occurrence (Arens and Van Beurden 1977; Hartmann and Boyce 1983), but there were certain flashpoints. Demands around dowry was one: if it was not paid on time, if it was not sufficient, if fresh demands after marriage were not conceded. A dissatisfied husband or his parents could make a wife's life miserable, subjecting her to violence and abuse, threatening to take another wife or divorce her. Alam (1985) observed that dowry had become an important factor in explaining growing marital instability. One young man told her: 'Today marriage has become a business. Men marry for dowries' (p.370). Poorer men, in particular, thought nothing of leaving one wife and marrying another so as to receive dowry.[11]

But violence was not always a display of power by men over women. It was often a product of poverty, an outlet for men's sense of powerlessness and frustration in the face of their failure to live up to their role as family bread-winner. Hartman and Boyce observed in the course of their fieldwork that quarrels about food were often a flashpoint for violence:

> We saw and heard of quite serious incidents in which women were beaten mercilessly with sticks, bricks, copper spoons and other tools. Such maltreatment may happen when a husband comes home hungry and the food is not ready yet.

As one of the women they interviewed said, 'When my husband's stomach is empty, he beats me, but when it is full, there is peace' (p.89).

Few women exercised the right to divorce – for a number of reasons. They were unlikely to be welcomed back by parents who could not afford to feed them or to pay dowry to arrange another marriage. The stigma attached to a divorced woman also made it harder for them to remarry. But, in addition, whether or not they agreed that heaven lay beneath their husband's feet, their security certainly did: 'submission to physical beatings and verbal abuse, or to the emotional pain of polygamy, is not too high a price to pay for social approval and physical survival' (p.92). Women with abusive husbands or husbands who took a second wife might suffer but they suffered in silence. For all the hardship their marriage might involve, they were better off with a bad husband than with no husband at all. Some took the desperate way out: Hartman and Boyce noted that the list of suicides in the village where they did their fieldwork was both long and exclusively female, spanning both rich and poor.

Gender and markets

Purdah norms were implicitly norms about male breadwinning responsibility. Men were expected to spend their time in productive work: cultivation on their own land, sharecropping other people's land, agricultural wage work, livestock rearing or businesses of various kinds. They rarely undertook any domestic responsibilities with the exception of going to the market for household food, clothing and other purchases, activities that would otherwise have taken women outside the home. Women, of course, were required to stay within the shelter of the home, looking after their family and the homestead, largely excluded from paid work and therefore financially dependent on male earnings over the course of their lives.

The work they did within the home went largely unrecognised in mainstream research because it was carried out as unpaid family labour and hidden from public view. Among the important contributions made by the research carried out in the 1970s was to make this work visible (Abdullah and Zeidenstein 1982). It included the post-harvest processing of crops, care and feeding of livestock, rearing poultry, homestead cultivation of fruits, spices, herbs and vegetables for family consumption, pickling, drying and preserving certain crops, weaving and spinning cloth and thread, and making and repairing the household and household utensils and equipment. These gendered patterns of specialisation in productive activities were established very early in children's lives.

As might be expected given the stratified nature of rural economy, there were class-based variations in the ability to abide by these normative prescriptions. Wealthy households sought to keep women in their families in strict *purdah*. Their homesteads were surrounded by bamboo groves and they had their own ponds where women could bathe. They hired poorer women, often poorer relatives, to undertake work that involved breaking norms of *purdah*: taking food to labourers in the field if necessary, carrying water and gathering firewood.

Most women from middle peasant households could not afford to hire in labour. They undertook all stages of home-based production as well as their domestic chores, working longer hours than any other group, with very little time to themselves. Poorer farming households also relied on female family labour but often had to deploy them in field-based tasks as well as within the homestead. The strength of social norms prohibiting women's presence in the fields meant that these women would carry out field-based tasks surreptitiously, hidden by hedges or in the dead of night, so as not to be seen by neighbours (Chen 1986; Hartmann and Boyce 1983; Schuler, Islam and Rottach 2010).

Women from landless households were the most likely to engage in income-generating work, often outside their homestead, but on very different terms to men from their households. There were few physical restrictions on men's search for work: they could work within their own village or other villages; they could migrate or commute to other districts or to urban areas. For women, the market for their labour was normatively demarcated, both physically and functionally. Cain, Khanam and Nahar summarised the nature of these restrictions in their study village:

> The physical limits of the market for a particular woman's labor are described by a circle with a radius of 20–400 meters, with her homestead as the center of the circle. The radius of the circle varies depending on the size of the village neighborhood (*para*) in which she lives, the homogeneity of her para in terms of kinship and other social criteria … The precise size and shape of the area demarcated is, of course, not important. What is important is that, geographically, the market for the labor of any given women is small, and the pool of potential employers is limited by the condition that some

> sort of prior social relationship exist between the woman seeking work and the employer. The relationship might be based on kinship, joint membership in a *mallot* (solidarity group), allegiance of a woman's husband to a faction leader, and so on. These criteria usually overlap. (1979, p.428)

The psychic and more tangible costs of work rose quickly when a woman left the confines of her 'circle'. It reflected the discomfort that she felt moving beyond the 'acceptable' boundary. She was also constrained in her search for jobs by the social expectation that she worked for families within her social network rather than for strangers. And, within the physical boundaries of the market for her labour, there were the normative boundaries about what kinds of work were appropriate. Most worked in the homes of employers, a few might work in vegetable fields planted close to their employers' house, but none undertook field operations in the main crops of jute and rice.

The limitations on the market for female labour led to sharp differentials in the average daily wages of males and females, with women's systematically lower than men's. There was no fixed schedule for women's work, no fixed payment and payments were often in meals and clothes rather than cash. The other consequence of these strictly segregated labour markets was the high rates of involuntary 'unemployment' among poorer women, their failure to find work despite their willingness to do it. Poorer women complained of too *little* work, too much 'leisure'. They had no cattle to look after, no crops to process 'and all too often nothing to cook' (Hartmann and Boyce 1983, p.87).

The poorest among this group were female household heads, women who were fending for themselves in the absence of an adult male breadwinner. Described as 'destitute women' in the literature of the time, they had lost the support of husbands, as a result of widowhood, divorce or abandonment, and had no adult sons or other male relatives to look after them. They had to support themselves and their dependents in an environment that gave them very few opportunities to do so. They had little choice about what, where and who they worked for. They did what work they could find, with some turning to begging or prostitution, often migrating into towns and cities on their own in search of work. Micro-level studies in urban areas found that a significant proportion of women who reported themselves as recent migrants were divorced or deserted women from poor rural families (Farouk 1976; Islam and Zeitlyn 1989; Jahan 1979).

Gender and community

Purdah norms ensured that the public affairs of the community were largely male affairs. The picture that emerged from studies of this period is one of relentless exclusion: women during my 1979 fieldwork compared themselves to 'frogs in a well' and 'oxen tied to the grindstone' to describe their sense of circumscribed lives (Kabeer 1989). They depended on husbands for news of the outside world. Most did not know who their village leaders were, when village meetings were held and what subjects were discussed. But their ignorance also extended to household matters, with many unaware of how much land their husbands owned or where their fields were.

The membership of *samaj*, factions and the informal committees that looked after different aspects of village affairs were all men, as were elected and government officials and anyone in the community who had connections with them. The Friday prayers, social occasions to mark life course events, such as births, deaths and marriages and various religious festivals were attended by men. The *shalish* who adjudicated local disputes was entirely male. A woman who was a disputant had to be represented by a male guardian, even if she worked outside her home for a living, or risk losing the case, regardless of its merits.

Leading members of the community saw themselves as guardians of the social order. They interpreted social norms and practices to restrict the movements and activities of women and policed their behaviour to ensure that it did not bring shame on the community. They could rely on the support of religious functionaries since they dominated the committees that ran the local mosques and *madrassas*, appointed the local mullahs, set their tenure, and determined the size of stipend they received. These functionaries were particularly instrumental in determining the boundaries between moral and immoral behaviour for women, often going well beyond what was written in the religious texts. But there were double standards at work: the norms of *purdah* were relaxed for the wives of the rich who might need to go to the town but similar actions by poorer women were condemned as *bepurdah* (Chen 1986, p.73).

This exercise of material and symbolic power to control their behaviour did not go unnoticed by poorer women. Writing about those who had become affiliated with BRAC, Chen (1986) writes:

> The real constraint, as the women see it, is that the rich control the paid labour opportunities within the village and dictate the norms that prohibit women from seeking work outside the village. If the rich disapprove of what poor women do, they can always threaten to or actually cut off their work within the village. Or if the rich disapprove of poor women working outside the village, they can put pressure on the woman or her family through the religious leaders. (p.72)

4.3 'Demographic inertia': the persistence of high fertility

As we saw in Chapter 3, the international donor community tended to explain the rapid rate of population growth in Bangladesh in terms of the unrestrained fertility of an illiterate peasantry dominated by religious prescriptions and superstitions of various kinds. However, for many researchers, attributing this demographic inertia to the peasant's 'blindness to choice' did not seem credible when the evidence on the ground suggested their willingness to exploit opportunities for even marginal gains and very often at considerable risk to themselves: 'people are quick to settle on the *char* lands in the delta mouth – land that appears and as quickly can disappear with the shifting patterns of siltation' (Arthur and McNicoll 1978, p.32).

At the same time, researchers had to find an explanation for the puzzling failure of fertility rates to decline despite declining mortality in the past half century, the worsening ratio of population to land and the accompanying impoverishment. While fertility behaviour was not expected to adjust automatically to changes in the mortality regime, a generation should have been a sufficient period of time for the consequences of unchanging fertility behaviour to have become visible. This had not happened. The claims of the population establishment that families would benefit from having fewer children did not appear to resonate with the families in question. More detailed research to investigate the reasons for this offered a variety of explanations but one unifying thread that ran through them was the significance assigned to risk and uncertainty as the backdrop to everyday life in the eastern delta.

A pro-natalist culture in the face of uncertainty

In the late 1970s, Maloney, Aziz and Sarker (1981) carried out what they described as the first in-depth anthropological study of folk demography in rural Bangladesh, which they combined with the collection of survey data. This allowed them to explore fertility behaviour as social practice: the meanings, values, know-how and action that it embodied. In response to a question about desired fertility, the overwhelming percentage of those surveyed responded with expressions of fatalism, their submission to the will of God. They had heard about certain forms of modern contraception, most often sterilisation, which was the main method being promoted by the government. Fewer seemed to know about traditional forms – rhythm, abstinence, withdrawal and indigenous herbal solutions. And even fewer said that they were using, or had used, any form of contraception.

Maloney, Aziz and Sarker suggest that this apparent indifference to birth control reflected the pro-fertility ethos at the core of the shared habitus of the region, the product of '3000 years of adaptation and symbiotic relationship between man and the land' (p.241). It was an amalgam of the 'little' and 'great traditions' that had helped the delta's inhabitants to make sense of and cope with the powers of the universe and its natural phenomena, including the human body and the processes of birth, death and sexuality. It had evolved gradually as the people of the delta sought to make a living against a backdrop of an unpredictable natural environment and a regime of disease and epidemics that for many centuries had led to an average life expectancy of just 20 years. It was an ethos that provided the population with the labour they needed to live off the land without destroying its resource base, but always in circumstances that were marked by sudden and unexplained misfortunes.

The nature of these circumstances are graphically illustrated in Appendix 4, Box 1, which records the major disasters experienced by Bangladesh in the 200 years between 1769 and 1974: floods and famines, cyclones and tidal waves, influenza epidemics, partition and war. It can say nothing, of course, of the less well documented but more frequent examples of some of these crises that were part of everyday reality in the region.

This pervasive uncertainty explained the importance of children in the worldview of the population. There was their symbolic importance: the number of children they had was determined by God, every newborn had to be cherished as a gift from God. There was also their material importance. The patriarchal bargain embodied an implicit intergenerational contract that spelt out the reciprocal responsibilities between parents and children. It was the moral duty of parents to have children, to nurture, support and arrange their marriages and to increase the lineage. It was the moral obligation of children to repay this debt. Sons in particular were expected to support their parents in their old age; those who did not were described as 'beasts and accursed' (p.244). Fatalism in matters of reproduction could thus be said to represent a rational response in the face of events over which they had little control. It also helped to reduce the psychological costs of knowing that many of their children would die before reaching adulthood.

Fertility behaviour and the persistence of risk

Maloney, Aziz and Sarker maintained that, as long as the objective circumstances that prevailed in the delta presented risks that could be best mitigated by a strategy of high fertility, the cultural rationale for high fertility would remain. However, in the light of the changes that occurred over the course of Bangladesh's history, it does not seem credible to argue that objective circumstances had remained unchanged. Materialist explanations for the persistence of high fertility in Bangladesh until well into the late 20th century suggested a reframing of the argument: objective circumstances had changed in Bangladesh but not in ways that undermined the pro-natalist ethos of the population. High fertility continued to represent a rational, though class-differentiated, response to these changing circumstances, at least at the level of households.

First of all, there was the question of mortality decline. As we have seen, the broad-based improvements in public health and infrastructure in the 20th century that led to a decline in overall mortality in the Bengal region were frequently discussed in the demographic literature as the reason for expecting a corresponding decline in fertility. However, as Arthur and McNicoll (1978) argue, mortality levels were still high, even by developing country standards. They were particularly high among children. Put bluntly, while overall life expectancy had increased from an average of 20 years at the start of the 20th century to around 40 by the middle, the simple case for continuing to have large numbers of children was that infant mortality rates were above 120 per 1,000 live births in the 1980s. Around 20% of children born during this period did not survive beyond the age of five (Cleland et al. 1994). At the very least, these considerations bolstered high fertility as a form of insurance to ensure that some minimum number of children survived into adulthood.

Furthermore, mortality had not declined evenly across the population. Mortality risks closely reflected the terms on which different groups were able to access opportunities in the local economy. Those who enjoyed livelihood security because of their capital endowments were most likely to have benefited from the broad improvements in the environment that had led to the onset of mortality decline. Any further decline in mortality for this group would require improvements in the provision of health services, which, at that time, were of abysmal quality.

A different set of considerations applied in the case of households living on the margins. They had been largely bypassed by the decline in mortality rates: studies reported that child mortality rates among poorer and landless households could range from double those of better-off households to nearly five times as high and that these differentials were even higher during times of crisis, such as the 1974 famine (Arthur and McNicoll 1978; Cain 1978; McCord 1976).

Nor were improvements in health services likely to bring death rates down in this group unless they were accompanied by dramatic improvements in their livelihood opportunities. Those living on the environmental margins, the fragile *char* lands in the mouth of the delta, had to cope with recurrent flooding, tidal bores and resulting high fatalities. Those living on the economic margins, numerically far more important, experienced high mortality through less dramatic causes: fragile livelihoods, declining real wages, hunger and malnutrition. There was no obvious rationale here for abandoning the high-fertility strategy.

Second, there was the role of family labour in helping households to cope with risks associated with their livelihood strategies – of course, it was generally male family labour that performed this role. While land was the most valued form of material capital in the countryside, the human capital represented by family labour helped households to utilise, defend and accumulate landholdings, potentially increasing the family's upward mobility or, at the very least, preventing its downward mobility. It helped them withstand risk and make gains in an environment that was characterised by various sources of uncertainty. For instance, Adnan (1978) points out that the near absence of the rule of law in the delta area had long presented a particular class of threat. In a society in which the shifting course of rivers constantly shifted the boundaries of settlements and landholdings, families often resorted to physical force to settle conflicting claims. The violence endemic to rural class relations imposed the imperative to ensure a sizeable number of males within the household, its *shakti shali*, as an important element in household livelihood strategies.

Family labour also helped households to diversify livelihoods where the vagaries of climate made sole reliance on agriculture extremely risky. Wealthier households invested their surpluses in non-farm enterprises – trade, moneylending and construction – and in strengthening links with the state and its functionaries. Sons were educated in order to take advantage of emerging jobs in the formal economy, including public sector jobs. They developed influential connections, social capital that could help their families to obtain a share of the substantial development resources that flowed from cities to countryside. Daughters could prove useful in securing strategic matrimonial alliances:

> In the flexible and fluid Muslim society it is not forbidden to climb the social ladder as an individual and to raise the rank of an individual with the help of a well-chosen son-in-law together with such practices as *parda*. (Vreede-De-Stuers 1968, p.7, cited in Feldman and McCarthy 1983, p.951)

For the poorest families, the risk of further downward mobility was their greatest fear, both in normal times, because of the extreme seasonality in the demand for labour in agriculture, and also during periods of accentuated crises: famines, floods, crop failures. Such risks were unlikely to be mitigated through reliance on other equally poor kinship networks but the number of adult males within the family could reduce the likelihood of decline. Households with more earners stood a better chance of avoiding distress sale of assets or recourse to usurious forms of credit. They were also better able to diversify income sources: petty trading, fishing and handicrafts supplemented wage labour (Arthur and McNicoll 1978). Having a pool of family labour to draw on also stood them in good stead in their efforts to cultivate patron–client relationships with wealthier households. They could provide labour, loyalty and muscle power in exchange for favoured access to sharecropping arrangements and wage opportunities in normal times as well as loans and other forms of support in times of crisis.

Finally, a third set of risks underpinning fertility strategies in Bangladesh related to a particularly critical stage of the household cycle, the death of the household patriarch, who was usually its primary breadwinner, while children were still young. Such a premature death could augur a period of intense uncertainty for surviving family members. In the absence of a mature son capable of taking over breadwinning responsibility and protecting the family property from predatory relatives or neighbours, the likelihood of downward mobility was extremely high. The resilience of the household at this stage of its lifecycle thus depended crucially on having had a sufficient number of children early enough to ensure that one or more sons had grown to adulthood by the time their father died (Cain 1978).

Separating out the interests of women within the household as distinct from those of men drew attention to the specific category of risks that women as a group faced. The literature on women's lives in Bangladesh at that time painted a bleak picture, with little prospect for improvement in the foreseeable future. The overlapping practices that assigned women a subordinate position within highly unequal gender relations spelt out an uncompromising patriarchal bargain. The deficits that underpinned women's dependence on male support over their entire life course, their lack of land and other valued material assets, the restrictions on their mobility and employment opportunities, imposed a severe penalty on those who lost this male support – what Cain, Khanam and Nahar (1979) describe as 'patriarchal risk'. This risk was increasing in the context of increasing poverty – with profound implications for the stability of the patriarchal bargain:

> The kinship, political, and religious institutions that support male dominance and authority remain strong and intact, while the associated sanctions that ensure that males carry out their responsibilities to women have weakened. With the pressure of increasing poverty, this outcome is predictable since male authority has a material base while male responsibility is normatively controlled. Normative control, while powerful, is nevertheless relatively malleable in the face of economic necessity. (p.410)

The erosion of the norms of male obligation saw increasing numbers of women who had been left, for one reason or another, to fend for themselves without the support of their husbands or families.[12] These women were driven outside the norms that prescribed their proper place in society to find ways of looking after themselves and their dependents. The materialisation of patriarchal risk thus brought with it a 'frightening financial independence' that had to be avoided rather than striven for (Adnan 1993). So, while women more generally may have shared the community habitus about the norms of gender propriety, they were also aware of the precariousness associated with their dependent status, of the harsh penalties suffered by those for whom this risk had been realised.

They responded by complying with the patriarchal bargain as far as possible so as to strengthen whatever familial bonds of security were available to them, and by resisting any form of change that might challenge these norms or threaten these bonds in any way. They accepted without question their parents' choice of marriage partner because it strengthened the moral obligations of parents to take them back should their marriage go wrong. They relinquished the share of the land that they inherited from parents to their brothers in order to maintain good relations with them and create a debt of obligation, which could be 'called in' in the event of divorce or widowhood. They proved their worth to their husband and his family by their modest and decorous behaviour, fulfilling their domestic obligations, abiding by what was expected of them as wives and daughters-in-law after their marriage. They put up with violent husbands and second wives without complaining.

But their best insurance was to produce sons, as soon and as many as possible. The production of sons assured their place in their husbands' family. The threat of abandonment and divorce was far greater if they failed to produce children or more specifically if they failed to produce sons. Given that sons were their most critical resource, an enduring preoccupation of mothers was to ensure the life-long loyalty of sons through favourable treatment of them from a very young age. And when their sons got married, they had a vested interest in the suppression of romantic love between their sons and their wives in order to claim their sons' primary allegiance and keep the conjugal bond secondary.

These arguments go counter to the assumption made in some of the literature cited in Chapter 1 that women were more likely than men to favour the egalitarian treatment of their children – on the contrary, it suggested that women had a stronger stake than men in ensuring the survival of an adequate number of sons because of their dependence on the support of sons in later life. As Cain (1978) points out, it was not surprising that informal interviews with village parents who had adopted some method of contraception found that wives were usually more adamant about postponing contraception until after the birth of at least a second son and more likely to articulate their awareness of the importance of sons to their future welfare. Husbands, on the other hand, when given the hypothetical choice between one and two sons, were more likely to express indifference.

4.4 A changing habitus?

The studies discussed in this chapter were carried out during the years when Bangladesh was widely viewed as an international 'basket case'. They offer the ground-level counterpart to the pessimism discussed in the previous chapter about Bangladesh's prospects for change that prevailed in policy circles. That there were very real grounds for pessimism during that period was succinctly summarised by the various litanies of grim statistics that were used to describe the country at the time.

A number of authors have suggested that this steady deterioration in the basic conditions of life was likely to have been accompanied by a collective transformation of their outlook, what could be described as their shared habitus. Osmani (1990), for instance, describes the 1970s as a watershed decade in Bangladesh, entailing massive political, economic and social shifts that forced people off the land and were likely to have forced them to rethink the taken-for-granted aspects of their way of life:

> The pressure to move out of land must have been irresistible under these circumstances. Yet in view of the centuries-old bondage to land in rural Bangladesh, it is unlikely that economic pressures alone can explain so massive a shift to non-agriculture in such a short span of time. Agriculture is not just an economic occupation but has been for centuries the way of life in rural Bangladesh. It must have needed a fundamental change in the socio-cultural psyche of the rural masses for them to contemplate an altogether different way of life. (p.73)

Osmani's comments were implicitly about men. But women had also had their own traumatic experiences. They had gone through a war of liberation that brought not only death and destruction but also mass rapes, dramatic evidence of the failure of men to protect the honour of their women. They had suffered the steadily rising poverty of the post-liberation period in gender-specific ways. The inability of increasing numbers of men to support their families was reflected in the growing incidence of divorce and abandonment by men of their wives and children. Studies from this period noted a rise in female-headed households: estimates varied between 6% and 16% of all households. As Cain, Khanam and Nahar (1979) observe, just as the proportion of landless households in the population provided an indicator of the extent of rural class differentiation, so too the proportion of female-headed households indicated the extent of 'patriarchal differentiation' (p.410).

The 1970s were, in other words, a watershed period for women as well, when many were 'irrevocably wrenched from the security of their homes and traditions' (Feldman and McCarthy 1983, p.955), when it was brought home to women from all classes that men could not always be relied on to live up to their side of the patriarchal bargain, that they would have to find ways of securing their own survival. It is likely to have brought about a change in their habitus, challenging traditional modes of thought and action. My own early and somewhat hopeful reflections on the growing awareness among women of the vulnerability of their position in society was that 'this period perhaps marks the beginnings of a feminist consciousness in the country' (Kabeer 1984, p.5). A more accurate assessment perhaps was provided by Feldman and McCarthy: 'The need for self-reliance, as women call it, was the primary lesson they learned during this period between 1968 and 1974' (1983, p.955).

This chapter opened with a quote from Arthur and McNicoll spelling out the nature of the impasse in which people found themselves: the social practices that had reduced them to life at bare subsistence not only worsened their conditions but persisted over time because they were fostered by these very conditions. But the observations in this concluding section suggest an alternative interpretation, that worsening conditions were leading to a change in the collective habitus. There was a growing realisation among many sections of the population that practices that had served them well in the past could no longer be relied on in the present, that they might need to modify and change them in order to prepare for an increasingly uncertain future.

Notes

[1] Bertocci (1972, p.30).

[2] These descriptions echo Khan's analysis cited in Chapter 2 that natural villages, the basis of rural settlements and local allegiance in much of Asia, were weak in Bangladesh, their boundaries 'elusive'.

[3] The violence that characterised competition for power and resources in the countryside can be seen from a report by BRAC (1983) that examined the wealth base of the most powerful men in 10 villages in which it worked. Very few had acquired their wealth through inheritance alone. Most had acquired it through various illegal activities, such as smuggling, cattle rustling, forcible occupation of disputed land, false documents, beating and murder of opponents or threats to do so, appropriation of public goods, fraud, forgery, corruption, litigation and theft.

[4] In Punjab in 1949, large landlords with more than 500 acres of land accounted for 10% of landownership, those owning 100 to 499 acres accounted for 11% of land owned, those owning 10 to 99 acres accounted for 47% of the land, while 32% owned less than 10 acres (Burki 1976).

[5] Wood (1999) cites one village study from Bangladesh around this time in which a large landholding family had land distributed over 18 different irrigation command areas in the village.

[6] The real wages of agricultural labourers in 1975 had fallen to less than two-thirds of their 1963 levels (Hartmann and Boyce 1983).

[7] See Yan and Roy (2019).

[8] The Health and Demographic Surveillance System (HDSS), funded by the United States, was set up in Matlab *thana* in rural Comilla in 1963 by a research institute originally known as the Cholera Lab and later renamed the International Centre for Diarrhoeal Disease Research, Bangladesh (CDDR, B). Since 1966, the HDSS has maintained registration of births, deaths and migrations in addition to periodical census. Over time it has added other variables to the system. It is considered the most reliable sources of longitudinal data in Bangladesh.

[9] See Appendix 3 for discussion about gender differentials in mortality.

[10] The shift to the dowry system as indicative of a deterioration in the value of women is also discussed in the wider literature (see Mason 1988).

[11] Dowry was named as a major factor in marital instability among poor people in a later UNDP study (1996).

[12] The Bangladesh Fertility Survey 1975 found that a fifth of all first marriages ended in divorce.

5. Defying the prophets of doom: the emergence of the Bangladesh paradox

> *Bangladesh has come a long way, defying the prophets of doom, and faring better than most had hoped, with an acceleration in growth and reduction in poverty in all its dimensions.* (World Bank 2003a, p.i)

> *The pragmatism that Bangladesh came to accept through a complex political and social process has yielded noticeable success, which has impressed—and to a considerable extent surprised—the world.* (Sen 2013, p.1967)

While the individual strands of change that made up the Bangladesh paradox have been discussed in various studies since the early 1990s, the language of paradox did not find its way into the development literature till the early 2000s, when it became clear that these individual strands added up to broad-based change across a range of social indicators. This chapter traces the processes of change that took place after the assassination of Mujib in 1975. The military regimes that followed him set about dismantling his vision of the new nation, seeking to build support among internal constituencies who had been opposed to his ideology and politics, as well as to end the country's isolation from the donor community. But, regardless of the complexion of the regime in power, of the later shift from military to civilian rule, the practice of politics through patron–client interactions remained the primary means through which different governments sought to gain support and reward loyalty. The poor quality of Bangladesh's governance was, as I noted in the introductory chapter, one of the factors that many believed would block its development trajectory.

This chapter explores why this did not happen. It examines the progress that was made on the economic front: the spread of rural mechanisation, growth of agricultural productivity and the rise of a successful export-oriented garment industry that took the place of declining jute exports. Its main focus, however, is on the pace of progress the country made on the social front, remarkable in the light of its adverse initial conditions. It unpacks different elements of the 'big picture' explanations referred to in Chapter 1: the key institutional actors that contributed to the change, the actions they took and, very importantly, the nature of the processes that made their efforts effective.

5.1 Shifting politics and policies: the turn to Islam and the market

The liberation of Bangladesh was, as noted in Chapter 3, greeted coldly by the Middle Eastern bloc. Bangladesh had broken up the world's first Islamic Republic and chosen to style itself a secular, socialist people's republic. Significantly, it was not till the assassination of Mujib and the assumption of power by Zia in 1976 that Saudi Arabia chose to recognise Bangladesh. Zia was prompt in redefining national identity in Islamic terms. The constitutional principle of secularism was replaced with 'absolute trust and faith in the Almighty Allah'. Citizens of Bangladesh were described as Bangladeshis rather than Bengalis to emphasise the nation's territorial boundaries and de-emphasise its common ethno-linguistic identity with Hindu-majority West Bengal. A Ministry for Religious Affairs was established to promote the practice of Islam among the country's citizens. He founded his own political party, the Bangladesh National Party (BNP). He also lifted the ban on religious parties, allowing them to become politically and electorally active. The process of Islamisation was continued by Ershad, who became president in 1982. He amended the constitution in 1988 to declare Islam the state religion – although the principle of secularism continued to be upheld.

By the time democratic elections were restored in 1990, there had been important changes in the political landscape. The familiar fragmentation of the left along ideological lines (pro-Soviet versus pro-Chinese) meant that progressive forces within the country had become increasingly ineffective in the political arena. Left parties had been clamped down on during Mujib's regime and further decimated by the military regimes that succeeded him.

By contrast, the official turn to Islam increased the influence of the religious parties. The largest among them, the Jamaat-e-Islami, was able to enhance its stature further by aligning itself with the two mainstream political parties, the AL and the BNP, in the mass protests to bring down the Ershad regime. While Jamaat-e-Islami never mustered a great deal of support in subsequent elections, the two main parties split the vote nearly evenly and so their search for coalition partners gave Jamaat, as well as other smaller and more extreme Islamic parties, an influence in politics and policies well beyond their share of votes and seats.

Religion became an increasingly visible force in public life. Although the AL was generally considered left-of-centre and the BNP right-of-centre, their economic policies were remarkably similar and bore the hallmarks of donor influence. They sought instead to differentiate themselves at the ideological level through their definitions of national identity and the role of religion. The BNP allied with Jamaat when it came to power in the 1991 elections and again in 2001. The AL continued to display remnants of its earlier commitment to secularism and was supported by the Hindu minority as more protective of their interests. But it also allied itself with other religious parties when politically expedient. This use of religion by the main political parties, Khan (2000) suggests, is best understood as an extension of patron–client factionalism rather than a commitment to ideological beliefs.

These moves in the direction of an Islamic identity, begun by the military regimes and continued by civilian ones, saw a growth in donor funds from the Middle East. Between 1971 and 1975, the countries of the Middle East, including Saudi Arabia, had provided just $78.9 million as aid. This rose after Mujib's assassination to $474.7 million between 1976 and 1981 and remained significant thereafter (Pattanaik 2009). The other major force connecting the country's economy to the Middle East was the rising flow of migration that had begun with the oil boom in the 1970s. Remittances from overseas migrant workers, mainly in the Middle East but other Asian countries as well, began to outstrip international aid as a source of foreign exchange.[1] Changes in government policy saw the emergence of a new middle class with strong business interests in the Middle East and 'professedly anti-democratic and anti-secular' (Pattanaik 2009, p.275).

If the assertion of its Islamic identity helped to restore Bangladesh's cred-ibility among the oil-rich Middle Eastern donors, its development policies were reshaped to gain recognition and aid from the West. Under Zia, the constitutional commitment to 'socialism' was amended to a vaguer commit-ment to 'economic and social justice', signalling his determination to steer the economy away from previous half-hearted attempts to institute a planned economy towards the liberalised model favoured by donors. Over the follow-ing years, and on a somewhat staggered basis, the country adopted the meas-ures associated with the classic structural adjustment package, cutting back on the role of the state, encouraging the private sector and moving towards a free trade regime.

The flow of foreign aid as a percentage of national income that had declined in the latter years of Mujib's rule rose again once Zia took power in 1975 to its highest level as percentage of the GDP and remained high through the 1980s (Hossain 2017, p.67). But the expected growth rates did not materialise; in fact, per capita growth in the 1980s at around 1.6% a year was lower than the rate achieved in the 1970s (Sen, Mujeri and Shahabuddin 2007). It was only in the 1990s that a significant break with this pattern took place. Per capita growth rates began to rise, reaching 3.6% by the end of the decade, fuelled by rising agricultural productivity and the export of ready-made garments (World Bank 2003, p.ii). Poverty rates declined from 70% in the early 1970s but remained high at 50% at the end of the century.

Rural entrepreneurship: breaking the agrarian impasse

The early years of liberalisation did little to dispel pessimism about the pros-pects for agrarian change. Agricultural growth rates were low and actually declined through much of the 1980s. They seemed to confirm the belief that the size and fragmentation of the country's landholdings ruled out the adoption of new technologies for most farmers and that its rural elites would monopolise whatever resources were made available. But, in the late 1980s, rural mechanisation took off dramatically, among not just large farmers but small and marginal ones as well.

Attempts to explain this disjuncture between expectation and reality pointed out that the Green Revolution literature had been dominated by the 'big machine' bias of the 'Punjab model' of rural mechanisation, the rapid spread of large-scale technologies well suited to the large landholdings and extensive irrigation, dating back to the colonial era, that characterised agriculture in the Punjab regions of both Pakistan and India. By contrast, the spread of rural mechanisation in Bangladesh was based on the adoption of small-scale 'everyday technologies' and 'locally distinct' pathways (Biggs and Justice 2017). This 'below-the-radar' model had been adopted in a number of Asian countries but overlooked in the literature because it lacked the visible symbolic power that modernisation narratives attributed to moments of 'take-off'.

Rural mechanisation took off in Bangladesh as a result of policy reforms undertaken at the end of the 1980s. A UNDP-funded Agricultural Sector Review (1989) into the causes of the sector's poor performance found that, although the government had embarked on agricultural liberalisation in the late 1970s, many of its previous policies remained, including restrictions on the duty-free import of farm machinery. It recommended full-scale privatisation of agricultural markets. The result was a rapid expansion in total irrigated area, the widespread adoption of high-yielding varieties of rice, the year-round cultivation of paddy and diversification into new crops. The country achieved self-sufficiency in food by the late 1990s.

Various factors converged to bring about this transformation. The obvious one, of course, was the availability of new and more appropriate forms of technology at a fraction of the price of imports before deregulation (Ahmed 1999). But change was also hastened by the accompanying reconfiguration of production relations in the countryside. The older agricultural economy, centred on the peasant farmer deciding how to use the resources at his disposal, gave way to a rural economy made up of a range of entrepreneurial actors, including farmers themselves, who found ways of using the new technologies and new strategies to circumvent the problems of both elite capture and the fragmentation of landholdings (Wood 1999).

Landowners unable to fully utilise the equipment they had purchased because of the size of their plots, or the fragmentation of their holdings, sold their surplus capacity as a form of business. But they had to compete with small and medium-sized farmers who could buy the now affordable irrigation pumps and power tillers. Farmers with scattered plots turned over different operations on their plots to a range of service providers: other farmers, private entrepreneurs and, in some areas, landless groups organised by NGOs like Proshika, purchased low-lift pumps to sell and deliver irrigation water. The 'operational consolidation' of holdings provided a solution to the problem of 'ownership fragmentation' (Mandal 2017).

These backward and forward linkages meant a wide range of actors benefited from rural mechanisation (Lewis 1996). The steady diversification of opportunities in the rural economy saw a shift from farming as the dominant occupation to entrepreneurial services. These changes were accompanied, and made possible, by the expansion and diversification of markets in credit. The classic loan relationship between landlord and tenant was supplemented by transactions between traders, employers and kin. There were also financial transactions between poor households, usually at the same high rates of interest charged by the rich but nevertheless providing borrowers with a desirable alternative to their dependency on richer patrons (White 1992).

The steady growth in rural migrant workers in overseas employment since the early 1970s and the increasing flow of remittance income lifted many households out of poverty and also helped finance infrastructural links, which accelerated the expansion of economic activity in the rural economy. The rural–urban divide was replaced by a rural–urban continuum that encouraged the mobility of people, goods and ideas, the proliferation of small/medium-sized market centres and a decline in poverty. Land-ownership was no longer the only determinant of rural power; capital and connections also mattered (Lewis 2011). Wealthier households continued to explore new avenues for livelihood diversification and status consolidation, but landless households were also able to diversify into the burgeoning non-farm sector and reduce their dependence on local patronage networks (Lewis 1991; White 1992). Consequently, while structural transformation in rural Bangladesh, as in many developing countries, was driven by rural–urban migration, it was also driven by changes with the rural economy itself, by the diversification of rural livelihoods and the expansion of the non-farm sector (Sen 2019).

Industrial entrepreneurship: 'the world's second largest exporter of garments'

Industrial growth had also stagnated after independence. While this was blamed on the inefficiencies and blockages associated with nationalisation, the move toward privatisation in the early 1980s did little to improve the picture for industry as a whole (Sobhan 1991). The main exception to this was the spectacular growth in the garment sector and, to a lesser extent, in leather and shrimp processing.

The export garment industry in Bangladesh began as a handful of assembly plants under subcontracting arrangements with East Asian entrepreneurs. That it went on to become second largest exporter of garments in the world (after China) was initially the result of some fairly ad hoc enabling factors rather than a grand government design to lift the country out of poverty.

One factor was the growing business class, who had become rich through 'primitive accumulation' strategies of the 1970s and was now seeking opportunities to invest and grow their capital. The other was that garment producers in East Asian economies had reached the quota limits placed on their garment exports to Europe and North America by the Multi Fibre Arrangement (MFA)[2] and were looking to set up assembly plants in nearby low-wage countries. They saw their opportunity in Bangladesh, which was part of the MFA but still quota-free because of its low-income status and insignificant textile industry.

Their initial forays into this territory took place in the late 1970s through joint venture agreements with local entrepreneurs, but the real take-off occurred with the adoption of the 1982 National Industrial Policy, which inaugurated a major programme of denationalisation and reprivatisation and put in place various incentives to attract investment. Largely unregulated factories sprang up in major cities where space could be found, very often in residential buildings. It was an easy business to enter in this early phase: it cost around £200,000 to equip a medium-sized factory of 500 workers with modern sewing machines, pressing irons and button machines (Jackson 1992). As a long-standing industrialist later put it, 'everyone saw a lot of money to be made here … Everybody and his uncle was getting into the business – engineers, police officers, military officers, civil servants'. His brother added, 'Everybody' (Labowitz and Baumann-Pauly 2014, pp.13–14). In fact, as the comment suggests, 'everybody and his uncle' was in fact quite a select group, mainly people with political contacts who had benefited from the 'primitive accumulation' opportunities of the 1970s. A 1993 survey found that 23% of garment factory owners had been in the civil service or the army (Khan 2013). The others were likely to have had close contact in politics that allowed them to accumulate funds.

The industry grew at an astonishing rate. In 1984, when the newly formed Bangladesh Garment Manufacturers and Exporters Association (BGMEA) started keeping records, there were 384 registered factories with around 120,000 workers. By 2008 there were 4,285 factories and 3.1 million workers. From near zero, ready-made garments (RMG) became the country's largest export item by 1988. By 2010, Bangladesh had become the second largest RMG exporter in the world after China. It had over 4,000 garment factories employing more than 5 million employees and generating further indirect employment through its linkages to other sectors – around 2 million in 2015 (BGMEA 2015; Haque and Bari 2021).

Even more astonishing was the fact that the vast majority of its work force was made up of women. A new female labour force of factory workers appeared to have come into existence almost overnight, growing as the industry grew to become 80% of its workforce. Their highly visible presence on the streets was astonishing for anyone who had known the country in earlier years. It was my main motivation for carrying out research on the phenomenon in the late 1980s. As I explained in the preface to my book *The Power to Choose*, it had come to my attention when I visited Bangladesh in 1984 after an absence of three years:

> I was struck then by the sight of thousands of young women mov-
> ing briskly around on the streets of Dhaka. In a city, and a country,
> where women had been conspicuous by their absence in the public
> domain, this was not merely a new phenomenon, but a remarkable
> one. (2000, p.vii)

The employment of a largely female work force was as unplanned on the part
of government and employers as the industry itself had been. Government
support for export industries reflected its need to earn foreign exchange and
to meet the demand for work by the country's surplus labour. Women were
not counted as among those demanding work nor was it imagined that they
might be (Feldman 2009). An early government publicity brochure spelt out
the advantages of the country's labour force to foreign investors, referring to
their productivity and undemanding nature – but *not* to their gender: 'The
light bodied Bangladeshis, who are recognised as very intelligent peoples, can
be turned into most productive and at the same time the least demanding
labour force' (Hossain, Jahan and Sobhan 1990, p.37). This was in striking
contrast to a Malaysian investment brochure designed to attract foreign
investment issued around the same time, which referred very explicitly to the
famous 'manual dexterity of the Oriental female', who was qualified by *'nature
and inheritance'* to work in assembly line production (*Far Eastern Economic
Review*, 18 May 1979, cited by Elson and Pearson 1981, p.149, authors' italics).

5.2 The emerging paradox: the disjuncture between economic and social progress

The rapid rates of growth achieved by Bangladesh despite its adverse initial
conditions had, as the World Bank put it in the opening quote to the chapter,
defied the prophets of doom. What was more impressive, however, was the
country's progress on the social dimensions of development at a faster pace
than most countries with similar levels of per capita income. And – most surprising of all – the earliest signs of this progress occurred where it was least
expected: in fertility behaviour.

Population growth rates were, as we saw, the overriding preoccupation of
the donor community. They had maintained their apparently inexorable rise
despite the fact that Bangladesh had become the largest recipient of foreign
assistance for population control (Cleland et al. 1994). In the mid-1970s, the
US ambassador expressed hope that there was light at the end of the tunnel.
He said that Zia had just taken power and had been anxious to reassure the
ambassador on this point:

> Uppermost on his mind, evidently, was a desire for us to under-
> stand that they had registered our concern that a really effective
> attack on Bangladesh's population problem was long overdue ... he
> wanted us to know they understood this was their top priority.

The ambassador in turn informed Zia that he was pleased to hear this because he was hearing increasing concerns about Bangladesh's unsatisfactory record:

> Questions were being raised about the purpose of the enormous amounts of aid we are putting into Bangladesh if there was so little to show in the way of checking population growth. (US Department of the State Office of the Historian 1976, cited in Hossain 2017, pp.150–51)

A decade later, in January 1984, the same despair was being expressed in a leaked memo written by the Bangladesh representative of the UN Fund for Population Activities (UNFPA) to its New York headquarters. There was little value, he said, in putting donor funds into primary healthcare services in the country if this was going to detract from their efforts to promote contraception. He suggested that voluntarist principles of family planning be put aside in Bangladesh in favour of the 'massive direct and indirect compulsion' employed by the Chinese government:

> As I see it, voluntarism is based on the idea that couples should have the right – the basic human right – to determine the number of its children. But what is a human right in one country may not be a right in another. (cited in Hartmann and Standing 1985, pp.37–38)

But, even as his memo was winging its way through policy circles, 'the couples' he referred to were in the process of changing their fertility behaviour at a pace that would later be described as a 'historic record in demographic transition' (Rahman, Da Vanzo and Razzaque 2002, p.317). Analysis of data from 1989 Bangladesh Fertility Survey and the 1993–94 Demographic and Health Survey found that lifetime fertility had declined from an average of seven children per woman in the early 1970s to three in the early 1990s (Bairagi and Datta 2001; Cleland et al. 1994). Since, according to demographic transition theory, some level of modernisation was considered a necessary precondition for fertility to decline, the idea that such a steep decline in fertility could have occurred in one of the poorest and least developed countries in the world was met with 'surprise, even incredulity' (Cleland et al. 1994, p.xi). But the findings were confirmed by a variety of sources: the decline was real, it was substantial, it had begun gradually in the late 1970s but gathered rapid momentum in the 1980s – and, furthermore, it was a poverty-led decline (Kabeer 2001a). As Larson and Mitra (1992) observed, Bangladesh set records for the fastest increase in contraceptive use, the swiftest fertility decline and the most substantial drop in desired family size, all accomplishments remarkable for one of the world's poorest nations.

Other signs of social progress, 'exceptional health achievement despite economic poverty' (Chowdhury et al. 2013, p.1734), began to surface. Analysis of the 1989 BFS data showed a substantial decline in infant and child mortality since the mid-1970s (Kabir, Chowdhury and Amin 1995). A major reduction in maternal mortality had also occurred – from 650 per 100,000 live births in the 1980s to around 320 in the early 2000s (Overseas Development Institute 2010). Life expectancy at birth, which summarises how populations fared on a range of different health indicators, increased from 44 years in 1970 to 59 in 1995 (Sen and Acharya 1997).

Aside from the facts of this progress, there were two aspects of it that attracted further attention: it was pro-poor, and it was gender-equitable. Comparing data from national Demographic and Health Surveys (DHS) between 1993 and 2011, Adams et al. (2013) reported that the rate of improvement in infant and child mortality had been faster among the poorest households than the wealthiest, closing differentials across the income distribution. Excess female mortality in the under-five age group mortality had declined to near parity by 1993 and then to lower rates for girls by 2011. Girls were now 20% more likely to survive childhood than boys, the pattern common in much of the world. As immunisation rates went up around the country, wealth differentials in coverage declined with higher rate of increase in coverage of the poorest households compared to the wealthiest. The ratio of immunisation rates for girls to boys also improved over time – from 0.89 in 1993 to 0.97 in 2011. And of course, as we have already noted in Chapter 1, there was no evidence to indicate prenatal gender discrimination. Analysis of the Matlab demographic surveillance system (see Chapter 4, Note 8) showed that sex ratios at birth had been constant since the 1960s when data collection began.

Other evidence showed a steady improvement in education. There had been a slow and fluctuating rise in primary enrolment rates during the Pakistan years and for some time after liberation, but boys' education had risen to a greater extent than girls, leading to gender disparities in education throughout this period.[3] Enrolment rates began to rise more rapidly and consistently since the 1990s, particularly for girls (Hossain and Kabeer 2004). By the early 2000s girls had overtaken boys at primary and secondary levels, though they continued to lag behind at tertiary level.

As noted in Chapter 1, Bangladesh had not merely achieved remarkable progress on its social development; despite high levels of absolute poverty, it had performed better on these indicators than other 'comparator' countries, i.e. those with similar or even higher levels of per capita income. Its status as 'positive outlier' was demonstrated by Asadullah, Savoia and Mahmud (2014) using cross-country regression analysis for time-series data between 1980 and 2010 for between 116 and 126[4] low- and middle-income countries. They pointed out that, although growth rates in Bangladesh had improved after the mid-1990s and income poverty had declined,[5] its per capita GDP still remained a fraction of the average for other developing countries.[6] Nevertheless, it performed better than comparator countries, including India and Pakistan (as we also saw in Chapter 1), on a range of social indicators, including births per woman and contraceptive prevalence, low-birth weight babies, infant and child mortality, immunisation coverage and primary and secondary, but not tertiary, education.

The study also investigated whether some of the common explanations for progress on human development could explain the country's outlier status. Here it used data for the period between 1971–75 and 2006–10. The explanations included economic variables (poverty reduction, per capita growth rates, levels of external assistance) as well as measures of governance and policy (quality of governance; investments in social expenditure and infrastructural development). None of these held up as explanations of the country's 'exceptionality'.

The study confirmed the poor quality of governance in Bangladesh. Throughout the study period, Bangladesh performed worse on governance indicators than other countries with similar levels of income. In other words, it had made social progress *in spite* of sub-standard governance.

It also found that Bangladesh had a higher incidence of poverty than comparator countries throughout this period, but it did note that intensity of poverty had fallen faster since the 1980s. Though progress on social development had begun before poverty began to decline, it was possible that the rise in per capita income from the 1990s and the decline in the intensity of poverty helped to sustain the pace of progress.

The share of expenditure on health and education in the total budget of Bangladesh had increased steadily between the early 1980s and the late 1990s, but its levels remained lower than other countries as a percentage of GDP. Public health spending was 1.82% lower, and education spending 2.1% lower than other countries in the 2006–10 period.

Bangladesh was one of the largest recipients of foreign aid among the world's poorest countries, but this did not appear to explain its performance. In terms of net official development assistance (ODA) received per capita and the share of ODA as a percentage of public expenditure on health, its levels were lower than other countries. It also found a decline in aid dependence over time, both in per capita terms and as share of the health budget.

Transport and communication infrastructure is considered a factor contributing to health and education outcomes through improved dissemination of information, lower transport costs and easier access to social services. But Bangladesh had fewer internet users, fewer mobile cellular subscriptions, fewer telephone lines per capita and a lower share of paved roads in overall mileage than other countries. It did, however, have greater road density (roads as percentage of land area), suggesting somewhat higher levels of physical connectivity, a factor that proved important in explanations of change.

To sum up, cross-country regression analysis suggested that Bangladesh's success in terms of social achievement did not lend itself to any of the conventional explanations for social development: it was neither growth-led nor policy-mediated nor reflective of good governance. It was this apparent failure to conform to received explanations of social progress that began to give rise to various epithets, such as 'unlikely success' (Larson and Mitra 1992), 'paradox' (Adnan 1998; Chowdhury et al. 2013), 'puzzle' (New York Times 2005[7]), 'surprise' (Devarajan 2005; Mahmud 2008), 'conundrum' (World Bank 2006a), 'outlier' (Asadullah, Savoia and Mahmud 2014) and even 'miracle'[8] to describe the country's performance.

Asadullah, Savoia and Mahmud did add a number of caveats to their findings. They pointed out that some of the conventional explanations for social progress may have been relevant to the Bangladesh case but could not be captured by the measures available for use in their cross-country comparisons. For instance, the comparison of overall per capita public spending on social services did not take account of its composition to distinguish expenditures that were more or less pro-poor in their orientation. So, while the share of the total budget allocated to health and education in Bangladesh was found to be lower than other countries, national estimates found that the distribution of benefit from public spending on both health and education among households was (weakly) pro-poor, a factor not captured in their regression analysis.[9]

They also could not easily capture the possibility of mutually reinforcing interactions between the causal routes through which change occurred nor could they capture possible interactions with contextual factors, such as history, demography, cultural heritage and geography, all of which shaped the environment in which development took place.

Explanations of the paradox that were more closely grounded in the specific empirical realities of Bangladesh took a different tack. They pointed to the role of different actors, the nature of their contributions and the importance of collaborations between them. They discussed aspects of the country's history and context that were likely to have made change possible or hastened its pace. And, finally, they considered possible interactions between various causal routes through which change had taken place. I explore these explanations in greater detail in the rest of this chapter.

5.3 Explaining the paradox: the role of institutional actors

One set of explanations revolved around the role of different actors and their contribution to the processes of change. The state was ascribed an important role in a number of studies, despite its widely recognised limitations. The World Bank (2003a), for instance, noted the persistence of poor-quality governance in Bangladesh but explained progress in terms of 'public policies that have complemented remarkable energy at the grassroots level' (p.i). These policies included sound macro-economic management, innovative human development policies through public–private partnerships, an environment in which NGOs could expand and reach out to the poor, and efforts to empower women and girls. A report by the Overseas Development Institute (2010) believed that 'policy continuity' had made the difference, with successive governments consistently adopting and implementing a range of pro-poor social policies and programmes.

The role of development NGOs also featured widely in these explanations. As Lewis (2011) points out, variations in how NGOs were defined and the plethora of informal and unregistered organisations co-existing alongside formal ones made numbers difficult to estimate.[10] But Bangladesh was recognised for its unusually high concentration of NGOs, more per person than any other developing country (Adams et al. 2013). The size, outreach and activities of the NGO sector distinguished it from other countries at similar stages of development.[11] Their outreach was extensive: between 20% and 35% of the country's population was believed to receive some services, usually health, education or microcredit, from an NGO (Lewis 2011). The majority of these organisations worked with the poor, some with the very poorest.

The important role of donors was also noted. Per capita aid to Bangladesh may have been lower on average than other countries at similar levels of development, but this estimate did not capture how this aid was used. For instance, unlike aid to Pakistan, which was largely military assistance, aid to Bangladesh was focused on development (Khan 2014). Apart from funding service provision, donor assistance also took the form of institutional support for both government and NGO services in basic health, education and social protection, as well as for advocacy and experimentation in these fields (Thornton et al. 2000).

Others pointed to the private sector as an important route for employment generation and poverty reduction. Here, Rahman (2006) highlighted the tendency in elite and donor circles to equate the private sector in Bangladesh with big business, celebrating in particular the phenomenal growth of the garment industry. He suggested that they failed to recognise the broader and longer transition through incremental reforms and physical connectivity to the market economy that Bangladesh had undergone since the late 1970s, the 'deepening of entrepreneurship that had taken place across micro, meso and macro levels of society' (p.14). The country was no longer primarily made up of peasant farmers but of small, medium and large-scale entrepreneurs in rural and urban areas, all of whom had played a part in driving economic progress.

Also relevant in discussions about the role of institutional actors was the importance of collaboration between them. This was the pragmatism referred to by Amartya Sen in the opening quote to this chapter, the willingness of rulers to forego the pursuit of ideological purity that favoured exclusive reliance on either private initiative or the state, and to opt instead for a 'potent' mix of public, donor, commercial and non-profit providers in the pursuit of public goals (Chowdhury et al. 2013). This policy of collaboration helped to compensate for the state's 'capacity deficit' in service delivery, partly a reflection of its reluctance to tax its wealthy citizens.[12] Donors had played a critical role here by providing large amounts of funding to the NGO sector as preferred provider in a context where markets in private social services were largely missing and by putting pressure on the state to partner with them.

Collaboration between government and the NGO sector, exploiting differences of comparative advantage, had an important role to play here. It helped the scale and pace of implementation and corrected for official biases towards neglected constituencies. Many of the better-known NGOs were characterised by their willingness to experiment with low-costs solutions suited to a poor population and by their outreach across the country. The state's subsequent adoption of these solutions helped explain the broad-based impacts found in Bangladesh, impacts that NGOs could not have achieved on their own.

5.4 Policies that mattered

Explanations of the paradox also singled out a number of policy interventions by the actors discussed that were considered to have played an important role in the country's social progress and highlighted what had made them effective. Some were related directly to the social domain in which the changes had occurred; others contributed indirectly.

Explanations also drew attention to key attributes of these policies that contributed to their effectiveness: their scale, speed and selectivity (Adams et al. 2013). 'Scale' referred to the willingness to think about and enact polices, on orders of magnitude that corresponded to the magnitude of the problem: 'small might be beautiful', as Fazle Hasan Abed, the founder of BRAC, observed, 'but big was necessary' (cited in Hossain 2017, p.19). 'Speed' referred to the willingness to roll policies out at a pace that reflected the sense of urgency that fired efforts to tackle seemingly insurmountable challenges. And 'selectivity' referred to the deliberate priority given in policies to two significant sections of the population that had been overlooked in past development efforts: namely, the poor and women.

Population

The predominant thrust of population policy in the early years of Bangladesh, dating back to the Pakistan era, had been a top-down, target-driven provision of a limited range of methods (high-oestrogen pills with negative side effects, IUDs and sterilisation) through government health facilities and rural dispensaries. Efforts were hampered by the structural bifurcation of the Ministry of Health and Family Welfare, with health activities assigned to men and family planning efforts to women, both mainly urban-based, and very little co-ordination between these parallel organisational structures.

Key to the success in bringing down fertility rates was a new approach to the delivery of family planning/mother-child health services which had been developed by ICDDR,B (see Chapter 4, Note 8) through experimental trials in Matlab starting in 1977. This was taken to scale by the government in 1989. At the heart of the new approach was the regular doorstep delivery of contraceptive services by trained female family planning workers, an acknowledgement of the nature of the cultural constraints that confined women to the home (Phillips et al. 1988; Simmons et al. 1988).

It also expanded the methods on offer: pills, condoms, foam tablets and injectable contraceptives were all brought to the doorstep. IUDs were provided at clinics, but appointments could also be made for home insertions. While sterilisation continued to be offered in clinics, the programme incorporated an incentive system with payments to women who agreed to the procedure, to the family planning worker who persuaded the women as well as to any individual intermediary who motivated women to come for sterilisation. Abortion remained illegal except to save the life of the mother, but in 1979 the government approved the provision of menstrual regulation (MR) services as a pragmatic alternative. This used vacuum aspiration to evacuate the uterus within the first 12 weeks after a delayed menstruation. It had to be provided by more qualified paramedical personnel than family planning fieldworkers but, unlike abortion, it could be provided without a pregnancy test for the purported health-related objective of 'washing out the womb' or as an 'interim method of establishing non-pregnancy' for a woman at risk of pregnancy, whether or not she was pregnant.

Health

The accelerated decline in infant and child mortality that began in the late 1980s took place in conditions of absolute poverty, lower levels of public health expenditure than other countries at similar stages of development and a poorly equipped and staffed public healthcare system in rural areas. Progress on health appeared to have occurred through three key pathways (Alam and Bairagi 1997; Kabir, Chowdhury and Amin 1995). One was through broad interventions that improved the general health of the population, such as access to safe drinking water[13] and sanitary latrines. The second consisted of low-cost, vertical preventive interventions to deal with common childhood diseases, such immunisation programmes and oral rehydration therapy. These were favoured by donors as they could be provided even in the absence of an established health system, but they also proved to be pro-poor. The third pathway consisted of massive publicity and educational campaigns combined with door-to-door visits aimed at improving everyday caretaking practices within the home, such as boiling drinking water, washing hands after defecation, and protecting food from flies and dirt. NGOs were important players in these pathways, through their own initiatives but also under contract from government (Sen, Mujeri and Shahabuddin 2007).

Education

From the early years of nationhood, education had been a domain of social policy in which concerns with skills and productivity had co-existed, and often clashed, with contestations over different visions of nationhood and national identity. These contestations were at their most obvious in two areas of education policy: religious education and the education of girls. Both expanded considerably from the 1990s: religious education was supported by Middle East aid and Islamic philanthropy, while female education was singled out by international donors.

The efforts of military regimes to demonstrate their religious credentials saw increased support for religion in education more generally as well as for improvements in the quality of state *madrassa* education. This increased the appeal of the state *madrassas*, removing the perception that they offered a second-class education and helping their graduates to enter mainstream employment (Bano 2008).

At the same time, female education had become identified in the international literature as a catalyst for a variety of positive development outcomes. Girls' education began to assume greater policy importance in Bangladesh. The BNP government that that came to power in 1991 put a number of initiatives in place that increased overall and female education. It launched a Food for Education programme in 1993 to provide free monthly rations of rice or wheat to poor families, conditional on their children attending primary school.[14] In 1994 it initiated the Female Secondary School Assistance Programme,[15] described by the World Bank as 'the world's vanguard program of this type' (cited in Mahmud 2003, p.3). A stipend and tuition subsidy were given to female students on three conditions: they attended school for at least 75% of the year, they obtained at least 45% in the final exam, and they remained unmarried till the completion of secondary education. A tuition subsidy was also provided to schools in which eligible female students enrolled. It covered both secular schools and *aleya madrassas* that were registered with the government.

The latter provision saw the number of secondary *aleya madrassas* for girls rise at a phenomenal pace accompanied by the rapid increase in female students, from 8% of *madrassa* students in 1994 to 48% in 2005 (Asadullah and Chaudhury 2008). The closing of the gender gap in secondary school enrolment noted in the paradox literature was thus partly a product of the increasing number of girls, particularly those from poorer households, in *madrassa* education.

The other important actor in the push to educate girls from poorer households was the NGOs. BRAC had begun experimenting with non-formal schools in the 1980s in order to reach children, mainly girls, from poor households who were either dropping out of primary education or had never been enrolled. In the early 1990s, national data showed that only a third of children belonging to poorer households were completing primary education. The BNP government agreed to allow a number of NGOs to expand their non-formal schooling programme as a bridge to government secondary education.

BRAC, along with some other NGOs, became leaders in the field of non-formal primary education, with BRAC alone running over 30,000 schools. They experimented with 'joyful' child-centred approaches in place of the rote learning then widely prevalent: they used well-trained voluntary teachers, simple textbooks designed to reflect rural life, continuous evaluation instead of exams, and flexible class times. NGO schools played an important role in increasing girls' school enrolment relative to boys – and in improving their test scores (Sukontamarn 2005).

Some five million children graduated from these schools, two-thirds of them girls from very poor and disadvantaged families. The majority went on to state-run secondary schools.

Safety nets and livelihood ladders

Bangladesh's safety net programmes were another factor in the pro-poor bias of its progress. These sought to both protect and promote livelihood opportunities for the poor, thereby enabling them to invest in the health and welfare of their families. The Vulnerable Group Feeding programme, set up after the 1974 famine to provide wheat transfers to those in need, was subsequently transformed in collaboration with BRAC into the Income Generation/ Vulnerable Group Development programme, which combined transfers with efforts to develop the entrepreneurial capacity of women from the poorest households. The Food for Work programme, also put in place in the aftermath of the 1974 famine, became an established programme providing work to both women and men in exchange for food during the slack agricultural season. CARE's Rural Maintenance Programme, based on the same principles, focused on poor women, not only providing wage work in construction for a period of four years but combining this with savings mechanisms and training for future entrepreneurship.

One of the more radical proposals adopted by the Ershad government was the distribution of all *khas*[16] land to the landless. While the more powerful sections of the rural elite were able to use to variety of tactics to appropriate this land, a number of radical NGOs working with groups of marginal farmers and landless labourers mobilised successfully to register some of this land with their members.

But Bangladesh's microfinance services were probably the most widespread and best known of its livelihood interventions. Microfinance began as a poverty-oriented strategy among NGOs, later also adopted by government, but over time, as donors began to stress the need for NGOs to become financially sustainable, programmes became more business-oriented. Membership of these programmes grew from 8 million in 1996 to 34.6 million in 2010 (Khandker and Samad 2014).

There has been considerable debate about the effectiveness of microfinance in poverty reduction based on conflicting findings, but a number of longitudinal surveys suggest that it made important overall contributions. One long-running survey that followed the same group of borrowers over 20 years concluded that continuous participation had made a difference, which varied by gender, to how they had fared: female participation in microfinance significantly reduced extreme poverty, boosting household consumption and living standards, while male participation was associated with accumulation of assets (Khandker and Samad 2014). Other longitudinal surveys found that borrower households had higher per capita income and lower likelihood of falling into poverty and that female borrowing had a positive effect on asset accumulation (Razzaque 2010); that access to loans had a positive impact on food consumption, self-employment and asset accumulation, more so for longer-term participants (Islam 2011); that it had a 19% increase in rural employment (Osmani 2015); and that it reduced rural poverty by 28% (Mahmud and Osmani 2017).

Gender equality policies

While some of the government's development policies were directly targeted to the reduction of gender disparities, many of its actions on the political and legal fronts contributed, somewhat unevenly, to the enabling environment in which progress occurred. Since the mid-1970s there had been growing interest in gender and development issues within the international development community and both Zia and, after him, Ershad saw the opportunity to signal their modernist credentials to the world.

Zia increased reserved seats for women in Parliament from the 15 mandated by the previous government to 30 in 1978.[17] In 1988, under Ershad, one-third of seats in union councils were reserved for women. These were initially based on nomination, but in 1997 direct elections were introduced to reserved seats at union level.

Successive governments undertook various administrative changes. In 1976, Zia established a Division for Women's Affairs in the President's Secretariat; it was upgraded to the Ministry of Women's Affairs in 1978, renamed the Ministry of Women's and Children's Affairs by the Ershad government in 1982, integrated with the Ministry of Social Welfare and downgraded to departmental status, restored to ministry status by the BNP government in the 1990s, and then combined with miscellaneous other groups to form the Ministry of Youth, Culture, Mass Media, and Sport.

As Goetz (1995) comments, this highly chequered history of national machineries for gender issues was symptomatic of their shifting utility at various periods in generating international political capital for regimes seeking to demonstrate a progressive national image. These gestures were not backed by resources. In the early years of Zia's regime, the Two-Year Approach Plan (1978–80) allocated 0.27% of the total budget to women's concerns (Feldman and McCarthy 1982). The Five Year Plan in the early 1990s allocated 1% of the total budget to the six ministries that were in any way connected with these concerns (McCarthy 1993, p.328).

There was considerable progress on the legal front but frequent gaps between formal and substantive change. A 1985 ordinance by Ershad had set up family courts at the local level with exclusive jurisdiction to deal with cases relating to parental and conjugal rights, thereby expediting their disposal. Other legal initiatives put in place by successive governments, very often in response to campaigns carried out by feminist and human rights groups, included laws that prohibited the payment of dowry and criminalised violence against women.

Bangladesh was also active in the international arena. It ratified the UN's Convention on the Elimination of All Forms of Discrimination against Women (CEDAW) in 1984, although, in deference to Islamic sentiment at home and abroad, it retained reservations to four articles on the grounds that they were against the *sharia*.

However, the government adopted the Beijing Platform for Action in 1995 without any reservations. In 1998, the Ministry of Women's and Children's Affairs under the AL government drafted a National Development Policy for Women to address its obligations in the critical areas identified by the Beijing Platform for Action. These measures ran into Islamic opposition and the National Policy was not adopted till 2011 and that too in a very watered-down form (Nazneen 2018).

In September 2000, the government of Bangladesh, along with governments from 190 other countries, signed the UN's Millennium Declaration to halve world poverty by 2015 and adopted the associated Millennium Development Goals. Many of these goals related to dimensions of social development on which Bangladesh performed well and it gained an international reputation as an MDG success story.[18]

The government's various efforts to project a progressive image on the international stage through support for the women and development agenda were often at odds with attempts to build their Islamic constituency (Guhathakurta 1985). Successive regimes were frequently forced to rein in these efforts because of the need to placate their Middle East allies abroad and their Islamic base at home. These shifts and contradictions within state policy were possible because the state generally regarded the issue of women's rights in essentially instrumental terms. At the same time, this ambivalence kept open a space for constant engagement between the state and feminist organisations – as we note below.

5.5 Context for change: the social composition of the elites

The state has been consistently singled out in explanations of the Bangladesh paradox, not only for initiating critical policy interventions but also for the continuity of its pro-poor policy commitments, regardless of the regime in power. But this begs an important question since, as Hossain (2017) points out, it required a degree of political will and policy coherence not typically associated with a state with such a poor reputation for governance. I want to spell out her attempt to explain this puzzle in some detail because it links to my earlier discussion of the country's history. It also highlights the importance of the context and culture in which policies are enacted for what they are able to achieve.

Hossain suggests that one of the lessons that the political elites of Bangladesh learnt after the terrible famine of 1974, and the deaths of over a million people, was that the political legitimacy of those in power in a poor country like Bangladesh depended at the very minimum on their ability to protect their population from crises in basic subsistence. However, such crises were not new to Bangladesh – far from it. As noted in Chapter 2, the history of the region was punctuated by periodic, and often calamitous, crises of various kinds without ever evoking the same degree of response from those in power.

So the explanation for the responsiveness of the post-independence elites had to be sought in what differentiated them from those who had led the country in earlier times. Hossain argues that they were, for the first time in the region's history, drawn from the ranks of the majority of the people of the region rather than originating from outside it. That difference on its own could have been a sufficient reason why they were more likely to have been affected by the scale of the deaths that took place as a result of the famine.

But what also differentiated them was that they did not come from a class of people long accustomed to the exercise of power. In fact, Hossain suggests that the defining characteristic of the Bangladesh elite may have been that it had not been, until very recently, particularly 'elite'.

National elites tend to be identifiably wealthier, culturally superior, and socially and sometimes racially or ethnically distinct from the masses. By contrast, the vernacular elite who came to power with independence were largely without inherited or culturally distinct status and few had held much economic or political power before independence. They constituted an 'intermediate' regime, dominated by middle-class professionals, small business-men and wealthy peasants, rather than landed or large industrial interests (Bertocci 1982; Nicholas 1973; Sobhan and Ahmad 1980). They were from recent peasant stock, from families who had taken up formal education or entered the professions only in the previous generation or so. They continued to have ties with extended families in their villages. Compared to groups that had ruled the region in the past, and to contemporary elites elsewhere, 'the Bangladeshi national elite was marked less by its distance and difference from the masses than by its affinity to them' (Hossain 2017, p.47).[19]

The same social history can be found among leading figures in the NGO sector and other civil society organisations who provided the 'remarkable energy at the grassroots level' commented on by the World Bank. As we noted in Chapter 3, one of the distinguishing features of the first generation of NGOs in Bangladesh was that, unlike many other developing countries, they were indigenous organisations, founded and staffed by Bangladeshis even if they received assistance from abroad. Their leadership was drawn from the same social class as the country's political elite and they shared the ideals of the liberation struggle. This explained why partnerships between them could be forged with considerable ease, particularly in the early decades after independence.

However, the NGO sector expanded considerably over time, became far more heterogenous and lost some of its radical edge. New organisations emerged because of the increased availability of official donor funding, and older ones adapted to donor demands to take on service provision roles. As a result, by the 1990s, it became possible to differentiate between a mainstream NGO sector and a radical subsector (Lewis 2017). Mainstream NGOs varied in size from organisations like BRAC and Grameen with millions of members to other smaller ones, unknown beyond the area in which they operated but also oriented towards service provision. The provision of microfinance services increasingly overshadowed other forms of service provision. Some, like the Association for Social Advancement (ASA), moved from their earlier radical agenda to the provision of minimalist microfinance services geared to promoting individual entrepreneurship. Others adopted a more mixed approach. Proshika, for instance, sought to combine credit services with social mobilisation while BRAC combined it with a programme of legal support to its women's groups and training on women's rights.

The radical subsector, on the other hand, was made up of organisations, like Nijera Kori, Samata and Saptagram,[20] that eschewed service provision from the outset and focused instead on popular education about rights and social justice and building the organisational capacity of the poor – men as well as women (Lewis 2017). Many of their members were now participating in the village *shalish* or convening their own, some were fielding candidates in local elections. They were much smaller than the mainstream NGOs, with the largest among them reporting membership in the hundreds of thousands rather than the millions.[21]

Lewis also included Gonoshasthaya Kendra (GK) in the radical subsector. While not a development organisation like the others, it nevertheless made major contributions in the field of health. It gained a global reputation for its 'barefoot doctors', a paramedic health worker programme based on the Chinese model; for being the first NGO to recruit female staff and to train its female paramedics to ride bicycles to carry out household visits, in defiance of social norms; and for the reduction of maternal mortality rates in its programme area to levels well below national levels (Chaudhury and Chowdhury 2007). It also fought a well-publicised struggle to curb the import of non-essential drugs. This was bitterly contested by the international pharmaceutical companies but it led to the adoption of the Essential Drugs Policy in 1982, which improved the local production and availability of essential drugs at affordable prices (Chaudhuri 2020).[22]

Also not part of the development NGO sector, and even smaller in size than the radical development NGOs, were a range of mainly urban-based civil society organisations that organised around women's rights (Nazneen 2017a). Despite their size, these organisations have nevertheless been able to punch above their weight because they concentrated their energies on strategic aspects of law and policy that had profound implications for large numbers of women in the country. Some, like Kormojibi Nari and Mahila Parishad, were loosely affiliated to left-wing parties, with one focusing on working women and the other on promoting women in politics. Others, like Ain-o-Salish Kendra (ASK), Bangladesh Legal Aid and Services Trust (BLAST) and the National Women Lawyers Association, were legal rights organisations, challenging discriminatory laws, providing legal training and helping victims of injustice to take their cases to court. Then there were feminist activist organisations like Naripokkho, which was particularly active around issues of sexuality and bodily integrity.

Along with the everyday struggles that all these organisations were engaged in, they periodically took on issues that brought them into national prominence. For instance, feminist organisations across the political spectrum mobilised to keep the issue of violence against women at the forefront of public consciousness. It was their efforts that led to the passage of the Cruelty to Women (Deterrent Punishment) Ordinance, 1983, the Prevention of Violence Against Women and Children Act, 1998, and the Domestic Violence Act in 2010 (Nazneen 2017b).

Feminist activism often brought these groups into direct conflict with the rising forces of Islamic orthodoxy (discussed in greater detail in Chapter 8). When Ershad amended the constitution in 1988 to declare Islam the state religion, Naripokkho activists took legal action against him on the grounds that the amendment marginalised minority religious groups and paved the way to undermine women's rights. He was toppled from power in 1990 before the case could be heard.[23] I noted earlier the government's decision to withhold ratification of four articles of CEDAW in deference to Islamic sentiment at home and abroad. Women's organisations also lobbied hard against this decision and in 1997 they succeeded in getting the state to withdraw reservations to two of these articles.

Legal organisations have been in the forefront of the fight to replace personal religious laws with a Uniform Civil Code that would make all women in Bangladesh, regardless of their religion, equal citizens in the eyes of the law (Pereira, Shahnaz and Hossain 2019). They have faced opposition from men from Islamist groups as well as from religious minority groups because it threatened male privileges upheld by their respective religions. BLAST mobilised against the use of fatwas by rural clergy seeking to police the behaviour of poorer rural women (see Chapter 8). In 2001, it succeeded in getting the High Court of Bangladesh to rule that fatwas could not overrule the law of the land but the Supreme Court stayed the operation of the verdict for fear of the Islamic backlash.

5.6 Interconnected processes of change

One other important dimension of social change that is not easily captured through econometric approaches is the mutually reinforcing nature of causal processes, the synergies between them and their interactions with the wider context. I will be investigating these processes in greater depth in the rest of the book, but I want to touch here on some of the hypotheses put forward in the paradox literature about how these interactions might have worked in the Bangladesh context.

Mahmud (2008) suggests that positive synergies and mutual feedback mechanisms between key social policies were likely to have been considerable because of the scale, and speed at which they were rolled out. Scale and speed would have been helped by the decision of the government to collaborate with NGOs that were engaged in service provision with considerable outreach to poorer populations. Density of settlements would have made outreach easier.

The sequence of interventions was also significant in that the establishment of certain prior conditions increased the likelihood of other forms of change. For instance, Bangladesh's demographic transition took place at unexpectedly low levels of income and education and, very unusually, before a discernible decline in infant and child mortality, generally seen as a precondition for fertility decline (Cleland et al. 1994). While the decline in fertility occurred because of the innovative nature of the family planning programme, it allowed the population to respond more rapidly to interventions intended to reduce infant and child mortality – and increase children's education – than would have been the case if families had continued to have large numbers of children.

Mahmud also draws on a version of the individual bargaining model outlined in Chapter 1. While declines in fertility and child mortality in Bangladesh took place before the rise in female education and employment, he suggests that it was possible that, once these began to rise, they led to an increase in women's bargaining power, which in turn expedited the speed of the transition to lower fertility and greater investments in children's welfare and education. In as much as women bore primary responsibility for the care of children and the family, it was plausible to argue that they would use an increase in their bargaining power in this way.

The increased connectivity between people and places as a result of accelerated rural infrastructure development was highlighted as an important contextual factor in promoting both synergies and spillover effects (Mahmud 2008; Sen, Mujeri and Shahabuddin 2007). Earlier I discussed its role in linking markets, diversifying livelihoods, deepening entrepreneurship, all of which led to a reduction in poverty levels (Ahmed and Hossain 1990; Khandker, Shahidur and Koolwal 2009). The spread of cellular mobile phones also had a major impact on rural markets: according to Murshid (2022), 80% of traders interviewed in 2008 had access to mobile phones enabling them to talk to clients readily and place orders over the phone without the need for face-to-face exchange.

But, beyond the impact on markets, improved connectivity also served to promote the mobility of people, ideas and attitudes. Rural electrification was found to be associated with increased adoption of family planning, while ease of access to health facilities increased the overall health of the population and reduced gender differentials (Ahmed and Hossain 1990). Proximity to paved (all-weather) roads increased the likelihood of secondary school enrolment for both boys and, to a greater extent, girls (Khandker, Shahidur and Koolwal 2009). Infrastructure development also influenced the kinds of schooling selected. Asadullah and Chaudhury (2016) found that parents were more likely to send their children to government schools than *madrassas* if they were in, or close to, urban areas, if their households had electricity and if their village had an NGO presence and satellite dish connection.

Finally, it has been argued that the relative homogeneity of the population was an important factor in enabling the rapidity with which ideas and interventions spread across the country. Local elites were not so detached or distant from the poor people they were supposed to serve that they could routinely afford to neglect them (Hossain 2017). The spread of opportunities and the chances of upward mobility were less constrained in Bangladesh by class, ethnicity or other social barriers (Mahmud 2008). If everyone, even the very poorest, saw a chance of escaping poverty, people were more likely to be proactive in their response to new economic opportunities. This, argues Mahmud, was an important reason why even poor families strove to send their children to school, despite the sacrifices it entailed.

But it is important to pause here and note that the pace of social progress has not been uniform – there have been systematic exclusions. These represent the country's achievement failures. Poverty remained a major factor in explaining who was left behind, but exclusions have been particularly concentrated among those at the intersection of poverty with the discriminations associated with devalued identities and disadvantaged locations. Populations in the poor coastal areas and urban slums as well as indigenous minorities in the Chittagong Hill Tracts lag behind in the country's health progress (Adams et al. 2013). The expansion of the primary schooling system has also been slow to reach children in the more remote locations such as the Chittagong Hill Tracts, the tea plantations in the east, and flood-prone districts (Sen and Ali 2009). Children from minority ethnic as well as non-Muslim groups have also been poorly served by the educational system in general but they are excluded by definition from the expanding *madrassa* system (Chowdhury et al. 2013).

I concluded the last chapter by examining evidence that suggested that the growing insecurity of people's lives led to a change in their habitus as they realised that practices that they had relied on in the past might no longer be viable in the future. It led men to give up their centuries-old attachment to the land as a source of livelihood and a way of life, to find alternative livelihoods in new and unfamiliar activities. It led women to realise that the patriarchal bargain that had been their main source of security over the course of their lives could no longer be relied on, that they would have to find other ways of securing their survival.

These studies were written in a period when the future did not appear to hold out much hope. Not surprisingly, the unexpected progress that began to appear in the literature not soon after gave rise to a more positive mood within the research community, a greater willingness to look beyond conventional explanations. For instance, since it seemed unlikely that this broad-based progress could be attributed to any single policy intervention, Alam and Bairagi (1997) wondered if 'something much larger', 'some socio-cultural changes in the country' had been at work:

> Perhaps a silent revolution, big or small, improving the status of women and female children took place in Bangladesh as a result of different actions taken by the government and non-governmental organizations. (p.216)

As the rest of the book will argue, some kind of revolution had indeed been taking place, a revolution that went beyond visible changes in the policy envi-ronment to a 'silent revolution' in how people thought about their lives, in the collective habitus. Let me conclude this chapter with a quote from Rahman (2006) that exemplifies this optimistic prognosis of the country's prospects. Like those quoted at the end of the last chapter, he also believes that a trans-formation took place in the collective consciousness, but it was a far more upbeat account of the transformation. It suggested the continuing evolution of dispositions and capabilities that were partly rooted in past struggles with an uncertain environment but that also looked forward to a future that seemed to hold the promise of expanded possibilities for women as well as men:

> Perhaps the over-riding story of Bangladesh is one not found in the statistics at all. The poor of Bangladesh have undergone something of a personality revolution and become more assertive, pro-active towards opportunities, clearer on life goals. This has not happened in a day. The egalitarian and democratic aspirations which under-pinned the attainment of independence, a resilient outlook born of a continuous struggle with the vagaries of nature, the demon-stration effect of mobility and livelihood opportunities, the return of competitive politics, all have played their role. The social real-ity may not have lost its oppressive features, but the poor men and women of rural and urban Bangladesh are new protagonists on the scene and societal outcomes are very much open. (p.16)

Notes

[1] Remittances accounted for 0.76% of Bangladesh's GDP in 1976 and rose to a maximum of 10.59% in 2012. It averaged 4.6% over this period (https://www.theglobaleconomy.com/download-data.php).

[2] The Multi Fibre Arrangement was signed in 1974 by the USA, Canada and a number of European countries as a short-term measure to 'facilitate' the process of trade liberalisation by allowing signatory countries time to make an orderly adjustment to rising imports from

the fast-growing East Asian economies. It turned into a longer-term measure, which was renewed every four years on increasingly restrictive terms until it was finally phased out in 2005. Under the MFA's 'anti-surge' clause, signatory countries were allowed to impose quotas on items imported from another country if the annual rate of growth in imports in these items exceeded 6% a year. However, in recognition of their particular development needs, the MFA allowed exemption from these quotas for imports from poorer developing countries. One of these was Bangladesh, which had no garment industry at the time and hence posed no threat to the US. But the rapid subsequent rate of growth of the Bangladesh garment industry, albeit from a base of zero, led to the imposition of quotas by France, the UK, the US and Canada in 1985. A campaign against the quotas in Bangladesh and elsewhere led to the lifting of the quotas by the UK and France in 1986, but they were retained in the US and Canada (Kabeer 2019).

[3] In 1970, a year before Bangladesh's independence, girls made up 32% of total enrolment in primary schools and just 18% in secondary schools.

[4] Depending on data availability.

[5] From 70% in the early 1970s to 50% in the mid-1990s to 40% by the mid-2000s.

[6] Its real per capita GDP in 2009 was $1,397, compared to $2,353 for Pakistan, $3,238 for India and $5,526 for developing countries as a whole. The trend growth between 1960 and 1971 had been 0.5% per year. This had increased to 2.4% in the first half of the 1990s and 5.5% in the second half (BIDS 2001). As fertility declined, economic growth rates began to outstrip population growth rates so that per capita GDP grew from 1.6% per annum in the 1980s to 3% per annum in the 1990s.

[7] See: https://www.nytimes.com/2005/05/07/opinion/philip-bowring-the -puzzle-of-bangladesh.html

[8] See: https://www.project-syndicate.org/commentary/bangladesh -economic-miracle-outperforming-india-and-pakistan-by-arvind -subramanian-2021-06 and also Sawada, Mahmud and Kitano (2018).

[9] The health subsidy of public spending represented 1.45% of the average per capita expenditures of the poor and 0.8% the non-poor (World Bank 2003b).

[10] Estimates cited in Lewis ranged from between 22,000, according to DFID and 206,000, according to the World Bank. According to the NGO Affairs Bureau, around 1,925 NGOs, most of them among the better known, received foreign funds.

[11] Some of its better-known NGOs were very large indeed. Membership of the four biggest NGOs was 5.2 million (Grameen Bank), 5.1 million

(BRAC), 5.7 million (ASA) and 1.9 million (Proshika) (World Bank 2006a; 2005 figures).

[12] The tax on agricultural land in Bangladesh was described as no more than a 'filing fee for annual ownership records', providing very little revenue for the government (Skinner 1991, p.505). A more recent study notes that the tax-to-GDP ratio in Bangladesh is one of the lowest in the world: 8.6% compared to averages of 17–18% for developing countries (Ahmed 2023).

[13] Access to safe drinking water registered considerable progress from the 1980s but in the second half of the 1990s, it encountered a significant setback when the haste to achieve goals led to failure to do proper testing of ground water and to the emergence of arsenic as a major health hazard in the second half of the 1990s.

[14] It was later monetised and became the Government's Primary Education Stipend Programme.

[15] The stipend was initially provided for lower secondary education (grades 6–10) and later extended to higher level. The programme was also expanded by the AL to reach boys from poor backgrounds.

[16] Unused government-owned land.

[17] When this provision lapsed in 2001 it was extended and later increased to 50 seats (Nazneen and Masud 2017).

[18] See: https://dailyasianage.com/news/6356/mdg-achievement--a-story-of-success

[19] The responsiveness of the political elite to the subsistence needs of the poor, regardless of which section of it was in power, may explain why successive surveys have found a surprising degree of trust on the part of poor people towards governments that they themselves might recognise as corrupt and inefficient (Hossain 2008).

[20] The full name of Saptagram was Saptagram Nari Swanirvar Parishad but it is generally referred to as Saptagram. The full name for Samata is Samata Samaj Samity.

[21] Nijera Kori, for instance, reported 275,700 members in its 2007–08 annual report. Saptagram at its height had just 26,000 members.

[22] See also https://rightlivelihood.org/the-change-makers/find-a-laureate/zafrullah-chowdhury-gonoshasthaya-kendra

[23] The case finally made it to Bangladesh's High Court in 2016, where it was rejected (https://www.aljazeera.com/news/2016/3/28/bangladesh-court-upholds-islam-as-religion-of-the-state). However, the provision for secularism was restored in 2011. The constitution thus designates Islam as the state religion but upholds the principle of secularism.

6. 'My children have a future': fate, family planning and the capacity to aspire

[Our mothers] were only busy with husking, boiling of paddy, cooking, and other household duties. They used to give birth to many children, but they did not care very much about their children, where they were going or not, what they were eating. (cited in Simmons 1996, p.256)

Many people are now using family planning to reduce their number of children, because it is not possible to rear a lot of children as it was in the past. Having few children and bringing them up nicely is much better than having many children not brought up well. (cited in Caldwell and Khuda 2000, p.245).

Academic research during the 'basket case' years was largely attuned to continuities in long-standing structures of power. Few sought out the meanings and motivations of the people whose behaviour was under study and hence few recognised the seeds of change that these might contain. A somewhat different picture emerged from research that 'talked' to its subjects. People came to life, spoke of their beliefs, aspirations and fears, and shed light on what led them to abide by certain rules and norms, as well as the tensions they experienced when their own desires took them in a different direction. It is through these 'emic' narratives that we can better understand how the changing circumstances of people's lives gave rise to ground-level changes in entrenched social practices such as those examined in this chapter, practices relating to bearing and caring for children.

The idea of the 'quality–quantity' trade-off in reproductive preferences comes from neoclassical household economics and refers to the choice that parents face between stretching limited resources across large numbers of children or having fewer children and investing more resources in each child (Becker 1981). Montgomery (1999) draws on this idea to offer a conceptual schema of how different stages in the process of demographic transition might embody different kinds of interactions between the objective possibilities for agency that they opened up and subjective changes in how parents saw their reproductive options. He suggests that, when mortality rates were extremely high and the survival chances of children uncertain, parental attitudes towards fertility were likely to be characterised by fatalistic attitudes: it was beyond human control; it was the will of God. Such responses could be interpreted as a rational stance in the face of pervasive uncertainty: if families had no way of predicting how many children would survive to adulthood, having as many children as God allowed was a means of maximising the chances that some of them might.

As health levels rose in the course of broad processes of economic development, and improvements in children's survival chances filtered into parents' consciousness, they were likely to become more open to the idea that greater care on their part could keep their children alive, not necessarily by helping them survive serious illness but perhaps through the kind of foresight that prevented accident or illness occurring in the first place and stopped minor illnesses turning into major ones (Caldwell 1996, p.613).

With the increasing likelihood of child survival over time, a different kind of agency became possible, 'one that involve[d] forward-looking strategies that play[ed] out over longer time horizons' (Montgomery 1999, p.12). Since the reduction in child mortality diminished the insurance rationale for high fertility, parents would begin to consider the possibility of taking action to reduce the number of births they had, rather than leaving it to chance or divine will. Initially, they would have adopted traditional methods of birth control, but, as more effective modern methods became available, the pace of fertility decline would have sped up. Moreover, modern methods would have brought an aspect of reproductive behaviour previously considered part of the realm of doxa, beyond the realm of human control, into the domain of conscious choice, of 'thinkability' (Mita and Simmons 1995, p.7). And, as parents began to look beyond the present, they would become willing to devote more resources to each child to prepare them for a future that they were now able to imagine. These shifts in shared worldview, the emergence of a forward-looking 'capacity to aspire' (Appadurai 2004) in the light of emerging possibilities, represented a profound change in the individual and collective habitus.

The process of demographic transition that took place in Bangladesh did not conform precisely to this model. Fertility declined before major declines in child mortality had taken place, in a society that remained 'predominantly conservative, traditional and agrarian' (Cleland et al. 1994, p.1) and within a fairly compressed period of time.[1] One result of this was that it was possible to collect personal narratives about childbearing behaviour from people who had borne their children at different stages of this demographic transition. These narratives suggested that the transition in Bangladesh had indeed been accompanied by a transition in the collective habitus, but that it was not the result of the long-drawn out, structural transformation of society predicted by classic demographic transition theory but to a great extent the consequence of deliberate policy efforts to make it happen. In this chapter, I want to draw on these narratives to tease out in more detail how these policies acted on, and helped to transform, the meanings, motivations and practices associated with bearing and caring for children in a context in which the reproductive belief system had long been characterised as stubbornly resistant to change.

6.1 The quantity–quality transition: controlling births

Signs of change in reproductive preferences

When Betsy Hartman and Jim Boyce went to do fieldwork in the village of Katni in 1974, most villagers they spoke to subscribed to fatalistic views about fertility: 'What can we do? It is Allah's will' (p.116). But information about modern forms of contraception was trickling in. A few years earlier, a wandering pot-seller had told villagers about a strange new pill that prevented pregnancy. Sometime later, a woman had passed through the village selling these pills at 20 times their price in town. She claimed they had miraculous powers but did not offer any instructions about their use. A few daring women purchased the pills but had no idea what to do with them.

The village mullah heard about the pill and condemned it as sinful. Village elders refused to believe it was humanly possible to control fertility but said that, even if it was, it went against the will of God. But not everyone in the village was equally hostile. Families who could not feed their children, who left them to glean the fields or collect fruit that had fallen on the ground, were open to its possibilities. So too were young men for whom population pressure had clearly demonstrable consequences: they would inherit less land than their fathers had and their children would inherit even less.

But the greatest interest was expressed by women in the village who knew only too well the toll that that continuous childbearing took on their bodies and lives. Older women, like Anis's mother, lamented that they were tired of having children and dreaded the thought of yet another pregnancy: 'My hair is getting thinner and my teeth are falling out … My body is weak. If I have another child, it will ruin me' (p.116). Younger women were also exhausted. Moni's wife was only in her early thirties but had 11 children, the last two separated by less than a year. To breastfeed the newborn, she had weaned the other baby, who was now thin and sickly. She was desperate:

> I have had so many children I don't know what to do. This little one is sick and cries all the time – she'll never be healthy. Sometimes I want to end her life, but how can a mother kill her child? They say Allah gives children and taking the pill is a sin. Even so, I want to try them. (p.116)

These women would question Betsy about contraception out of earshot of their husbands: 'What is it? How does it work? Is it a sin?' (p.116). The couple's efforts to help them provide a telling sketch of the state of family planning services at the time. They went to a government family planning office in the nearest town to see what help was available. In response to the request by the 'foreign' couple, two young women were sent to the village. Mothers were summoned, lectured about birth control, promised IUDs and pills – but the women did not return. The couple made a second visit. Two more women arrived, distributed pills and informed villagers about the availability of the IUD and sterilisation in government clinics. A few women started using the pill provided by the visitors, but their supplies ran out and they were too shy to ask their husbands to purchase fresh supplies from the town. Efforts came to a halt.

We catch other glimpses of the nascent changes in beliefs and attitudes about fertility that was under way in the study cited in Chapter 4 by Maloney, Aziz and Sarker (1981). While the overwhelming response to questions about desired fertility repeated the familiar fatalism and submission to the will of God, these responses also included ambiguities and contradictions, stirrings of change below the surface. For example, while over 80% of survey respondents agreed that the number of children depended on God, a sizeable percentage of this group were clear that they did not want any more children, with women more likely to express this view than men. This apparent inconsistency could be seen to reflect the gap between the possible and the desirable.

Limited access to contraception meant that the number of births could indeed be said to depend on God. But dependence on God was not seen to rule out the possibility of action by people in what they believed to be in their interest. The inconsistencies in responses therefore suggested that, for many of those questioned, the belief that smaller families were in their best interest was beginning to take shape.[2] Among those who still wanted more children, the single most important reason – and this was more frequently stated by women than by men – was the desire for sons. Those without a surviving son were more likely than those without a surviving daughter to say they wanted more children, but the percentages went down with each surviving son or daughter.

From fatalism to fertility control

These studies were carried out in the 1970s, when contraceptive prevalence among married women was less than 5% (Cleland et al. 1994). It had risen to 25% by the mid-1980s and to 40% in 1991. A number of qualitative studies carried out in the early 1990s explored the motivations behind this turn to birth control by 'the first generation to control family size' (Caldwell and Khuda 2000).

These studies suggest that individual rationales for limiting family size were embedded within broader stories of social change. One set of stories related to the growing pressure of population on a limited resource base, the steadily declining size and growing fragmentation of farms over successive generations, rising landlessness and scarcity of work: 'they cannot get jobs so they fall into drug use and criminal behaviour' (Caldwell and Khuda 2000, p.246). Contrary to the predictions of demographic transition theory, it was poverty rather than prosperity that led to the onset of fertility decline.[3]

A 25-year-old woman echoed the point that young men had made a decade earlier about the consequences of population pressure on land: her father-in-law had not had to face hardship because he had inherited 16 acres, but, when his land was divided, her husband and his seven brothers received just two acres, too little to support their families through farming. A poor sharecropper explained that he and his wife had decided to limit their family size after observing his older brother's nine children, who could be seen wandering around the village with plates in their hands: 'He has sold almost all of his share of the family land and his children are as miserable as beggars. Everyone scorns him' (Schuler et al. 1996a, p.68). And in one of the quotes at the start of this chapter a 30-year-old woman spoke of what it had meant to grow up in a large family in which mothers were too busy to pay much attention to their children.

Another set of stories related to rising aspirations. Not everyone could hope to purchase a Japanese motorbike like the landlord in Katni, but everyone could hope to eat better food and to live in better housing. The route to a better life was seen to lie in the new livelihood opportunities emerging outside agriculture, the most coveted being government jobs. But demand for these jobs far outstripped their availability, required the payment of bribes or useful connections, and were largely confined to men with educational qualifications. So, while sons continued to be valued for their potential to help families improve their living standards, education was becoming an important precondition, adding to the cost of bringing up children. The explanation for the spread of family planning offered by the 50-year-old woman quoted at the start of the chapter essentially summed up the quality–quantity trade-off as it played out around her: having fewer children and bringing them up well was preferable to having many children who could not be looked after.

Recognition of the advantages of small families did not translate instantaneously into the adoption of contraception. The doorstep delivery of contraceptive services was a major improvement on the services offered in the past, but it still represented an intrusion into the most intimate aspects of human relationships, aspects that continued to be governed by powerful social norms. Not surprisingly, it encountered a great deal of hostility, resistance and ambivalence.

There were denunciations of the family planning programme by religious leaders who preached hell and damnation for women who promoted or accepted family planning. Wealthy families refused to hire women who had been sterilised because they did not want their food cooked by someone who had interfered with the will of God (Schuler et al. 1996a). Conflicting views on contraception were expressed by women within rural communities, although the positions taken did not always divide neatly between those who opposed it on religious grounds and those who were willing to defy or reinterpret religious norms to adopt it (Caldwell and Khuda 2000). There was contradiction and ambivalence on both sides. There were women whose resistance to contraception was based not on religion but on fear and anxiety about new, unfamiliar technologies, exacerbated by accounts of very real and alarming side effects.[4] There was the case of the woman who refused to use contraception on religious grounds but prayed to God every day not to send her any more children and then asked to be forgiven for such a prayer. Others who considered themselves good Muslims expressed a kind of moral relativism to argue for family planning, the need to balance the 'sin' of family planning with their responsibility for the welfare of the family (Caldwell and Khuda 2000).

The interviews also suggested a degree of flexibility in the interpretation of religious injunctions. The earlier traditional methods, like abstinence or withdrawal, had gone largely unremarked by religious authorities because, as one husband explained, they did not introduce anything artificial into the body or interfere with its normal functioning. With modern methods, this was unavoidable, but as the concept of family planning began to take hold in the local culture, distinctions began to be made between different methods.

Temporary methods were generally viewed as more acceptable because they merely postponed births rather than eliminating their possibility. Moreover, the pill was already a familiar form of medicine for various ailments. There was hostility to the IUD because it entailed insertion of an object into women's bodies. There was greater hostility to abortion as a direct challenge to God's will since the foetus had already been created. Menstrual regulation did not attract the same opprobrium since it had to be carried out early in the pregnancy and was seen as 'washing out the womb' for health reasons. The greatest hostility was reserved for sterilisation because it terminated women's procreative capacity, overstepping what was permitted to human beings.

Co-operation and conflict within the household

While one set of contestations over the idea and practice of family planning was carried out at the community level, another took place within the domestic domain. The need to secure their status within their marriage, the fear of 'patriarchal risk', still provided women with a powerful incentive to produce sons, but they were also aware that it was their bodies that bore the costs of early, frequent and prolonged childbearing. Studies carried out during this period showed that conflicts within the family most often pitted younger married women against those in authority within the family.

Women had not been enthusiastic about traditional methods of contraception not only because they were not reliable but also because they required men to co-operate – and many did not. As one woman put it, men 'do not leave women alone' (Caldwell and Khuda 2000, p.244). They were now being offered forms of birth control that did not have these disadvantages.

But the actions of those receptive to the new technologies depended a great deal on the responses of family members, their husbands in particular, but also their in-laws. Many received such support: indeed, without family co-operation, it is unlikely that contraceptive prevalence would have risen so fast. There were many husbands who, as primary breadwinners, were well aware of the difficulties of supporting a large family. There were many mothers-in-law, particularly those who had interacted with family planning workers, who were favourably disposed towards contraception because they could see the rationale for it. But such support was not always forthcoming. There were husbands who forbade it, extended families who issued threats: 'My father-in-law and mother-in-law were completely against such methods. They told me that I would have to leave their house if I used a family planning method' (Schuler et al. 1996a, p.70). In the face of such opposition, responses varied.

When women responded with open defiance, it tended to be confined to defiance of elders in the family. Both Simmons (1996) and Balk (1997) note that there appeared to be a transition in progress by the 1980s in the influence exercised by the older generation. Women who lived with their in-laws generally had less decision-making authority than those who did not, but, as long as women had the support of their husbands, they were willing to override the wishes of the elders, sometimes concealing what they were doing, often with the collusion of husbands. One 24-year-old had been warned by her mother that she was 'killing babies' by using the pill, while her mother-in-law warned her she was poisoning her insides. She went ahead anyway because she believed having fewer children would allow her to look after her family properly and 'also, many other people were practising family planning' (Caldwell and Khuda 2000, p.243).

Far fewer were willing to openly defy husbands whose presence and support continued to define their lives. One pleaded in vain with her husband to let her go for sterilisation, telling him of her anguish when she heard her children cry because he had not earned enough money and she could not feed them. Others were cowed by husbands' threats to ban them from the house or to refuse to pay for any medical treatment needed in case of possible side effects (Schuler et al. 1996a; Caldwell and Khuda 2000).

Not all women gave in to family pressure. Their accounts tell us about the kinds of agency they sought to exercise in the face of opposition. Some relied on argument and persuasion. One told her husband that she had to take the pill because it was she who suffered, not him. Another resorted to the moral balancing act referred to earlier: 'Family planning is sinful but not to practice would also be sinful, because a woman is ultimately responsible for her family's welfare and family planning is essential for this' (Caldwell and Khuda 2000, p.243).

Others resorted to clandestine defiance. Among the 104 women interviewed by Schuler et al. (1996a), 21 had adopted, or said that they were willing to adopt, contraception without letting their husbands and families know. In their cases, preferences with regard to method was less about compatibility with religious norms and more about potential for concealment. They spoke of possibilities for secrecy associated with readily available pregnancy termination methods such as herbs, roots and oral contraceptive pills. Injectables had the advantage that they could be administered secretly. A 41-year-old woman had an IUD inserted without her husband's knowledge:

> I did not discuss it with my husband because he doesn't approve. He asked me why I did not get pregnant, and I replied 'I don't think I will ever conceive again. You have become old.' [After that] my husband did not ask any more. (Schuler et al. 1996a, p.73)

These women believed that they were justified in disregarding husbands on this matter:

> Committing a small misdeed to postpone childbirth and to keep the family small is not something to feel guilty about. It will bring happiness and peace to the family. (Schuler et al. 1996a, p.73)

Most accepted that husbands were likely to find out sooner or later but were willing to take the risk because they were convinced that husbands could either be persuaded or that their opposition would weaken over time.

But of course this strategy could carry costs. One of the women interviewed by Schuler et al. (1996a) had told her family she was visiting a relative but had gone for sterilisation instead. When her husband found out, he was furious. He informed the rest of the family and they ostracised her: they refused to eat food she had cooked or let her near them. She decided she would work as an intermediary for a sterilisation clinic to earn some money of her own. Her earnings seemed to soften her husband's attitude towards her but the rest of the family remained adamant and arranged a *shalish* to pronounce a verdict on her behaviour. She attended it, informed its members that she had not done anything that was against the law of the land, and left before the proceedings were over.

Her story makes a number of important points. It testifies to the desperation of women who were willing to go against the wishes of those in authority in their families, including their husbands, to bring childbearing to a halt. The fact that her husband's anger dissipated when she started to bring home an income (even though it was earned by taking other women to the clinic for sterilisation) spoke of a certain degree of pragmatism on his part. Her decision to stand up to the *shalish* by invoking the law of the land suggested that women were looking to the state as an alternative source of authority to that of community elders – though it is likely that her husband's support bolstered her courage. The willingness to defy those in authority within the household and community by other women in the study suggests a further point. Relations of power within households were not absolute, despite their portrayal in the literature. Women had their own ways of getting around them and, even when they were penalised, seemed willing to wait it out in the expectation that anger would subside over time.

While the family planning programme had made it possible for many women to realise their reproductive preferences, this was most often the case when their preferences were aligned with the priorities of the programme. Those who went to the clinic to ask for IUD insertion were treated well. Those who went for an IUD removal reported harsh treatment. IUDs were inserted during menstrual regulation procedures without their knowledge; menstrual regulation was often made conditional on the acceptance of an IUD; false claims were made that IUDs had been removed as requested; pressure was exerted to keep an IUD in despite side effects (Schuler and Hossain 1998).

The reality, of course, is that the family planning programme was never concerned with women's reproductive preferences but with population control. While the earlier single-minded focus on sterilisation had given way to a broad range of contraceptive options, the government had its own order of preferences. Sterilisation remained its preferred option because it was irreversible, hence the incentives offered (Hartmann and Standing 1985). It was followed by other methods, such as the IUD and injectables, that could not be easily reversed at the discretion of women. The pill was regarded as least reliable – although it was the most widely accepted by the better off.

'Spreading and rooting': the dissemination of family planning

While the growing acceptance of family planning methods on the part of women and families was a response to challenges and opportunities associated with the changing environment, the rapid pace at which it occurred is unlikely to have happened if it had been left entirely to their individual agency. But the urgency attached to population control by the government and donor community meant that they were not content with merely ensuring the effective supply of modern technologies to those who wanted it; they were also determined to create new demand and to construct an environment that made that demand socially acceptable.

Findings from the early years of the new approach, when efforts were being made to incorporate it into the government system, offer very positive assessments (Simmons, Mita and Koenig 1992). This was a period when the programme was being closely supervised and monitored as part of the ongoing experiment. There was no guarantee that the same quality of services would, or could, be maintained as the programme was rolled out on a national scale. But these early findings are important because they cast light on what it was about the programme that allowed the idea of family planning to put down sufficiently deep roots that it continued to flourish as the programme went to scale. It also continued to flourish when, in the late 1990s, the government reduced door-to-door contraceptive delivery in favour of service provision through clinics, satellite clinics and rural village depots. The idea of small families had taken root in social practice.[5]

At the heart of the ICDDR,B experiment were the 13,500 young, educated women who were hired in the late 1970s to become frontline workers providing contraceptive services free of charge to women in their homes. Their presence at field level contained an interesting contradiction: it required the departure from *purdah* norms by those who provided the services in order to accommodate the compliance with these norms by those who accepted the services.

The early years were not easy. The workers had to venture into 'male space' outside their homes and interact with strange men in order to engage in a form of work that was denounced as immoral and indecent. They were considered to have lost all honour, shaming not only themselves and their families but their entire community. Religious leaders issued moral threats:

they would not be buried in the village graveyard when they died and the *imam* would not say prayers for them. Workers recalled this period:

> They used to say, one person's wife is working with another man. A *khanedarjal* [devil] has come, that is why there is poverty everywhere, there are no crops. They are working and going through the fields during monthly menstruation. Hence there is no paddy. The country is becoming a hell. Evil will fall on us. (Simmons, Mita and Koenig 1992, p.100)

Interviews with this early cohort of workers document their struggles to win social acceptance by playing up their professional competence and service ethics while also emphasising their virtuous conduct, keeping a distance from male supervisors and talking with them only when necessary. Organisational strategy played a role in gaining acceptance for the workers by upholding *purdah* norms as far as possible, limiting violations only to what was essential to the work. It expanded the range of health-related competencies provided to family planning workers beyond the delivery of contraception. This stood them in good stead with the community who began to address them as 'little doctors'.

Workers were also trained in arguments that would help them overcome the resistance they encountered within the community: to advise women who were anxious about the possible side effects of the contraception; to point out that family planning was not forbidden in the Quran; to cite statistics showing the decline in child mortality to allay the fears about children's chances of survival; and to counter the equation customarily made between the size of families and their strength and status by pointing to the actual effects of family size on the ability of a family to look after itself.

The other aspect of family planning efforts that contributed to the widespread acceptance of contraception was through both the planned and unanticipated routes that allowed knowledge of new practices to travel. In the early years, women had learnt about contraception through family planning workers since they had restricted mobility and radios were rare, but knowledge about birth control spread beyond them through informal networks within communities. Mita and Simmons (1995) relate the case of Shamiran, who was a schoolgirl in the late 1970s when the family planning worker started to visit her village. She discussed what she learnt with her friends in school; they were all impressed with the nice saris worn by the worker, the ease with which she moved between villages and the money she was rumoured to earn. They decided then that they would practise birth control when they got married so that they did not have the problems associated with too many children and could keep their saris 'clean and nice'. Years later, as these young women grew up and got married, they acknowledged the significance of this early learning for their receptiveness to contraception: 'the root of the decision was founded then'.

Later cohorts of women did not need the same degree of close interaction with family planning workers. Most had grown up with one or more members of their *baris* using contraception and knew what it was about. A telling phrase used by a woman interviewed in the late 1980s was that 'family planning has become like *dal-bhat*' (Simmons 1996, p.253) – as mundane as the typical daily meal of rice and lentils.

Along with these interpersonal routes of dissemination, mass media and social marketing campaigns took on increasing importance. By the late 1980s, radio, television and printed publicity came up routinely in interviews about the subject of family planning. The government used media channels to spell out the benefits of fertility regulation and portray the small family as an aspect of a modem lifestyle: 'The two-child family is a happy family'. Radio programmes about family planning and happy families were broadcast so frequently that 'people listened to it whether they wanted to or not' (Schuler 2007, p.192).

These attempts created a broader discursive environment in which matters once considered too controversial for public discussion were now discussed routinely. What worked particularly strongly in favour of the programme was its association with the government. The widespread trust that ordinary villagers appeared to have for *sharkar* (the government), regardless of which set of politicians was in power, gave its interventions a legitimacy in their eyes that was not enjoyed by other institutional actors. The association with government meant the programme's vocabulary, concepts and arguments provided women with an authoritative discourse to counter the forces of custom and tradition. Faced with denunciations of family planning as un-Islamic, they would retort that this could not be the case or the government would not be promoting it. But religious objections to family planning faded with surprising rapidity (Caldwell and Khuda 2000). People agreed that they had once believed that family planning was against God's will but now accepted that God's will could work through the family planning programme, that it was 'in best interest of family and country'.

In the final analysis, however, what made these messages effective was that they resonated with the needs and experiences of people on the ground. Schuler et al. (1996a) note that, while women's explanations were often sprinkled with declarations about the benefits of small families that appeared to be parroting government propaganda, further probing made it evident that programme messages provided these women with the language to express what they had come to realise through their own experiences, that their lives would be worse off in the absence of birth control, 'a sense not so much of economic gain but rather disaster averted or deterioration slowed down' (p.68).

6.2 The quantity–quality transition: saving children's lives

A second critical moment in the quantity–quality transition in Bangladesh related to the increase in children's chances of survival, particularly in the fraught early years of their lives. Here policy interventions faced a very different set of challenges to those encountered by the family planning pro-gramme. There were no religious or patriarchal grounds for resisting efforts that could be shown to improve the health of family members, particularly the health of children. Public efforts resonated with local values. The challenge lay instead in disseminating new practices and demonstrating their effective-ness to a population which already had its own understanding about disease and cure in which folk beliefs about supernatural forces were interwoven with religious beliefs about divine intervention. The early stage of the health tran-sition was therefore characterised by considerable experimentation to find solutions that took account of these pre-existing belief systems as well as of the material constraints of the local population.

One important reason why Bangladesh was able to improve child survival despite prevailing conditions of absolute poverty was that household income was not the only factor contributing to poor health (Bairagi 1980). Although child malnutrition was higher in poorer households, it was found at all lev-els of income, suggesting other factors were also at play. Gender was one: girls were more malnourished than boys, regardless of income levels. Numbers were another: malnutrition was higher among higher-birth-order children. Mother's education was a third: even a basic level of female literacy improved children's nutrition levels, with the impact increasing with income levels.

The importance of maternal education was not unexpected, given mothers' primary responsibility in the provision of care to children and family. But female education levels were low and it would take some years before an edu-cated cohort of mothers could be created. Efforts focused instead on finding ways to incorporate forms of behaviour that contributed to child survival into the routine caretaking practices of the current generation of mothers. And, if mothers were to be reached, the recruitment of women with some minimum level of education into community-based health provision by government and NGOs was recognised as central, thereby expanding the employment oppor-tunities available to this category of women.

A pinch, a fistful and half a litre: making cholera history

The development and dissemination of oral rehydration therapy (ORT) to tackle cholera and other diarrheal diseases has been described as a 'piece of history of the late 20th century that may have saved more lives than any other medical advance in our time' (*The Lancet* 1978, p.300). An important part of this history took place in Bangladesh and has been narrated by Chowdhury and Cash (1996). As Rohde, the UNICEF country representative in Bangla-desh, wrote in the foreword to their book, it was a:

> tale of how a medical technology was adapted, revised and pre-sented to an illiterate public through house-to-house health educa-tion by a small army of dedicated health workers ... health history at its best. (1996, p.xx)

ORT is a form of fluid replacement that treats diarrhoeal dehydration, the most common cause of death from cholera and other diarrhoeal diseases. When it was first developed, it had to be applied intravenously, putting it out of reach of rural populations in low-income countries. By the late 1960s, a solution of sugar, salt and water that could be taken orally was developed by doctors working in the ICDDR,B and the Infectious Diseases Hospital in Kolkata.

In the early years of independence, the government's diarrhoea control programme consisted of the distribution of packets of these ingredients through small shops across the country. It had limited success; poor households could not read the instructions or afford the packets. The obvious solution was to teach people how to make the solution at home since it used ingredients commonly found in village kitchens but publicity campaigns in the 1970s would not have reached those who were unable to read posters or did not have access to radios. Face-to-face interactions with primary care providers to teach them how to make their own solutions was the alternative option.

World Health Organization officials were opposed to the idea of homemade, non-standardised solutions. Studies had shown that American nurses had not been able to prepare the oral rehydration solution correctly and it was thought unlikely that illiterate mothers in Bangladesh could do better. Instead officials encouraged the government to embark on a national oral rehydration programme to produce and distribute the solution at village level. It quickly became clear that the government had neither the budget nor the capacity to take this task on at the necessary scale in a country with very poor infrastructure. Moreover, its primary healthcare programme was largely staffed by male workers who found it difficult to reach rural mothers.

This was when BRAC entered the picture. It had begun development work in 1973 in the remote district of Sulla in rural Sylhet, where it had tried, without much success, to introduce a health insurance scheme and a family planning programme. It decided to collaborate with ICDDR,B to take ORT to rural mothers across the country through a door-to-door education programme – starting in Sulla itself. Research into local understandings of diarrhoea had found major gaps in knowledge about the causes and treatment of cholera, but no evidence of cultural antipathy to ORT. Some villagers had heard of it, some had tried it but many did not believe it to be effective, possibly because the effects were not immediately obvious. BRAC set out to make the technology available and persuade families of its effectiveness.

It recruited local young women with a minimum level of education to become its frontline oral replacement workers (ORWs). It came up with an easily communicated version of the formula: one pinch of salt, one fist of *gur*[6] and half a seer of water. Household pots would be permanently marked to indicate what half a seer of water looked like. The effectiveness of the solution would be demonstrated by treating villagers with diarrhoea. ORWs were instructed to taste the solution in front of the mothers to assure them it was safe. They also taught mothers a structured seven-point health message about behavioural change, including keeping the house clean through the frequent use of brooms, covering food to protect it from flies, drinking tube-well or boiled water, washing hands properly with soap or ashes.

When the programme moved beyond Sulla into villages where BRAC was unknown, they met with hostility from villagers who believed they were family planning workers pretending to provide health advice. Since the only female workers that were beginning to be seen in rural areas were family planning workers, the confusion was understandable – but also indicative of the hostility surrounding family planning. Accommodations had to be made to patriarchal sensibilities to increase the chances of programme effectiveness.

The organisation hired male supervisors to go ahead of the ORW teams and explain the purpose of the programme and the role of the female workers to leading figures in the village community. This paved the way for female workers to reach village women. The teams travelled by foot, rickshaw and country boats and set up temporary quarters in villages. BRAC drew up strict rules to ensure that staff complied with gender norms so as to avoid hostile attention. Female workers were required to wear *sarees* rather than *shalwar kameez* (the more practical option) within villages, were not to talk to any men in the village without another ORW present, lived in separate quarters from male workers and could not leave their quarters without informing the supervisor.

These early efforts met with success and BRAC decided to scale up the programme in 1980 with the goal of covering the country by 1990 (Chowdhury 1990). It was given government clearance to do so and BRAC in turn made a point of involving local government officials in its activities, both to give them a sense of partnership and because it increased the credibility of their field staff.

Experience had already taught BRAC that the support of men within the wider community was essential to its efforts to reach women. It started village health committees with local leaders, village doctors and social workers, with equal representation of men and women wherever possible. The committees were used to mobilise community support for BRAC's efforts. Staff held spot forums to initiate discussions about health issues in spaces where men congregated, such as markets and tea shops. Male staff attended the Friday prayers and with the consent of the *imam* held discussions about these issues, knowing that people tended to listen more attentively to what was said within a mosque.

It also adopted a strategy for 'spreading and rooting' knowledge on a wider scale. Billboards were installed in public places and posters were put up in schools, *bazaars*, pharmacies and restaurants. Information was disseminated through adverts in journals and periodicals, through spots on Radio Bangladesh, through 60-second commercials broadcast periodically on Bangladesh Television and through the Post Office, which stamped the following message on all letters between 1993 and 1994:

> Mix with loving care
> Half a seer of clean water,
> A pinch of salt, a fistful of gur,
> Do away with this menace for good.

By 1986, health workers had visited and trained mothers in eight million households, more than half of all the households in Bangladesh. They had covered all but one of the 20 greater districts – the exception was the Chittagong Hill Tracts, where indigenous groups were engaged in an armed struggle for greater autonomy. In the tea estates, BRAC workers taught *sardars* and estate officials who then taught mothers in their respective lines. As BRAC's efforts became better known, it was able to switch from its intensive individual teaching methods to group-based teaching. By the late 1990s, it became possible to shift to pre-packaged solutions at affordable prices. According to UNICEF (2012), the promotion of ORS led to an 86% decline in deaths from diarrhoea among children under five over a period of 30 years.

Immunising children

Immunisation against the six most common communicable diseases was the other vertical intervention that contributed to child survival. The government launched its Expanded Programme on Immunization (EPI) in 1979 but achieved less than 2% coverage over the next five years. Low levels of contact between government workers and households were a major constraint: only 26% of the households in a 1986 BIDS survey of these efforts had been contacted by a village-level government worker over the three months prior to the study. The picture on clinic-based services was equally dismal, with inadequate supplies, limited equipment and little or no supervision of staff.

In 1985, with a UN declaration committing member states to universal child coverage by 1990, there was an intensification of government efforts in Bangladesh, with strong donor support. On donor advice, the government enlisted two large NGOs, BRAC and CARE, to take on responsibility for mobilising demand for immunisation and monitoring coverage in 122 *upazilas* and 96 *upazilas*, respectively.

A detailed study carried out by BRAC in 1988 on how government health and family planning workers performed their duties in one *upazila* provided revealing insights into the nature of the problem (BRAC 1989). Workers were vocal in speaking to the researchers about their problems and expressing their resentment that no one listened. They in turn showed weak commitment to their responsibilities. BRAC researchers shadowing the health workers for a week found that few actually spent the claimed amount of time on their duties. Some spent time looking after their own farms or visiting relatives and friends. The sanitary inspector took the BRAC researcher to the local sweetmeat shop, ostensibly to inspect it but in reality to consume sweets that he did not pay for or let the observer pay: 'if I need to pay … then what the hell [have I been] serving as a Sanitary Inspector for so many years?' (p.21). The medical officer, a recent graduate, was in culture shock at finding himself posted to a district town and was busy lobbying for a more central posting.

The study also found that even when the workers did carry out their assigned responsibilities, their performance was perfunctory. For instance, government health assistants were supposed to visit households, register eligible population for immunisation, motivate families, particularly male members, to adopt contraception and provide health education. Shadowing one of them, the BRAC researcher found that his performance was characterised by one-way communication and haphazard information, with very little effort to greet people and explain his purpose:

> Once a man was bathing on a tubewell platform. On the spot, the HA (health assistant) started to give him health education. The man was hardly listening to the HA. The HA was hardly bothered with the man for not listening to him. And thus, the bathing and health education were going on simultaneously, [neither] disturbing the other. In another house, a woman was cooking in her kitchen. The HA then and there started giving health education on the top of his voice from the veranda. Here too health education and cooking went on simultaneously without the HA trying to understand if the mother learnt or had any questions. (p.13)

The next phase of the programme strengthened the collaboration between the government and its NGO partners, with the NGOs taking on responsibility for providing training to mid- and lower-level government health workers. There were also nationwide efforts to promote immunisation through TV, newspapers, religious leaders, and film and sports celebrities, while immunisation sessions were held at all hospitals at district and *thana* levels. This appeared to have been effective as immunisation rates increased from 2% in 1986 to 60% in 1993–94, an achievement described as a 'near miracle' (Huq 1991).

6.3 The quantity–quality transition: educating children

We drew earlier on the idea that processes of demographic transition were accompanied by an evolution in habitus as parents moved from attitudes of fatalism to more purposive efforts to look after their children, knowing they were likely to survive. It is evident from the narratives cited that, for many parents, 'looking after children' meant going beyond just feeding and clothing them to also educating them for a better future. Everybody had dreams for their children, a 25-year-old woman told Simmons (1996), and, for both rich and poor, education was at the centre of these dreams (p.256).

In fact, as the steadily monetising economy moved from agriculture into a broader range of economic activities, education appeared to be an important factor driving the shift to smaller families. It was seen as the route to better livelihood opportunities for children and also, increasingly, a way to secure their willingness to look after parents in their old age. As land became scarce, investment in education appeared to be taking its place as a form of bequest to children.

From the parents' perspective, the desire to educate children was primarily a desire to educate sons. From the policy perspective, on the other hand, a strong rationale for girls' education had emerged as the result of accumulating evidence of the impact of female education on a range of desirable demographic outcomes. While the causal pathways through which education, even the low levels and poor-quality education that characterised low-income countries like Bangladesh, managed to have such an impact was not properly understood, the fact that it did had given it the status of an axiom in development policy circles.

Studies of policy efforts suggested the importance of targeted incentives to ensure that parents sent their daughters to school. An evaluation of the non-targeted Food for Education programme found that its main impact was on the enrolment of boys in primary school, with negligible impact on girls' enrolment – except in the case of female-headed households (Sukontamarn 2013). The Female Secondary School Stipend programme, on the other hand, was credited with increasing gross enrolment rates for girls aged 11 to 15 from 44% in 1995 to 60% in 2005, while the rates for boys rose from 48% to 52%. In just two decades, the number of girls enrolled in secondary school increased from 600,000 in 1980 to 4 million in 2000 (Hossain 2017).

The many promises of education

The reasons for investing in boys' education were fairly straightforward. They were the family breadwinners, they were responsible for parents in their old age and they could perform these functions more effectively if they had the educational qualifications they needed to access new off-farm livelihood opportunities, particularly urban, formal employment. The motivations for sending girls to school were more complicated and reflected many different sources of change.

Government financial incentives clearly played an important role. So did efforts by government and NGOs to alter cultural norms about raising daughters. Ideas about gender equality and girls' education were woven into government campaigns to promote the small family norm. Posters depicted the happy two-child family as made up of a girl and a boy, while others advised parents that sending daughters to school would delay their age of marriage, protect their health and improve their chances of a happy family life. One woman related how, many years ago, a 'Health Apa' (sister) had shown the women in her village a picture of a sick and ailing girl to illustrate what happened to girls who married and got pregnant too early. She had warned them that early marriage meant:

> the family is submerged in unrest and the husband-wife relationship deteriorates. They always quarrel and argue with each other. And the wife does not recover easily from illnesses. If she recovers from one illness, she becomes sick with another. (Schuler 2007, p.193)

The narrator remembered those words clearly: she had waited till her own daughter had completed her 10th grade before she married her off at 19.

Research into parents' motivations suggested that other changes in the wider environment were also reshaping their views about their daughters' futures. Whereas, in the past, the qualities sought in a bride related to her age, her complexion, family status, compliant behaviour and ability to work hard (Aziz 1979; Ellickson 1988),[7] by the early 1980s it was clear that her education was becoming an increasingly important consideration (Lindenbaum 1981). There was a general belief that educated brides made better wives and mothers, and that they were more able to look after their family and educate their children, obviating the need for the private tuition that many parents considered essential for children to do well at school (Schuler 2007).

Some parents believed that educating daughters increased the likelihood that they would secure an educated husband in formal employment – and some also believed that educated husbands treated their wives better. As one mother said,

> If my daughters did not have any education, then I would have had to marry them to van pullers or cobblers ... she would have to begin each day being tortured physically by her husband and go to sleep at night again being physically tortured. These people do not have any sense of gentleness. But if a girl gets a husband with an educational background, there will be no quarrels or physical torture, and the girl will be happy in her married life. (Schuler 2007, pp.197–98)

Others linked daughters' education with independent access to good jobs, the chance to make something of themselves. In the opinion of a 29-year-old woman interviewed by Simmons (1996), 'if girls are properly educated, they can look after themselves well. They can get themselves good jobs. They can stand on their own feet' (p.256). Another 27-year-old declared: 'It is my conviction that even if I won't be able to take food, I'll get my daughter passed the matric exam. I'll never allow her to remain a fool like me' (p.256).

There was also evidence that education could reduce the amount of dowry demanded or even act as a substitute for dowry. In their study in Rajshahi district, Amin and Huq (2008) found that, while 70% of all marriages had involved dowry payments, its incidence varied considerably by the education of the bride: just 39% of girls with higher education in their study had paid dowry at marriage, compared to 79% of those with less than primary school education. Nasreen's mother confirmed that the topic of education had been discussed when a proposal was brought for her daughter and that the prospective in-laws had asked for a much lower dowry once they found out that she had completed higher education. Others hoped that the improvement in the job prospects of educated daughters might have a similar effect. A mother whose husband was a rickshaw puller was educating her daughter in the hope that it would allow her to transcend her humble origins and make a good marriage:

I am sure that when she passes the IA [Intermediate Exam], nobody will brand her as a rickshaw driver's daughter ... if she can manage a job in a [garment factory] in Dhaka and earn 2,500 to 3,000 takas ... a month, people will take her as their daughter-in-law seeing her monthly salary. I will not have to pay any dowry. (Amin and Huq 2008, p.197)

In some cases, mothers said that they had learnt from their own bitter experience of having been denied an education and been married off at too young an age to know what they wanted from life. They were determined to educate their daughters so they would escape a similar fate and be able to work and support themselves should anything go wrong with their marriage.

My own home is like a hell on earth ... If I had been educated, I would have been able to feed myself by getting a job, and I would not have had to tolerate this oppression. I would have left this place and returned to my father's house with my daughter and my son ... The smallest thing out of place and [my husband] begins scolding and beating me. I have learned from my own life! (Schuler 2007, p.198)

For many poorer parents, education represented a form of cultural capital, of knowing how to behave in polite society, of becoming *manush* (human). They described the attributes and lifestyles they associated with families from the educated classes: they were polite and genteel, less prone to loud and quarrelsome behaviour; their women were refined and well-spoken. A rickshaw puller described what had inspired him to educate his daughters:

I was poor, and [in those days] nobody like me could even think of educating his children, but I dreamt I would educate mine when I saw the students in front of their schools. I used to carry the daughter of a *daktar apa* [sister doctor] to and from her school. That *daktar apa* had such a nice manner! Educated people are usually well behaved, and they talk differently. We illiterates do not even know how to talk. (Schuler 2007, p.191)

Others had observed examples in other families that led them to value education for their daughters. A mother spoke of a niece who had trained as a nurse after she completed secondary school, got a nursing job and then had helped her parents rebuild their house and her father to buy land and had also got jobs for her two brothers. Moreover, no dowry had been demanded when she married. The mother had been inspired to encourage her own daughter's education in the hope that she too might find a job that would allow her to help her family financially. She had two sons but they were indifferent students, so she was pinning her hope on her daughter (Schuler 2007).

It is worth noting that this mother's aspirations for her daughter reflected attitudes that appeared to be gaining ground among families in Bangladesh: that new employment possibilities would allow daughters to look after their parents in the way sons were expected to – but often did not. Many of the women interviewed in the Matlab area in 1983 by Lindenbaum, Chakraborty and Mohammed (1985) referred to the value of education in increasing women's access to *chakri* ('proper' jobs), most often in teaching or family planning. Some added that such jobs might allow daughters to look after ageing parents in the future. These views were expressed again in the study carried out by Simmons (1996) in Matlab in the late 1980s:

> Opinions are divided over the issue of whether sons can still be relied upon to provide support to aged parents. Some feel that because parents cannot necessarily count on their sons, they may have to depend upon their daughters. The possibility of financial support from daughters has become a realistic expectation in a few rural families. (p.257)

And, based on her interviews carried out in the early 2000s in a different region of rural Bangladesh, Schuler (2007) commented that a 'substantial minority' of parents in her study expressed hopes of receiving support from daughters if they could educate them sufficiently to become employable.

Finally, some kind of 'tipping point' also seemed to be at work in explaining the rise in girls' education: parents were sending their daughters to school because it was taking on the status of a new norm. For instance, a mother of a five-year-old girl said that she planned to send her daughter to school and to keep her there at least till the fifth grade. Asked why, she had nothing to say about the benefits of education, only that all of the parents in the community were sending their children to school so she would do the same (Schuler 2007).

Walking a tightrope: age, education and dowry

The rapid rate of increase of girls' enrolment in primary and secondary school was clearly remarkable, but gender discrimination with regard to education had not disappeared. While more girls than boys enrolled in primary and secondary education, more girls dropped out than boys. Of those who enrolled in school, only 10% of girls went on to pass the secondary school certificate examination, compared to 25% of boys (Amin and Huq 2008; Mahmud and Amin 2006).

One major reason for this was parents' greater reluctance to use their own incomes to pay for the additional costs associated with schooling for daughters compared to sons (Xu, Shonchoy and Fujii 2019). These additional costs included private tuition and school materials, which were essential for the quality of education but were not covered by the government stipend. So, while the stipend eased parents' budget constraint sufficiently for them to send girls to school, they were less willing to use their own resources to ensure the quality of their daughters' education or to send them on to post-secondary education.

This reluctance can be partly explained by the problematic interaction between age of marriage, dowry costs and labour market opportunities. While marriage was universal for both men and women, it was a particularly crucial aspect of women's prescribed life course, marking their transition from the guardianship of fathers to that of husbands and constituting the only legitimate context in which they could fulfil the childbearing roles that defined womanhood. Parents who did not succeed in marrying off their daughters were viewed as failures, regardless of how marriages actually turned out. There were a number of pressures on parents that led many to opt to marry daughters off at a relatively young age rather than waiting till they completed their education.[8]

One set of pressures related to dowry. Most parents had no choice but to pay dowry if they wanted to marry off their daughters. While the amount of the dowry was set at the discretion of the groom's family, a number of factors came into play in regulating how much could be reasonably demanded. While it was the case that the bride's education reduced dowry demands or even substituted for dowry, earlier considerations, such as age and appearance, continued to matter. The older the bride or the darker her complexion, the larger the dowry that could be demanded.[9] There was no similar premium on the youth or appearance of the groom – men could marry at a later age, with some marrying multiple times into old age, and physical appearance rarely featured as an attribute sought in husbands. Given the expenses associated with educating daughters, some parents sought to reduce the size of dowry demanded by marrying their daughters off before they completed their schooling.

The other pressure was anxiety about sexual risks. Sex outside marriage was considered immoral and shameful – but far more so for girls. Once they reached puberty, they were seen as dangerously seductive to men as well as dangerously vulnerable to male sexual predation. There were fears that they might make an unsuitable match through a 'love' marriage or become the object of malicious gossip frequently circulated about young girls of marriageable age who were seen to have transgressed cultural norms in some way. Adolescence was also a period of heightened risk for girls of sexual harassment of various kinds.[10] They were discouraged from reporting it out of shame, out of fear of being blamed, out of fear of retaliation by harassers, and, of course, out of fear of what it might do to their marriage prospects. These fears were another source of pressure to marry daughters off as soon as possible, cutting short their education.

All this meant that parents had to walk a difficult tightrope in the decision to educate daughters, balancing it against the various factors that determined the amount of dowry they would be called to pay. While Amin and Huq (2008) found that far fewer girls with higher education in their study villages had paid dowry, those that did pay had to pay larger-than-average amounts. Because the norm was for women to marry men who were not only older than them but also at least as well, if not more, educated, the pool of men in the right age group with appropriate levels of education shrank as girls became more educated – so higher dowry could be demanded. One way to avoid such demands was to marry daughters off before they completed secondary education.

Finally, the parental calculus also had to factor in the job market for educated girls. A secondary school certificate appeared to be the critical threshold for gaining access to more desirable forms of formal employment but there were limited numbers of these jobs to go round. Despite the hopes that many parents expressed that education would lead to better jobs for their daughters, the reality was that bribes were required for these jobs and men tended to monopolise them. Most women remained concentrated in home-based enterprise.

Parents' reluctance to spend their own money on daughters' education and the higher rates of dropout by girls at secondary levels of education testify to aspects of gender relations that remained resistant to the forces of change and to the complicated relationship this set up between education, age of marriage and dowry. The reality of the broad context in which these decisions were weighed up was still one of relative scarcity of employment opportunities for women, especially in rural areas, and of the continued centrality of marriage in marking their transition to adulthood. For many parents, concerns about the marriageability of daughters and the size of the dowries that might have to be paid for 'over-educated' daughters served to limit to how far they wanted to educate daughters. But what had undoubtedly changed was that the value of education for daughters was no longer in question.

6.4 Policy efforts and reproductive practice

The analysis in this chapter provides important insights into the micro-processes of structuration in the reproductive domain, how existing practices were gradually changed through the reconfiguration of their constituent elements into new forms of routine behaviour. The changes in question were initiated by various policy actors and brought together new or modified material resources (modern technologies such as contraception and vaccinations, home-made remedies such as oral rehydration solution and familiar objects such as brooms and cooking pots), new or improved forms of knowledge and competencies (the purpose of contraception, how to make up oral rehydration solutions, better feeding practices) and new meanings and values, such as what it meant to be a 'good' mother or a 'modern' family. These new meanings carried weight because they were disseminated by the government which gave them a certain degree of legitimacy, but their spread also reflected the efforts that governments and NGOs put into 'grounding and rooting' these meanings within local practices. As one family planning worker put it, constant repetition of the same messages worked on people's minds: 'if one keeps rubbing a stone in one point, the stone begins to wear away' (Simmons, Mita and Koenig 1992, p.103).

It is evident from this chapter that there were different degrees of receptiveness and resistance within the community to these policy efforts to change different aspects of reproductive behaviour. Some practices were clearly more deeply rooted in the shared habitus of the community. The greatest hostility was encountered by efforts to intervene in the childbearing process through the promotion of modern contraception. These went directly against the grain of norms and beliefs about sexuality and reproduction that had evolved over centuries to ensure the survival of a society that was at the constant mercy of natural forces. These had come to constitute the core of the collective habitus and the foundations of its patriarchal order.

That they were overcome reflected the multitude of efforts simultaneously carried out by governments and NGOs. Every village had some kind of regular exposure to family planning outreach: radio programmes exhorting the use of contraception, market outlets where contraceptives were advertised and sold at subsidised prices and periodic visits from family planning workers offering free supplies (Cleland et al. 1994). Once the idea of family planning took root, change happened relatively fast, partly because, as I noted earlier, fatalism was not as deeply ingrained in the local culture as initially believed. Schuler et al. (1996a) found that, while those who were among the first to adopt family planning were harshly condemned for violating social norms, those who adopted it just 10 years later had an easier time because the norms of the community had begun to change.

Efforts to change practices around the care of children met less resistance. There was considerable receptivity within the population to public efforts to improve the health of family members – particularly when it involved the health of children. There was also considerable receptivity to the idea of children's education, though greater effort had to be put into the promotion of girls' education. Here the hesitation seemed to be less a matter of hostility to new ideas and more a concern about balancing the gains from girls' education against the possible impact of delaying age of marriage on their marriage prospects and on likely dowry demands.

At the same time, and somewhat counterintuitively, the analysis suggests that, even though women encountered far fiercer resistance to their efforts to access modern means of contraception than they did to changes in other aspects of reproductive practice, this was not the gain that had the most transformative impact on their lives – at least not on its own. Control over their fertility might have had the unanticipated effect of expanding their potential for other forms of agency, but their own motivation was desperation to escape the relentless cycle of childbearing. There was little evidence in the literature to suggest that they sought greater control over their fertility in order to gain access to jobs or to avail themselves of other new opportunities or that it had the effect of transforming their subordinate position in society. Indeed, the programme was designed so as to allow them to conform to patriarchal norms as far as possible. Exploring this question, Schuler et al. (1996a) conclude:

> Although family planning has had a profound and positive impact on the lives of women, and on Bangladeshi society in general, we contend that the isolation, economic dependence and low status of women is a deep-rooted problem that family planning alone cannot address. (p.76)

The same could not be said of female education. Not only did the women – and men – cited in this chapter believe from the outset that it embodied the potential for significant positive change in women's lives, there was also a strong and growing body of quantitative evidence supporting this belief – documenting impacts that ranged from age of marriage, reproductive preferences and behaviour, child health and survival as well as voice and agency within household and community.[11] These findings testify to the lasting effects of early experiences of education in shaping habitus in later life. Why such effects could be brought about by the very poor quality of education that prevailed in Bangladesh at that time has not been investigated in any ethnographic detail but I would like to conclude this chapter with some insights provided by Lindenbaum, Chakraborty and Mohammed (1985). Theirs was one of the few attempts to explore the factors behind the inverse association between maternal education and child survival reported in the Bangladesh literature and more widely. Their findings cast a helpful light on how the transformative effects of education might have worked in practice.

They point out that young village girls were likely to have their first lessons in hygiene and cleanliness at school. The textbooks of the time showed the importance of washing hands before eating, keeping food covered from flies, and burying rubbish and refuse. Schools gave girls from poorer households the opportunity to observe how those from higher-status households behaved. It implanted new aspirations, the desire to emulate higher-status behaviour and, with it, new practices which had health implications: educated women and girls washed with tank or tube-well water in the home rather than public bathing in ponds and canals, where water was likely to be contaminated. The act of going to school allowed girls public mobility in a society that confined women to the home. Education provided new sources of authority to family and community and opened up new sources of information. Most schoolgirls in the village listened to the radio and, while their passion was Bengali songs, they also listened to broadcasts on health and family planning and sometimes to the evening news. And, with the school bell ringing periodically, they absorbed the habit of structured, time-defined existence, a habit that was important in later life.

These impacts appeared to have a bearing on the habitus that girls acquired through their time at school. Younger educated women spoke of a 'newfound consciousness, a sense of mental change which empowers them to act' (p.12).

Some of the villagers spoke disapprovingly of the self-sufficiency of educated women, their independence of their parents, their lack of care of husbands and family. Others approved of their ability to deal with people, to live harmoniously with husband and in-laws, to handle financial and domestic affairs of the family, and to tutor their children so saving the need for private tuition.

Educated women were also likely to exercise greater negotiating power within the family, to have greater say in the allocation of household resources and the care of children, to be treated better by their in-laws and to be able to stand up for themselves in the marital home. These enhancements of women's capabilities were prominent among the reasons that the later generations of parents from different parts of Bangladesh who are cited in this chapter gave for wanting to educate their daughters. In addition, Lindenbaum, Chakraborty and Mohammed report early evidence of changing views about the role of daughters that would become more widely held over time, early evidence of subjective counter-currents, and views that education gave daughters access to proper jobs (*chakri*) and that the income they earnt would allow them to look after their parents in later life. This led Lindenbaum, Chakraborty and Mohammed to speculate on the possible longer-term consequences should this happen:

> It might be said that daughters are becoming like 'sons' in many rural families. This new focus on employable daughters suggests that male and female infants might receive equal nurture and that the greatest shift in the morbidity and mortality of children under five should occur with the better survival of daughters, particularly those of educated women. (p.10)

Notes

[1] It took Britain 95 years (1815–1910) for fertility to fall from more than six children per women to less than three children per women. It took Bangladesh 20 years (1982–2002) (Roser 2024).

[2] Maloney, Aziz and Sarker caution that, while a deep-rooted peasant culture might lead people to express their resignation to God's will, these were generally expressions of resignation to matters outside their control, as fertility outcomes were. These belief systems did not rule out people's ability to take action in their own interest where this was seen as rational but they nevertheless appeared to protect them from the consequences of such actions: 'In this ethos, happenings which are a matter of chance and not dependent on personal choice are attributed to Allah. Happenings not dependent on chance, but on personal choice are also attributed to Allah' (p.39). But, where the exercise of choice did not yield the hoped-for results, they were attributed to the workings of *shaitan* (Satan) or *jins*.

[3] In Kabeer (2001a), I used data from the 1989 Bangladesh Fertility Survey to show that fertility began to decline earliest among older women from the poorest households. It was among younger cohorts that it also showed decline among the better-off and more educated women.

[4] Only extreme high-oestrogen pills were being distributed at that time.

[5] Fertility rates in Bangladesh continued to decline. Total fertility rates are currently estimated at 2.3 births.

[6] *Gur*, a form of molasses, was a cheap, locally available substitute for sugar.

[7] Among Hindus, rules of caste endogamy, i.e. marriage to members of the same sub-caste, meant that caste considerations restricted the choice of marriage partner to a limited group of families. Breaches of caste endogamy were, as Aziz (1979) writes, till recently punished by excommunication (p.40).

[8] The age of marriage for girls in Bangladesh has risen very gradually and still remains extremely low: the average age was estimated at 16 in 2012.

[9] A woman's complexion is a key indicator of beauty across the subcontinent.

[10] Studies show that the harassment that female students encountered on their way to, and from, school was also a major reason why they dropped out, and that the highest rates of dropout occurred as they attained puberty (Alam, Roy and Ahmed 2010; Karim 2007).

[11] Evidence of various immediate, longer-term and intergenerational impacts associated with female education in Bangladesh has mounted over the years. Educated women were likely to marry later than uneducated ones and more likely to marry educated and formally employed men who were closer to their age. They were more likely to use contraception and to report lower desired and achieved fertility rates and weaker son preference (Ahmed 1981; Duvendack and Palmer-Jones 2017; Hahn, Islam and Nuzhat 2018; Kabeer 1986; Kabeer, Huq and Mahmud 2014; Khuda and Hossain 1996). They were more likely to be immunised during pregnancy, their child feeding practices were better, and their children were healthier and survived longer (Brown and Zeitlin 1991; Hahn, Islam and Nuzhat 2018; Piechulek, Aldana and Hasan 1999). They were more likely to favour additional expenditure on education for their children and to believe that girls should be educated along with boys (Amin and Das 2013). Maternal education increased the likelihood of education of both boys and girls over time, reduced the overall likelihood of daughters dropping out of secondary school and also increased the age of marriage of daughters (Bates, Maselko and Schuler 2007; Mahmud and Amin 2006; Razzaque, Streatfield and Evans 2007).

Educated women were more likely to be in formal employment. They were more likely to exercise voice in household decision-making, to have savings of their own, to be consulted for advice by others in the community, to decide how they would vote and to report a strong sense of agency over their own lives (Balk 1997; Kabeer et al. 2013; Kabeer, Mahmud and Tasneem 2018). And, very recently, Bora et al. (2023) conclude that women's education had not only been the single most important driver of fertility decline in Bangladesh but that it had important spillover effects: the proportion of educated women in a community influenced the fertility behaviour of less-educated women. Studies documenting the positive impacts of female education found that they remained even after controls that been introduced for other variables, including household economic status and male education, and were generally more consistent and larger than those associated with male education.

7. 'Standing on your own feet': the making of a female labour force

I have to go door to door in search of work ... There is no work that I have not done. I work mainly for food. I don't get to see cash that often ... I earn from day to day and we consume what I earn. (Humera, 25 years old, casual wage labourer, divorced, LSE/BIGD fieldwork 2014)

But even if a husband is a millionaire, there is still a need for women to earn their own income because otherwise they are not valued by society. They should have some means of strengthening their position. (Lily, 24 years old, NGO worker, cited in Kabeer et al. 2018, p.246)

Women's agency in relation to their reproductive behaviour received considerable coverage in the paradox literature. Their agency in the productive domain featured less, possibly because women's labour force participation was seen to be low and unlikely to exercise much influence. But in Bangladesh, as in most countries with large informal economies, official labour force estimates have consistently failed to capture women's economic activity. A study from the late 1970s described the official estimate that rural female labour force participation was 3% as 'frankly irrelevant' as a description of their actual activity (Begum and Greeley 1979). Smaller-scale surveys consistently found higher rates of labour force participation by both women and children.[1]

Later official surveys suggested a gradual rise in female labour force participation, from 8% in the mid-1980s to 24% by the end of the century and 36% in 2010. Male activity rates fluctuated around 80% throughout this period. However, these estimates still failed to capture the full picture. This was demonstrated by our 2008 IDS-BIGD survey of around 5,000 women from different parts of Bangladesh.[2] It used the same ILO-based definition of economic activity as the official surveys[3] but estimated participation rates of 67% compared to the official 2005–06 estimate of 30% (Mahmud and Tasneem 2011). The difference reflected the exclusion of a great deal of women's home-based economic activity from the official survey. Moreover, the home-based activity that it did capture was largely classified as 'unpaid family labour' (Rahman and Islam 2013, p.24). The IDS/BIGD survey, by contrast, found most of it consisted of market-oriented activity within the home.

This chapter has a number of objectives. First, it brings together the findings of various studies since independence in order to trace how women's labour force participation has evolved over the years. These confirm the steady rise in participation rates documented in the official data but suggest that the official data has continued to both underestimate the actual size of the female labour force at any given time and also failed to capture changing patterns over time. As this chapter shows, women's livelihood activities have come to include not only those prescribed by long-established practice but new ones, practices-in-the-making.

Second, it explores women's agency in the making of this labour force. Studies have talked about women being 'discovered' by capital or 'sent' to work by patriarchy (Feldman and McCarthy 1983, p.211; Siddiqi 1996, p.120) but they have also talked about the active choices that many women made in response to the changing circumstances of their lives, about the motivations that led them to opt for one set of livelihood options over others and about their efforts to justify choices that went against the grain of prevailing cultural norms.

Third, the chapter explores the potentials for change associated with these expanding options. The livelihood activities studied in this chapter, like any form of social practice, were constituted by material elements, such as land, equipment, credit and physical labour; by skills and know-how; and by the social meanings ascribed to them. But they were also characterised by intentionality on the part of workers themselves, the motivations that took them into forms of work outside the socially prescribed boundaries of the home and their efforts to reconfigure these prescriptions. The chapter will explore the motivations and meanings that workers associated with their work.

Finally, I want to consider what the analysis in this chapter tells us about the hypotheses put forward in Chapter 1 about possible routes through which an increase in women's participation in the productive domain might contribute to the social progress captured by the Bangladesh paradox. One was the individual route and drew on the idea that women's access to paid work increased their voice and influence in household decision-making, including decisions that contributed directly to the changes documented by the paradox literature. The other was a societal route and pointed to the social value given to women in acknowledgement of the greater visibility of their economic contribution. The chapter will consider the evidence for both of these hypotheses.

7.1 Variations in past patterns of women's work

Unpaid family labour: from home to field

The early research on women's productive work described in Chapter 4 sought to address gaps in the prevailing literature by providing detailed descriptions of what they did. It depicted a gender division of labour in rural areas that adhered faithfully to prescribed norms. Men worked in the field-based stages of the agricultural process while women worked 'inside' the homestead, processing crops once they were brought home, looking after small livestock and poultry, and cultivating the homestead plot.

When better-off households hired wage labourers, they allocated them to tasks that reflected this approved division of labour with female wage labour in home-based productive and domestic work while male labourers worked in the fields. Poorer farm households who could not afford wage labour had to send their female family members to carry out field-based tasks, but often under the cover of darkness.

With growing impoverishment in the post-independence years, there were limits to how long farming households could continue to rely on the surreptitious use of female family labour. This was revealed by a survey of women's rural activity carried out as part of the Agricultural Sector Review (Safilios-Rothschild and Mahmud 1989). The survey departed from normal practice by asking women about the primary use of their time, *aside from housework*. Forty-three per cent described agricultural work as their primary occupation, while 15% described it as their secondary occupation. Twelve per cent described non-farm employment as their primary occupation, while 6% described it as a secondary occupation. These suggested much higher rates of rural labour force participation than official estimates.

It also found that, while few women in farming households worked in field-based operations on their own, a sizeable percentage undertook such work jointly with men from their households. So, for instance, only 10% of women reported they undertook harvesting, a conventionally male activity, on their own but 40% undertook it jointly with men. Similarly, only 5% said they planted rice on their own but 40% planted rice alongside men. As might be expected, it was the smaller farms that, under the pressure of poverty, were most likely to report female family members working openly alongside men in the fields. The presence of male family members alongside women in 'outside' work appeared to mitigate its apparent break with norms. Significantly, women in these smaller farms were more likely to report joint decision-making in agriculture, a contrast to the male-dominated decision-making reported for larger farms. This association between women's productive contribution and their voice in household matters was a recurring theme in the studies reviewed in this chapter.

The hidden economy of women's trade

The report also drew attention to women's non-farm employment. This had gone largely unnoticed in earlier analysis but qualitative studies, such as White's ethnography of a Rajshahi village (1992), had begun to record women's involvement in the growing entrepreneurial economy. Most buying and selling was still conducted in the *bazaar* and *haat*, quintessentially male domains that women could only access through male intermediaries, but there had been a proliferation of minor markets that allowed them to engage directly in market transactions from their homes. These involved buying, selling, and bartering a variety of goods and services (such as eggs, milk, fodder, fuel, homestead vegetables and fruits, quilts, tailoring) with travelling pedlars and local village shops as well as neighbouring households.

Social custom recognised women's 'ownership' of minor assets, such as poultry and small livestock, and allowed them to keep the small sums of money they earnt from these assets, although they were expected to spend their earnings on family needs. By contrast, it was accepted that men would keep back some of their earnings for their own personal consumption, such as cigarettes or tea at the local stall. But it was evident that many women sought out small areas of financial autonomy through clandestine economic activities that did not appear to dispute the terms of the patriarchal bargain but managed to circumvent some of its constraints. Older studies had referred to the practice among women of keeping aside *ek mushti chal* (a fistful of rice) before cooking the daily meal, a hidden reserve for their own use or as an emergency fund (Abdullah and Zeidenstein 1982). As their access to income increased, they undertook other strategies. They sold their produce to the middlemen who came to their door rather than relying on male family members to sell it in the *bazaar*: the prices might be lower, but the proceeds came directly to them. Or they sent young sons to sell their produce in the market, increasing the likelihood of control over the proceeds. There was also a great deal of borrowing and lending of money and rice, mainly among women themselves, although better-off ones also lent money to local traders.

White pointed out that the growing involvement of women in these own-account activities in the study village occurred in the absence of microfinance services, contrary to the widespread misconception that it was the advent of microfinance services that kick-started female enterprise. She also found that women's increasing involvement in trading activities, although still home-based, had important implications in reshaping gender identities. In contrast to women's unpaid productive efforts, their business activities, when pursued successfully, resulted in greater recognition for the economic value of their contribution, both within their own households and in the wider community.

The distress sale of labour

Women from the poorest households faced a far more limited range of livelihood options. They had no land, assets or savings of their own, while fear of indebtedness kept them from taking loans to set up their own businesses. They sought instead to make the most of their unskilled labour. They entered share-rearing arrangements with women from wealthier households to translate their labour into a goat or poultry; pursued midwifery as a low status form of service provision with payments varying according to household means; relied on ecological reserves for fuel, edible wild plants and roots; and gleaned the rice fields after the harvest (Kabeer 1989).

In addition, of course, they took up wage labour in the homes of affluent neighbours. Initially, they were drawn from the 'destitute category', widowed, divorced or abandoned women, usually heading their own households, who in the mid-1980s made up just 15% of overall rural households but 25% of the landless (Safilios-Rothschild and Mahmud 1989). Growing impoverishment made it difficult for poorer households to continue to 'carry' dependent members. There was a gradual breakdown of the obligations that held families together and the emergence of a 'fending for oneself' pattern (McCarthy and Feldman 1983). Women who might not have thought to take up waged work outside the home found that the economic costs of not doing such work outweighed status concerns:

> What need have the poor for self-respect or propriety? Everything is dictated by scarcity (*abhab*): scarcity of food, scarcity of clothes, scarcity of shelter, there is no end to scarcity ... there are mothers who cannot feed their children – can they afford propriety? (Kabeer 1989, p.7)

These pressures led to a steady increase in the female wage labour force and a change in its profile. Destitute women were joined by married women whose husbands earnt too little to support the family or were too old, ill, or disabled to work, and then by young, unmarried women, previously secluded by stricter *purdah* norms, and by the children of the poor.

There was also increased diversity in the kinds of work they took up (Feldman and McCarthy 1982; Kabeer 1989). As men moved into the non-farm economy, women began working in selected activities in the fields, harvesting potatoes, chillies and sometimes paddy, weeding rice fields and vegetable plots, drying chillies and stripping jute. They took up work in commercial rice mills, small-scale rural workshops and road construction, often on government or NGO public works. They also began migrating on their own into towns, most often to work as domestics.

These were not desirable jobs. 'Outside' work in fields, roadsides and construction sites was physically demanding and exposed women to casual sexual harassment by the men they encountered. Domestic servants worked 'inside' but made barely enough to survive, suffered physical and sexual abuse, worked long hours at the discretion of employers and could be dismissed at any time.

Wages were invariably higher for men,[4] who were physically stronger and had greater freedom of movement in the search for jobs. Women were disadvantaged on both these criteria, but on others as well. Husbands could be a major obstacle, objecting, often violently, to wives taking up work outside the home because of its threat to their status as family breadwinners. Employers were reluctant to incur the wrath of the community by hiring women if a pool of male labour was available (Rahman 1986a). Village elites policed the behaviour of poor women, pronouncing the spectacle of women from 'their' village working outside the home to be a matter of shame for the entire community (Chen 1986).

Women from poorer households considered casual wage labour in the public domain to be socially demeaning, employers to be disrespectful and the pay to be inadequate, yet many of those interviewed by Rahman (1986a) in the mid-1980s said they were willing to do such labour if male family members did not earn enough and if it were available within a certain distance from their village. Rahman also found that a 'surprisingly large percentage' (p.82) were positive about regular formal employment in urban factories.[5] But their preferred option was self-employment since working for oneself was considered 'more prestigious' than working as wage labour for others but it was not an option open to them because they did not have the finance necessary to start their own businesses.

7.2 The emergence of new opportunities: the rise of the 'female petty entrepreneur'

Women did not have the necessary finance because formal and informal financial markets in Bangladesh had always been dominated by men – as lenders as well as borrowers. The informal credit market where the poor generally sought loans was made up of specialised moneylenders, but also landlords, traders and shopkeepers. Interest rates in informal markets varied between 120% and 240% a year and were charged till the full loan was repaid as a lump sum, a major reason for high levels of indebtedness among the poor.

The advent of microfinance services represented a major departure from these practices. Grameen Bank, which was set up in 1976, lent small amounts of money at interest rates of 16% a year[6] to borrowers from poor and landless households who were organised into groups and required to repay their loans in small but regular instalments at weekly group meetings held after the Friday prayers. They were also required to act as guarantors for each other's loans. The failure to meet the repayment schedule by any group member jeopardised access to loans for all members. The organisation exerted various forms of informal pressure to bolster formal rules of loan repayment, publicly reprimanding members who fell behind on their repayments and summoning them to the bank office to answer to more senior officials. These practices were intended to address the challenge of lending money to borrowers conventionally regarded as high credit risks.

Grameen started out with mainly male borrowers; they made up 60% of its 28,000 members in 1980 (Hossain 1988). But it began to shift its focus to women so that, by 1986, women made up 75% of its membership. They made up 95% of its 2.23 million members by 1997 (Rahman 1999). The official explanation was that women were the poorest of the poor and also more likely to use their loans to improve family welfare. The unofficial reason was that the organisation – and institutional lending in general – was facing a crisis in male repayment rates (UNDP 1989). Field staff complained that men were difficult to work with: 'they do not come to meetings, they are arrogant, they argue with the bank workers and sometimes they even threaten and scare bank workers' (Rahman 1999, p.73). Women borrowers, by contrast, were more easily disciplined, more likely to attend group meetings, less able to leave their homes or locality to evade officials and easier to shame through public reprimand (Karim 2008; Rahman 1999).

But the organisation was also aware that the capacity for regular repayment of loans required the regular flow of income that only male earners could provide. This led to the near exclusion of female household heads who had no reliable flow of male earnings – even though they really did constitute the poorest of the poor. Single women were also excluded because it was assumed that they would move to a different village after marriage. As a result, microfinance lending was largely targeted to married women from moderately poor households with husbands who could repay the loans. Other development NGOs adopted the Grameen model, most prioritised women in their lending programmes and, by 2005, around 22 million rural women were involved in microcredit organisations (World Bank 2006b).

Loan use and women's agency

According to Rahman (1999), although microfinance lending had ostensibly shifted from men to women, there was little opposition from men. This, he suggests, was because, although they might not have time or inclination to submit to Grameen's group discipline, they knew they would exercise ultimate control over their wives' loans. This interpretation was supported by an informal survey by Karim (2008) that reported that 95% of loans to women were 'really used' (p.14) by men and went on consumption and repayment of old debts. The 5% of women who presumably managed to retain control over their loans engaged in 'the practice of usury' (p.18) from their homes, leading to what Karim describes as the making of a new neoliberal subject: the female petty moneylender (p.20).

Other studies suggested a less uniform picture, drawing attention to the diversity of relationships that existed within households, and the varying responses by men. They reported men welcoming women's access to loans for the reasons suggested by Rahman but also because they saw its benefits for the family. In addition, they reported men refusing to let their wives take loans, of wives refusing to hand over their loans, of poor households being prevented from taking loans by the local landlord, of reluctant women being persuaded to join by others who had benefited and of would-be borrowers patiently explaining to their husbands that the household would benefit collectively if they took out a loan (Goetz and Sen Gupta 1996; Kabeer 1998; Kabeer 2001b; Shehabuddin 1992; Todd 1996). Studies also reported considerable variation in the use of loans and the frequent divergence between the official sanctioned use of loans (e.g. business, paddy stocking, livestock, trade and rickshaw vans) and their actual use (e.g. moneylending, loan repayments, land transactions, international migration, housing improvement, health expenditure, consumption, dowry and marriage expenses), uses that the borrowers clearly valued.

Finally, studies also found considerable variation in patterns of decision-making related to loan use. Here we can distinguish between three broad patterns: male-dominated, female-dominated and joint decision-making. Male borrowers were systematically more likely than female borrowers to report male-dominated decision-making in conformity with accepted social norms (Kabeer 2001b; Montgomery, Bhattacharya and Hulme 1996). They were also more likely to forbid their wives to take loans (Kabeer 2001b).

There was greater variation in decision-making patterns in female-borrower households. A number of studies suggested the voluntary surrender of loans to men. In Karim's study, for instance, this pattern was so taken for granted that any other course of action was inconceivable:

> Rural men laughed when they were asked whether the money belonged to their wives. They pointedly remarked that 'since their wives belong to them, the money rightfully belongs to them'. Women also told me that, as a Bangladeshi woman, I should know that they would give the money to their husbands who labour outside the home. (2008, p.15)

Other studies suggested that male use of women's loans was not always a matter of consent. It could also take the form of straightforward appropriation by men in authority, often leading to tensions and violence (Goetz and Sen Gupta 1996) In fact, Rahman (1999) noted that some of the violence reported by women loanees in his study occurred because they had refused to give their loans to their husbands.

Joint decision-making appeared to be the most common pattern reported by female borrowers (Hashemi, Schuler and Riley 1996; Kabeer 2001b; Montgomery, Bhattacharya and Hulme 1996; Todd 1996). They explained this in terms of the perceived jointness of household welfare and the collective stake that family members had in how their household fared, echoing the view expressed by one of the women interviewed by White: 'What is his is mine and mine, his. Isn't that how it is in your country?' (1992, p.141).

In some cases, joint decision-making resulted in the investment of some or all of the women's loans in male enterprises – in recognition of the greater productivity of their enterprises or their greater responsibilities as primary breadwinner. Such investment could also represent class-inflected manifestations of familial solidarity. Women were aware of the hardships their husbands faced as they struggled to feed their families and they spoke with satisfaction of their ability to use their loans to free them from the usurious clutches of moneylenders or the exploitative demands of landlords. As one said, 'My husband now works alongside me. He no longer has to hear harsh words if he does not pay his debt on time' (Kabeer 2001b, p.72).

In other cases, joint decision-making could result in the investment of some or all of women's loans in female enterprises. The fact that a variety of studies have reported women's higher engagement in paid work in the households of female borrowers compared to women in male-borrower households suggests that investments in women's enterprises were most likely to happen when women were the loan recipients (Hashemi, Schuler and Riley 1996; Kabeer 2001b; Pitt and Khandker 1998). While both male and female borrowers used their loans to purchase homestead land, women borrowers were more likely to register the land in their own name, a break from past practice (Kabeer 2001b; Todd 1996). Women's access to loans was also associated with their ownership of other productive assets and with providing children's schooling (Pitt and Khandker 1998).

Women's greater role in household livelihood efforts led to a qualitative change in their relationships with their husbands. A woman vendor who had been able to expand her business considerably said her husband, who had never been a violent man, nevertheless loved her more now that she was earning more money. Asked if he had not loved her before, she replied:

> Did he love me before? Well, the difference between then and now is like day and night. I did business before, but it was small business, 200–300, is that proper business? Now I work hard, I earn well … won't he love me more? (Kabeer 1998, p.49)

While a number of female borrowers reported increased domestic violence as a result of their loans for some of the reasons mentioned above, others reported a decline (Kabeer 2001b; Schuler et al. 1996b). Various explanations were given for this. Schuler et al. found that it went down because men became afraid that wives who had previously stayed at home now had a group forum where household matters might be made public. Ahmed (2005) found that domestic violence went up in the early years of a woman's membership of a microcredit organisation but it subsided over time as women attended NGO training programmes and were better able to negotiate conflict.

In my own study, many women said that the improvement in their households' economic situation as a result of loans had led to a decline in the tensions and frustrations caused by scarcity. One woman reported how, in the past, her husband sometimes came home without enough to feed the family and the children would cry with hunger:

> There would be words, I would say angry things to him, he would respond angrily: 'I don't have it, how can I give it'. But now, she said, they sat down to eat together, 'the tears were gone and there was no longer any need to fight'. (Kabeer 2001b, p.72)

Another reported that her husband worried that the loans would dry up if project staff found out about his behaviour at home. He also thought that now that she was earning an income, she was in a position to leave him if his behaviour did not improve: 'My husband sees I am working as hard as he is. He thinks that if he makes me suffer, I will leave him' (Kabeer 1998, pp.50–51).

Finally, in the third and least frequently reported pattern of decision-making, women made the main decisions regarding loan use – a departure from patriarchal norms. This was predictable in female-headed households where there were no adult men to exercise authority. In the less predictable cases of married women, some women claimed, and their families agreed, that their husbands were too pious or too simple to handle household finances. As a daughter explained, 'My mother has got a head for business' (Kabeer 1998, p.40).

But there were also a number of women in my study who had taken on primary decision-making responsibility in response to extreme and sustained violence at the hands of their husbands. Violence in these cases was attributed to the husbands' bad character rather than the frustrations of poverty. Despite the fear harboured by some husbands that loans might empower their wives to leave them, this was not considered a realistic option for a number of reasons: women did not want to leave their children behind, they did not think that they would be welcomed back by their natal families and the alternative of setting up an independent household was not easy in rural communities: 'If I left him, somebody would be pulling at me, somebody would be passing comments at me' (Kabeer 1998, p.52).

These women invested some of their loans in their husbands' businesses in the interests of peace in the household, but they used the bulk of it to set up their own businesses. Their financial autonomy gave them a position of authority within their household, the role of household provider. As one put it,

> My courage has increased step by step, loan by loan ... I keep all the household accounts. If my son wants a *lungi*, he says, mother buy me a *lungi*. My husband's *lungi*, shirt, I buy it all. Soap, oil, whatever, they ask me. (Kabeer 1998, p.45)

Another had not forgotten the abuse her husband had inflicted on her in the past. She used her loans to essentially effect a 'divorce within marriage'. She set up her own separate enterprise, she opened two deposit pension schemes (DPS) in the bank in her own name and she had her own savings with her market *samity*, as well as a fund of 60,000 takas that she used for lending to local traders. She cooked her husband's meals only if he contributed his share: 'If he gives me money for the bazaar, I will cook for him, if he doesn't, I won't' (Kabeer 2001b, p.75).

An examination of the economic activities reported by women borrowers makes it clear that microfinance did little to challenge the gendered segmentation of livelihood opportunities in the countryside, as most continued to work from home in a limited range of businesses: livestock rearing, rice-processing and setting up shops within the home as well as lending to others. But what it *did* do was to allow many more women to earn an income within the home.

For those who had been confined to domestic responsibilities or unpaid family labour, the expansion of their livelihood options through access to loans may have added to their work burdens, but they evaluated these options differently from their unpaid work obligations, work that was not recognised or valued by their families, by their communities or by women themselves. Those engaged in such work had no choice but to accept the status of perennial supplicant as the price they paid for male support, but the lived experience of dependency could be a humiliating one when they had to plead with husbands for money to buy the most basic essentials. It explained the importance that they attached to their new income-earning capacity: 'If you have money in your hand, you feel joy. If you have no money, you feel pain. My labour has increased, but I don't feel it because the money is also coming in' (Kabeer 2001b, p.71).

For those already engaged in some form of enterprise, access to loans allowed them to expand and diversify their efforts. And, for those who had been working in backbreaking and exploitative forms of wage labour – in people's homes for left-over food or in the fields where they stood knee-deep in water with leeches crawling up their legs – access to loans allowed them to move into forms of work, most often within the home, that did not take such a toll on their bodies or on their sense of self-respect. Rural elites complained that the supply of agricultural wage labour had fallen since microfinance came to their village: one woman told Shehabuddin:

> Even a few years ago, I could find a local girl to come in and sweep the floor, to wash the dishes and do the laundry in exchange for a cooked meal at mid-day and half a *sher* of rice at the end of the day. Now, they are all too busy making *pati* (cane mats) and *jal* (fishing nets) … with Grameen Bank money. (Shehabuddin 1992, p.135)

7.3 The emergence of new opportunities: becoming a factory worker

Microfinance was a largely rural phenomenon, allowing married women with little or no education from moderately poor households to take up income-generating activities within the shelter of the home. Entering the new export garment industry, by contrast, represented a radical departure from past norms. Although it was urban-based, the bulk of its workforce was made up of rural women who materialised almost overnight, migrating from the countryside, often on their own, to take advantage of the new opportunities. It took women into a form of work that was not only located outside their homes and neighbourhoods but outside their villages.

The first generation of women who found work in the industry were young, mostly under 25. Many were divorced, separated or widowed, but there were also large numbers of married women and a sizeable percentage of young single women. Most had not completed primary education and some had no education at all, picking up the basic skills required – a smattering of English and proficiency on the sewing machine – while working as helpers.

The poorer ones were likely to have been employed previously, most often in domestic service, so that affluent housewives began to complain that that 'good maids [were] increasingly difficult to obtain' (Siddiqi 1996, p.120). Others had been engaged in agricultural wage labour, construction work and home-based cultivation. They found out about garment factories when factory girls came to visit their village home with tempting stories of higher wages and better conditions (Kabeer 2000). The more educated were unlikely to have worked before, even if their families had needed the money. The fact that garment work was considered 'clean', that it was carried out within the four walls of factories often located in residential areas of the city, gave it an aura of respectability that allowed these women to consider joining the factories.

But entering factory work presented many hardships. First-time migrants into the city had problems finding accommodation. Landlords either refused to rent to young single women or charged them exorbitant rents. Workers interviewed in 1984 had complained: 'we have no place to live ... no one will rent to us' (Feldman 2009, p.282). They spoke of being crammed into a single room with restricted use of water for washing, bathing and drinking, but still having to pay rents of 200–250 takas each. Over a decade later garment workers were making the same complaints: 'Landlords don't want to rent to us' (Amin et al. 1998, p.194).

There were the daily costs of working in an industry that failed to observe already-weak labour regulations. Trade union activity was repressed, contracts were rarely written, wages were low. The short delivery times imposed by buyers meant a relentless pace of work to meet unrealistic quotas. Young women, fresh from the countryside, were subjected to the harsh discipline of an export factory regime: regulated toilet breaks, abusive supervisors, long hours of work and compulsory overtime, not always remunerated.

Then there were structural hazards. Export manufacturing had come into existence in a hurried and unplanned way; as we saw, 'everybody and his uncle' had jumped on board what appeared to be a lucrative bandwagon. Small workshops and factories were set up wherever empty buildings could be found, with little attention to industrial safeguards. As a result, the history of the industry has been one of periodic industrial accidents, leading to numerous fatalities and injuries.

This attracted the attention of trade unions and human rights activists within national and international forums. There were regular calls for the boycott of the industry and a proliferation of codes of conduct by buyers seeking to improve their reputations, but progress was extremely slow. It was only with the collapse of Rana Plaza in 2013, resulting in the death of over 1,000 workers and the injury of many more, that a concerted effort was made by international buyers, the ILO, governments of importing countries and international trade unions to put pressure on the industry to improve its health and safety conditions (Kabeer, Huq and Sulaiman 2020; Labowitz and Baumann-Pauly 2014).

Women workers had to cope with the weight of unfavourable public opinion, the symbolic costs associated with their work. The sight of large numbers of young women crowding the streets of cities, living in unconventional arrangements with other young women, working alongside men, often late into the night, constituted a very visible challenge to the socially prescribed invisibility of women. It inevitably attracted harsh criticism. Garment work was widely seen as disreputable and garment workers were constructed as shameless, cheap and immoral – no better than prostitutes. The media offered lurid representations of this new phenomenon:

> A group of girls … with faces in cheap makeup, gaudy ribbons adorning their oily braids and draped in psychedelic-coloured sarees with tiffin carriers in their hands are a common sight [these] days during the morning and evening hours. These are the garment workers, [a] new class of employees. (*New Nation*, 22 December 1986)

Islamic economists devoted learned treatises to this question and concluded that not only did such employment take away work from men, the natural breadwinners of the family, but it represented a threat to the very fabric of the moral order:

> Men and Women sit in the same working place face to face. Whatever liberal arguments are put forward in favour of this arrangement, in reality the close proximity of opposite sexes arouses lust and love for each other which on many occasions lead to immoral and scandalous affairs between them. (Hossain 1980, p.270)

The religious community thundered about the breakdown of the 'natural' principle of the sex-segregated spheres. It organised *waz mahfils*, religious meetings often lasting several days and nights, within the vicinity of the factories, during which time various mullahs used loudspeakers to denounce the behaviour of the 'bold' garment women who moved around the streets of Dhaka unaccompanied by any male guardian.

Women workers had to deal with the unwelcome attentions of the men they passed on the streets, which ranged from leering, suggestive comments and abusive catcalls to more direct sexual overtures. Those coming home late at night after extended overtime were particularly fearful because, in addition to the 'normal' quotient of sexual harassment they experienced, they could be picked up by police, for whom any woman on the streets after dark was automatically labelled a prostitute.

Many male co-workers were also negative. While they recognised the contribution that these women were making to their families, they disapproved of what the work entailed: women working alongside men, going home late, earning their own income, becoming too economically independent, threatening to divorce their husbands on the most trivial grounds.

Their value may have gone up, as one put it, but their status had gone down (Kabeer 1997, p.271).

Given the various practical obstacles they had to overcome, the disapproval they had to endure, what explained the continued waves of migration of women seeking jobs in the garment industry? The answer has to be sought in the interactions between the wider context and the imperatives, incentives and aspirations these generated for different groups of workers and their families. It was clear that the industry was tapping into the 'latent' demand for paid work that women had been expressing since the 1970s, a demand that intensified as more and more families experienced difficulties in making ends meet. Studies had already identified the willingness of extremely poor women to do waged work wherever they could find it. What had remained invisible was the need for paid work among families who did not suffer from abject poverty, who nevertheless struggled to maintain their place in society on male earnings alone but who shrank from the prospect of female members engaging in the forms of waged work previously available to women.

For these reasons, as Siddiqi (1996) comments, 'the spectrum of families in which daughters, sisters or wives have been "sent" to work in garment factories [was] quite wide' (p.120). But, of course, not all these women were 'sent'; many came on their own volition, often in the face of stiff opposition from family members. The motivations that brought these women into the industry varied according to their family's economic condition and social status and to the expectations associated with their position within it. Their accounts help us understand what it was about their circumstances that led them to overcome their inhibitions about engaging in an unconventional form of work.

The push of poverty

One group of workers had been sent to work by their families under the pressure of poverty. Some were young unmarried women who came from very poor families, the kind that were accustomed to sending daughters out to work as part of the family's survival strategies and saw factory work as an improvement on their previous options. Many were sent while still very young, often on their own. They had to find their way in the city, having lived in the countryside all their lives. Runa, who had started work when she was about 13, spoke of the trauma of her first few months:

> I would cry all the time when I first came to work, but I told myself, my father is poor and he has five children to feed. He has to send them to school ... so I convinced myself to stay. (Amin et al. 1998, p.190)

Others who joined the factory under pressure of poverty belonged to the traditional 'destitute' category, female household heads in desperate straits who had to earn in order to eat. A young mother who had been married off at the age of 15 to a 'vagabond' husband and deserted a few years later said:

> In our society, women are left with nothing when the marriage does not work. I have taken this job so that I can take care of myself, and not depend on anybody. I do not care what others have to say either. They are not feeding me. (Siddiqi 1996, p.133)

But there were also women from better-off households who had expected to remain within the shelter of the marital home all their lives. This prospect had been shattered by their husbands' desertion or premature death. In the past, they would have been looked after by their in-laws or natal family, but they were increasingly regarded as a burden. With the emergence of factories as a relatively respectable option, they were expected to contribute to their own living expenses.

Maintaining the myth of the male breadwinner

A second category of workers was made up of married women who had come of their own volition. In cases where their husbands supported their decision, the process was relatively smooth. Happy, for instance, decided to join a factory because she was just 'sitting around and wanted to do something useful' (Siddiqi 1996, p.133). Her wages paid her son's school fees. Her husband accompanied her to and from work in a covered rickshaw so she avoided unwelcome attention on the streets.

But there were other husbands who opposed the idea. Their objections were partly practical: who would do the housework? Who would look after the children? How safe was it on the streets? There were also emotions involved: how would it look to others if their wives were involved in such a public form of work? Anxieties about propriety were frequently shot through with sexual anxiety about the idea of their wives working alongside men who were not their kin.

Shanu's account was very revealing of the sexually loaded nature of these emotions (Kabeer 2000). Her husband had six daughters from a previous marriage and a baby daughter with Shanu. His trading activities offered very uncertain income flows so he decided to send his older daughters into factory work. But when Shanu decided that she also wanted to work – her stepdaughters were taunting her for 'eating' out of their earnings – her husband was opposed: she would be working late, the child was still young, the family would not be looked after properly, they would have to eat stale food. Shanu herself confided that his real fear was that she might get involved with other men.

Most married women understood very well what the nature of their husbands' resistance was since it was rooted in a shared habitus. They avoided confrontation, using their *boodhi*[7] to devise strategies of 'wielding and yielding'. As Monowara put it, 'The woman who understands won't show her power; the one who doesn't, will' (Kabeer 2000, p.128). They presented their desire to work in terms that invoked the welfare of the family, the need to educate their children, to save for their daughters' dowry. They ensured that their domestic responsibilities were not neglected, even if it meant getting up earlier than the rest of the family and going to bed later. They made strategic decisions about the disposal of their wages, with interesting differences that reflected the differing concerns of status-conscious middle-class husbands and economically insecure poorer ones (Kibria 1995). Among the former, it was a matter of honour and pride that men did not take money from women in the family. These women retained virtual control of their salaries but generally earmarked it for expenditures on collective welfare: the children's tuition, for instance, or house rent. In poorer households, women were more likely to hand over their wages to their husbands to bolster his precarious status as primary breadwinner.

Laying husbands' jealousies to rest was a more difficult matter. Shanu had finally succeeded in overcoming her husband's objections by reassuring him that her behaviour would be virtuous, that she would not neglect her domestic duties and that she would hand over her wages to him. Hanufa's husband only agreed to her factory employment on condition that she wore the *burqa* he had bought her to and from work (Kabeer 2000).

Regardless of the motivations that propelled women into factory and how their wages were managed, it was evident that, for many, earnings had led to a shift in their position within the household. Some described this acknowledgement in emotional terms: 'When you contribute to the family, they love you more, they give you respect' (Kabeer 2000, p.161). But acknowledgement was also manifested at the level of practice. Zohra handed over her wages to her husband but pointed out that, in the past, she always had to provide an account for any requests for money that she made. This was no longer the case:

> When I want to buy something, I just ask for it – it may be his income or mine. He never asks why I need it. Nor would he spend without asking me. (Kabeer 2000, p.161)

In Shanu's case, both husband and wife explicitly acknowledged a change in their relationship but in somewhat different terms. He said:

> I manage the household finances … But the money she earns is very useful. She gives the entire amount to me … But when she brings me the money, I have to buy her whatever she wants. (Kabeer 2000, p.172)

Shanu, on the other hand, said:

> [Women] couldn't say a word before they started working. If I had
> not been working, my husband would have ordered me to look after
> his children and see to their needs … If one works, one has different
> rights. (p.172)

There was also a subcategory within this group for whom entry into garment work provided a way of carving out a degree of security for themselves
(Kabeer 2000; Kibria 1998). Some feared that, through no fault of their own,
they had failed, or might fail, to live up to their side of the patriarchal bargain, giving their husbands grounds for leaving them. For others it reflected
a more generalised sense of insecurity, the belief that the patriarchal bargain
had become much shakier than the past, that husbands did not need any justification for abandoning their wives.

These women used their earnings to secure themselves against these different
forms of patriarchal risk. Their precautions were rarely taken openly for fear of
risking the very outcomes they sought to avoid. Instead, they took the form
of information withheld, half-truths and outright deceptions. Amena had five
daughters and no sons. She joined the factory because she calculated that the
financial burden of dowries for her daughters would feel less onerous for her
husband if she was able to contribute. She had opened two deposit accounts in
the bank, one in her husband's name, which he knew about, and one in her own
name, which he did not. Every month she scrupulously paid an equal amount
of money into both (Kabeer 2000). Other married women who had failed to
conceive entered factory work in anticipation of what might happen. Salma, for
instance, worried constantly about what fate had in store for her:

> Men don't always feel the same; he treats me well now but what will
> happen if God does not give me any children … What will become
> of me if he decides to remarry? (Kabeer 2000, p.162)

Recasting the dutiful daughter

A number of daughters had taken the initiative to seek work because they saw
their families struggling to manage. The costs of dowry were often the primary push factor. Seventeen-year-old Feroza knew that her father was finding
it hard to arrange a marriage for her because prospective husbands wanted
'money, a cow, a bed, a watch', demands that were beyond his means. She had
followed other girls in her village into factory work:

> At least I will be feeding myself. I will not be a burden. And if I
> can learn the work well, then maybe in some time I can pay for the
> education of my younger brothers and sisters. (Kibria 1998, p.12)

Some fathers had come to terms with the fact that their daughters would have to earn their own dowries:

> When I was younger there were families that were rich, there were families that were poor. But no one would consider sending their daughters to work in garments. Your responsibility as a father was to arrange your daughter's marriage. But now for those who are poor, there is no way out. All the marriage proposals that come ask for money or for other things. (Kibria 1998, p.12)

But some daughters had to work hard to gain parental permission. Rehana's family had opposed her joining factory work because they believed she would lose her innocence: she would be living alone in Dhaka, mixing with men and all kinds of 'low people'. She had responded:

> How long can I eat your rice? Now there's not enough food for two meals a day, and I'm just another mouth to feed. They had no reply to what I said. (Kibria 1995, p.303).

Reluctant parents sometimes gave their permission only on the under-standing that any money their daughters sent home would be kept aside for their marriage.

An interesting reinterpretation of the idea of the dutiful daughter surfaced in some of these accounts: the desire to compensate parents for not having sons who could share the father's breadwinning responsibilities. These daughters strove to prove that they were as good as any son. One 16-year-old declared:

> Just as a son can be a guarantee against poverty for parents through his income, so can a daughter if she is given the opportunity. Just as a son can earn money, so can a daughter look after her parents. In fact, the truth is that *daughters can turn out to be more reliable than sons in this respect.* (Siddiqi 1996, p.127, author's italics)

Then there were young women had become all too aware of the disjuncture between the promise of the patriarchal bargain and its reality. As Aleya said,

> The *maulvis* object to garment work because they say we come into contact with strange men, but we say to them, 'Can you feed us? If you want to object, then you have to feed us'. (Kabeer 2000, p.89)

Heaven no longer beneath her husband's feet

The discussion has focused so far on women whose decision to enter the gar-ment industry was taken either by their families or with their (often reluctant) consent. To that extent, these women were respecting the social norms that governed family relations, even as they sought to reinterpret them. But there were others whose entry into the industry was associated with an open break with these norms.

Some were married women who had taken the initiative to leave their husbands and fend for themselves, knowing that they could earn regular wages and live on their own in the anonymity of the city, away from the surveillance of their village community. The decision to leave a marriage was rarely a bid for freedom, more often a response to a husband's failure to honour his side of the patriarchal bargain.

Among poorer women, it was most often related to his breadwinning obligations. Renu had suffered from her husband's violence and irregular contributions throughout their marriage but it was his irresponsibility as a breadwinner rather than his violence that drove her to leave. Her first son had died and she hoped that, if she had another, he would change his ways, but she had a daughter, nothing changed 'and my heart broke and I came away'. She explained why it took her so long to leave her husband:

> When I was married, even if I was not earning, at least I was with him. No one could say anything to me. Now, even if they say nothing, I feel afraid, I feel they might. That fear is always there. Don't all women have this fear inside them. I am a woman on my own; I have to go to the bazaar, I have to go here, I have to go there; men stare at me, they pass comments. (Kabeer 2000, p.103)

Hanufa was able to throw her husband out of the rented room in which they lived after a particularly violent episode. She took him back later, but she had made her point: she was capable of feeding herself:

> Garments have been very good for women, even for me. I have become more courageous ... Now I feel I have rights, I can survive ... Suppose my husband says something, I won't care because I can feed myself ... I can earn and survive – I have got the courage. (Kabeer 2000, p.175)

In more middle-class households, the decision to leave often revolved around the issue of other wives. Jahanara, an educated young woman, lived with her husband and their five-year-old daughter in Khulna. He had been married before and his continued relations with his first wife was a perennial source of tension in their marriage. After a major quarrel she left for Dhaka with her daughter but she visited the local shrine regularly to pray that her husband would come for her: 'After all, a woman should always obey her husband because a wife's paradise is under her husband's feet' (Siddiqi 1996, p.131).

Other women had decided that paradise was no longer beneath their husbands' feet. Sathi Akhter had moved from an attitude of passive acquiescence – 'there is no difference between a woman's fate and a prisoner's fate and it is no different for the daughter of a prime minister' – to taking active control over her life (Kabeer 2000, p.175). She found out within the first month of her marriage that her husband was already married. She felt deeply betrayed by this deception. Her stepmother did not welcome her return so she lived with her uncle's family:

> I swore I would eat from my own income. If I can feed myself, I will eat or I will not eat at all. My greatest satisfaction today is that I do not have to put up with anyone's gibes. (p.176)

She had no interest in remarrying: 'The thought of the future no longer troubles me. Marriage proposals come but I just say I am already married' (p.176).

Not all women were as adamantly opposed to remarriage but they had firm opinions about the kind of man they would consider. Hosna's marriage had broken down because of continued dowry demands by her parents-in-law. When one of her co-workers sent a marriage proposal, she told him the conditions on which she would consider it: she would not leave her job, she would not give any of her earnings to her husband if she did not want to and, as long as her parents were alive, she would send them money (Kabeer 2000).

Her account highlighted the new models of marriage that were being negotiated by women who were no longer prepared to pay the bitter price of economic dependency within marriage:

> Some women think that they can't do anything if they are married. They think that their husbands have turned them into beggars. Some women are afraid that they will never find a husband so that he becomes more important than money. But other women think there is no reason to live with a husband if he makes you suffer, it is better to live on your own ... I think that it is good for women of our country to work, to educate themselves and to stand on their own two feet. They can marry after that. (Kabeer 2000, p.178)

Many of these women now headed their own households, but they no longer resembled the traditional category of destitute women, whose 'frightening' financial independence had long served as warning of the dire consequences of losing male support. Furthermore, their experience of dependency with marriage, of being 'beggars without a voice', had instilled in them a powerful determination that their daughters should not suffer the same fate.

The previous chapter spoke of rural mothers who wanted to educate their daughters so that they would have a better chance in life. I heard the same views passionately articulated by garment workers who had been left fending for themselves when their marriages broke down. They felt that they had been married off when they were 'too young to be able to evaluate their own benefits and losses', that they were 'having babies when they were still babies themselves', and that they had been ill-equipped to earn their own living when their marriages broke down (Kabeer 2000, p.180). Denied the opportunity to make something of their own lives, they wanted fiercely that their daughters' lives should not be similarly circumscribed: in a phrase used by many, 'our lives are over, but our daughters have a future'.

Like the women who featured in the previous chapter, these women put a particular emphasis on the emancipatory potential they saw in education. Hanufa's bitter experience of marriage had led her to this view:

> If I had known before, I would not have got married. So many girls of my age have not got married or have got married at a later age. I do not want my daughter to suffer … If she is educated, then she can read, write and understand … I want her to get married when she has the capacity for understanding and deciding what is good for her future … I don't want her to blame anyone else for her life. She should make her own choices. (Kabeer 2000, p.183)

A 25-year-old woman told Ahmed and Bould (2004) that she had been put under pressure by her husband to have a third child in the hope of having a son but she had been able to override him because they both knew that the family depended on her earnings. That she had two daughters was enough for her and she wanted the best for them:

> I told him there is no difference between sons and daughters these days … I want my daughters to be educated and have a better life than I did. One able daughter is better than 10 illiterate sons. (p.1335)

Momta had left her husband, taking her baby with her, when he expressed his disappointment that she had given birth to a girl. She decided she would not marry again but would work to support her daughter and herself. Her dream was to educate her daughter till MA level, to marry her off only when she was old enough to understand the world. She might then realise the sacrifices her mother had made so that her daughter had a better life: 'Then maybe she will give me respect. If I am lucky, she will look after me' (p.179). Hers was a narrative in which maternal altruism and the search for future security meshed seamlessly together.

The shift in habitus that led mothers like Momta to increasingly look to daughters for support and security in their old age can be seen as a continuation of some of the changing perceptions reported in rural areas in the previous chapter. They expressed the view that sons were increasingly less reliable: 'boys tend to fall into bad company more easily and become troublemakers' (Ahmed and Bould 2004, p.1339). They also observed that a significant percentage of daughters, even those who were married, were sending money home to their natal family. Women's future economic security was no longer as closely bound up with having adult sons as it had been in the past.

Making their own way in the world

Young, unmarried women were also beginning to raise questions about the terms of the patriarchal bargain. Some believed that the intergenerational dimensions of the patriarchal bargain, the contract between parents and children, had begun to unravel. Daughters found that they could no longer expect the kind of support from their natal families that had once been the case, that they were increasingly required to become responsible for their own future. These young women did not send money home, not because they did not earn enough but because there had been a shift in attitudes: the need to look after oneself was displacing the need to contribute to the natal family:

> My father and mother can't feed me, my brothers can't feed me, my uncles can't feed me. So that is why I am working in garments, to stand on my own feet. Since I am taking care of my own expenses, I have no obligation to give money to my family. (Kibria 1995, p.289)

One young woman had left home to take up garment work after a major fight with her family. She was a good student but before she could sit her SSC exam she was told the family could no longer afford to finance her schooling. She felt that they simply did not value her education enough. Yet another said she had refused to cave in to her family's demand for her wages when they had done so little to look after her (Kibria 1995, p.304).

We also see signs of rebellion on the part of some of these women at the culture of son preference and their personal experience of discrimination within their families. One young woman said that her entry into garment work had been an angry response to her father's decision to invest virtually the household's entire assets to finance her older brother's migration to the Middle East. She did not believe that he would repay their parents out of his earnings abroad and that, as a result, her younger siblings would be deprived of the chance to continue with their education (Kibria 1998, p.10).

The traditional family system held little meaning for these women. They saw a future in which they would 'stand on their own feet', a phrase that we can see had become increasingly common in relation to women's shifting place in society. They did not share their parents' preoccupation with marrying them off as early as possible to keep dowry demands to a manageable size. They wanted marriage on their own terms:

> If you work in garments, you can better yourself. What's the use of sitting at home? If I lived in the village, I would be married by now, but

I'm glad that my life is different. Because I am self-sufficient, I can go where I want and marry whom I want. Even after I'm married, I will continue to live my life in my own way. (Kibria 1995, p.304)

Sixteen-year-old Lily had been able to avoid an unwanted arranged marriage by escaping to work in a garment factory (Amin et al. 1998). She had not ruled out the prospect of marriage, even an arranged one, but she wanted to be in a position to decide what kind of man she would marry. She wanted to earn enough money to build a nice house near her parents, buy a cow and save for her dowry. After that, she would be prepared to marry, preferably a boy from her area, one who had passed high school and had a job in an office or as a supervisor in a garment factory.

But, while these young women were resisting the customary early arranged marriages, another important change was taking place as a result of their large-scale entry into factory employment. They were meeting men in the course of their working lives, falling in love and arranging their own marriages. While the idea of 'love marriages' had been widely condemned in earlier times, it was becoming an increasing trend, particularly within the garment workforce.[8] Parents themselves were less resistant to it than they had been in the past. Garment employment jeopardised women's chances of conventional arranged marriage so letting daughters arrange their own marriage provided parents with a way out.

Love marriages had the additional advantage that they did not involve dowry demands. Since the daughter had not married according to her parents' choice, parents could not be expected to pay dowry for her. But a second reason was that the earning capacity of garment workers made them an 'asset' in a marriage rather than a liability. The idea that dowry was being waived in the case of working women, whose 'value had gone up even if their status had gone down', was a plausible one. The practice of dowry in Bangladesh did not have the sanction of religion or long-established custom, but (as detailed in Chapter 4) came into existence sometime in the latter half of the 20th century. If it was indeed a reflection of the declining value of women's economic contributions in the move from the subsistence to the market economy, as some have argued, then logic seemed to dictate this decline would be reversed, or at least halted, when women moved from unpaid labour within the home to visible participation in the market economy.

Certainly, given the pragmatic, rather than romantic, view of marriage taken by some of these women, they appeared to find the waiving of dowry to be a logical outcome of their transition to the status of asset. Suraya, a young unmarried woman, had explained why she gave greater priority to finding a job in the garment factory than to her parents' priority to finding her a husband:

You never know, after marriage my husband may abscond with my dowry money or divorce me after some time. So what's the use of spending so much money on dowry incurring great debt in the process? It is better I work and stand on my own feet first ... If I can earn, there will be no shortage of men willing to marry me. (Begum 1988, pp.119–20)

Dilu was of the same opinion:

If a woman is earning something, the man's family is interested in her. The more she earns, the more interested they are. They aren't interested if she is poor. The difference is that rather than asking for a huge dowry, they may be willing to just take the girl. (Kabeer 2000, p.171)

Or, as Milu announced (with some amount of pride), 'How can they ask for dowry to marry us? *We* are the dowry' (Kabeer 2000, p.171).

It is evident that these young, unmarried girls were imagining a future for themselves very different to the one that had been mapped out for them; they had 'big dreams' that challenged their prescribed destiny. They had grown up in a rapidly changing environment where rising costs of living combined with rising aspirations about the standard of living. They had migrated from the countryside with others like themselves to enjoy some increase in their personal freedom, some degree of financial autonomy. They were acutely aware of the physical demands of their work, the stigma still attached to it, the rumours about their morality. Delowara felt that these rumours were unfair: 'Don't say *women*. If one woman has done something bad, then say *woman*, don't say *women*. You can't judge a whole group of people by one woman's misconduct' (Kabeer 2000, p.94). These costs were partly offset at the personal level by their enhanced sense of agency. They could live on their own, they could fulfil demanding quotas, they could move factories in search of higher wages, they enjoyed the sociability of factory life, they wanted some say in who they married and when they married. They were exposed, far more than previous generations, to cross-cutting influences that led them to hold views about themselves and the lives they wanted that were far removed from the habitus of the older generation.

7.4 The rise of new opportunities: service providers to the community

I want to pick up briefly here on the stories of women workers in community-based service provision that I touched on in Chapter 6. Although they constituted a fairly small percentage of the female work force, they had expanded considerably in recent decades and exercised a disproportionate influence on the aspirations of parents and daughters. When parents educated their daughters to improve their chances in the labour market, these were the kind of jobs they hoped their daughters would get.

These jobs were characterised by varying degrees of formality. They could be located in offices, in banks, in schools or in the field, and could involve full or part-time salaried employment or voluntary work for an honorarium, but they were considered desirable because, first, they required some level of education and hence were not open to all and, second, because they involved work for formal institutions, even if their own jobs were not necessarily formal. However, the very desirability of these jobs meant that the demand for them far outstripped the supply – indeed, educational levels rose partly in the hope of accessing these jobs – so that various informal practices, including bribes and personal contacts, came into play as rationing mechanisms.

The earliest cohort of workers in this category dated back to the 1960s, when the government had recruited village women to act as organisers for the women's co-operatives set up as part of the Comilla programme. McCarthy (1967) found that they mainly came from land-poor households, that they were either divorced or separated women heading their own households or whose husbands were old, sick or unemployed. Their poverty meant that they had little to lose in taking up work that required them to move around their village or attend meetings at the programme centre where village men were also present. They encountered the familiar threats, abuse and hostility that greeted women breaking with cultural norms, but they had little choice. As one said, 'If I sit at home is Allah going to put food in my mouth?' (Feldman and McCarthy 1983, p.954).

While the economic deterioration of the post-independence period led increasing numbers of poorer women to take up jobs wherever they could find them, it also exerted pressure on middle-class families to find employment for female members that was commensurate with their status. Factory work did not qualify for many, particularly as it required them to migrate, but they were willing to contemplate community-based employment within family planning, health, nutrition and, later, microfinance programmes. There were minimum educational requirements for these jobs so they attracted the first generation of educated women from respectable rural families to take up work outside their homes. Starting with the handful of women who were hired in regular posts in the IRDP's Co-operative Programme, this group grew to well over 100,000 female development workers in state and NGO programmes, according to a 1987 World Bank report (Jiggins 1987, cited in Goetz 2001).

In the early days of these programmes, women workers reported regular confrontation with hostile villagers. Many years later, a government health officer expressed his view that the government's decision to hire women as community-based service providers in that initial period had been groundbreaking (Mahmud and Sultan 2016). As government employees, these women had been in a stronger position to absorb the initial hostility and their presence had made such work more socially acceptable for other women.

Over time, what had appeared to be entrenched norms became less rigid as communities became accustomed to the sight of women working alongside men in the public domain. Whether or not these 'norms became history', as claimed by Chowdhury and Cash (1996, p.75), rules were certainly relaxed, particularly for those working in NGO programmes. Male and female NGO workers began to stay in the same hostels close to office quarters. Women were allowed to wear *shalwar kameez* for ease of mobility in place of the earlier insistence on saris. GK had been the first NGO to require its female health workers to ride bicycles and motorbikes so the organisation could expand its outreach. Others followed so that, by the 1990s, the bicycle-riding female fieldworker had become a familiar sight. Each of these departures from cultural norms encountered fresh hostility but, in each case, this appeared to subside over time as villagers became accustomed to the new practices and appreciative of the services they provided.

The motivations that led women into these jobs were not that different from the more educated sections of the garment workforce. Financial considerations were most frequently mentioned – they were seeking to contribute to their families, to supplement their husbands' income, to improve their standard of living, to educate children or siblings or to save for daughters' marriage. But there were intangible considerations as well: the desire to put their education to use, dissatisfaction with their dependency status, problems in the marital or parental home. A health worker whose family had been in the process of arranging an early marriage for her confessed that she had stolen money from her parents to run away from home and join GK (Mahmud and Sultan 2016). A government fieldworker said she had always planned to work after completing her studies: 'I don't want to be dependent on anyone.' Her husband did not approve but she told him that she was only willing to leave the job if he found her a better one (Goetz 2001, p.136). But many husbands were supportive, expressing appreciation of their wives' financial contributions and pride in their achievements: 'she has earned a status of her own from this job' (Mahmud and Sultan 2016, p.11).

In addition, we also find evidence of awareness about the instability of the patriarchal bargain, most often framed by these women in terms of the insecurities of old age, the fear that they might not have the family support they needed. They were saving for such an eventuality with banks or with NGOs. A common aspiration was to buy land or build their own houses.

Like earlier cohorts of workers in these jobs, these women spoke of gaining acceptance through their virtuous personal deportment and their professionalism. They defined their roles as providers of needed services to the community: 'everyone calls me a doctor' (Mahmud and Sultan 2016, p.15). They saw themselves as role models for the next generation of girls, encouraging parents to invest in their daughters' education. But their emphasis on their professional expertise was not necessarily instrumental. The sense of personal satisfaction that many expressed about their jobs was conspicuous by its absence from the narratives of other categories of workers. As one BRAC health worker said,

What I like best is serving others. After a child is born, the mother will let me hold the child before she gives it to the father … I am satisfied with my work because my work gives me peace. (p.17)

7.5 Paid work and pathways to social change

The livelihood activities that women took up over the years, like any form of social practice, embodied different kinds of capital, including symbolic capital, the social meaning ascribed to them. But they were also characterised by the changing meanings that workers themselves ascribed to their work and by the changes they made possible in workers' lives. In this final section, I want to examine how 'intentionality' was exercised in relation to new forms of livelihood activities, how women workers sought to reconfigure the social meanings attached to their work, particularly work that took them outside the socially prescribed boundaries of the home. I also want to explore what they were able to achieve through their work, how it changed their sense of themselves as well as how they were viewed by others. These changing perspectives and practices were all part and parcel of the larger changes in gender relations within society, contributing to the reconfiguration of particular aspects of the patriarchal bargain, but also made possible by changes that were occurring in other aspects.

Redefining the meaning of work

Unlike the changes that took place in the reproductive domain that had been initiated through the purposive efforts of policymakers, women's growing presence in the domain of production were spearheaded by their individual responses to the push of household need and the pull of market opportunities. A great deal of this activity was carried out at home in compliance with cultural norms, but even this could involve attending NGO meetings or gathering fodder for cattle at some distance from home. Other forms of work constituted a very visible break with norms. Women's mobility in the public domain had increased over time but there was still loss of status associated with being seen to be working for a living in the public domain.

They sought to legitimise their departure from accepted norms by drawing on the cultural repertoires of the community to reinterpret their work in ways that did not reject the boundaries of gender propriety but claimed that these boundaries had not been transgressed. Deployed by successive generations of working women, their discursive manoeuvres helped to shape the processes of social change, allowing gradual modifications in the meanings and doings of gendered social practice in the domain of work.

For instance, long-established norms had required women to work inside their own homes or, if they were forced to work outside, only within a strictly defined radius around their homes. As women went further and further afield in search of work, steady redefinitions of the 'inside' and 'outside' were evident in their conversations: the boundaries of 'the inside' were constantly shifted outwards as what had previously been 'the outside' were invested with the qualities that had defined 'the inside' as a safe and honourable space. Women who once worked surreptitiously in their own fields or under the cover of darkness had begun, by the late 1980s, doing this work openly, though often alongside male family members to retain some degree of respectability.

Similarly, the boundaries of the neighbourhood were gradually extended to encompass the rest of the village and its environs as they started to take on waged work in fields, orchards and roadsides. In place of emphasising that they worked 'only' within their own neighbourhoods, they took to saying that they worked 'only' within their own villages or 'only' in nearby villages or else 'only' close enough to allow them to return home before dark.

Garment workers had their own spatial strategies. They sought to render factory space respectable by stressing its 'inside' qualities: their work took place within the protection of four walls and gates were kept locked and guarded throughout the day, symbolic of the strict regulation of factory life and reconstituting the inside/outside divide as the divide between factory and street (Kabeer 2000).

Along with *where* women worked, there were also strong social proscriptions about *who* they worked for. The normative ideal was to work for one's own family but, if women were forced into wage work for others, they were expected to work only for members of their kinship network. These proscriptions became harder to adhere to as increasing numbers of women had to take up whatever work they could find. Here the long-established practice of claiming 'fictive kinship' was drawn on strategically to establish familial relationships. Women said that they cooked in a roadside restaurant owned by someone who was 'like an uncle' or 'sort of a brother' or that they had been informed of an opening in a garment factory by their mother's brother's cousin's uncle, who would be presented as close kin.

Women garment workers claimed kinship with others in their factories, describing their employers and managers as 'guardians' whose role it was to ensure moral behaviour on the factory floor. They described their relationships with male co-workers as 'like brother and sister' in an effort to desexualise these relationships (Kabeer 1991b; Siddiqi 1996). These relationships could be scaled up as required: as Todd notes (1996), female staff working for Grameen would invoke the metaphor of 'brother and sister' to describe their relations with fellow male workers, thereby extending admission to family status to the 10,000 mostly male members of bank staff!

There was also the problem of visibility in the public domain. A continuing thread in the literature on women's participation in outside work has been their ongoing struggle to reconcile their presence in the public domain with the norms of female seclusion. These had taken the form of efforts to reinterpret the meaning and conduct associated with *purdah*. Women from the poorest families had little choice but to work in full public view in jobs that made efforts at modesty difficult. At most, they would drape their *anchal*, the edge of their saris, around their heads, pulling it over their faces when the need arose.

But those from households with some status in the community had to find ways of justifying publicly visible forms of employment. Based on research in the 1960s, McCarthy (1967) reported that, among the small group of women who participated as facilitators in the Comilla co-operative programme, the better-off had donned the *burqa* to carry out their duties. It acted as a form of 'portable seclusion' (Papanek 1973, p.295) that allowed them to enter public spaces without violating moral boundaries.

Other interpretations of *purdah* centred on meanings and conduct. They spoke of an inner morality: I take my *purdah* with me. As Feldman and McCarthy (1983) point out,

> Even in this early period, one can see, in the responses of the women who were leaving the village, the kind of argumentation and response that carried them though the turbulent period of village opposition. (p.955)

In a later period, similar reinterpretations were offered by those who entered the urban garment industry (Kabeer 1991b). They were painfully aware of the aspersions cast on their morality, their reputation as women of loose virtue. They too emphasised 'the *purdah* of the mind', the purity of their intentions and the propriety of their conduct in the public domain: they would cover their heads and upper bodies with their *orna* (scarf), walk rapidly to and from work, preferably in groups, and keep their eyes downcast so as to avoid eye contact with any men on the streets.

Individual pathways to social change

While these discursive strategies to redefine the meaning of women's work were intended to make such work compatible with social norms, the motivations that led women to take up such work reflected the changing material circumstances of their lives. Survival needs were important but there were other considerations as well. The 'classic' patriarchal bargain had defined women in terms of their dependency status within the family, a status they had embraced because of what it promised in return. But, starting with the watershed decade of the 1970s, their faith in this bargain had been severely tested. The kinship, political and religious institutions that supported male dominance and authority had remained intact, but the associated sanctions to ensure that men observed their corresponding responsibilities to women had been weakening. The growing number of female-headed households, where women had to earn for themselves and their dependents in the absence of a male breadwinner, was becoming an increasingly common indicator of 'patriarchal differentiation'. I cited earlier the point made by Cain, Khanam and

Nahar (1979) that the increasing pressure of poverty made such an outcome predictable since male authority had a material base but male responsibility was normatively controlled: 'normative control, while powerful, is nevertheless malleable in the face of economic necessity' (p.410).

They were referring here to malleability in relation to norms of male responsibility. However, with the wisdom of hindsight, we can also extend the possibility of malleability to norms of female dependence which were exacting increasing costs for families that sought to uphold them as well as for women themselves as they saw the greater uncertainty of returns to compliance. It became clear to all categories of women, not just the destitute, that the old bargain could no longer be relied on, that men in their families were often unable or unwilling to shoulder their responsibilities as family breadwinners.

For women from poorer households, the decision to take up paid work was undoubtedly motivated by survival imperatives. We can best appreciate what paid work meant for them if we consider the deprivation that characterised the lives of so many during the 'basket case years', when men from landless and land-poor households laboured long hours for meagre wages and there was little or no work for women. Material hardship had been bound up with social humiliations. Women would beg for food from neighbours. Children were left to fend for themselves, gleaning the fields for fallen grains after the harvest, collecting fruit that had fallen on the ground. On days when there was nothing to eat, the family went to bed hungry, having chewed betel leaf or tobacco to blunt the hunger pangs (Kabeer 1989). As the quote from Humera at the start of this chapter illustrates, the ability to feed themselves and their families remained central to the search for paid work in the narratives of these women.

But women from households with a modicum of livelihood security were able to use their earnings to fulfil small and large dreams, dreams that contributed to the changes captured in the paradox literature. Whether as mothers, wives or daughters, they helped to raise the household's standard of living through better food, better clothing and better housing, they contributed to household savings and assets, they bought small everyday treats for children in the family, helped to educate them, both boys and girls, and they took on responsibility for dowry payments, reducing the pressure on the male breadwinner.

Their contributions did not go unnoticed. A number of studies drew on McCarthy's concept of 'centrality' to capture the shift from the margins of household decision-making to its centre that often came with women's increased capacity to take on breadwinning responsibilities (McCarthy 1967, p.91). In some households, this centrality could be experienced as a renegotiation of power. As Shanu put it, women who worked had very different rights from those that didn't. In others, it was experienced as 'mattering', a relational emotion that expressed the value of being needed by others, being important to them (Ashwin, Keenan and Kozina 2021). Daughters spoke of being valued like 'sons' by their parents, mothers spoke of the gratitude of children whose life chances they had helped to improve, wives spoke of the affection and appreciation they received from husbands: 'Now if anything happens to me, it is *his* head that hurts. That is how it seems' (Kabeer 2001b, p.74). These women could be seen as renegotiating the terms of the patriarchal bargain, using their earnings to position themselves within the family as breadwinners rather than dependents.

There were other women whose faith in the patriarchal bargain had been weakened to the extent that they used their earning power to carve out a greater degree of independence for themselves. Some were married women who pursued their goals in clandestine ways because they did not want to threaten relationships they still valued or depended on. But there were also women who no longer cared to protect their marriages. They had been married to husbands who were abusive, who failed to discharge their breadwinning obligations, who took second wives or else lied about their first wives. They used their access to paid work to end their marriages, often migrating to urban areas where they could fend for themselves in relative anonymity.

Finally, there were young unmarried women for whom the intergenerational bargain had begun to unravel. Their parents were not willing to discharge their responsibilities to them, their brothers were constantly favoured over them and they were aware that they were regarded as burdens who had to be married off as early as possible. These women wanted to be in a position to meet most of their own needs, to pay for their own dowries if necessary and to marry men who respected their independence. It was not simply their access to an income of their own that led to these big dreams. It was changes in the wider context – the availability of more regular employment, the possibilities for living on their own, the opportunities to fall in love – that had made it possible for these dreams to emerge.

One thread that ran through the narratives of these various groups of women, regardless of whether they remained within a traditional family set up or struck out on their own, was their ability to use their earnings to promote some of the changes that helped to close gender inequalities in different aspects of life. Whether it was married women investing in their families in ways that no longer upheld earlier forms of gender discrimination, parents valuing what daughters were able to provide, sometimes more reliably than sons, or unmarried women taking control over their own lives and life choices, these were examples of the routes through which paid work allowed women to dismantle some of the structures of patriarchal discrimination in their lives.

Dowry and the societal value of women

The societal route hypothesised to link women's increased labour force participation to the gender equality reported by the Bangladesh paradox shifted attention from individual agency to changing societal perceptions of women as they transitioned from the status of dependents within their families to the status of providers. Lily, who is quoted at the start of the chapter, certainly believed that earning women were valued by society, but how generalisable was her belief? One way to assess the societal impact of women's changing economic status is through its impact on dowry. As I noted in Chapter 4, the rise of dowry was widely explained in terms of the spread of markets, the integration of men into the wider cash economy and the erosion of women's traditional role in subsistence agriculture. The shift from bridewealth, which had previously symbolised the bride's worth as a person to the groom's family, to dowry signalled the fact that men's income potential now surpassed the previously valued attributes of the bride (Lindenbaum 1981; Westergaard 1983). Daughters, as I noted, had become 'a rope around their parents' neck' (Chapter 4). The question I want to address here is whether the fact that women were now entering the market in larger numbers had any impact on dowry demands.

The narratives in this chapter point to examples of impact through individual routes. One was through the use of women's earnings or loans to share or assume the costs of dowry. This was a change from the past, when the payment of dowry had been the sole responsibility of men within the household. Another was the investment of mothers' earnings in their daughters' education because it reduced or dispensed with dowry demands – either because education was a desired quality in a bride or because it increased the bride's earning capacity. We also saw that women who had access to financial resources, whether through microfinance or their own earnings, were often regarded as 'assets' rather than 'liabilities' in marriage transactions. A fieldworker cited in Goetz and Sen Gupta (1996) believed that loans that women were giving to their husbands were replacing what their fathers might otherwise have had to pay: 'Actually, this credit is a form of dowry' (p.51). I cited Milu, the garment worker interviewed in the late 1980s, who made a similar point. How could prospective husbands ask for dowry to marry an earning woman when 'We *are* the dowry'? Then, of course, many garment workers were reporting love marriages, where dowry was not required. In fact, according to Geirbo and Imam (2006), love marriages were often encouraged by parents in urban slums as a way of avoiding the payment of dowry, while Rashid (2006) found it had become more widespread among young women in low-income urban neighbourhoods.

But, while there is a range of positive evidence of the impact of women's work status on dowry payments of the kind I have cited in this chapter, it is generally based on small-scale studies. For the larger picture, I turned to a number of nationally representative surveys of married women of different age groups carried out in 2005 and 2006, which included questions about dowry payments (Amin 2008; Amin and Das 2013; World Bank 2008).[9] These confirmed that the incidence of dowry had been rising: only 8% of older women, mainly Hindu, reported dowry payments when they married compared to 46% of younger women (Amin and Das 2013).[10] They also showed considerable regional variation in the spread of dowry: for instance, only 13% of women living in Sylhet division reported dowry, compared to 65% of those in Rajshahi (Amin 2008). Since women's labour force participation also varied across country, it is possible that its impact on dowry demands played out locally rather than at the societal level. However, this was not supported by the evidence. While women's religion, education levels, household wealth and community norms and practices all played a role in determining individual and community-level variations in the incidence of dowry payments,[11] neither the work status of individual women nor the proportions of women in different districts who worked for 'cash or kind' proved significant (Amin and Das 2013; World Bank 2008).

Findings from the 2008 IDS/BIGD survey offer a possible explanation for this absence of impact (Kabeer et al. 2017). The survey asked women a number of questions about how their work was valued. The distribution of responses was telling. Women in formal waged work were most likely to believe that their productive contribution was important for their household (over 80%), followed in order by those in informal waged work, those in informal self-employment outside the home, those in paid self-employment within the home and, finally, those in unpaid family labour, only 47% of whom expressed this view. The same ranking was evident in relation to whether their families considered their work to be important. Positive responses here varied from 84% of those in formal employment to 44% of those in unpaid family labour. However, it was clear that these same women believed that there was far less recognition of their economic contributions on the part of the community. While those in formal employment still reported more positive perceptions on the part of the community than others, the percentages were far lower for all forms of work – from 26% of those in formal employment to just 9% of those engaged in unpaid work at home.

In other words, women and their families gave far more importance to their market contributions than did their communities, but the importance they gave varied considerably according to visibility and remuneration associated with the work: outside waged work was ranked considerably higher than self-employment outside or within the home. What this meant was that the overwhelming majority of working women were concentrated in informal home-based activities to which they gave little value and the community even less. It is not surprising then that their work status per se had not had a great deal of impact on whether or not dowry was demanded when they got married. Any impact it did have operated through the individual routes described in this chapter.[12]

Notes

[1] Begum and Greeley (1983); Rahman (1986a); Westergaard (1983).

[2] See Appendix 1 for details.

[3] Including a reference period of seven days

[4] Female wages could vary anywhere between 30% to 70% of the male wage, depending on time and location. Women were more likely to be

paid in kind rather than cash: they might receive a portion of the harvest for harvesting chillies and potatoes or a certain amount of rice for domestic work and post-harvest processing. Alternatively, they might be paid in the form of meals or clothing.

[5] This may have referred to the export garment factories that were emerging in emerging areas around this time.

[6] This estimate comes from Hossain (1988). Later estimates of NGO interest rates vary considerably. The Grameen Bank website stated it to be 20% in 1998. Various hidden costs mean actual rates are much higher. Naher (2006) and Faruqee and Khalily (2011) set it between 25% and 35% per annum. What was agreed was that they were considerably lower than the interest rates of 120–240% a year charged by moneylenders (Faruqee and Khalily 2011). Commercial banks charged around 13% but did not lend to the poor.

[7] While *boodhi* refers to intelligence, the use of the brain, it was often used by women to refer to the canny strategies they adopted to get their own way without appearing to do so.

[8] Paul-Majumder and Begum (2006) noted the unusually high proportion of women factory workers who had 'love marriages'.

[9] The 2005 survey was carried out by Population Council in collaboration with BRAC and covered 15,492 adolescents across Bangladesh. The 2006 national survey was carried out by the World Bank and covered 5,000 respondents: the results from this survey reported here were based on 1,500 married women in the 15–25 age group and 1,500 married women in the 45–49 age group.

[10] However, the estimate of 46% does seem low, given the extent to which dowry dominated the conversations about daughters' marriage reported in the qualitative literature, an observation also made in World Bank (2008). Since this is cross-sectional data, we do not know if this is an underestimate reflecting reluctance to admit to taking dowry or it represents a decline or levelling off from higher rates in the past.

[11] The survey found that at the individual level, Hindu women were more likely to pay dowry than Muslim, as were less-educated women and women from poorer households. At the community level, attitudes rather than economics proved significant: dowry was less likely to be reported in communities with more gender-egalitarian attitudes. It was also less likely to be reported in more religious communities as measured by veiling practices. For these communities, dowry continued to be regarded as an anti-Islamic practice.

[12] Findings from studies support this interpretation. Women in paid work, whether at home or outside, generally reported more positive impacts

than those who did not earn but the impact of their work varied according to type of activity, with work outside the home, particularly formal paid work, generally associated with more positive impacts than work within the home. The impacts in question related to voice in decision-making, children's (particularly girls') education, the purchase of assets, experience of domestic violence, sense of self-worth and agency and status in the community (Anderson and Eswaran 2009; Kabeer 2016; Kabeer, Mahmud and Tasneem 2018; Kabeer et al. 2013; Pitt and Khandker 1998; Rahman 1986b; Salway, Jesmin and Rahman 2005; see also a review of the literature in Kabeer 2016).

8. 'We follow *shariat*, but we follow *marfat* too': contestations over gender and Islam in the nation-making project

Their mothers, grandmothers and the women before them may have been God fearing and even practicing, but if they did not distinguish their religious obligation from social convention, grounding faith and practice in a thorough knowledge and understanding of texts, that faith was merely an extension of 'cultural Islam'. (Huq 2011, p.340)

[Poor rural women] make choices on the basis of both material and spiritual concerns, of how to both improve their lives in this world and to ensure a good akhirat (afterlife) in a manner that appears quite irrational in strictly secularist and Islamist understandings of self-interest and rationality. (Shehabuddin 2008, p.5)

The Bangladesh paradox has been framed in the development literature in terms of the unexpected pace of social progress, including progress on gender equality, in the face of high levels of absolute poverty and a dysfunctional state. What has gone largely unremarked is that this progress was achieved during a period that saw the visible rise of a particularly orthodox version of Islam. The paradox here lies not only in the antithesis posed between Islam and gender equality in the international literature, which tends to brush aside differences in the practice of Islam in different parts of the world, but also in the fact that the place accorded to women within this orthodoxy was deeply opposed to many of the gains that they had made in the Bangladesh context. This is the aspect of the paradox I want to explore in this chapter.

Bangladeshi Muslims have always been a devout people and religion has always played a role in daily life. But Islam is not a monolithic belief system.[1] It may have originated in the desert lands of West Asia but it has taken root in many different parts of the world and been nourished in very different cultures. Chapter 2 traced how the religion was brought to the Bengal delta by Sufi preachers, who espoused a mystical form of Islam and the mutual process of adaptation and accommodation that took place with the pre-existing Hindu, Buddhist and indigenous belief systems.

It was this syncretic version of Islam, a version that accommodated different interpretations of Islam, that formed the worldview of the mass of Muslims in East Bengal since that time – despite periodic attempts to promote more purist versions. It did not disappear when the newly independent Bangladesh declared its commitment to secularism. Mujib was a practising Muslim, as is his daughter, Sheikh Hasina, who has led the country off and on since elections were re-established in 1990. His commitment to secularism did not refer to a strict separation of state and religion, as in the Western variant, but to an ethics of religious tolerance that banned the use of religion for political purposes:

> Secularism does not mean the absence of religion. Hindus will observe their religion; Muslims will observe their own; Christians and Buddhists will observe their religions. No one will be allowed to interfere in others' religions ... Religion cannot be used for political ends. (Government of Bangladesh 1972)

But it is not this tolerant version of Islam that has been on the rise in recent decades but the purportedly more authentic Wahhabi version that has been aggressively promoted across the world through Middle Eastern oil money and influence (Choksy and Choksy 2015). This is a version of Islam that sees the syncretic religion practised in Bangladesh as hopelessly contaminated by Hindu influence.

There have been a number of studies discussing the rise of this orthodoxy in the Bangladesh context. While frequently presented in terms of a binary opposition between secularism and religion within competing national imaginaries (Nazneen 2018), the underlying tensions are in fact about what *kind* of Islam should prevail in Bangladesh. However, what I want to explore in this chapter is what kind of Islam *does* prevail in Bangladesh when we step out of these politicised debates to examine the 'lived Islam' of ordinary people. I also want to ask how these everyday practices relate to the broader story of progress on gender equality related in this book.

I will be using four key issues that have featured prominently in this literature as case studies for understanding how tensions between 'what should' and 'what is' played out in this lived Islam. These relate to the efforts of the Jamaat-i-Islam, the main Islamic party, to win women's votes; the attacks by Islamist groups on NGOs as vehicles of Western values about gender equality; the spread of Islamic study circles to promote orthodox practices among women at grassroots level; and, finally, the perennial question of veiling by women in public places. On the basis of this analysis, I will be arguing that one reason why it has been possible to make progress on gender equality in Bangladesh, despite the rise in Islamic orthodoxy, is that the country's population has, so far, resisted the imposition of a single monolithic belief system.

8.1 Islamic revivalism and the rise of Jamaat

A global Islamic revival, made up of the proliferation of various transnational movements, has been ongoing since the 1970s in response to a complex set of developments: the growing hegemony of the West; tensions between Westernised ruling elites in the Muslim world and orthodox sections of their populations; the Iranian revolution; the occupation of Palestine and the violation of the rights of Muslims in other parts of the world; the rise of the petrodollar and, with it, the power to exercise international influence; and the large flows of labour migration between Muslim countries and the Gulf states (Ali 2023; Lakshman 2006; Hasan 2012; Hossain 2012; Momayezi 1997).

The ideas associated with this revival have travelled to Bangladesh through various routes. The flow of official funds from the Middle East and its support for Islamic institutions has been one. Then there have been steady flows of migrant workers to the Middle East who have been deeply influenced by the Islam practised in a region that they deem closer to its origins, and hence more authentic, than the locally embedded Islam they grew up with. These ideas were also disseminated within the country through new means of communication such as global and regional satellite TV stations and social media, through older means of communication such as newspapers, television, radio, cassettes and videos, and through the long-established traditions of Friday sermons and *waz mahfils* often lasting several days and nights, with recordings made of the lectures for further distribution.

The dissemination of orthodox Islam found a hospitable environment in Bangladesh as a result of the steady desecularisation of public life by successive regimes after Mujib who were anxious to demonstrate their Islamic credentials to conservative constituencies within the country and the Islamic bloc outside. Zia's lifting of the ban on religious parties in 1976 allowed them to return to the political arena. The largest and oldest of these was the Jamaat-e-Islami. It had been founded in 1941 by Maulana Maududi, an Islamic scholar from north India, who saw politics as an essential precondition for the establishment of an Islamic state strictly governed by *sharia* law. Jamaat's policies towards women drew on his interpretation of *sharia*, subscribing to what has been described as a 'complementary' model of gender relations based on a 'natural' division of roles and responsibilities that placed men in authority within the family and the public domain and required women to remain in *purdah*.

Jamaat acquired considerable influence during military rule as both Zia and Ershad sought their support to shore up their Islamic credentials. It also gained legitimacy with the wider political establishment when it joined the main political parties in the popular movement to bring down Ershad in 1990 (Kumar, 2017). When elections were announced, Jamaat assumed that the 'natural faith-motivated' voting preferences on the part of the country's largely devout Muslim majority would bring it to power (Shehabuddin 2008). In fact, its support came largely from sections of the educated middle classes and it won only 18 of the 222 seats that it contested, or 12% of the vote (Riaz 2010). Nevertheless, by forming an alliance with the BNP, which had fallen short of a majority, it became part of the government that took power in 1991.

Its poor electoral performance led Jamaat to campaign far more actively for the next round of elections held in 1996, exhorting voters to support the only party committed to establishing an Islamic state. It won even fewer seats: three out of the 300 that it contested (8% of the vote). It blamed its defeat on unfair tactics by the AL and on the efforts of the NGO sector to discredit it. This was partly true. As discussed below, the period under BNP/Jamaat rule saw a series of attacks by Islamist groups on the country's NGOs for their gender strategies. The country's NGOs responded by spearheading an 'unprecedented mobilization' (Shehabuddin 2008, p.197) of poor rural women against the party, one of the factors in the ruling party's defeat.

These dismal electoral results led Jamaat to reconsider its public image and find ways of strengthening its appeal to the rural poor and to women. It watered down its version of the Islamic state in its 2001 manifesto: there would be no more chopping off the hands of thieves or stoning of persons convicted of adultery or banning of interest payments on loans (Lintner 2004). Instead, it foregrounded poverty alleviation and declared its support for NGOs as legitimate partners in development. It toned down some of its rhetoric on gender, attempting to project its support for a modernised version of female piety. It modified its earlier hard-line position that women be strictly confined to the domestic sphere with proposals for gender-segregated educational institutions and workplaces in which women dressed modestly and interacted only with other women. It also began to directly target women in its various dissemination efforts, including *madrassas* and *taleem* (Quranic) classes.

These intensified efforts also failed to pay off: it won just 17 seats or around 4% of votes in the 2001 elections (Riaz 2010). Despite dire threats about the 'bed of fire' that awaited those who did not vote for it, its brand of Islamic politics clearly did not have wide appeal. However, given the extreme hostility between the two main parties and near complete split down the middle in voting patterns, Jamaat – and other Islamist parties – have played 'king-making' roles in the coalitions that determined which party took power. Their poor performance in garnering votes has not prevented them from exercising disproportionate influence in the policies of successive ruling parties.

8.2 The attack on NGOs: defending the patriarchal order

Although NGOs were celebrated in the paradox literature for their contribution to the social progress of the country, they also attracted considerable criticism. Sections of the left within the country saw them as agents of Western imperialism, funded by donors to distract the rural proletariat from revolutionary action (e.g. Umar 1996). Others charged them with institutionalising a neoliberal agenda, shifting from their earlier concerns with social justice and redistribution to individualism and entrepreneurship (Feldman 1997; Karim 2004). There were also criticisms about the inordinate influence exercised by the Western donor community, the NGOs' lack of accountability to their grassroots constituencies, the absence of internal democracy and the promotion of new forms of patronage (Devine 2003; Karim 1995).

But far greater hostility towards NGOs was expressed by Islamist groups within the country. The 1990s were, as we saw in Chapter 5, a period when

NGO efforts to promote girls' education and women's livelihood opportunities and, in some cases, their political participation, had taken on nationwide significance. The pace and visibility of women's progress in these fields drew the ire of Islamist groups and this period also saw concerted effort by these groups to galvanise opposition to NGOs at local and national level.

A great deal of their hostility crystalised around the NGO focus on women and they called on all pious Muslim women to take a stand against 'our mothers and sisters who believe in Western civilization and follow the path of godlessness' (Shehabuddin 2008, p.202). The fatwa emerged as a new instrument in this effort. Once extremely rare, fatwas began to increase in number and frequency with the installation of the first BNP–Jamaat coalition. They were initially directed at individuals, mainly women. According to Ain o Shalish Kendra (ASK), a feminist law centre, fatwas were issued against around 200 women between 1993 and 2000 on grounds of immoral behaviour and led to their punishment by whipping and stoning. At least 18 committed suicide (Shehabuddin 2008, p.10).

Fatwas also were increasingly issued against NGOs. These were supported by Islamist-controlled national newspapers and magazines that published sensationalised news stories about the allegedly anti-Islamic activities of NGOs. Two central themes featured prominently in these stories – the alleged promotion of Christianity by NGOs and their corruption of women's morals (Naher 2006).[2] BRAC was accused of converting innocent children to Christianity by injecting turtle's blood into their bodies, of failing to teach Arabic in their schools, of preferential recruitment of non-Muslim teachers in order to promote Christianity, of timing their classes in the early morning when children studied Arabic at *madrassas* in the villages and of teaching the pupils songs and dances contrary to Islamic values. Mullahs expressed particular objections to the education received by girls and women, claiming that it was making them shameless, too knowledgeable about their own bodies and raising their awareness of 'un-Islamic' legal rights. Islamist groups attacked NGOs offering health and family planning services, denouncing their bicycle-riding female health visitors.

Microfinance organisations came under fire for the un-Islamic practice of charging interest on loans, making both the organisations and their borrowers guilty of dealing in *haram* money. According to one mullah, 'it would be hundred times more sinful for anyone to take loan from Grameen Bank than to have extra marital sex in holy Mecca' (Naher 2010, p.319). Verbal and written attacks were accompanied by physical actions. NGO schools were set on fire or prevented from opening, teachers were physical assaulted, teaching materials destroyed. *Imams* and *madrassa* teachers instructed parents to withdraw their children from NGO schools or face social ostracism (Hashmi 2000). Grameen Bank officials were attacked, its offices closed down. Pregnant women were prevented from accessing NGO health services on the grounds that they were being converted to Christianity and the offices of a women's health NGO were burnt down (Kabir 1996).

There was naturally a great deal of discussion within secular circles about what lay behind these attacks (Karim 2004; Riaz 2004; Shehabuddin 1999). Some put the blame on the elitist politics of the NGO sector. Karim (2004), for instance, saw the attacks as reflections of the fault line within society between a 'small coterie of Western educated urban elites who advocate women's rights, secularism and social justice' and a 'large rural population that is poor, illiterate, unemployed/underemployed' and had no voice in the nation-making project (p.301). NGOs were part of this coterie, engaged in pressing women from poor and illiterate rural masses into the service of the market economy, 'not as informed agents but as clients' (p.301). One of the reasons she cited for the hostility on the part of the rural clergy to the NGOs was that 'in the 1990s, BRAC, with support from its donors, began to lobby for the privatisation of rural primary education, which would bring rural education under NGO (and indirectly, donor) jurisdiction' (p.299). This was not, in fact, true.[3] What did appear to be the case is that both *madrassa* teachers and teachers from mainstream government schools saw themselves in direct competition with BRAC schools for students (Naher 2006, p.170).

Others believed that the attacks were a manifestation of a wider antagonism on the part of conservative forces in society towards various changes they saw as threats to the traditional order. These included government initiatives to reform *madrassa* education and to improve female literacy and increase their political participation, as well as the private sector's export factories, which encouraged women workers to display themselves on the streets, satellite television and various forms of new media that broadcast risqué films from Bollywood. In fact, the anti-NGO campaign followed a more general pattern of verbal attacks on secular and radical writers, journalists and intellectuals in which women – from female garment workers generally to individuals such as the outspoken feminist writer Taslima Nasreen – were particular targets (Naher 2010).

The attacks on the NGOs reflected the very specific power dynamics of the rural communities. They were orchestrated by a coalition of those sections of the rural power structure – mullahs, *matabors* and *mahajans* – who felt their position in the social order was under direct threat from NGO activities. Rural mullahs played a leading role in the coalition. They were paid by the village elite and hence beholden to it. Their purported knowledge of Islamic laws and their power to issue fatwas in turn provided legitimacy to the actions of the rural elite. Mullahs controlled the unregistered *madrassa* system and could rely on support of its students. BRAC's informal schools were seen as a direct threat to their incomes and their ideologies.

The *mahajans* (moneylenders) found their business undermined by microcredit programmes. They continued to charge exorbitant rates to the very poorest, who were excluded from microfinance services, but large sections of their previous clientele now borrowed primarily from NGOs (Berg, Emran and Shilpi 2013). Interestingly, while mullahs were loud in their denunciations of microcredit NGOs for the un-Islamic practice of charging interest, they maintained a deafening silence about the traditional *majahan* system despite its far more exploitative interest rates and lending practices (Naher 2010, p.320). Indeed, Naher found a number of *madrassa* teachers were involved in moneylending as an additional source of income.

And as noted in Chapter 7, village *matabors* had lost their pool of captive female wage labour as a result of the opportunities promoted by the NGO sector. As poorer women used NGO loans to withdraw into self-employment and those who continued in wage work bargained for higher wages, the rural elite began to find it harder to find cheap female labour to work in their homes and fields.

There was one other important factor at play (Naher 2010). The promotion of women's participation in rural development activities was an issue on which the views of significant sections of men from different classes tended to converge. The reasons were not difficult to find. As Siddiqi (1996) observes,

> regardless of the degree of their success, NGOs have become a powerful symbol of change in the domain of gender relations. Their intensive activities have opened up new spaces for mobilizing women, making them literally more visible, and offering possible alternatives to lives circumscribed by existing structures of domination. (pp.216–17)

In a climate of general anxiety over the ways in which development activities were seen to be weakening male authority over women in the villages of Bangladesh, the mullahs found a cause that could mobilise large numbers of people against NGOs, amplifying and legitimising patriarchal grievance through the use of Islamic rhetoric.

8.3 Constructing the pious female subject

Islamist groups recognised from the outset that education was an important site for the construction of devout Islamic citizens but were somewhat late in recognising its importance for the construction of the pious female subject. This changed with the nationwide adoption in 1994 of the female secondary school stipend in government schools, including registered *madrassas*, and the dramatic expansion that took place in secondary-level *madrassa* education for girls (Asadullah and Chaudhury 2008). Studies suggest that religious education had an impact on attitudes. Students from *madrassa* schools, both male and female, were more likely than those from government secondary schools to express unfavourable attitudes towards women's intelligence and political abilities and to prioritise higher education for boys (Asadullah, Savoia and Mahmud 2019). And female students from registered *madrassas* were more likely than those from government secondary schools to favour Islamic rule, to believe in the primacy of the male breadwinning role, to attach greater importance of higher education for boys than girls and to prefer large numbers of children (Asadullah and Chaudhury 2010).

But a more widespread effort to construct the pious female subject took the form of women-only Quranic study circles or *taleem* classes, which were held at neighbourhood and village levels. Some were organised by religious parties like Jamaat and some by popular piety movements such as Tablighi Jamaat, while others were organised by individual women who were recognised to have knowledge of Quranic teachings but did not have any explicit organisational affiliation. This diversity in the organisation of *taleem* classes meant that they could not be seen as part of a planned political agenda. At the same time, it was significant that these groups began to proliferate in the early 2000s, after it became clear that Islamist political parties were not making much headway with women voters, that the co-ordinated attacks on NGOs had petered out without significantly eroding women's NGO membership and that Jamaat had been forced to publicly acknowledge NGOs as legitimate development partners. *Taleem* classes offered a quieter and more promising vehicle for spreading Islamic values among women from different classes and across the urban–rural divide.

What was taught in these classes varied according to whether they were intended as part of the Islamic state building agenda or as part of a spiritual agenda of self-purification, but they shared a common core goal: to cultivate the 'correct' understanding of Islam among participants and to promote the model of gender roles sanctioned by Quranic texts.[4]

Qualitative studies of *taleem* classes have analysed the interactions between teachers and students. One of these is Samia Huq's insightful study of *taleem* classes organised in an affluent suburb of Dhaka by a devout teacher who was not affiliated to any political party (2011). The educated middle-class women who attended these classes expressed beliefs that seemed common to a range of these classes, regardless of who organised them. They believed that the Islam practised in Bangladesh had been corrupted by its Sufi origins and assimilation of local, including Hindu, beliefs and needed to be stripped down to its authentic core. They agreed that *purdah* was 'one of *the* most important practices to adopt if one truly desires piety' (p.230, author's italics), a significant marker of whether goals of piety have been attained. They subscribed to a rigid interpretation of the veil as full covering of head and body: 'they did not grant themselves any leniency in interpretation' (p.231).

They expressed their support for complementarity in gender relations as prescribed in the Quran rather than the equal rights argued for by feminist and women's groups in Bangladesh, the 'liberal torchbearers of change' (p.294). They were taught that the Western liberal belief that women should confront men head on had given rise to a battle of the sexes in which marriages frequently ended in divorce. *Taleem* participants were advised instead of the importance of acting in ways that men always retained their sense of authority, of wielding their power 'calculatingly and strategically in such a way that the man does not realize that he is being worked on' (p.221).

There was a great deal of discussion of religious texts in these classes but not a great deal of dissent – with one memorable exception. It related to the *taleem apa*'s explanation of Islam's position on polygamy. Islam, she said, recognised that men were naturally polygamous, they had greater sexual needs than women. If a wife was not willing or able to satisfy her husband, it was better that he took other women as wives so that they had a respected status in society rather than treating them as mistresses, condemning them to hell-fire.[5] This religious sanction of what many of the urban, educated and affluent women who attended these classes saw as lewd male behaviour left them in state of 'shell shock' (p.314). It seemed to have been the only time they expressed reservations about what they were being taught.

Studies of *taleem* classes by other feminist scholars generally recognise Huq's point that the women who attend them often experienced a sense of inner fulfilment from the knowledge that they were following a righteous path. There was less consensus on her view that these classes 'empowered' women. According to Huq, empowerment did not require women to 'cry out loud for an overthrow of all existing structures, systems and relations' (p.221), a view she attributed to secular-liberal feminists. Instead, changes in women's 'suffering from subordination' could come about through indirect challenges and the gradual reconfiguration of existing roles and relations (pp.43–44). Such indirect challenges and gradual reconfigurations have, of course, been the stuff of the processes of social change documented in earlier chapters of this book, memorably captured in Monowara's sage observation back in 1987 that a smart woman did not show her power (see Chapter 7), but they were not motivated by the teachings of the *taleem* teachers. Instead, for most women, they were born out of the direct experience of the costs of dependency and the unfairness of real-life 'complementarity'.

Critical scholars have also noted the limited range of texts that students were given to read in *taleem* classes, regardless of who organised them, and the limited space allowed for interrogating what they were taught (Gardener 1998; Hussain 2010; Rozario 2006). There was little scope for developing the kind of critical consciousness that would allow them to question what was 'given' in religious texts and to reconfigure those aspects of ascribed roles and relations that they found to be unjust. Indeed, it was unlikely that such questioning would be encouraged. Maimuna Huq (2008), who attended *taleem* classes conducted by Jamaat's women's wing, concluded that their aim was not the construction of Islamic intellectuals, the diversification of Islamic thought or the promotion of independent reasoning. It was rather the creation of a body of committed followers capable of convincing others to join the Jamaat project. While this political motivation may have been absent from other forms of *taleem* classes, they shared the common aim of creating a following of the faithful who could spread what they defined as the authentic message of Islam to the rest of the population.

Two aspects stand out in these studies of *taleem* classes. One is the emphasis on fear, the constant warnings about the divine retribution that awaited those who deviated from the path of righteousness, versions of the bed of fire that Jamaat promised awaited those who failed to vote for them. The *taleem* preacher discussed in Samia Huq's study drew on vivid imagery to make more real to her listeners the horrors of hell that awaited those that did not follow the true path:

> How will we drink boiling water in Hell when it's so difficult for us to bear the summer heat in this world? How restless we become when there is no electricity and hence no fan even for the briefest of periods! How painful the slightest burn can be. And yet, hellfire will be so many times more intense than this earthly fire. (Huq 2008, p.475)

For ordinary village women as well, *taleem* classes on the rules to be followed by devout Muslims were accompanied by efforts to instil fear if they were not followed. According to Hafiza Bibi, a young woman who was interviewed as part of our LSE/BIGD study,

> There are rules for everything – whether you are walking, eating or sleeping. There are prayers for when you get out of the house, board a vehicle, eat, go somewhere. You have to say your prayers, fast, recite the Quran in the morning, cover your head, go about in a way that you don't look into a man's eyes. Be careful women! You should buy and read the book called 'Why don't women stay within *purdah*'. You will feel as if Azrael has come to your door. If I read it at night, I feel scared going from this room to that one. (Fieldwork, Comilla, 2014)

The use of fear to recruit people to the righteous path meshes, as White (2012) points out, more easily with critiques of religion as a form of ideological domination than as a pathway to women's empowerment. Nor does it sit easily with the more tolerant understanding of religion that many people in Bangladesh continue to subscribe to. Kanta, a young woman in Samia Huq's study explained her reluctance to attend *taleem* classes:

> I suppose what puts me off is that they believe that they're better, and that's arrogant. After all, it's up to God to judge who He favours and why. We really shouldn't worry about that … And I don't really want to be frightened into connecting with God. (2011, p.331)

The other feature that stands out is the extent to which these classes, and the Islamist agenda more generally, embodied a form of 'cultural *jihad*', the determination to uproot local practices considered to be antithetical to purist Islam. *Taleem* classes were an effective vehicle for taking this cultural *jihad* to women from different sections of society. The religious rules that Hafiza Moni was pointing to were attempts to teach participants the correct way to express their devotion to God. Learning the correct way meant unlearning the incorrect ways of the past.

These included long-standing religious rituals followed by Bengali Muslims: *milad mahfils*, where people met to engage in religious prayer and song to mark special occasions; visiting of shrines and seeking guidance from pirs; and holding *qul khani*, a mourning ceremony 40 days after a death. They included long-standing cultural practices: elaborate wedding ceremonies marked by various rituals, folk and Sufi music festivals and the celebration of the Bengali New Year with flowers, dances and song. They also included modern day cultural practices, watching soaps on TV or films or listening to popular songs and music on the radio, since all were fraught with the danger of exposure to a polluted world (Rozario 2006). The quote at the start of this chapter summarises the attitudes of *taleem* participants in Samia Huq's study, who dismissed 'their mothers, grandmothers and women before them' whose failure to separate out their religious practices from local cultural conventions meant theirs had been merely a 'cultural Islam'.

8.4 Grassroots responses to the rise of orthodoxy

I want to turn now to what various studies tell us about women's responses to the contradictory forces of 'religion' on the one hand, as represented, for instance, by the politics of Jamaat and *taleem* classes, and of 'secularism' on the other, as represented, for instance, by NGOs and feminist organisations. The strongest support for the Islamist agenda in the countryside tended to come from women from elite rural families, those whose material conditions made it possible for them to follow its strict prescriptions (Gardener 1998; Shehabuddin 2008). Their ability to embrace the new Islamist practices reinforced the older traditions that had positioned them as bearers of honour and status in their families, engaging in forms of behaviour that could not be easily adopted by those from less privileged backgrounds.[6]

The Islamist agenda was also frequently supported by women somewhat lower down the status hierarchy who sought to emulate elite notions of propriety in order to distinguish themselves from those even lower down. They attended *taleem* classes and adopted new forms of veiling and other visible signs of the new orthodoxy. They also sought to keep their distance from NGOs, a distance they could afford because of the regularity of male earnings in their households. Their aloofness sometimes expressed a religious opposition to microfinance but also, quite often, status considerations: As one said, 'I have not fallen so low that I would degrade myself by parading in front of strangers from other districts, doing physical drills and loudly chanting slogans about Grameen Bank' (Shehabuddin 2008, p.147).

But there were also large numbers of women from mainly poor households whose views about NGOs and religion were likely to vary a great deal from those better off than themselves and possibly from each other but whose limited livelihood opportunities meant that they benefited considerably from NGO activities. Their refusal to succumb to the overtures of the Islamic parties or be cowed by the attacks on NGOs suggested that they did not necessarily subscribe to the values that inspired the Islamist agenda. Equally, however, their continued membership of NGOs did not imply that they had turned their back on religion – as the Islamists maintained or secularists might claim. As the quote from Shehabuddin at the beginning of this chapter put it, poor rural women were anxious to improve their lives in this world and to ensure a good *akhirat* (afterlife). They had to find a way of keeping on the right side of those in power in their locality without jeopardising their access to services and opportunities provided by NGOs but they also looked to spiritual concerns for their afterlife.

Women had made up nearly half of the 75% voter turnout for the elections in 1996 and 2001, so it was clear that they played an important role in the defeat of the Islamic parties. Why had so many of the women who voted, who said that they prayed, fasted, read the Quran regularly, conformed to notions of *purdah* and female modesty and generally saw themselves as good Muslims, failed to support Jamaat when it presented itself as the standard-bearer of these practices? This was the question that Shehabuddin (2008) set out to answer.

She notes that an informal survey carried out by ASK after the 1996 elections into the voting behaviour of women in different parts of the country found that 95% reported that they had not voted for Jamaat. Their reasons included pre-existing loyalties to other parties, obedience to husbands' instructions, scepticism about Jamaat's chances of winning and dislike of their local candidate but the overwhelming reason appeared to be that they were not prepared to support a party who clearly believed in women's inferiority, constantly found fault with them, and refused to field women candidates in elections.

One woman pointed out that Jamaat might condemn dowry as an un-Islamic practice, but it simultaneously blamed women for its rise. It claimed that women had cheapened themselves through their immodest behaviour in the public domain so that men's natural attraction to women had been transformed into repulsion; dowry had replaced the Islamic practice of *mohrana* as a payment to persuade men to marry them.

There was also fear that a Jamaat victory would take away women's option of deciding for themselves how they chose to follow Islam. In an Islamic state, as they understood it, religion would no longer be left to an individual's personal judgement but would be dictated from above. As one declared, 'The Jamaat? I will never vote for them. My religion is my business' (Shehabuddin 2008, p.184).

Finally, most women, and many men, were concerned that Jamaat would impose codes of conduct and dress that would make it impossible for women to work for a living outside the home. For all their efforts to appeal to women voters and to uphold the spiritual equality of men and women, Jamaat continued to insist on a strict form of *purdah* as the most important marker of authentic Islam, advocating restrictions on women working alongside men as they did in the garment factories and in NGOs, the two largest and most visible employers of women in the country. Its counter proposals to offer interest-free loans for home-based enterprise, to train women in income-generating skills and to uphold the payment of *mohrana* to prevent divorced women from sliding into poverty fell far short of the support that women thought they needed.

Consequently, poorer rural women had little interest in a party that would take away the few freedoms they had won. One woman interviewed in the ASK study said:

> If the Jamaat comes to power, they'll say that I can't leave my house anymore to earn a living. Who's going to feed my children and me then? I'll tell you this: none of those people who are so concerned about purdah now will rush forward to feed me. (Shehabuddin 2008, p.184)

However, as Shehabuddin notes, this scepticism about Jamaat's agenda was expressed in the privacy of the ballot box rather than openly in the public domain. A Jamaat activist had explained to her how Jamaat sought to influence rural female voters:

> We tell them that this world does not matter, that it is the next one that counts, that goes on forever. And if you do not behave as you should here, you will have to pay the price when you face God on the Last Day. Does a mother not reprimand an unruly child? Similarly, God punishes those who break His rules. In hell, one is made to lie down on a bed of fire and then covered with a blanket of fire. One cries out for it to end, but one does not die there. This continues forever. (p.200)

Shehabuddin inquired whether this method of communication had proved successful. The Jamaat activist shook her head and lamented, 'The village women usually sit at our meetings and nod in agreement with everything we say. But then they leave and forget it all!' (p.201).

This low-key, non-confrontational response by poor rural women to the efforts of Islamist parties also characterised their responses to Islamist attacks on their NGOs. The practicalities of earning a living and caring for their children were at the forefront of their willingness to defend their NGO affiliation. In fieldwork carried out in 2006, White (2012) noted how NGO credit had become a routine practice in the local economy, just one option among others in helping families get by. Shehabuddin suggests that the NGO experience had made many women more articulate and self-confident, participating in, and even running, regular meetings, conversing with strangers and managing their own small businesses.

But few NGOs took a collective stand against the Islamist attacks and few sought to build women's capacity to take collective action on their own behalf.

Most left their members to work out their own responses. Naher's research in the village of Miyapur in the late 1990s describes some of these responses (2006). One was to investigate for themselves the veracity of the anti-Islamic accusations being levelled at NGOs. They solicited the views of relatives more educated than themselves, asked high school students to read them BRAC's education texts and used their position on BRAC school committees to make their own assessments. They found little to support the accusations. Another was to persuade NGOs to change those aspects of their practices that appeared to draw particular hostility. BRAC, for instance, dropped elements of its 'joyful education' programme, such as clapping hands, singing and dancing, requested girls to cover their heads when they came to school and started offering weekly classes in Arabic. Grameen Bank members gave up the performance of physical exercises at the start of group meetings.

There were also examples of women drawing on their cultural repertoires to frame dissent, using the resourcefulness familiar from previous chapters. They argued that NGO officials were like members of their own family who (depending on age difference) addressed them as their sisters or aunts. They emphasised their own virtuous behaviour:

> We directly go to the centre to attend weekly meetings and for money transactions, and then come back to our homes. We do not talk to any male strangers on the way, neither do we spend time with the *sir* gossiping. (Naher 2010, p.322)

They stressed the pains they took to dress with modesty: wearing the *burqa* if they could afford it or covering themselves in other ways if they could not.

Several invoked the terms of the patriarchal bargain to justify their actions. They had been 'sent' to take loans by their husbands or they had only done so with family's permission. If such activities were now regarded as un-Islamic, the moral responsibility lay with household patriarchs, not with them. Most were supported by men in their households as few men wanted their wives to give up NGO membership or their daughters to lose out on educational opportunities. In Naher's study village, a group of fathers kept watch over the local school at night to protect it from attacks.

Women also pointed to the failure of the 'moral' community to give them the protection and provision embedded in the Islamic patriarchal bargain. One woman's rejoinder to a mullah critical of her membership of Grameen Bank was that she would never have taken a loan if she had got financial support from virtuous Muslims like him (Naher 2010, p.321). Another expressed her anger at a community that was ready to criticise but not to help:

> People said a lot of things when we first took money from the Grameen Bank – that we are becoming Christian, that we were losing our religion. If we are, then we must. When have they ever lent us ten takas? We must do what we can to survive. Sometimes they

say these things because they are afraid that the poor will become rich. (Shehabuddin 2008, p.145)

They levelled accusations about the double standards of religious leaders similar to those women had been making in the 1970s: 'When the female members from rich households go to town for shopping or to watch the cinema, nobody says anything about them. Mullahs always speak against the poor people' (Naher 2010, p.322).

8.5 Building a culture of rights: the radical NGO sector

The mainstream NGO sector was largely focused on service provision, primarily microfinance. Building the organisational capacity was not among their aims and without such capacity, it was not surprising that their members adopted non-confrontational responses to the Islamist attacks on their organisations – but there were exceptions. Shehabuddin (1999) describes one of them:

> At a waaz mahfils in November 1995, in the village of Chaita, Jama'at leader Abdur Rahman Azadi began, 'Today I will not talk of Allah but of NGOs … I have burnt many schools of BRAC.' His tirade, however, was directed at another NGO, Saptagram, which ran an adult-literacy program for women using a unique gender-sensitive syllabus. 'Saptagram is conducting un-Islamic activities. They are forming cooperatives with women. They are educating women but not men; they are making women immoral. The books used by Saptagram talk of divorce and dowry and include anti-Islamic teachings—these will turn people into Christians and send them straight to hell.' He referred to the largely female staff of Saptagram as 'the offspring of traitors and dogs,' who deserved to be tied up with a rope and their tongues cut off. When village women involved with Saptagram heard about this waaz, they banded together, brooms in hand, and confronted Azadi. They warned him, 'In your next waaz, talk about Islam only, do not say such filthy things about women. If you do this again, we will beat you with our brooms.' (pp.162–63)

Saptagram was part of the radical NGO subsector referred to in Chapter 5 that had eschewed a service delivery role in favour of building the collective capacity of the poor. McCarthy (1993) provides early examples, drawn from the 1980s, of the kinds of collective actions being undertaken by members of these organisations: women from a Nijera Kori (NK) group who took on the local landlord and his muscle men who were trying to close their group down; Saptagram groups working on the Integrated Rural Works Programme who marched on the district commissioner's office when they found they were being cheated of their wages by programme officials; and Proshika's groups, which banded together to confront violent husbands in their community.

These were isolated examples. Other studies carried out more in-depth analysis of these organisations, highlighting key elements of their approach and what they were able to achieve (Devine 2002; Kramsjo and Wood 1992; Paprocki 2021; Westergaard 1994). A few, like Saptagram, worked primarily with women, but the majority worked with both men and women. As I noted in Chapter 5, most had started in the 1970s, part of the country's 'liberation dividend', inspired by the values of the struggle for independence to frame their vision of social justice. They used regular savings by their members and weekly meetings as the basis of group formation but the primary emphasis from the beginning was on challenging the collective habitus through popular education, drawing on variations of Freire's pedagogy of the oppressed (1972) along with theatre, role plays, songs and storytelling to promote a critical consciousness among their groups and the collective capacity to fight for their rights.

Over the years I have carried out my own studies of this sector, using both surveys and qualitative research in order to both quantify and to understand the kinds of changes their members believed had been brought about in their own lives and within their communities (Kabeer and Haq Kabir 2009; Kabeer and Huq 2014; Kabeer and Matin 2005; Kabeer and Sulaiman 2015; Kabeer et al. 2012). The survey results suggest that members of these organisations had greater awareness of their constitutional rights than others in their community, including those belonging to mainstream NGOs; were frequently called on for advice by others in the community; interacted routinely with elected officials; were more likely to vote, campaign and stand during local elections; were more likely to be elected to village committees; and were more likely to be called on to participate in *shalish* called by local elites or by the *upazila* chairman but also to hold their own *shalish*. Both men and women from these organisations engaged in collective action and protests around a variety of issues, including the unfair distribution of public goods, rights to *khas* land promised by the government, bargaining for fairer wages and, most frequently, violence against women. Finally, they were more likely to believe that the quality of justice had improved over recent years.

Qualitative research provides insights into changes in consciousness that had been brought about by their membership experiences. According to Ibrahim, his years with NK had allowed him to imagine a radically different vision of society – and a radically different future for himself. His father had been a sharecropper, he himself had been a sharecropper and he believed that this was the preordained order of things: those who had assets would remain rich, the poor would remain poor. But through his membership he had learnt that the wealth of the country belonged to its people and that their fundamental rights as citizens were written into the constitution. He no longer looked to the landlord for support and advice but to his organisation (Kabeer and Haq Kabir 2009).

A similar shift occurred in Nilu Begum's thinking. She had grown up accepting her preordained fate as a woman, an early marriage and a life that revolved entirely around her husband and household: 'I have seen my grandmother, my mother and my aunts, they all did the same'. But she found herself changing through her membership of NK: 'I am an illiterate woman, so was my mother. But I have dreams for my children which my mother never had for us' (Kabeer 2011, p.336). She had not been able to send her older son and daughter to school but was determined to educate her youngest daughter till college level.

According to Rasheda, Saptagram had taught her the most important lessons of her life: how to mix with people, how to sign her own name, how to stand on her own feet and the value of unity. She had learnt that she had the same rights as her husband:

> I didn't get rights earlier and I cannot say that I get them all even now. But at least I now know what they are and I can teach my children … If I didn't know that we have a right to my father's property, then I wouldn't have been able to get it from my brothers … Whether I get my rights or not, I can still demand them. (Kabeer and Huq 2014, pp.262–63)

Nasima related how her participation in the struggle by NK groups for the rights of the landless to government *khas* land had crystallised her own thinking about women's land rights. She recalled how her grandfather had willed his 30 *bighas* of land to his two sons, thereby depriving his daughters, including her mother: 'In a case where a father can deprive his daughters, what are the guarantees that a husband would not do the same to his wife?' (Kabeer 2011, p.515).

The *khas* land allocated to her household by the government had been registered in her husband's name, but if the opportunity arose again she would insist that it was jointly registered. In the meanwhile, she had managed to persuade her own father to write half of any land he had acquired over his own lifetime in his wife's name:

> My father did not agree at first, though I have only one brother. But both my mother and my father have been toiling hard and so any land he buys from their income should be shared with my mother. My father is a very peaceful, simple man. If a person like him does not easily want to surrender any ownership to his wife, what will other men do? (Kabeer 2011, p.516)

These struggles also opened men's eyes to the discrimination that they themselves had practised. Abdur Rahman said:

> Before joining Samata, I hardly recognized women's roles. We really had no idea that women worked as hard as we did in running the

family. Now I realize that our family is a result of our joint effort. When we received two bighas of land in 1994, it was in both our names ... because I now believe that land should be allotted jointly in the name of both husband and wife. (Kabeer 2011, p.516)

These organisations never achieved the mass membership of the mainstream microfinance organisations and most had begun to disappear by the late 1990s for a variety of reasons, including internal mismanagement, the inability to scale up their operations and the decision by some to prioritise microfinance under pressure from donors to become financially sustainable. The NGO sector is now dominated almost entirely by microfinance organisations, with the exception of Nijera Kori, though BRAC continues to offer legal education (Lewis 2017). Despite their disappearance, radical NGOs are part of the paradox story. They were not able to bring about the transformation of society they had sought, but their achievements were proof that there was nothing inherent within the local culture that made it impermeable to 'secular' ideas about justice and human rights. These could be seen as perfectly compatible with religious beliefs as long as religion was not defined in orthodox and exclusionary terms.

8.6 Interrogating the veil

Beyond the intense contestations about women's place in society that were being conducted in the political arena and within civil society, ordinary men and women were enacting their own interpretations about the right and proper ways to conduct themselves as they went about their daily lives – interpretations that were by no means homogenous. I want to continue my exploration of conflicting ideas about female virtue, this time through an examination of an aspect of everyday life that had become very central to these contestations: how women dressed in the public domain.

This has, of course, been a perennial preoccupation within Bangladesh society. Traditionally, a woman covered her heads with the *anchal* of her sari in deference to the norm of female modesty. The *burqa* was imported into the country some 50 or more years before liberation by those who had gone on *hajj* (pilgrimage), but it was confined to women from more affluent conservative families as a signal of their status (McCarthy 1967). There was a period after liberation when it was generally believed that the observance of *purdah* was declining because of poverty, the need for many more women to work and because increased education was leading to new ways of thinking and behaving. Women from respectable households continued to cover themselves, but the additional clothing represented by the *burqa* remained a minority practice.

As a result, Siddiqi (1996) was able to observe in a study in the early 1990s that Bangladesh had not been characterised by a 'return to the veil', the phenomenon evident in a number of countries in the Middle East where large numbers of women were voluntarily adopting full veiling in protest against excesses of consumerism and westernisation. 'Nor,' she added, 'is the veil itself a central subject of political discourse and contestation' (p.143).

This began to change some years later as a very visible increase in veiling, and a proliferation in the forms it took, began to take place across the country. It is not easy to pinpoint exactly when this began but a comparison of narratives by different generations of women (or even different cohorts of siblings within the same family) in fieldwork carried out in 2010 suggests that it coincided with the spread of *taleem* classes across the country, in other words in the early 2000s. So one interpretation of the rise in veiling was that it signified a growing adherence to Islamic orthodoxy, and that *taleem* classes with their focus on everyday practices had succeeded in promoting a degree of modesty on the part of Bangladesh's women that the Islamist political forces had failed to enforce.

This was the interpretation offered, for instance, by Samia Huq on the basis of her study of *taleem* participants. She found that 'most women covered first and foremost out of religious obligation' (2011, p.233). It marked them out as women who were striving towards piety. But, of course, her study was based on a highly selective sample of affluent, educated and urban women. In a population the size of Bangladesh in which large numbers of women were opting for the veil, it was highly unlikely that any single motivation could explain the trend.

In exploring some of the different meanings and practices associated with veiling by women from different walks of life, I will draw on the secondary literature, but my main source will be the 2008 IDS/BIGD survey and qualitative interviews carried out between 2014 and 2017, supplemented with information from the 2015 LSE/BIGD survey (Appendix 1). Table 8a in Appendix 5 provides information on changes in veiling practices for different age groups of women in 2008 and then followed up in 2015.[7]

In 2008, the percentages of women saying they always veiled themselves when they left the house and the percentages saying they never veiled themselves was evenly divided for the different age groups. By 2015, a much higher percentage of the same women, particularly in the younger age groups, reported that they always veiled themselves when they left the house and far fewer reported never veiling. Though not shown in the table, women who belonged to NGOs were as likely to veil as those who did not. The surveys did not distinguish between different kinds of veiling, nor did they ask about the reasons for veiling. For this, I will draw mainly on qualitative research that was carried out with 80 women from four study districts carried out in 2014 as part of the LSE/BIGD study.

The meanings that emerged from this research had cultural as well as religious dimensions. Cultural interpretations expressed concerns with gender propriety and social status, with men's ability to act as breadwinners and guardians of family honour and the need for women to behave in a seemly manner in the public domain to uphold the family's standing in the community. These concerns could be found in Hindu households as well, emphasising the fact that they cut across religious boundaries.

By contrast, religious interpretations sought conformity to Islamic norms of female piety. These had been undergoing considerable change in recent times through efforts to promote the more 'authentic' forms of veiling associated with the rise of orthodox Islam. The practice of veiling now included the customary covering of the head with a sari or the traditional *burqa* but also variations of veiling imported from the Middle East, the *abaya* (a long outer garment or cloak worn over normal clothes), combined with the *hijab*, a scarf which completely covered the head and, often, the *niqab*, which covered the face. Many *taleem* teachers also encouraged additional items, such as gloves, socks and even dark glasses for more effective covering.

Religious interpretations of *purdah* emphasised differences between religious communities. Those who subscribed to them disapproved of Hindu women who were willing to move around in the public domain without fully covering themselves but they disapproved equally of Muslim women who did not abide by strict *purdah* norms. Hindu women, in turn, were bemused by the preoccupation with ever-increasing forms of veiling among Muslims. Radha Rani, for instance, believed it was important for women to cover their heads in public or men would stare at their breasts but did not see the point of some of the new forms of covering that women were wearing: 'They look like banana trees' (Fieldwork, 2014, Comilla).

Both interpretations of *purdah* encouraged women to stay within the home and imposed restrictions on their mobility and conduct in the public domain so that the distinction between them was not always clear-cut. Indeed, the same person could articulate both versions, weaving them together seamlessly in her account. Consequently, while the more extreme forms of veiling (socks, gloves, dark glasses) could generally be taken to signify strict adherence to religious norms, the explanations given by other women suggested that a somewhat fluid and diverse set of meanings and motivations characterised other ostensibly similar practices, in line with the diversity of ways in which women practised Islam.

Veiling, piety, and status

Let me begin with women who said that they wore full veiling when they went out, either the traditional *burqa* or the new *abaya–hijab*, very often with the addition of face covering, socks, gloves and perhaps sunglasses. Women who regularly attended *taleem* classes – the affluent suburban women in Haq's study, as well as most *taleem* participants interviewed by Huq and Khondaker (2011) and by Rozario (2006) – were in this category and subscribed to strict religious views about female piety.

Some of the rural women in the LSE/BIGD study also fell into this category. Jahura (Comilla) said that not only did she cover herself fully every

time she stepped out of the house but she only ever left the house for a limited number of reasons, to go to the doctor or visit her daughters. Lutfa (Comilla) lived with her in-laws, a very religious family. Her husband worked in Oman. He had sent her a *burqa* and she wore it whenever she went out, adding an *orna* (long scarf) over her head and a mask over her face (*niqab*). Her sisters-in-law also wore gloves and socks but she herself did not because 'it was too hot'.

Full veiling on grounds of piety was not confined to better-off women. A number of garment workers reported that they wore a *burqa* to and from the factory, expressed their appreciation of employers who made provision for workers to pray and said that they attended *taleem* classes in their neighbourhood whenever possible.

A feature that recurred frequently in the narratives of these women was their disapproval of 'improper' forms of veiling. According to Jahura, standards of morality had deteriorated considerably:

> In the past, our mother and aunts would wear 18-feet long saree, they would wear it in a way that their body and head was fully covered. But today's women can't cover themselves well even if you provide them 21-feet long saree.

Najma (Narayanganj) expressed similar disapproval and took it on herself to reprove others:

> Everyone wears a *burqa* these days, but no one wears it the way it should be worn. Some wear a *burqa* but behave in the worst possible way. They are giving those who wear a *burqa* a bad name. You are supposed to wear it to cover your dignity and your honour (*izzat*) so that no man gets to see you, your beauty … I love wearing the *burqa*. Sometimes I stop people on the road and say that you haven't worn the *burqa* properly. Your head may be covered, but the outline of your body is showing.

There was also a number of women in this category whose motives for full veiling were a mixture of religious beliefs and status concerns. Nushat from Comilla, for instance, said she wore a *burqa* to ensure her face and body were covered: 'Wearing *burqa*, *hijab* has increased because it is beneficial in terms of Islam, it guards against sinning.' But she added:

> People criticize anyone who goes out without wearing one. A daughter-in-law of a reputed family can't go around casually. People might say, 'That Member's wife wasn't wearing a Burqa when going out.'[8]

Veiling, poverty and work

The majority of those who said that they did not veil were from poorer households. This did not mean that they rejected veiling. Some yearned to be in a position to adopt the veil, combining the desire for piety with the protected life associated with the ability to observe *purdah*. A domestic worker spoke of her regret that her need to work made it impossible for her to avoid sin by observing *purdah*. She would have liked to hide away from everyone's sight so that she could claim a pious life on judgement day but she had to earn to support herself and her children.

But Hafiza (Tangail), who had been to *taleem* classes in her village, did not see how injunctions about the veil applied to her:

> These instructions are given to us who work but the *taleem apa* does not have to work so she does not understand ... If you have to feed yourself by working, then you cannot wear *burqa*. They tell us what we have to do, we comply as much as we can ... But I raise cows, if my cow runs out of the house or my goat escapes, then I have to go out and catch them, with or without a *burqa*. What we can observe, we observe, what we can't, we can't.

Others, like Shirin (Chapainababganj), expressed anger at those who defined piety in ways that were out of reach for women like herself whose husbands had remarried and who had to work as wage labour to earn their own living:

> They tell us about the right way to live our lives, to observe *purdah*, to wear *burqa* when going out, they discuss the *hadith* and Quran. They talk about the religious restrictions on women regarding going outside and working. But women of poor families have to work for their survival ... They may forbid poor women to go outside, but will that hold them back? ... After all, those women at *taleem* meetings will not help a poor woman with even 10 takas, will they?

Purdah of the mind

As noted, many of the women who subscribed to orthodox views about veiling expressed their disapproval of the ways that others chose to veil. It was their view that veiling did not count as virtue if it was not done with virtuous intent. A version of this view was, interestingly, also subscribed to by women who chose not to veil. They argued that the veil signified very little; it was possible, even easier, to engage in immoral activities while fully veiled. A version of this argument was put forward by Mochona (Comilla):

> *Taleem* is within yourself ... You can find out things by reading a book and looking it up on the internet. In the *taleem* classes they

tell you to pray and fast, remain within *purdah*, wear a *burqa*, recite your prayers. But you can carry out robbery wearing a *burqa* … A man can enter an empty house wearing a *burqa*. Would I be able to recognize him if he is wearing a *burqa* and covering his face?

These women did not reject the idea of *purdah* but by defining it as state of mind, as purity of thought and intention, something they carried inside them rather than an expensive outer garment, they defined themselves as pious Muslims even as they went about their daily business in the public domain (Rozario 2006). I discussed versions of this in Chapter 7.

Also within this group were a number of women who were extremely devout in their religious practices but followed Sufi *pirs* and were satisfied that their own efforts at modesty were sufficient. Rubina (Chapainababganj) had left her husband when he took a second wife. Since then she had been earning her own living selling snacks in a small stall by the ferry. She was a devout follower of the Atroshi Pir, the holy man of Faridpur. She actively recruited disciples for him and regularly attended his classes. She was taught about prayer and fasting, the need to put on the veil, what prayers to say before igniting the stove, and all about *tariqat, shariat, marfat*.[9] She wore a *burqa* when she went to Atroshi, but otherwise a sari and a scarf around her head: 'People who know how to cover their body well with their sari don't need to wear a *burqa*.'

Fashion *burqa*

The pious women in our study reserved their most scathing criticism for those who treated the veil as a form of fashion. In the view of Rekha (Bagerhat),

It is the new fashion now. People wear tight-fitting burqas. They are available in multiple colours, different collar and sleeve styles. But they don't cover their face so what's the point of wearing *burqa* anyway?

Momena (Bagerhat) was also disapproving: 'In the old days you could not tell a woman's age or the shape of her body when she veiled.'

These criticisms had validity. For some of the younger generation, veiling had indeed become part of fashion rather than an expression of piety. In place of the standard loose, tent-like black *burqa* that had been the old way of full veiling, these women wore many different styles and colours.[10] As Hussain (2010) observes,

During my study women argued that as a result of cultural flows from abroad, modern westernized women are accepting jeans and shirt as a style from the West, while modern Muslim women are accepting *hijab* as a fashion from the Middle Eastern countries. (p.326)

Joya (Narayanganj) was of the opinion that women wore *burqas* to look beautiful: 'There are so many fashionable burqas now and many designs. My daughters and granddaughters have bought them because they look beautiful.' Marufa, who worked as a tailor in Narayanganj, reported an increase in the number of orders for 'fashion' *burqas* she was getting from young women:

> In fact, it has become the new shalwar kameez. Take for instance, my daughter – she has four *burqas*. She goes for coaching – she doesn't feel like wearing this *burqa*, she will wear another. She doesn't like that one, she will wear another one. They tend to wear different *burqas* instead of different shalwar kameezes. Some older women wear it as *purdah*, but the young women especially wear it as fashion.

The instrumentality of the veil

Finally, there were examples of women who veiled for instrumental reasons – with their reasons ranging from the mundane to the strategic. Among the mundane reasons was that veiling dispensed with the need to worry about ironing clothes every day or about wearing the same clothes as the day before or about wearing cheap and unfashionable clothes (Huq and Khondaker 2011). As Shona (Narayanganj) said,

> Girls think, why waste time changing into a good shalwar kameez … Now each girl has 10 scarves, what we call *hijab*. They pleat the *hijab* and wear it around their head, put on a *burqa* and off they go.

More strategic reasons related to the anonymity that full veiling provided. For women working outside the home, it helped to mitigate the trade-off between women's economic value and social status. Veiling allowed women to go to work in garment factories or provide community-based services or attend NGO meetings without drawing attention to themselves. Anwara (Bagerhat) told us how, when her husband was posted out of town, she would put on a *burqa*, load a hired rickshaw van with fruits and vegetables from her farm, instruct the driver to park near the bazaar in town and sell her produce to passers-by safe in the knowledge that she would not be recognised by anyone who knew her.

Nilufa (Comilla) had been engaged in smuggling saris across the border from India. She said that she subscribed to the idea of 'inner *purdah*'. But she also spoke of the instrumental advantages of full veiling when she was engaged in her smuggling activities:

> It gave me an advantage … If we were bringing back saris and we were traveling without covering ourselves, they would catch us and

put us in jail. If we wore a *burqa*, they would not be able to catch us ... they wouldn't be able to see the saris tied to our bodies under the *burqa*.

There were women who opted to veil in response to the kind of behaviour that they frequently encountered from men when they moved in the public domain: leering, suggestive propositions and unwelcome touching and grabbing. They hoped that by veiling themselves they might avoid, or at least minimise, this sexual harassment. Veiling was also reported as a form of assurance to families. Families were more likely to feel secure about the safety and reputation of their female members if they dressed in ways that signalled their virtue to others. Young girls wore the *burqa* so that they could get their parents' permission to attend university. Married women veiled themselves to get family approval to take up work. Bano, an educated young woman from a middle-class rural family in Chapainababganj, who worked in BRAC bank, told us that, when her husband found out that she would be working alongside men, he asked her to wear a *burqa* to work. She said she complied willingly:

> If I don't ... I will be the one facing problems. Maybe many people in society will say I am bad ... It's good from society's point of view and from the religious point of view.

But, according to her, neither she nor many of the young women she knew wore the *burqa* because of *taleem* instruction: 'If I am to worship God, I will do it voluntarily, not because someone else tells me to.' She turned her veiling into a form of fashion:

> The reason I am saying that *burqa* is a fashionable attire is because usually *burqas* are supposed to be loose. But see the one I am wearing, this one is tight-fitting, see there is a lot of design on it. *Burqas* are supposed to be black and without any designs. Why black? Because there is no beauty in black. People will not look at you. But when the *burqa* is bright and your scarf has a design, then it becomes fashionable ... Wearing *burqa* is not mandatory; it's everyone's own choice.

Reviewing these various rationales for veiling, it would appear that they were generally characterised by some degree of voluntarism but there were cases when this was clearly not the case, when women were required to veil themselves by husbands, in-laws and other family members. Nor was voluntarism evident in the comments of women who asserted that veiling had spread to such an extent that, in a fairly short space of time, it had taken on the status of a norm. Not veiling could be interpreted as the absence of modesty and hence likely to attract unwanted attention.[11]

8.7 Alternative pathways to personhood

The contradictory views and practices reported in this chapter suggest that ordinary men and women in Bangladesh varied considerably in their practice of religion and the extent to which it incorporated the orthodox version of Islam being actively promoted across the country. The phrase used in the title of this chapter was repeated in a number of interviews I have carried out over the years, and, while different meanings were intended by different people, they all referred to a certain approach to religious belief: the moderation of the strict rules of the *sharia* by the reflexivity of individual conscience.[12] It allowed them a greater space to carve out alternative pathways to personhood, while still considering themselves devout Muslims, a possibility that would have been ruled out had the new orthodoxy attained hegemonic status.

Identity and exclusion

To understand better why there had not been a more uniform acceptance of a version of Islam that was powerfully backed, both internally and externally, I want to draw on Stuart Hall's proposition that the politics of identity-based movements can be evaluated based on how narrowly they define their boundaries and the degree to which these boundaries are open or closed (Hall 1996). While movements built around a sense of shared identity, as Islamist movements are, may carry a great deal of significance to their members, Hall suggests their broader appeal must be judged by asking whether they function primarily as modes of exclusion, so that those regarded as 'the other' are firmly relegated to the outside, or whether they are sufficiently open to differences around them to be able to recognise and move beyond their own exclusionary tendencies. There is, he says, a critical distinction between movements that are able to live with 'difference' and those that must eradicate it, destroying, or expelling the despised 'other', in order to survive.

I would argue that the orthodox Islamic groups that are seeking to embed their worldview in the social order in Bangladesh operate as modes of exclusion. They welcome those who subscribe to their religious worldview and indeed actively recruit adherents but are intolerant of those who do not. The steady desecularisation of political and civil life, the declaration of Islam as state religion, the growing strength of Islamist groups and their stigmatisation of all non-Muslims as 'infidels' have, as the UN Special Rapporteur on Freedom of Religion and Belief reported, heightened feelings of vulnerability and insecurity among religious minorities.[13] Islamist groups are not unique in the persecution of Hindu minorities. Systematic discrimination and sporadic riots over the years has seen a steady but 'quiet' migration of Hindus from Bangladesh to India and a decline in their share of the population from 22% after partition to 9% in 2001. But attacks on religious minorities tend to escalate when Islamist groups are on the political ascendant (Riaz 2004).

The non-Bengali indigenous minorities in Bangladesh, who make up around 1% of the population, follow Buddhist, Hindu, Christian and animist religions and are largely concentrated in the Chittagong Hill Tracts. Efforts to assimilate them into the dominant nation-building project following Bangladesh's independence led to an extended period of attempted 'pacifica-tion' through military means. It was not until the 1997 Peace Accord steered by the AL that a degree of self-governance for indigenous groups was recog-nised. While it remains poorly implemented, it is significant to note that it was opposed by the BNP and Jamaat-i-Islami. Moreover, the only NGO allowed to operate in the Hill Tracts till the AL came to power in the mid-1990s was a Saudi-funded Islamic organisation whose mission was to convert the local population (Chakma 2010).

Islamists have also sought to expel the 'other within'. They have denounced the Sufi traditions of Bangladesh, targeted Sufi shrines and called for the arrest of Sufi folk singers. In 2020, the Baul singer Shariat Sarker was arrested after a complaint by an Islamic scholar that he had 'hurt the sentiments of Muslims': he had told the audience at his concert that neither the Quran nor the Hadith had forbidden singing and announced a reward of Tk. 50 *lakh* if anyone could prove the contrary.[14] Islamists have called for the law to declare the Ahmadi sect within Islam to be non-Muslims, mounted increasing physical attacks on their people and mosques, had their publications officially banned in 2004 and issued a fatwa in 2005 against any interaction with them. They have also demanded the introduction of an anti-blasphemy law that would carry the death penalty for anyone who hurt Islamic sentiment. They show little con-cern for hurt caused to other religious sentiments.

It is these exclusions and closures, the inbuilt intolerance of 'the other' within as well as outside the Islamic *umma* that feminist organisations, human rights activists and other progressive secular forces in the country, many of them practising Muslims themselves, continue to resist. They have not been able to rely on the state because the ambivalence and contradictions that different regimes have displayed on the issue of secularism and toler-ance have made it an unreliable ally. At the same time, as I have noted, this ambivalence has at least allowed a space for contestation rather than closing it down altogether. Bangladesh has so far not, despite the pressure from its Islamist forces, adopted *sharia* law or declared itself an Islamic state. It is also the unusual example of a country, and a Muslim-majority one at that, that has been governed for the last 30 years by women leading both the party in power and the opposition.

Nor has it only been a 'small urban coterie' that has resisted the intolerance of Islamic orthodoxy. The studies cited in this chapter provide a small glimpse into the diversity of ways in which ordinary people continue to understand and practise Islam, despite efforts to impose a singular meaning and practice. It is evident in the contestations in the political domain between 'secular' and Islamic parties and in the quiet resistance of so many women to the efforts of Islamists to win their votes. It is evident in the range of meanings given to the practice of *purdah* and in conflicting views expressed about the relationship between veiling and piety. It is also evident in the efforts of NGO members to navigate their own pathway between those who denounce NGO membership as antithetical to Islam and those who interpreted it as an acceptance of secular values. The affluent suburban *taleem* participants who featured in Haq's fieldwork in Dhaka reserved their greatest contempt for 'women's lib' and liberal/secular groups. By contrast, many of the poor rural women cited in this chapter who featured in research by Shehabuddin and by Naher focused their antagonism on the *matabors, mahajans* and mullahs who singled them out in their denunciations of immorality and un-Islamic practices.

There are strong reasons why many women, but poorer women in particular, are ambivalent about the Islamist agenda. Its rhetoric of the spiritual equality of men and women does not disguise its support for the fundamental material inequalities between them and its intense preoccupation with policing women's conduct and clothing. It has failed to acknowledge the changes that have led many women to question the terms of a patriarchal bargain that has become increasingly unstable and unreliable. Instead, it has asked them to give up the material gains that they have won in recent years in return for the promise to shore up the old bargain through appeals to the authority of the Quran.

Identity and belonging

The Islamist agenda also asked women to give up important aspects of their cultural identity, aspects they have come to value over the course of their lives. As I noted, it contains a strong critique of the Islam that flourishes in Bangladesh, including its use of music and song as both devotional practice and an integral aspect of Bengali culture. For Islamists, music is seen to take away from the cultivation of an ideal pious disposition and has to be banned from the lives of those seeking to become good Muslims. I want to conclude this chapter by drawing attention to the role that music and song played in the lives of three women who have featured in different research projects.

The *taleem apa* who taught the urban middle-class women in Samia Haq's study equated music with the culture of the 'secular-liberal' Bengali. She exhorted her students to shun it at all costs as they struggled to leave behind their Bengali middle-class notions of femininity and emerge as pious Muslim women. Suhaila, one of her students, was an accomplished classical singer and had long enjoyed singing: it gave her peace, it carried her away to another world, a better place. When she learnt that singing was un-Islamic, she resolved to give it up as part of her journey to authentic piety. It was a difficult struggle because of what her singing meant to her. She began by singing alone in her room, hoping that she was still complying with the discipline required of her but she came to realise it was not enough. It still took her two years before she finally gave up her singing.

We interviewed Jobeda in 2014. She was in her late 50s, lived in Narayanganj with her husband and son and sold saris in the neighbourhood to earn her living. She said that it was in the *shariat* to live within *purdah* but she had to go out to sell clothes because of family need: she respected the *shariat* but she followed *marfat* too. In fact, expressions about her desire to remain at home in virtuous seclusion were half-hearted efforts to 'perform' propriety for the benefit of her interviewer. She soon announced that she was an enthusiastic disciple of the *pir* Babaji and had travelled to different parts of Bangladesh with her Bhandari sisters to participate in religious events. They travelled by bus to these places and sang and danced throughout the entire journey. What was memorable about her narrative, which was periodically interspersed with bursts of song, was the importance of music and song in her life. She spoke about the hardships of her life that made her sometimes think that death would be a welcome release. At such times, she would go to the Kollar Chat tomb or to Bhandar Shorif, where she could find peace singing the songs of Shorif. The music that she spoke about was not the same music that Sohaila struggled to give up but each was as much a part of Bengali culture as the other.

My third example comes from fieldwork I carried out in rural Comilla in 2002 as part of a project that explored how households believed they had fared economically over the previous 10 years. Out of interest, I sometimes asked the people I interviewed what made them happy. The answers generally revolved around the issue of livelihood security, but one woman responded by talking about what music meant to her:

> People now and again will sing a song. We hear them and we say, look there is a wave coming out from a lake with no water. To free your mind from sorrow, you sing a song … I have no brother, no sister, no father, no mother, when I think about that, I want to weep. At that time, if I can hear a song somewhere, my sorrow diminishes a bit. If I can't hear a song, then I have to cry away my sorrow.

Notes

[1] The terms in the chapter title refer to different doctrines of Islam: *shariat* refers to external adherence to doctrinal Islam, while *marfat* refers to inner conscience. *Tariqat*, referred to later, is the pursuit of inner vision.

[2] While the language of the campaign against NGOs was couched as the defence of Islam against 'Christianity and its agents', Naher (2006) notes that the Islamists did not seem particularly concerned with the activities of NGOs that could credibly labelled 'Christian' such as Caritas and the Christian Commission for Development. They reserved their energies to attack 'secular' Bangladeshi NGOs such as BRAC and Grameen Bank, which no one seriously thought were seeking to convert people to Christianity. She suggests that reason for their emphasis was that their main audience for their propaganda were rural peasants, for whom the

category 'Christian' was probably the nearest equivalent to the word 'Western', which would have no ready meaning to the vast majority of villagers. In this sense, it could be seen as an attempt, in part at least, to articulate how many villagers must have viewed these organisations in the rural setting – as an 'alien' presence.

3 In response to frequent allegations of this kind, BRAC issued a statement in 2008: 'BRAC strongly believes that it is the responsibility of the state to ensure quality primary education for all. BRAC does not believe in the privatization or commercialization of primary education' (http://www.brac.net/latest-news/item/356-). What BRAC had done in the 1990s was to target the third of children, particularly girls, from poorer households who were left out of the primary school system and, with UNICEF support, start a system of non-formal schooling geared to reaching these children (see Chapter 5).

4 While Jamaat did not generally approve of the Tabliq because of their lack of commitment to building an Islamic state, a Jamaat activist nevertheless viewed its members as performing a valuable function in creating a population likely to be generally receptive to Islamist ideas. Equally a women follower of the Tabliq, while distancing herself from Jamaat, accepted that they shared the same vision and she had no quarrel with the idea of a state governed by *sharia* law (White 2012).

5 A similar justification for polygamy was given by Jamaat's secretary general when questioned about this in 1996: 'This matter is tied up with conjugal life. However, if one person experiences a practical need and the other person does not recognize that need and it is not dealt with, if a person feels a need and it is suppressed, then he may drift in the direction of anti-social behaviour and indiscipline' (Shehabuddin 2008, p.93). Marrying a second woman legally was a preferred alternative to illicit relations with multiple women.

6 Our IDS/BIGD 2008 survey also suggested that women from the wealthiest third of households were far more likely than those from poorest third to 'always' cover themselves when they left the house (78% and 55%, respectively).

7 Table 8b provides the same information for the sub-sample of women from Amarpur.

8 She was married to a member of the local union council.

9 See Note 1.

10 It is worth noting that, even among the older-style *burqas*, there were differences between the 'newer, more stylish long black satin burkhas of the more economically secure families' with netting around the eyes so women could see and the 'white or green cotton cloth ones where only two holes have been cut for eyes' (Hussain 2010, p.953).

11 This may partly explain why a higher percentage, particularly of younger women, in our 2015 LSE/BIGD survey said they always veiled themselves outside the home than did younger women in our IDS/BIGD 2008 survey.

12 It was generally used by my respondents when they wanted to explain forms of behaviour that seemed to go against stricter versions of Islam.

13 Office of the United Nations High Commissioner for Human Rights (2016). Report of the Special Rapporteur on Freedom of Religion or Belief on his mission to Bangladesh (A/HRC/31/18/ Add.2). United Nations.

14 https://advox.globalvoices.org/2020/01/20/baul-singer-shariat-sarkar -arrested-in-bangladesh-for-insulting-islam

9. Unruly sons, compassionate daughters: reconfiguring the intergenerational bargain

People are happier when they have sons ... A son will bear the torch of the family. Girls cannot do that. They cannot live in their father's house their whole lives. When you have daughters, you get them married and they leave. (Rokeya, 60 years, fieldwork, Faridpur 2010)

I hear from a lot of people now that they prefer daughters. No, earlier their faces would fall if they had a daughter ... My aunt had a daughter – she tried to smother her with her hand, but if Allah decides to make her breathe, who can stop Him? They were happy with sons because they would be able to bring their earnings home. They don't feel like that anymore, now they think girls are better. (Farah, 48 years, fieldwork, Faridpur, 2010)

This chapter returns to the original impetus behind this book, the decline in son preference in Bangladesh and the revaluation of daughters. Chapter 1 noted that the ensemble of patriarchal structures in Bangladesh – and the northern plains of South Asia more generally – could not have been more purposefully designed to ensure that parents longed for, and cherished sons, while subjecting their daughters, 'the neighbour's tree', to malign neglect. Yet there has been a steady decline in key aspects of gender discrimination in Bangladesh – health, nutrition, survival rates, education and work. Fertility has also declined but, in marked contrast to neighbouring India, it has not been accompanied by the resort to female-selective abortion by parents seeking to reconcile persisting son preference with their desire for small families.

These facts point to a decline in son preference, which in turn suggests important shifts in the underlying structures of patriarchy. Preceding chapters have explored the processes by which the long-established desire for large families gave way to the small family norm and why it was accompanied by a decline in discriminatory practices in the care of children. This chapter focuses more closely on this shift in reproductive preferences and practices. It explores how the changes in social meanings and material practices described in previous chapters contributed to this shift and to the accompanying change in the value that parents attached to sons and daughters. It therefore brings together disparate strands of the analysis in preceding chapters and links them more directly to the central concerns of this book.

9.1 Tracking changes in reproductive preferences

Findings from a series of studies on reproductive preferences and practices since the late 1960s are summarised in Box 2 (Appendix 4). They show some clear trends. First, there has been a marked decline in both desired and achieved family size. Second, there has been a weakening in the desire for sons as measured by behavioural outcomes, as well as by expressed preferences with regard to ideal sex composition of children. Notably, early studies showed that mortality rates were considerably higher among second and higher-birth-order daughters than sons (Muhuri and Preston 1991) but this parity-specific effect faded after 1995 (Alam, Roy and Ahmed 2007). Later studies show a shift towards balance in the preferred sex composition of children, with a sizeable minority of women saying that they did not want any more children even if they had only daughters (Talukder et al. 2014). The latest study cited in the box suggests that women wanted small families and a balanced composition, with one boy and one girl as the ideal – although it also suggests that male preferences for larger families, and for more sons, could override this in practice (Asadullah, Savoia and Mahmud 2021).

Some of these trends are evident in comparisons of findings from my surveys of Amarpur village during my PhD fieldwork in 1979 and from the 2008 IDS/BIGD survey, listed in Appendix 5. Table 4 shows that all women who were, or had been, married at least once (who I refer to as ever-married women) covered by my 1979 village census reported a mean parity of seven children by the end of the childbearing period – similar to fertility rates prevailing in the rest of Bangladesh. By 2008, mean parities had declined to 5.76.

Table 5 reports on the value of number and sex preference scales in the two periods. The 1979 estimate is based on my survey of ever-married women. The majority of women, particularly the younger ones, were clustered at the lower end of the numbers scale but around half of the women in the survey, particularly the older ones, were clustered at the strong son preference end of the sex preference scale.

The 2008 estimates in Table 5 show that the desire for large families had declined since 1979 and that there had been a marked shift in son preference: 50% expressed a preference for daughters, while most of the rest opted for a balanced composition. In response to a question asking women what their preference would be if they could have only one child, 47% expressed a preference for a son, while 47% said they were indifferent (Kabeer, Huq and Mahmud 2014).

A follow-up survey of the same women was carried out by the LSE/BIGD team in 2015 along with a survey of men from the same districts. We added an additional question to our questionnaire that allowed an alternative assessment of preferred number and sex composition of children. We asked women and men whether they wanted any more children and compared their answers with the number and sex composition of their surviving children. The results for men and women in the age group 15–49 in the total survey samples for the two years are reported in Tables 6a and 7a, respectively – with findings for Amarpur reported separately in Tables 6b and 7b. The results for the full samples and for Amarpur show similar patterns but, since the sample for Amarpur is very small, I will focus the discussion on findings from the larger samples.

Tables 5 and 6 divide their samples into three groups. The first group is made up of men and women with one son and one daughter. The result for this group supports the finding that one boy and one girl has become the ideal: the largest percentage of men and women in the survey samples were in this category and very few wanted any more children: just 6% of women and 7% of men.

The second group is made of those with either zero sons or zero daughters. While both men and women with zero sons were more likely than those with zero daughters to want more children, the desire for more children diminished rapidly with numbers of children. So, for example, among women with one daughter and zero sons, 77% wanted another child, while, among those with one son and zero daughters, 69% wanted an additional child. On the other hand, among women with three or more children, only 11% of those with zero sons wanted more children and just 3% of those with no daughters. We find a similar pattern among men, but the results suggest that men want more children than women. A total of 88% of men with zero sons and one daughter wanted more children, compared to 84% of those with zero daughters and one son. Once again the desire for additional children declined with more children. Of men with three or more children, 24% of those with zero sons and 15% of those with zero daughters wanted more children.

The third group was made up of those with three or more children, including at least one son and one daughter. The desire for additional children was very low in this group and it was generally lower among those who had the same number of sons and daughters. Among women, only 0.7% of those with the same number of sons and daughters wanted more children, compared to 0.4% of those with more sons and 0.8% of those with more daughters. Among men, the figures were 1.6%, 2.9% and 3.3%, respectively. The general pattern in Amarpur mirrors that of the larger population but suggests an even weaker desire for large families. Most men and women with three or more children did not want more children regardless of whether they had only sons or only daughters.

These results support the findings reported in Box 2 (Appendix 4). They suggest that small families have become the norm for both men and women; the ideal is one boy and one girl. While both men and women were more likely to want more children if they did not have a son, they generally did not want more than three children, regardless of the sex of their children. In fact, many were prepared to settle for children of one sex, particularly if they had only sons but even if they had only daughters. Although not shown in the table, 35% of women with only daughters said they did not want any more children, compared with 50% of women with only sons. (In Amarpur these figures were 51% and 58%, respectively.) Among men, 39% with only daughters and 49% of those with only sons said that they did not want any more children. (In Amarpur, the figures were 45.7% and 50%, respectively.)

In the rest of this chapter, I draw on detailed interviews with 40 married women and 22 of their husbands carried out in Amarpur in 2010, along with some follow-up interviews in 2014. These explored the life histories of different generations and their views on the social changes that had taken place during their lifetime. I have added, in brackets, ages of the men and women cited in the discussion that follows; these are very approximate in the case of the older generation. Their narratives tell us how social practices have changed over time and what had led people to adopt new ways of thinking and doing. They discuss the shift in reproductive preferences and the aspects of change in the larger context that helped to explain it. These, as we will see, include many of the changes described in previous chapters.

As background to the analysis, Table 8a provides information on relevant data mainly drawn from the full 2008 survey sample, with the Amarpur data presented separately in Table 8b. The tables present information for three cohorts of women – an older generation of women aged 50+, a middle generation of women aged 30–49 years and a younger generation aged less than 30. This allows us to track some of the changes highlighted by the qualitative analysis across generations. I will focus here on the Amarpur results.

9.2 Amarpur revisited

Life trajectories in the past: the way things were

In 1979, Amarpur was a rural economy, although it was just four miles from Faridpur town. It was far poorer than it is today. There were very few brick houses; most of the older generation had lived in huts of bamboo and mud with thatched roofs. Over 80% of the male population aged 15+ were economically active, mostly in agriculture, as farmers, agricultural labourers and sharecroppers. Others were fishermen, weavers and traders. A few worked in formal government jobs. Only 12% of women were in paid work, most often in paid domestic work in other people's homes. The rest were engaged in household work and crop processing or helped husbands with weaving, making fishing nets or bamboo work. The older generation had thus grown up with the idea that women did not undertake paid work. Even if poverty led some to search for it, it was not easy to find and they were generally paid in kind: 'Women would go to five different places and never find any work. They never held a five taka note in their hand that they had earned' (Bharati, 40).

That this was also a generation that had grown up in the pre-demographic transition era was evident in their frequent references to loss of mothers, siblings and their own children, both in the actual numbers of deaths reported by some but also in the vagueness of others about these numbers: 'my mother lost three or four children' or 'several of my father's wives died'.

Births took place at home, sometimes with the assistance of a midwife, and were shrouded in mystery and danger; miscarriages were described as giving birth to turtles or blood clots; babies were at the mercy of evil spirits and could die any time; fatalism about births was matched by fatalism about deaths – both were outside the control of human beings:

> At that time babies would get tetanus while in the *atoor ghar*, but people didn't understand. They thought that something had possessed the child. They would simply say that the baby turned red first, then blue, then black … a lot of children died this way. (Nadera, 58)

Education was not widespread. If a family were well-off, they might send sons to school; if not, they would put them to work. But going to school was rarely an option for girls. Schools were few and far between, people made disapproving comments, but most importantly it had no place in the future mapped out for them: to marry and go to live in their husband's house where all they would do would be to 'cook, wash dishes and take out the cow dung'.

Women were married off early, often while they were still children before they had a chance to know what they wanted but even if they knew what they wanted, it counted for very little. Sufia (55) had wanted to stay on in school, her parents could afford it, but her eldest uncle, a *pir* and the senior authority in the family, had advised them to marry their daughters off before they reached puberty. She still resented the fact that her parents had chosen to educate her brothers, regardless of their interest or ability: 'one did not even finish school because he didn't have the discipline'.

There was sorrow too that mothers had been too busy looking after large numbers of children, in too much of a hurry to marry their daughters off, to have much time to care for them:

> If my mother had had just two children, then our lives would have been very different. It was because she had so many that she did not have the motivation to keep me with her. (Sohela, 40)

Marriage was arranged by parents or elders in the family. Neither bride nor groom was asked if they consented to the marriage. Most of the older women had been married at a time when dowry demands were not common, when the groom's family would gift money, jewellery or clothes to the bride. But, by the time I did my fieldwork in 1979, the practice of dowry previously associated with higher-caste Hindus had displaced bridewealth as an established practice among Muslims.

Once a daughter was married, she was regarded as 'belonging' to her husband's family. If the marriage did not turn out well, there was little her parents could do but exhort her to put up with her fate. Jamila (39) remembered her aunt, who had been married off at the age of seven or eight:

> Her husband sometimes beat her into pulp, but her father would say that he had married her off to that family, so whether she lived or died, she would have to remain with them. A husband's house was the same as a grave.

Marriage was a major transition in women's lives. They left behind their families and the village they had grown up in. They left behind the names they were given and would be known henceforth as the wife of their husband (Moni's wife) or the mother of their sons (Anis's mother). They would not be able to visit their own families without permission and it was a mark of generosity on the part of in-laws when this permission was granted. Given the poor state of communications at the time, they had to travel by *tom-tom gari* (horse-drawn vehicles) or covered *palkis* (palanquins) if their families could afford it. If not, they simply did not see their parents for long periods of time.

Many spoke of their fear of husbands they had never met before and mothers-in-law who would monitor their every action to ensure that they did not shame the family in any way. Some were fortunate in having mothers-in-law who were kind to them, but most less so. Jorina (60+), who had been just 12 when she was married off, described the servitude of her early years of marriage: sweeping the house, washing pots and pans, cooking and serving food, threshing paddy, feeding the young children of the house, washing their clothes, bathing and preparing them for bed and then tending to her father-in-law. There was no time for play.

Then there was the pressure to have large numbers of children to ensure surviving sons. Modern forms of family planning were still rare. Safura (51) could recall when the first family planning workers had come to her village:

> I remember clearly when I was nine years old, these women used to walk around the village to distribute the medicine. My mother and aunts used to chase them out. My grandfather and uncles would tell them not to enter our house and forbid my mother and aunts to allow them to sit in the house.

Life trajectories in the present: the way things are

Amarpur had prospered since those days. By 2010, most homes were made of durable materials, they had electricity, diets had improved, people ate fish and meat on a regular basis, they owned modern consumer durables, like cable TV ('dish') and mobile phones. Transportation links to Faridpur town had turned Amarpur into a peri-urban village, with people moving easily between town and village for work, trade, shopping and social events. There had been changes in the structure of economic activities. Male labour force participation rates remained high but there was now much greater diversity in how men earnt their living. Many had moved into off-farm employment, working in trade and services, commuting to other districts and towns and migrating abroad. Female paid activity had risen from 12% in 1979 to 56% (Table 8b). The majority of women were engaged in home-based market activities, but there were also women in office jobs, wage labour, factory work and outside self-employment.

While the way that people lived and the options available to them had also changed, one thing remained constant. Despite rapid fertility decline, the average age of marriage had risen very slowly over time and still remained stubbornly low at 17, similar to the national average (Table 8b). Parents may have become more aware of the health risks of early marriage and childbearing, but anxieties about reputational and sexual risks continued to exercise a downward pressure on their daughters' age of marriage.

However, they were now far more likely to seek their children's consent to the marriages being arranged for them. Just 29% of those over 50 reported that they had a say in who they married, rising to 83% of the youngest (Table 8b).[1] While having a say generally meant that parents sought the opinion of their children about the partners they chose for them, there had also been a rise in the incidence of 'love' marriages. The general increase in mobility among girls and the greater opportunity to meet boys at college or at work had made this possible. Mobile phones had also expanded the circle of men and women between whom unsupervised interactions could take place – to the disapproval of many of its older generation:

> People are constantly saying 'hello' on the mobile. This 'hello' business has taken over. A girl from one district talks on the phone to a boy from another district and the next thing you know, he appears on her doorstep. (Shukurjan, 60+)

Love marriages did not meet with the kind of social disapproval they had in the past. They were regarded as a sign of changing times and associated by many of the older generation with greater affection between couples, a contrast to the distance that had characterised their own marriages. Hajera (55) recalled that, in the past, husbands and wives did not understand each other properly, they had separate beds once they had children, and they never seemed to talk to each other, especially in front of elders.

The shift to smaller families in Amarpur, as elsewhere, was linked to the improvement in child survival that resulted from the expansion in health and family planning provision described in Chapter 6. Many of the younger generation still delivered their babies at home, but they were more likely to seek pre- and post-natal consultation than the older generation (Table 8b). As Joygun (50s) commented:

> Four or five of my mother's children died, no one knew why they died. They couldn't take them to the doctor, they were not given any advice. Nowadays if a child just farts their parents will take them to the doctor.

Women were well versed in various contraceptive methods and experimented to find one that suited them. They adopted it when they decided they did not want any more or when they wanted to space births. Abortion remained illegal but menstrual regulation was easily available. It was often used if women got pregnant by accident or too soon after the previous birth or if they thought they had enough children – though what was considered 'enough' had changed considerably. Julekha (50s) had an abortion after her sixth child because she thought she had enough. Dipa (26) spoke of women she knew who had abortions because they considered two or three children 'enough'.

The issue of ultrasonograms came up in relation to the increased practice of prenatal consultation. Ultrasonograms were routine among better-off women, but usually five or six months into the pregnancy to see if there were any problems and make sure the baby was positioned properly. By then it was too late to ask for an abortion. Some women said that doctors used to reveal the sex of the foetus after the test but they believed that there had been a government directive forbidding it, possibly related to the issue of son preference.[2] A number said they knew of women who had sex-selective abortions but it was not clear if they knew them personally or had heard public service announcements on Indian TV cautioning against this practice.

As elsewhere in Bangladesh, the 'quantity–quality' transition was very much in evidence in the explanations offered for the desire for smaller families. Ensuring a proper upbringing for their children, *bhalo bhabe manush kora* (bringing them up as proper human beings) meant feeding and clothing them and providing them with as good an education as parents could afford. The phrase 'this is the era of education' was repeated in several interviews to describe this trend, as was the phrase 'we had eyes but we could not see', slogans used by the government to persuade parents to send their children to school. And, as elsewhere in Bangladesh, greater value was given to girls' education than in the past. As Hameda (50s) put it, the days of *purdah* when girls had to be kept at home were over: 'My husband I both took the decision to educate our daughters. Now everything is lit up with education.'

The desire to educate daughters was bound up with various aspirations about their future of the kind discussed in earlier chapters: their status in society, finding a good husband, reducing or offsetting dowry demands, becoming better mothers and wives, helping their children with their studies, gaining respect in the eyes of their in-laws and as the route to a good job. In fact, education was singled out by the overwhelming majority of women in Amarpur (and in the larger survey) as the single most important force for change in women's lives in general (Tables 8a and 8b). In their own lives, access to credit was more frequently mentioned by less-educated women.

Joygun Begum was educating her daughter as far as she could so that she could find a good job and make a good marriage: 'I won't have to give dowry for Jhuma. No one wants money from a girl who has a job. My daughter will be the dowry.' For Shamsunahar (23), it did not matter that they had to pay twice for their daughter – once for her education and once for her dowry – 'the benefit of her education was that she will have something of her own. She will have a different value.'

For Shefali (32), education and work were bound up together in the 'big dreams' she had for her daughter:

> I want her to be educated, to have a job, to build her own future. And she too will be motivated to educate her children. This cannot be seen as a question of profit and loss. You educate your daughter and she leaves for her husband's home. Where is the loss? I see only that my daughter being educated and happy in her life. She is my only child. I wish I could keep her with me forever.

As elsewhere in Bangladesh, a particularly poignant force in bringing about these changes was the regret of mothers who had been denied an education by their own parents. Sufia, for instance, whose desire to study beyond primary level had been overridden by the strictures of her religious uncle, was determined that the same would not happen to her children. All three of her children, two daughters and a son, were graduates and, as her husband told us, it was largely due to her determination.

There was also awareness that men had been changing as part of the broader processes of change in gender relations. Like women, they learnt from the educational endeavours, seminars and awareness programmes conducted by government and NGOs, they watched TV programmes on these topics and they heard successive prime ministers declare the importance of women's rights. Kulsum's husband summarised what he saw as the main changes that had taken place in women's lives: they were now educated, they had mobile phones, they knew which bus to take, where to get off, they knew how to go to different places: 'They have shaken off the shackles of a restricted life.'

But views about social change were not unanimous. The more orthodox sections of the population decried the new talk of equality, the idea promulgated by the government and NGOs that boys and girls were equal, were equally entitled to jobs, and equally free to move around in the public domain. According to Islamic principles of equality, men were lords of work in the fields while women were lords of work in the home. Women did not have to leave the house to be equal; there was no need for women to try to over-achieve.

When summing up the nature of these changes, a number of villagers made an interesting distinction between 'the Islamic perspective' and 'the social perspective'. This was intended to relay their awareness that many of the gains that women had made would not meet with approval from more orthodox believers but that they themselves considered these gains in a positive light. So, for instance, Yasmin's husband said:

> All these things put together are bringing about changes in women's lives. It is not good from an Islamic point of view, but otherwise it's a good thing. Women are now ahead, with laws against dowry and violence backing them up. So they are more courageous ... Now people cannot get away with doing anything they want to do, with harming women for no reason.

9.3 Shifting sex preferences

There was general agreement among those we spoke to in 2010 that 'most people' wanted small families and that strong son preference was a thing of the past: people valued both sons and daughters. However, it was not always possible to establish what their *own* preferences were because these were so often tangled up with their opinions about what other people wanted or with what other people might want now.

For the purposes of the analysis, I will distinguish between two broad groups. The first were those who either stated their own clear preference for sons or spoke of the importance of both sons and daughters but came down in favour of sons or else said that they wanted, or had wanted, their firstborn to be a boy because this reassured them of having at least one son. They were expressing a bias towards sons and hence some continuity with past norms. I draw on their narratives to better understand the persistence of son preference.

The second category consisted of those who were unqualified in their desire for *both* sons and daughters or who said that they wanted their firstborn to be a girl or who expressed a clear preference for daughters. They were engaged in a reassessment of reproductive preferences and hence a departure from past norms. I draw on their narratives to better understand what had led them to reassess the value they attached to sons and daughters.

The persistence of son preference

The explanations that people gave for their expressions of son preference reflected many of the beliefs and practices that had bolstered it in the past. The intergenerational dimensions of the patriarchal bargain had remained intact for them. They favoured sons in the distribution of their property and resources in the expectation that they would remain with, or close to, their parents after their marriage and, together with their wives, look after them in their old age. Parents might no longer have land to bequeath to sons but they invested what they could in their sons' education and job prospects. Even if their sons moved to other parts of the country or went abroad in search of work, they would remain bound by duty to look after their parents in their old age and to bury them when the time came. Daughters, on the other hand, would leave for their husbands' household after marriage; they would be lost to their parents.

This was how Hamida (50+) saw it. She had been married off at 15 to a distant relative. Her husband worked as an accountant and they had been able to educate their children, one son and two daughters. Her daughters were married and she hoped to marry her son off to a nice, quiet girl to whom she would hand over responsibility for household affairs. Then she and her husband could devote themselves to prayer and visiting relatives. She did not have any expectations from her daughters but hoped that they would live well.

Some younger women also expressed these views. As Rohima (27) put it, whatever affection a daughter might have for her parents, she would only live with them for the first 17 or 18 years of her life. Once she got married she would have her own husband and children to look after. Even if she wanted to support her parents, her husband would insist that his parents should take priority: 'Are you going to support your parents or mine?'

According to Kulsum (23), even if sons did not look after their parents, there was little that daughters could do: 'they live in someone else's house and they live under someone else's rule'. They had to obey their husbands and in-laws; they had no right to support their own parents, the right that sons could take for granted. Sufia (26) spoke of the shame of being looked after by a daughter and son-in-law in old age when it was a son's duty:

> Listen, it doesn't matter how old one is or how helpless ... no parent wants to be looked after living in their daughter's house, they don't want to have to die there.

Concerns with the preservation of the patrilineage was another factor that bolstered son preference. As Sona Rani (36) pointed out, such concerns were common to both Hindus and Muslims:

> A son bears the torch for his lineage, the family expands when he gets married. But if you have a daughter, she leaves once she is married ... That is why people, whether from your community or ours, want a son.

Without sons, Shaheda (46) pointed out, parents faced a lonely old age and would be forgotten after they died:

> Of course I have a strong connection to my daughters, but girls leave for another home. If I have five daughters and I marry them all off, they will all leave and the house will be empty ... When we die, no one will remember that we once lived here.

And finally, of course, there were the costs associated with marrying off daughters – in contrast to the benefits that flowed from the marriage of sons. Whether people agreed with the practice of dowry or not, it appeared to many to be the price they had to pay to marry off their daughters. While parents might educate their daughters in the hope that it would reduce the burden of dowry, they could not always be sure that this would happen:

> If you have a daughter then you have to educate them and then give a dowry when she gets married ... Take our situation, my husband is working, I am also working. If we have to give fifty thousand for our daughter, is that not a problem? If we had a son, I wouldn't have had to give dowry. How will I save so much money, where will I get it from? Is this not a cause for tension? I am wasting away with tension. This is why everyone wants a son. (Rahela, 43)

The revaluation of daughters

By and large, however, strong son preference was described as a thing of the past. The older generation recalled the time when people preferred sons because they could work on the farm or because they studied, got jobs and improved the condition of the family. They would have up to 15 or 16 children in the hope of sons. But now most men and women in Amarpur favoured small families and a balanced sex composition. In some cases, the desire for 'balance' overrode the desire for small families. Mahfuza (38) ended up with three daughters in the hope of having a son. Her husband said they had stopped trying as it was clearly not God's will. Keya (39) had gone in the opposite direction, ending up with four sons in the hope of having a daughter. She consoled herself that at least she had been spared the worry of saving for a daughter's dowry.

More generally, however, the desire for small families overrode any preference for balance that parents might have had. They were willing to stop at two children, or even just one, regardless of sex, so they could be sure of looking after them properly:

> I don't want any more children. With the little income that my husband earns, if I cannot bring up my one daughter properly, then there is no point in having more children. It's not a question of simply deciding to have more children, there is a question of bringing them up. (Fawzia, 28)

> Now is the age of education ... Now parents hope for two children – a son and a daughter. Even if they have two daughters, they do not have any more children. They think let me stop at two daughters. (Jamila, 49)

As we can see from the quote from Farah that opened this chapter, there were also some who believed that there had a been shift in favour of daughters or who expressed a preference for daughters themselves. Dolly (24) had wanted a daughter first:

> I like girls. You can dress up a little girl, do all sorts of things. But I prayed to Allah for a son the next time … My husband didn't express any particular preference. He wanted whatever Allah gave.

Shaheda said that she had not cared when her firstborn was a daughter but had cried when the second was also a girl. Her husband's reactions were very different. According to her, when he first saw his daughter's face, it was as if he had been given the world: 'He told me that I had no idea that I held heaven in my arms. Both his daughters are his love, his heart and soul.'

While dowry costs were mentioned in these narratives, they did not seem to be a strong enough reason for disfavouring daughters but rather a cost to be borne, as with their education, to improve their prospects in life. Worth noting, though, is the unexpected number of parents who declared that they would not demand dowry for their sons or pay dowry for their daughters. They wanted their children's marriages to start off on an equal footing, something that dowry transactions were seen to jeopardise.[3]

The other noteworthy feature that emerged from these narratives was the difference in the language that parents used when they explained what they valued about sons and daughters. Their regard for sons was often expressed in the language of expectation, of anticipation of the filial duty of sons towards ageing parents written into the intergenerational bargain. Their language was more emotional when they spoke of daughters:

> If you don't have a daughter, then you have no affection. A house is brightened and filled with love if there is a daughter. Yes, of course there are expenses. But even though there are expenses, daughters bring a lot of joy. (Purnima, 35)

> Daughters are a big asset. You can tell your daughters everything. Son's wives don't listen to your tales of sorrow. You look like someone who does, but there are not many daughters-in-law who are willing to listen to the long-winded stories of their mothers-in-law. Whereas you can tell your daughter everything, she listens and understands. (Hameda, 52)

It was also very frequently the language of hope that their daughters might be able to look after ageing parents if sons did not. It was believed that the affinity between daughters and their parents was different from that between sons and their parents, that it was based on love and care rather than duty. Mothers believed that there was a special bond between mothers and daughters. Fathers claimed that daughters had a special place in their hearts for their fathers.

But there was a further dimension to these shifting preferences. Daughters had not suddenly started to become more loving and loyal, more attuned to their mothers' feelings, more attached to their fathers. What had changed was, on the one hand, the relationship between parents and their sons, and the associated relationship with daughters-in-law, and on the other, the daughters' emerging capacity to back up their feelings of love and loyalty for their parents with material support.

Unruly sons, insubordinate daughters-in-law

A growing disillusionment with sons was evident in many of the interviews: boys had become undisciplined, parents could no longer exercise control over them, command their loyalty or count on their sense of duty. Here is how Farzana's husband explained the loss of faith in the old intergenerational bargain:

> The tradition was that sons would work and feed their parents, daughters would get married and leave their parents' home. When sons got married, their wives would take care of his parents. But it is not easy to bring up sons these days. They do not listen to their parents. Once they are a little grown up, they no longer fear their parents. They get into trouble ... They wander around, they get involved in dubious activities. They steal or get into fights ... Many unemployed boys are into drugs now. They get money from doing bad activities.

Underlying this story of unruly sons was a broader one about the steady nucleation of family life and the expansion of markets for male labour. In the past, it had been parents who decided when it was time for married sons to set up their own households, within the same *bari*, of course, and they continued to expect their sons' support. This had changed. Sons had become increasingly independent of their parents. They were the ones who made the decision about when to separate from the parental home. They went to college, they migrated to other parts of the country or abroad in search of work, they mixed with different people and they fell in love with and married unsuitable women.

Some parents accepted that they had to reconcile themselves to these changes, to accept that their sons' first responsibility was to their wives and children: 'They have their own future to consider. How will they manage if they have to feed everyone?' (Suraiya, 53).

But the more common reaction was a sense of bitterness and betrayal. A son's decision to set up a separate household, often very early into his marriage, often at his wife's instigation, was seen as an indication of his shifting loyalties from his natal to his conjugal family. A great deal of the resentment expressed by parents, particularly mothers, about their changing relationships with their sons singled out daughters-in-law as the root of the problem. They were seen to be selfish and independent-minded, very different from how they themselves had been in relation to their own mothers-in-law.

It was, of course, true that the younger generation of daughters-in-law were different from those of the past. They were more likely to have entered their in-laws' families as a result of their husband's choice rather than through arranged marriages and to have a closer relationship with their husbands from the outset. But, even with arranged marriages, this generation of women were starting married life with higher levels of education than the past, greater knowledge of the world and more ambitious dreams for themselves and their children. They had been less socialised into displaying the docility and obedience that their mothers-in-law had displayed when they had got married and that they had expected in turn from their daughters-in-law.

So, for the older generation of women, the daughter-in-law who had once lightened their burden of work at home, over whom they could exercise one of the few forms of authority available to them, now appeared to exercise an authority over their sons that they, as mothers, had expected to have. I have synthesised what various women said about their daughters-in-law in order to convey both the strength of their bitterness and the reasons for it. First, they recalled how it had been when they had entered their husbands' homes:

> In earlier times, our husbands remained in their parents' household. We had to cook the rice, fetch water for our mother-in-law, wash their clothes, served them food. We used to fear her, creep around her … We lived on whatever she gave us to eat, wore what she gave us to wear. If we made a mistake, we knew we would have to face her anger. We were the ones who suffered but we made sure our elders lived in peace.

They contrasted this with the insubordinate and uncaring behaviour of daughters-in-law today:

> Daughters-in-law used to fear their mothers-in-law but not these days. These days they enter the house as *matabors*, they strut around with self-importance, go wherever they please, swear at their husbands, swear at their mothers-in-law, refuse to cook. They don't look after parents-in-law because they don't like doing it, no one wants to clean other people's faeces. If their mother-in-law tells them not to do something or not go to certain places, they will get into a fight, they will talk back and argue at every instance. So now elders are in a weaker position … They have no rights, they suffer, they are stuck in the house with no one to look after them. Older

people are suffering, but daughters-in-law are doing well, they are living in contentment.

They attributed this insubordination to the fact that daughters-in-law were likely to be educated and to have jobs:

> Sons are educated, their wives are educated. They both have jobs, there is no scope for looking after aging parents. Will their wives wash their mother-in-law's clothes? Serve her food? They come to visit us with grim faces. They do not recognise that even if their mother-in-law never had a job like them, she worked hard to bring up her children. When I ask my daughter in law what she would do if her sons' wives behaved towards her in this way when she grows old, she says she will employ someone to look after her.

They also attributed it to the fact that their sons were afraid that their wives would leave them and return to their parents' home:

> If the mother-in-law says anything to her daughter-in-law, she gets angry, she returns to her father's house and refuses to come back. Nowadays girls say that they will only stay with their husbands if they want to and if they don't like it, they will return home. It is girls these days who break off their marriages, they say things like: 'I won't stay with you, I'll divorce you and this and that'. Sons listen to their wives because they want to minimise discord within their marriage, because they are afraid their wives would leave them, especially if they came from high status families. Earlier, no one dared to leave their husbands. It is the wives these days who want a separate household, not the sons. They want to earn their own money and live their own lives.

Capable daughters

So even parents who still looked to their sons for support in their old age did not do it with the unquestioning confidence of earlier times. This had a number of repercussions. It meant that parents were willing to stop having children once they reach the desired family size, regardless of the number of sons they had. If having sons did not guarantee their security in old age, the patriarchal risk associated with not having a minimum of sons was no longer as great as it had once been. It also meant that they started to make their own provisions for the future through savings, investments and pensions.

But the other repercussion was the emerging hope with regard to daughters. While it had never been part of the patriarchal bargain that daughters would support their parents in their old age, and it was still spoken of in the language of hope rather than expectation, this possibility had certainly begun to enter into discussions about the value of daughters. As Firoza (34) explained,

> People had wanted sons because boys earned incomes but daughters bring peace in the house, they look after their parents much more than boys do. Even when a girl is married, she comes and tells her brothers' wives to take good care of her parents, to look after them properly.

Farah (48) expressed a view that was held by many: a son's love for his parents had become fickle; a daughter's love was steadfast:

> If I had to have only one child, I would want a daughter … As soon as boys grow up, all they are interested in is finding a beautiful girl and once they find one, they take no further notice of their mother or father. But girls are pulled by feelings for their mother … Yes, they can keep a look out for you even after marriage if they want to.

For Jorina's husband, who received a government pension and hence enjoyed a degree of financial security, money was not the main issue. He had an elderly bed-ridden mother; what he wanted for her was care:

> Money is not going to buy me the things I need, the care … Is the government going to clean up when my mother urinates or defecates, lying in bed or will somebody else? It has to be your own family who will do it … That is the thing for which you have to look to them. When you become old, you cannot walk, you become disabled, and you need help with everything – eating, walking, talking.

Shireen's husband had wanted a daughter from the outset and believed that this was the case with a lot of parents. He was of the view that they were more loyal to their parents. He cited the example of someone he knew who had five daughters and no sons. The daughters all worked and sent money to their parents whenever they needed it. When one of their husbands raised objections, she had retorted that she wanted to send money to her parents because they had educated her and it was her money she was sending, not his.

As his comment shows, the idea that daughters could be 'like sons' had been taking root in local perceptions on the basis of observations of others in the community. Asma pointed to the case of the local landlord:

> Even when people have two daughters, they accept it and bring up their daughters like sons. That means educating them properly. [The local landlord] has two daughters and no sons, but they are like sons. They are studying and one of them is going to be a lawyer.

If that girl earns an income, will she abandon her father who has done so much for her?

Thus, while the qualities of caring and compassion attributed to daughters were part of the reason for the value that parents had begun to attach to daughters and for the efforts they made to assure their daughters' future happiness, we can also detect the emergence of a new kind of intergenerational bargain, an instrumental rationale to the revaluation of daughters.

Parents had become more discriminating about who they married their daughters off to. The study in rural Rajshahi by Amin and Huq (2008) cited earlier had found that, though many girls had wanted to be married off within their natal village so as to remain close to their parents, societal norms and parental preferences generally dictated marriage outside the village. This seemed to be changing in Amarpur. Along with looking for a groom with a good education and job prospects, many parents wanted to marry their daughters into families living close by so that they were not lost to them after marriage. Even if married daughters did not live within the natal village itself, improved transport and mobile phones made it far easier than in the past for them to visit their parents regularly and to enquire after them on a routine basis to ensure they were looked after properly.

I have already discussed in previous chapters how many parents wanted to bring their daughters up with the capabilities they needed stand up for themselves, to earn their own income, to exercise greater voice in their marriages – in other words, the very 'voice' that mothers in Amarpur were decrying so passionately in their daughters-in-law. Kamrunahar (36) spelt out what these new capabilities made possible for the young generation of women – including the previously disapproved of, and almost unthinkable, possibility of walking out of marriages:

> It is good that girls are now able to stand on their own feet … Her husband is earning, she is also earning. She doesn't have to listen to anyone … If her mother-in-law says something, she can go off and live in a rented house with her husband … This was not the case in the past. At that time, even if the mother-in-law harassed you, you had no option but to put up with it, you did not know how to earn a living. The present situation is better. Now children are educated and they know everything. If they don't like life with their in-laws, they can always leave.

Morjina (33) was divorced. Her experience had taught her that happy marriages were not preordained. She had suffered a great deal in her life and she did not want her two daughters to suffer: 'Fate will determine what kind of life they have, but a mother can influence fate.' As such a mother, she planned to educate her daughters so that they could get jobs and they would not have to look to their husbands for everything as their mother had.

She spoke of the values she sought to instil in her daughters that would allow them to be self-reflective, to constantly ask themselves:

> What should I do, what do I want to do? I want to do well in my studies, I want to get satisfactory results, I want a good job. I want to be able to do things my way, freely and independently. I want to be able to hold my own in good society.

They might accept their husbands' authority within marriage but, if he let them down, they had their education to fall back on, they could leave their marriages and set up their own households.

What is significant, of course, is that the same capabilities that allowed a daughter to consider walking out of an unsatisfactory marriage also gave her the ability to support her parents after marriage, often in the face of opposition from husbands and in-laws. So, even as mothers contemplated the shifting power dynamics in their relationship with their daughters-in-law with varying degrees of resentment and resignation, they were bringing up their own daughters with the ability to stand up to *their* husbands and in-laws if necessary in order to help their own parents who had made so many sacrifices to bring them up. Rabeya Begum (50s) summed up this new thinking succinctly: 'Girls can look after her parents these days. They couldn't earlier … because they didn't have jobs, they didn't have rights and they had to obey their husbands' commands.'

Rahela (43) said that she had been beaten and mistreated by her mother-in-law because she came from a poor family and had no education. She had educated her daughter to make sure the same thing did not happen to her. She also hoped that her daughter would remember her parents' sacrifices as she grew older:

> If you bring up your daughter properly, then when she marries, she can get a job and earn five thousand takas, she can send some to her parents. But if you don't help her to get to that level, how will she give anything? If she can stand on her own feet, if she can work independently, then she can tell her husband: 'My parents have given me an education, they have spent money to educate me and now they are suffering … I want to give them something in return'. A good husband will allow her to do so but if he does not, a daughter with earnings of her own can always use different strategies to send money anyway.

Kulsum (37) believed it was important that daughters were brought up to be strong and independent:

> Even if there is a cost if you have a daughter because of dowry, she can do the work of five sons. But not all parents bring up their daughters the right way … Women have a value nowadays but only

if they can act independently. Those whose hands and feet are tied can have no value. If she cannot look to the left or right, or go out, or be able to learn things, then she will have no value.

Sabura (47) explained why she had educated her daughters as well as her sons:

We could not leave them any financial assets but if we gave them a high level of education, then they could not say at a later stage that their parents left them nothing.

But her son and his wife had grown distant and, when she spoke of her own future, it was in relation to her daughters:

I have no claim on my daughters but if I make them qualified, then they will tell their husbands that 'just as you are responsible for your parents, because they educated you, so too my parents qualified me and therefore have a claim on me'. But that won't happen if you only teach your daughter to boil rice and throw out the cow dung.

To sum up, therefore, we can see that, while strong son preference persisted among some parents in Amarpur, preferences were changing among the majority, simultaneously reflecting and contributing to shifts in the patriarchal bargain. The intergenerational terms of the bargain had, in the past, been a taken-for-granted aspect of social practice, rooted in the realm of doxa, but many parents were losing confidence that they could rely on it in their old age. As they sought to reconfigure these terms in ways that shifted some of the responsibility onto daughters, their narratives took on a more explicitly transactional element, spelling out a bargain that was not sanctioned by tradition but that they were bringing into existence through new kinds of practices. They attached greater importance to daughters' education than they had done in the past, fed and looked after them more equally, and put greater effort into finding the right husband for them and marrying them closer to home so that ties remained strong. In return, they hoped that daughters would recognise the sacrifices that their parents had made and reciprocate by supporting them in their old age.

9.4 Gendered pathways of social change

In Amarpur – and elsewhere – the decline in family size had been accompanied by a weakening in the intensity of son preference. Son preference lingered on, but most families wanted a daughter as well as a son, with one of each the ideal. This chapter has gone into explanations for this revaluation of daughters in some depth in the context of Amarpur, but the changes it has discussed did not happen overnight nor were they confined to Amarpur. Early signs of these changes are evident in studies dating back several decades and carried out in different locations.

We caught sight of them in research by Lindenbaum, Chakraborty and Mohammed (1985) in Matlab *thana* in the early 1980s, where new job opportunities for educated women were beginning to emerge and there was speculation about whether daughters could play the role of 'sons' when their parents grew old. These views had become more widespread in Matlab by the late 1980s when Simmons et al. reported that opinions were divided as to how reliable sons were likely to be as support to parents in their old age. During their fieldwork in rural Jessore in 1996, Caldwell and Khuda heard complaints from parents that sons were becoming less reliable, that they were looking to their daughters for old age support. When research was carried out in Matlab in the late 2000s, the belief that parents would be looked after by their daughters in their old age if their sons failed to do so appeared to have become widespread, along with reports by a number of married daughters that they were indeed looking after their parents (Schoen 2018). Studies with garment workers in the late 1980s and 1990s noted how working daughters spoke of being 'sons' to their ageing parents and how working mothers were educating their daughters in the hope of their support in later life. The 2006 World Bank survey cited in Chapter 7 found much higher percentages of younger married women than older ones said they would be willing to accept financial help from their daughters in their old age or to live with them (World Bank 2008). In addition, a number of earlier studies had also commented on the weakening authority of the older generation over the young (Balk 1997; Simmons 1996), an early sign of the growing precarity of the intergenerational contract.

As the possibility of financial support from daughters grew among many rural families, Lindenbaum, Chakraborty and Mohammed speculated that this might, in the future, lead to a more egalitarian treatment of sons and daughters. Over a decade after their study, Alam and Bairagi (1997) reported that the survival chances of girls were indeed improving relative to boys and that this improvement appeared to be occurring independently of the expansion of health and family planning services. They wondered if perhaps the various programmes undertaken by government and NGOs were bringing about a 'silent revolution' in the status of women and girls.

Adnan (1998) makes a similar point:

> Changes in women's position still remain far from universal in Bangladesh, but the emergent trends were sufficiently recognizable by the 1980s. Insofar as these have had an impact on prevalent social norms and cultural perceptions, it is possible that a reassessment of the value of female children might well have begun, even if it is not always consciously articulated. Since many of the factors which made girls less preferable than boys are ceasing to hold, it is likely that parents have also begun to find female children less undesirable than before … It … seems reasonable to postulate

the hypothesis that the preference for sons is on the decline, given increasing value of female children to parents. (p.1344)

Different chapters in the book have spelt out some elements of the ongoing silent revolution. As government stipends made girls' education more affordable, parents were able to imagine a different future for their daughters. Some hoped that education would secure more desirable husbands for their daughters while also reducing the amount of dowry demanded. Others hoped education would lead to better jobs and that education and employment would allow their daughters to stand up for themselves within marriage. And, of course, as the view that sons were becoming increasingly unreliable as support in their parents' old age appeared to be spreading, it was being replaced by the belief that the role of daughters had changed and would change even further in the future: they were no longer dependents within the patriarchal family but were taking on breadwinning responsibilities; they were becoming 'sons'.

So the explanations that we found in Amarpur for the weakening of son preference can be seen to some extent as reflecting material changes and attitudinal shifts that were unfolding across Bangladesh over the years. However, if we accept the validity of accounts of 'unruly' sons and 'compassionate' daughters that were circulating in Amarpur and elsewhere, what explained this divergence in views? For the answer, I believe we need to juxtapose the changes that I have described in the lives of men and women in Bangladesh with the continuities that characterise the wider context.

The long-established tradition of sons remaining in close residence to their parents had been based on the land they expected to receive as bequest when their fathers died. Such expectations were not relevant among the growing number of landless families; not only did nucleation set in much earlier among these families but they became more dispersed as landless sons became increasingly mobile in their search for work. Over time, as agriculture shrank in importance within the economy, it was not only the landless that became mobile in search of economic opportunities. Men from across the class structure took up work in a variety of non-farm occupations within their communities, in village and towns outside it, with many more now going abroad in search of more lucrative work.

The steady nucleation of family structures and a greater likelihood that sons set up their own independent households soon after, or even before, marriage, was accompanied by a decline in their willingness to support their parents in their old age; at least, that was how many parents in Amarpur saw it. The growing incidence of love marriages, the greater likelihood of educated wives, the joint aspirations of couples for their own children also added to the likelihood that sons focused their attention more on the welfare of their own families than on the welfare of their parents, particularly as the old material rationale for providing support, the expected inheritance of land, had weakened. Sons no longer looked to their parents for economic support in the way they had done before but looked instead to their own efforts to make their own way in the world. They did not need their parents' approval to decide who to marry and, if their marriages broke down, they could simply marry again.

Change had also occurred in women's lives but their lives evolved very differently. In the past, they had been permitted few, if any, resources of their own. They had been expected to move from dependence on their fathers in their early life to dependence on husbands as adults to dependence on sons as they grew older. This had changed in that they were now increasingly able to earn a living and to exercise some degree of independent purchasing power but their livelihood options remained limited by continued restrictions on their physical mobility and continued discrimination in favour of men. Their education and employment gave many a greater voice in their own lives but patriarchal risk had not vanished. Marriage was not a stable institution; husbands were not reliable sources of security. Both mothers and daughters spoke of the need for women to have an income of their own should their marriage break down or their husbands die before their sons had become adults. Divorce might be more frequent, less stigmatised, but the possibility of a woman on her own setting up an independent household was still rare and still frowned upon, particularly in rural areas.

So, while their earnings provided greater financial security to women than they had enjoyed before, they continued to need the support of their natal kin. If their husbands behaved badly or their marriages broke down, it was to their natal families that they turned. In the past, women had waived their rights to parental property in favour of their brothers so that they would still have their familial networks to fall back on if needed. Now they had the means to invest in their relationship with their natal family, particularly with their parents who were now more willing than in the past to struggle and make sacrifices to give daughters a better chance in life. Their natal families still remained their primary source of security. It remained in women's interest to keep these family ties strong.

Notes

[1] The 2006 World Bank survey also noted this pattern of increasing consultation of women in marriage negotiations (World Bank 2008).

[2] In fact, as Talukder et al. (2015) note, disclosure of the sex of the foetus was not legally restricted and was found to be widespread in the two districts they studied – but sex-selective abortion was extremely rare.

[3] This seems consistent with the finding reported by Amin and Das (2013) that communities that reported more egalitarian attitudes on gender also reported a lower incidence of dowry. See Chapter 7, Note 11.

10. Resolving the paradox: concluding reflections

Some paradoxes are resolvable by showing that a premise was slightly false, that the inferences included unjustifiable steps, or that the conclusions turned out to be more plausible than initially thought. (Quine 1981, p.178)

This book took the idea of the Bangladesh paradox as its point of departure. My final chapter returns to the idea. The quotation from Quine above prefaces the argument that I want to make. Some paradoxes are more apparent than real: they can often be resolved by reassessing the validity of their premises, the logic of their inferences or the plausibility of their conclusions. I argue, on the basis of the analysis in this book, that the social progress that Bangladesh made despite high levels of poverty and poor governance may indeed have been 'surprising', even 'astonishing', but that characterising it as a paradox reflects misplaced premises about how progress was going to happen in the country. There are important insights contained in this analysis into the actual processes of social change that took place in the country. I will be drawing them together in this chapter.

I also want to return to the 'reverse paradox' in India that was touched on in the introduction. Despite its higher per capita income, more rapid rates of growth and a near-uninterrupted record of democratic governance, India has not only reported continued inequalities in the survival chances of girls relative to boys but also rising sex ratios at birth since the 1980s: the new phenomenon of prenatal discrimination. I offer a brief account of how the practice-based approach adopted in this book might explain the diverging patterns in the two countries. Finally, I conclude by asking whether the social progress reported by Bangladesh is likely to be sustained in the foreseeable future.

10.1 Privileging sites of knowledge production

In her book on the production of scientific knowledge, Krause (2021) points out that it is generally organised around two basic elements: a set of research objectives, the conceptual focus of inquiry, and the concrete empirical forms through which researchers seek to achieve these objectives. While the conceptual concerns are rooted in the specific disciplinary and intellectual traditions to which researchers belong, a common practice across these varying traditions is to use specific empirical objects of their research to 'stand in' for the general phenomena they are interested in, since it is rarely possible to study such phenomena in their entirety.

Moreover, within the different disciplines, certain empirical objects acquire privileged status in that they are used repeatedly to 'stand in' for the more general phenomena they are taken to represent. For instance, while cities are generally taken to stand in for processes of urbanisation in general, particular cities, such as Berlin, Chicago and Mumbai, have been repeatedly selected in such studies, to the neglect of others like Monaco City, Jacksonville or, for that matter, Dhaka. Well-known classics in the sociology of work have been more likely to deal with doctors and lawyers than with priests or exterminators. And, while revolutions in general are used to 'stand in' as instances of political upheaval, the French Revolution has featured far more frequently than others, such as the Haitian Revolution or even the American one. These privileged 'stand-ins' become what Krause calls the 'model cases' for their discipline, shaping its understanding of categories and concepts in disproportionate ways, generating knowledge that becomes part of the general knowledge in that field.[1]

The privileging of certain stand-ins over others in the construction of model cases has not been random. In some instances, the selection process reflected scientific criteria, the closeness of 'fit' between the research question and specific empirical choices. So certain research objects and sites were elevated to the status of the model case because they were assumed by collective consensus within the discipline to have the capacity to generate important and generalisable insights. In other cases, the selection process reflected practical concerns: convenience, funding availability, job opportunities and sponsorship deals have all made certain empirical choices more appealing than others.

In addition, researchers' ideological predispositions have often created a strong bias towards empirical examples that are framed as 'the most advanced' within the category under study. For instance, there has been a tendency to focus on growing cities on the assumption that they would provide insights into what other cities would later become. Similarly, within the study of work, activities using the latest technology attract disproportionate attention because they are seen to offer insights into the future world of work.

This ideological predisposition towards 'the most advanced' has been particularly clear in the field of development studies. The field emerged at the end of the Second World War and the beginning of the Cold War, a period when many of the previously colonised countries in Africa and Asia were gaining their independence and preparing to embark on state-led processes of import-substituting industrialisation that would allow them to catch up with the West. From the viewpoint of the major capitalist powers, there was a real danger that, without adequate socio-economic progress, these countries would be drawn into the communist sphere of influence. This had to be pre-empted through large-scale financial aid and policy advice to steer them towards a capitalist road to development. The inception of the aid industry can be traced to this historical moment.

An important objective of the new industry was investment in research that could inform its policy efforts. Developed countries looked to their own past for lessons on how to shape the future of developing countries in their own image. Europe, and the West more generally, became 'model cases' in this field of research, an approach Chakrabarty (2000) dubbed 'first in Europe, then elsewhere' (cited in Krause 2021, p.48). The unilinear stages-of-development narratives that characterise its early theories – of growth, modernisation and demographic transition – reflected attempts by researchers to capture stylised facts about the processes through which capitalism evolved in the model cases (Lerner 1958; Notestein 1945; Rostow 1960).[2] Their narratives formed the basis of the industry that grew up around the provision of aid to less developed countries, offering funds, job opportunities and sponsorships to promote their ideas and policy prescriptions.

Of course, these theories have been modified over time. The rise of neoliberalism saw the displacement of the state's earlier role in steering the development process, the deregulation of markets, the opening up of economies to free trade and a greater stress on 'good governance'. But there has remained a strong strand within development studies that continues to evoke the logic of the early 'model cases'. It reflects the persisting belief that historical experiences of the West could provide a generalisable account of how developing countries were likely to evolve should they follow the West's advice. Their progress could therefore be monitored by classifying them according to the stage of growth, modernisation or demographic transition they had achieved.

This belief held back the recognition that the countries in question represented sites of research in their own right, that they could offer valuable insights into how change was likely to happen in contexts that were very different from those that had prevailed in the West. Indeed, many developing country contexts had been reshaped to suit the interests of the West, most dramatically through the colonial encounter. It was unlikely that any progress they made would follow faithfully in the footsteps of model cases. Many of the so-called paradoxes that litter the field of development studies reflect the fact that these other sites had their own dynamics of change that failed to conform to 'the model'.

The idea of the Bangladesh paradox emerged out of this intellectual tradition. It reflected the general puzzlement that the country appeared to be reporting a pace of social progress that the development canon assumed could only occur after it had achieved a certain stage of socio-economic development. Efforts to explain the paradox have tended to follow a pattern. Starting from the observation that Bangladesh had not conformed to the canonical model of change, they sought out the deviations from the norm that might explain why this was so. The deviations in question were generally dictated by the development canon itself: an interventionist family planning policy that had not been considered necessary in the demographic transition that took place in the West, the adoption of vertical low-cost health solutions that made it possible to bypass the country's poverty, the role of NGOs in compensating for governance deficits, and continuity in policy across different regimes dictated by donor interests. As I have noted, these are valid elements of any explanation but they do not explain why these enabling factors occurred in Bangladesh in the first place, allowing it to defy the doom-laden prophesies that accompanied its independence.

An alternative approach would be to study the processes of change in Bangladesh as phenomena of interest in their own right. This would certainly include the enabling factors mentioned above, but it would locate them within the history, culture and economy of the country. And it would seek to deepen its understanding of the processes in question by exploring the role played by different actors, those in privileged positions in the country as well as ordinary men and women, and tracing how their actions translated these factors into social change.

10.2 Multilevel stories of change: structure, agency and practice

'Big picture' stories and structural change

A particular manifestation of structural change motivated my interest in the 'Bangladesh paradox': the steady 'normalisation' of child sex ratios and the continued 'normality' of its sex ratios at birth. The increased value given to daughters indicated by this change was part of the larger story of social progress that the idea of the paradox sought to capture. My desire to retell this story from the bottom up, to take the perspective of ordinary people and how they responded to the changing world around them, explains the theoretical framework that guided my analysis (Chapter 1). The open-ended methodological approach I adopted to tell the story allowed me to draw on a range of different sources representing different forms of data collection at different time periods. I have sought to weave these together to form a coherent narrative about the processes of structuration that had taken place in the country, the changes in its structures and in the social practices that mediated how these changes played out on the ground.

Chapter 2 offered a very compressed history of Bangladesh, tracing its transition from an agrarian subsistence economy to its current status as a semi-industrialising country in an unequal global order. This 'big picture' account drew attention to what it was about the history and geography of the country that explained its context at the time of its independence: its abject poverty, its population density, the oppressive nature of its patriarchy – but it also hinted at a certain fluidity of social relations and practices that lay below an apparently intransigent surface (picked up in greater detail in Chapter 4).

While the fertility of the land in the Bengal delta lent itself to cultivation by waves of migrants, the vagaries of its natural environment gave rise to a society that had to adapt to sudden shifts in its circumstances. Its location on the eastern margins of the Indian subcontinent isolated its people from the cultural, political and economic mainstream of the north Indian plains for many centuries. This did not prevent various rulers, mainly from outside the region, from attempting to impose their rule on it. But it did mean that the belief system that flourished in the region had strong roots in its early indigenous culture, albeit shaped by these different external influences.

This history helps to explain why the achievement of national sovereignty in 1971 represented such a major watershed, despite the dire situation that persisted for many years after the country's independence (Chapter 3). It marked the transition from several centuries of rule by elites from outside the region with little in common with the majority of the population to a new era of rule by an emerging domestic elite that shared its culture and beliefs. More responsive to the needs of the people, it undertook bottom-up policies that sought at the very least to meet their subsistence requirements (Chapter 5).

A second important structural element contributing to progress in the country were different kinds of 'connectedness'. One was social in nature (Chapter 5). The domestic elite who took up leadership roles in politics, administration, NGOs and the emerging private sector shared similar backgrounds: their families knew each other, they may have been students together. This elite cohesiveness, combined with its social proximity to the majority of the country, was an important factor in explaining the extent and effectiveness of collaboration across sectors that has been commented on in the paradox literature. The same social homogeneity and the relative absence of rigid social barriers also enhanced the likelihood of upward mobility in the general population. The 'capacity to aspire' could take root, even among the poor, as new possibilities came into view because they believed that many of these possibilities were within their reach.

The density of population generated physical connectedness, contributing to the speed with which new ideas took hold and spread. Increased investments in roads, transport, media and digital technology meant that the population could reach each other easily. The widespread presence of NGOs contributed further. Connectedness also enabled growth in non-farm activities, the diversification of rural livelihoods and the spread of social services, contributing to the decline in different dimensions of poverty.

Also part of the big picture was the influence of different institutional actors. Western donors played a major role in opening the country to global competition and seeking to modernise it in their own image. Impelled by Malthusian doomsday scenarios, they promoted a degree of state and NGO intervention in the intimate sphere of family-based reproduction that had not been dreamt of, or considered, necessary, when the West was undergoing its demographic transition. They also made modern technologies of birth control and child survival, which had not been invented in the 19th century, widely available to the population. Important early changes in women's lives were thus programme-led. NGO activities had a particularly important role to play in opening up new possibilities to women, different futures to those they had grown up with, futures frequently premised on secular ideas about women's rights and gender equality.

The pressure exerted by donors combined with the interests of the emerging national elite to open up the country to global forces, creating both new livelihood opportunities in the shape of the export garment sector and international migration and increasing the cross-current of ideas and images that shaped consumer aspirations and models of modernity.

External forces also included the flow of orthodox Islamic beliefs into the country through the aid provided by countries in the Middle East, through the beliefs and practices brought into the country by migrants returning from the Middle East and, of course, through the efforts of Islamist forces operating within the country. These were adopted by successive regimes in search of legitimacy and disseminated through various channels, including media, education and religious NGOs. While they offered an alternative form of modernity to that associated with the West, they did little to contest the privatisation agenda of Western donors or the structures of classic patriarchy.

'Small picture' stories and women's agency

A key objective of this book was to bring together the multitude of 'small picture' stories that featured in ground-level research carried out over the years. I wanted to understand how the actual processes of social change unfolded in people's lives and, in particular, to explore the agency exercised by women from different social groups in driving processes that led to greater gender equality. Fieldwork carried out in Amarpur in 2010 helped to formulate the key research questions that guided my research. In a patriarchal system which deprived women of material resources of their own, of knowledge about the outside world, of symbolic capital that would allow them to challenge the gendered limits to permissible behaviour and of social networks other than those they were born or married into, what led women to seek to reconfigure some of the more oppressive manifestations of this system and what forms of agency did they draw on in order to do so?

If I had to summarise the main forces that motivated women to seek change, I would single out poverty on the one hand and opportunity on the other. Poverty brought home to many women the precariousness of the patriarchal bargain on which they had relied for protection and provision from male family members and which had led them to accept the unfairness of its terms. Opportunity gave them the means to renegotiate these terms in a way that mitigated their status as perennial dependents without necessarily jettisoning the entire bargain. A great deal of the agency that women exercised in these processes of negotiation relied on their cultural capabilities, the creativity and resourcefulness they could bring into play as a result of their intimate knowledge of how the structures that shaped their lives played out for their families and communities. This knowledge helped to shape the tactics and strategies they could use to expand their 'room for manoeuvre' without jeopardising the relationships they valued or at least depended on.

Where their 'preferences' aligned with government policy objectives, they benefited from the legitimacy bestowed on their efforts by the official discourse (Chapter 6). The messages that accompanied government interventions in the intimate and value-laden domain of reproduction were often as critical to bringing about change in practices as the actual resources they distributed. So we found that women's family members were generally receptive to the idea of change in certain aspects of reproductive behaviour – those relating to the care of children, for instance – so that new practices were adopted without much opposition. But where women's own desires diverged from those of their family or community, as in the adoption of new contraceptive technology, government endorsement gave them the courage and the arguments to stand up to opposition.

Such officialising discourses were absent in the processes through which women began to take up paid work outside the socially approved boundaries of their homes (Chapter 7). These processes were driven by the responses of individual women – often in defiance of their families and communities – to the circumstances of their lives rather than to incentives offered by government policy. One reason that so many women opted to take advantage of the new microfinance services that became available from the 1980s onwards was that it made home-based income generation possible. It allowed some of them to move out of backbreaking and demeaning wage labour in the fields and by the roadsides and others to move from unpaid family labour to earning an income of their own.

But there were others who were either excluded or excluded themselves from microfinance services or else wanted to avail themselves of better-paid opportunities outside the home. While they did not constitute the majority of working women in the country, their growing presence in the public domain was a clear departure from past norms and a visible challenge to the patriarchal status quo. Women from poorer families had long been forced by the imperatives of survival to break with the norms that governed their economic activities. But the entry of educated women from better-off households represented the exercise of a certain degree of agency on their part. In the face of hesitation or outright opposition from family members or hostility from the community, these women drew on the cultural repertoires of the community to downplay or even deny transgression of its norms (Chapter 7). As practice theorists have pointed out, there are limits to the change that can be brought about by discursive strategies in the face of resilient material constraints but, where reinterpretations of norms are reflective of, and made possible by, cracks and openings in the structure, they become part of the process by which old ways of doing things are modified and gradually evolve into new ways of doing things.

Women from poorer households were the main beneficiaries of the activities of development NGOs who played a major role in providing access to various social and financial services as well as to new kinds of social networks.

It was these gains that shaped their responses to the rising tide of orthodox Islam in the country (Chapter 8). While affluent women in urban and rural areas could afford to adopt the restrictions imposed by the orthodox version, poorer women resisted interpretations of Islam that sought to block off economic opportunities and to close down the organisations that had been instrumental in providing them. Most opted for non-confrontational forms of resistance, but those from the radical NGO subsector were less compromising. It was among its members that we found the greatest willingness to challenge the realm of the doxa as well as the new orthodoxies, the clearest articulation of 'bigger dreams' for a fairer society.

While the history of the region helps us to understand the larger structures that were in place at the country's independence, one of the important insights that emerged through the analytical focus on women's agency was the motivating power of individual histories as a force for social change (Chapters 7, 8 and 9). Women spoke passionately about what it felt like to grow up as a daughter whose mother's attention was focused on cherished sons. They had seen their brothers favoured in the distribution of household resources as the future breadwinners of the family, while they themselves were regarded as liabilities for whom dowry would have to be paid to marry them off and who, once married, would be cut off from their natal home.

They spoke of the abuse and harsh treatment that many had faced at the hands of their husbands and in-laws, their knowledge that their parents were unlikely to come to their aid since they now belonged to their husband's lineage. Their bitter memories of coming to adulthood in a society in which they were only ever regarded as the 'neighbour's tree' shaped their dreams and aspirations in later life and the value they attached to 'standing on your own feet'.

It explained their efforts to mitigate their dependent status within their families by taking up the forms of paid work that were newly available as part of larger changes taking place. In some cases, they reported that their greater role in the household breadwinning activities made them more central in household affairs, gave them a greater sense of 'mattering' in the family, the feeling that their preferences and priorities were heard and taken account of. In other cases, it allowed them to seek out greater independence, turning their backs on uncaring parents or abusive husbands and taking responsibility for their own future.

It also explained the determination of these women to ensure that their daughters would not have to experience the costs of dependency that their mothers had, that their happiness and wellbeing would not depend in the same way on what others decided for them. We saw a concerted effort on the part of parents, and mothers in particular, to invest in their daughters, in the hope of giving them a sense of self-worth, a 'strength of their own', so that they had the ability to stand up to the arbitrary exercise of power on the part of husbands and in-laws and to take responsibility for their own lives if necessary.[3] While each of these dreams for their daughters represented a departure from the conventions of the past, the fact that many mothers – and fathers – seemed to contemplate with equanimity the possibility that their daughters might walk out of marriages if these proved oppressive was probably the most radical departure from the past. In these narratives, as Reay (2004) puts it,

> we begin to get a sense not only of the myriad adaptations, responses, reactions and resistances to 'the way the world is', but also of individuals struggling to make the world a different place. (p.437)

Middle-range stories and changing practice

While women's agency was an important part of the story of change that featured in the Bangladesh paradox, it was not exercised as the isolated acts of individuals. It contributed to, and was made possible by, changes initiated by other actors in society around the same time. The chapters in this book illuminate some of the mechanisms that allowed these individual responses to coalesce into new social practices that redefined the wider social context.

As I noted in Chapter 6, the speed at which policy-initiated changes in reproductive practices occurred owed a great deal to the dynamics of sequence and synergy within the policy process. The adoption of the doorstep delivery of contraception by female family planning workers was credited with the dramatic decline in fertility rates, but the close sequence in which different interventions in the reproductive domain occurred and the synergies between them is likely to have hastened the pace of change and amplified its impact.

Parents were motivated to adopt family planning to look after their children better and they were able to adopt new ways of looking after their children better because they could control the number of births. Policy dissemination efforts intended to change reproductive practices built on each other in ways that reinforced and amplified the messages of each: small families consisting of a boy and a girl were 'happy' or 'modern' families; the happiness of the family and the health of the mother required daughters to be sent to school and to marry later.

There were gains also from institutional collaboration in the delivery of social services, which were particularly important when they went against social norms. Fieldworkers found their efforts eased when they were part of government programmes that had the stamp of public authority and when their workers were regarded as the government-in-person. NGOs sought to associate their efforts with government, to involve local officials when they could, so as to benefit from this authority. NGOs, in turn, compensated for the government's capacity deficits, reaching poorer sections who government officials failed to reach and experimenting to find out what worked best, lessons that the government then adopted.

Programmes used various routes to communicate new meanings and practices to the population at large, creating a discursive space for the spread of these practices. The metaphor of the 'pebble in the pond' (Mita and Simmons

1995, p.4) used in the family planning literature provided a vivid description of how these efforts worked. The community-based health worker was the 'pebble' who brought about changing practices among the women and families they encountered, changes that rippled outwards through conversations between these families and others in their community, conversations that took place across generations so that the younger generation grew up familiar with the idea of family planning. These ripple effects were further amplified by more generalised forms of communication such as poster campaigns, radios, newspapers and TV that were aimed at the large population.

While the widespread promotion of education by government and NGOs assisted the transition to quality in parental strategies, making education more affordable for both boys and girls, the increased investment in girls' education proved to be a potent force for change. Parents themselves put a great deal of store on the transformative power of education (Chapter 6). As we noted, women in the 2008 IDS-BIGD study were almost unanimous in declaring that access to education was the resource that had had made the biggest difference in women's lives (Tables 8a and 8b). These emic views were supported by a large number of quantitative studies testifying to the strength of the association between female education and a range of immediate, longer-term and intergenerational outcomes in their lives (see Chapter 6, Note 11). Education worked in indirect ways as well to catalyse change in the public domain. The requirement of some level of education for various government and non-government jobs helped to legitimise the employment of educated women from higher-status households in forms of work that could be defined as respectable – partly because they were closed off to women from poorer households.

The narratives related in this book gave us a 'close up' view of the workings of some of the mechanisms of change that feature in the social science literature: role models, demonstration effects, tipping points, spillovers and feedback effects. In particular, they uncovered their relational dimensions. These mechanisms may have been put into motion by individuals as a result of their changing ideas and aspirations, but these changes were the product of their observations of those around them, observations that helped them to change their views of what was possible or desirable and provided them with the impetus to make change.

I have cited many examples of the power of role models to generate change, role models that were themselves products of wider change. There was the rickshaw puller who observed the polite behaviour of the children he took to school every day and decided that he would educate his daughters so that they would also learn to conduct themselves with dignity. There was Shamiran and her schoolfriends living in a village in the early 1980s who had been so impressed by the dress and confidence of the family planning worker who came to advise married women in their village about birth control that they decided that when they grew up they too would take up jobs distributing pills and helping others to have fewer children while being able to buy nice clothes for themselves. There were the young women in rural Bangladesh who observed with envy the confidence and earning power of the garment workers who came to visit their village home and gained the courage to migrate themselves in search of such jobs. As one young woman told me in my earlier research, 'If they could do it, why couldn't I?' (Kabeer 2000, p.359).

Demonstration effects were also at work. There were the negative lessons learnt from observing families who had too many children and could not afford to feed them so that they could be seen wandering around the village with plates in their hands, begging for food. Sights like this persuaded a number of women that birth control was a good idea. There were the positive lessons reported by women who decided to join microfinance organisations after initial reluctance because they observed the increased prosperity of those who had taken loans. There were also mothers and fathers who were motivated to educate their daughters because they knew of people whose educated daughters got good jobs and assisted their parents in a way that had not been possible before.

There were spillover effects that worked through the diffusion of ideas. Schuler and Hashmi (1994) found that, while Grameen Bank members were more likely to adopt family planning than non-members, non-members in villages with a branch of Grameen Bank were more likely to adopt family planning than non-members in villages without such a branch. Bora et al. (2023) report that the proportion of educated women in a community influenced the fertility behaviour of less-educated women in that community.

There was the feedback effect reported by Heath and Mobarak (2015), who note that the observed availability of garment jobs for women with some level of education by families living in close proximity to garment factories increased the likelihood that they would invest in their daughters' education.

There were also examples of 'tipping points', change that became self-sustaining after a critical mass of people had adopted it. One reason why fertility decline was so rapid in Bangladesh was that, while those who were among the first to adopt family planning were harshly condemned for violating social norms, those who adopted it just 10 years later faced far less criticism; the norms of the community had undergone change (Schuler et al. 1996a).

Similarly, the early cohort of garment workers had borne the brunt of the social condemnation directed towards women who had departed from cultural norms in such a visible way. Delowara, who I interviewed in 1987, protested at how unfair it was for the public to judge all garment workers by the 'misbehaviour' of just a few: 'don't say women, say woman' (Chapter 7). Over the years, their numbers grew and their presence on the streets became a familiar sight. The workers interviewed three decades later did not attract the same disapproving comments and when they did they dismissed them with a firmness that was in marked contrast to their earlier defensiveness:

> What is so bad about falling in love, it is a natural thing and could happen anywhere. Do girls in schools and colleges not also fall in love, elope with men of their choice? No one points a finger at them.

Why is it only garment girls who are given a bad name? (Kabeer, Huq and Rahaman 2021, p.19)

More generally, the presence of large numbers of women engaged in various kinds of income-generating activities may not have displaced the dominance of the male breadwinner model, but it gained wide acceptance for the idea of women as 'secondary' breadwinners and, implicitly, for the dual breadwinner family.

The process by which growing familiarity led to the routinisation of practice that had once been seen as a departure from norms was also evident within the policy domain. It meant that the extra effort necessary to bring about early stages of behavioural change did not necessarily have to be maintained over time in order to sustain these changes. We saw the efforts made by government and NGOs at the start of their field-based programmes to ensure the social acceptability of their female work force in order to minimise any hostility they might encounter. They sought to accommodate the community habitus as far as possible, using familiar materials and images, invoking religious authority to legitimise their efforts, enforcing proper behaviour on the part of their staff. These efforts were relaxed as the new practices became more familiar and the changes self-sustaining. Family planning became as mundane as the daily diet of rice and lentils; parents sent their daughters to school 'because everyone was doing it'; microcredit was absorbed into the routine of everyday livelihood activities. As new practices took root, rules of behaviour for field staff became less strict. Organisations were able to move from the doorstep delivery to fixed location clinics for the distribution of contraception. Nutritional education through face-to-face interaction with mothers gave way to more impersonal forms of communication. Microfinance organisations relaxed the principle of group liability as timely repayment of loans became the norm. As time went on, assumptions about what women could and could not do had to be rethought in recognition of the fact that 'times had changed and so had gender relations' (Hossain 2017, p.116).

Finally, the book has provided some important insights into structuration processes as they played out in relation to the patriarchal bargain. In the introduction, I discussed the power of habitus in enforcing conformity to social norms through the internalisation of these norms by individuals and by those around them. Gender injustices were taken for granted, part of the realm of doxa. This changed over the period studied in the book through processes which modified and attenuated this habitus as perceived and real gaps opened up between the promise of the patriarchal bargain and its practice.

A great deal of the agency that women sought to exercise was a response to this widening gap, the increased instability of the patriarchal bargain it signified and the realisation that they could no longer rely on men to fulfil their side of the bargain, regardless of how faithfully they themselves observed theirs. Unquestioning compliance became rare, although compliance continued to be performed in the effort to evade sanction by husbands and in-laws or by the wider community. More often, though, the research cited in this book uncovered a repertoire of tactics and strategies through which women sought to destabilise or renegotiate the terms of the patriarchal bargain, ranging from hidden forms of subversion, the performance of outward compliance with norms even as they circumvented them, to more overt dissent and even open defiance.

I found that many of the factors that had led to growing uncertainty about the patriarchal bargain also increased uncertainty about its intergenerational dimension. Parents no longer had the same faith that the support in old age by their sons that they had once assumed would be forthcoming. Their uncertainty reflected the great mobility of young men as they sought jobs in various parts of the country and spent a great deal of their adult lives living independently of parents. It also reflected the shift away from arranged marriages among the younger generation. Children expected to be consulted about potential spouses or to select spouses of their own choice – although daughters were still more likely than sons to seek the approval of parents. Sons, on the other hand, did not require parental approval to the same extent, nor did they look to parental support to the same extent if their marriage did not last.

This led to altered relationships between parents, on the one hand, and their daughters and daughters-in-law, on the other. Patriarchal risk had not disappeared from the lives of young women and they sought to retain their ties with their natal families as insurance against abusive husbands or the breakdown of their marriage. As a result, parents spoke of greater closeness with their married daughters than had been the case in the past while at the same time speaking of the greater distance from their increasingly independent daughters-in-law. The greater compassion they attributed to daughters came to the foreground as the expectations they had of their sons' support in old age receded. Indeed, there were growing expressions of the belief that daughters were 'becoming like sons'. Thus, just as structural changes had changed the context in which the individual agency of men and women was exercised, so too, shifting relations of co-operation and conflict brought about by the exercise of this agency translated into changes in the terms of patriarchal bargain. These forms of change go a considerable way to explaining the increased value attached to daughters.

10.3 Son preference and daughter aversion in India: a paradox in reverse?

In the earlier stages of the book, I referred to what appeared to be a reverse version of the Bangladesh paradox that was unfolding in neighbouring India. India was extremely successful by standard development criteria. It had an almost uninterrupted record of democratic governance along with higher rates of per capita income, higher rates of economic growth and lower levels of poverty than Bangladesh. But, as we saw, not only did it perform less well than Bangladesh on a range of social indicators (Chapter 1), its fertility decline was accompanied by a steady rise in its child sex ratios, evidence of intensified gender discrimination: the ratio of boys to 100 girls in the 0–6 age rose from 105.8 in 1991 to 107.9 in 2001 and then to 109.4 in 2011 (John 2011).

While adverse child sex ratios have long reflected excess female mortality in the under-five age group, and excess female mortality remained high, it did not appear to have risen over this period (Das Gupta and Bhatt 1997). Instead, as noted in Chapter 1, the rise in child sex ratios reflected the emergence of female-selective abortion and rising sex ratios at birth (SRBs). The resort to female-selective abortion reflected effort on the part of parents to reconcile their desire for smaller families with their continued strong, even intensified, preference for sons and the deepening 'emotion and practice of daughter aversion' (Borooah and Iyer 2004; Das Gupta and Bhatt 1997; John et al. 2008, p.72).[4]

From the 'normal' SRBs of 105 that had prevailed in the country till the 1980s, India recorded a rise to 111 in the late 1990s and then to 113.6 in 2004 before declining to 110 in 2012, an improvement but still above the norm (Kaur et al. 2016). In fact, these national averages obscured regional differentials: in the classic patriarchal states of northern India, SRBs had reached 120 by the end of the century (Guilmoto 2009).[5]

Moreover, although the deterioration in sex ratios at birth was first reported among the landed upper castes in these northern states, which already had a long history of adverse sex ratios, and, while it was remained pronounced among these groups, it gradually spread to lower castes and to the southern states, where adverse sex ratios had not previously been a problem (Agnihotri 2000; Basu 1999; Das Gupta and Bhatt 1997; John 2011; Kaur et al. 2016; Siddhanta, Agnihotri and Nandy 2009). This went directly against the expectation that fertility decline in India would involve a natural progression from the high-fertility, inegalitarian gender regime that characterised northern India to the lower-fertility and more egalitarian pattern that prevailed in the south – in line with the predictions of demographic transition theory that fertility decline was brought about by improvements in women's status (Basu 1999).

The other unexpected finding related to the religious differentials, specifically those between Hindus, the majority religious group in India, and Muslims, the largest minority. The depiction of Islam as antithetical to gender equality has long been part of the 'common sense' in the Indian context (as elsewhere): as Lahiri and Self (2005) cautiously put it,

> It is possibly not wrong to say that the conventional wisdom – at least outside the Islamic World – is that bias against women is more pronounced among Muslims than among other religious groups. (p.17)

While demographic data had established that Muslims had higher fertility rates than Hindus in India, the conventional wisdom was proved wrong on the matter of sex bias in the treatment of children (Borooah et al. 2009; Government of India 2006).[6] Despite lower levels of education and employment and the greater poverty of their households, Muslim women were less likely than Hindu women to express a preference for sons relative to daughters when asked to specify their ideal sex composition of children; they were less likely to report gender differentials in infant child mortality and nutritional levels; and they were less likely to report male-biased sex ratios at birth (Borooah et al. 2009; Visaria 2015). In regional terms, Muslim preferences and practices did not vary a great deal between the north and south, but as son preference was somewhat weaker among Hindus in the southern states, religious differences tended to be larger in the north than in the south (Borooah et al. 2009).

As Borooah et al. point out, a number of studies sought to explain these religious differentials in reproductive behaviour in terms of a 'pure religion' effect. They drew on theological sources to search out doctrinal differences in such matters as the value ascribed to sons and daughters, contraceptive behaviour and so on. However, not only is it possible to find pronouncements on the subordinate status of women in both sets of theological sources, but these pronouncements are themselves highly debated within each religion. Furthermore, it is difficult to believe that doctrinal differences in beliefs and values could, on their own, constitute an adequate explanation for religious differences in reproductive preferences, given the considerable diversity in sex ratios and son preference reported by Hindus by state, caste and class across India and the differences reported between the Muslim-majority countries of Bangladesh and Pakistan.

A more plausible explanation is likely to be found in the interaction between social norms, values and beliefs, of which religion is one aspect, and the organisation of kinship and family life within different communities and across different contexts in South Asia.[7] The rules, norms and values governing the intergenerational contract are of particular relevance here because of their significance for how different communities seek to preserve, reproduce or transform their status and identity within the larger society and, more immediately, for how the costs and value of sons and daughters are structured within these communities.

The early literature from South Asia reviewed in Chapter 1 told us that the interlocking elements of the intergenerational contract that characterised classic patriarchy in northern India and Bangladesh underpinned what appeared to be an enduring culture of son preference and a history of adverse child sex ratios. But more recent studies suggest that the processes of growth and modernisation that have since taken place in India and Bangladesh have led to a divergence in the 'emotion and practice' of son preference and in accompanying patterns of sex ratios.

I would like to draw on the practice-theoretic approach that has informed the analysis in this book to explain these diverging patterns. I will provide a broad-brush account of the processes of socio-economic change as they played out in India and summarise explanations for why they led to the intensification and spread of adverse sex ratios across the country. I will then draw on the analysis in previous chapters to explain the absence of this phenomenon in Bangladesh. The main argument that I want to make is that, while religious norms are an important dimension of social practice among different communities, their significance varies. There is an important distinction to be made between communities in which religious norms constitute the prescriptive core of the collective habitus and those where religious norms are interwoven more loosely with other aspects of that habitus.

Stories from the Indian context

The 'big picture' story of economic development in India can be divided into two broad phases. The first phase was in the three decades or so after independence when India adopted a capital-intensive, import-substituting and largely state-led industrialisation strategy in order to build its industrial capacity and infrastructure. Economic growth through this period was low, fluctuating around an average of 3.5% a year, which, given population growth rates, translated into per capita growth rates of 1% a year (Varshney 2017). Growth also failed to generate much employment and large swathes of its population continued to live in abject poverty and remained concentrated in agriculture (Basu 2018). There was a spurt in growth rates in the late 1960s with the onset of the Green Revolution and rising agricultural productivity. This began in the highly irrigated wheat growing regions of northern India and later spread, but unevenly, to other parts of India, mainly coastal areas and areas with canal irrigation. The main beneficiaries in all cases were the wealthier landowning castes (Basu and Maertens 2007; Patnaik 1990; Sen and Ghosh 2017).

With the adoption of market-oriented reforms in the 1980s and its acceleration in the 1990s, growth rates began to rise rapidly – an annual average of 6.3% between 1980 and 2015 with per capita growth rates at 4.5% – but still failed to generate sufficient employment to absorb the working population. So, while agriculture's rates of growth and share of the GDP declined over time, a typical feature of structural transformation, agriculture continued to account for a disproportionate share of the country's work force, indicative of the incomplete nature of the transformation (Dev 2012; Varshney 2017). The jobless pattern of India's growth contributed to a widening of regional and urban–rural disparities and to growing inequalities between different classes and occupational groups (Deaton and Drèze 2002; Varshney 2017).

The other aspect of the big picture story was the persistence of a dualistic employment structure. Since the colonial era, the employment structure had been stratified into, on the one hand, a highly coveted formal, largely public sector, monopolised by members of the educated upper castes, and, on the other, a large informal economy that accounted for over 90% of the labour force. Economic growth in recent decades was spearheaded by the service sector, particularly the more advanced sectors of ICT and finance, but generated relatively few formal jobs and did little to challenge the stratified structure of the economy.

For rural families, an important goal was to escape from reliance on uncertain agricultural livelihoods into the non-farm sector, preferably into 'good' jobs: white-collar, service and government jobs. Education was essential for gaining access to these jobs and became a key dividing factor within caste and kin groups; not all families could afford to educate their children and not all who were educated would get salaried jobs. It was once again the prosperous upper and middle castes who were best positioned to take advantage of these new opportunities.

Opportunities were also stratified by gender. As the economy modernised, women's traditional roles in the agricultural economy declined, but they were largely excluded from employment in the modernising economy. In the context of a largely jobless economic trajectory and given the various norms that restricted women's economic mobility, men were better positioned to take advantage of the emerging opportunities and hence favoured in family investment strategies.

While this divergence in economic opportunities varied in different regions of the country, the consequences were generally unfavourable to women. They were either confined to the shrinking agricultural sector or else dropped out of the labour force altogether. As a result, women's labour force participation, already low, declined further over time (Duvvury 1989; Jackson and Rao 2004; Lahoti and Swaminathan 2016; Pattnaik et al. 2017). According to 2015 estimates, India's female labour force participation rates of 21.7% were, after Afghanistan and Pakistan, the lowest of eight South Asian countries (World Bank 2014).

This gendered divergence in access to market opportunities was a major reason for the spread of dowry across the country to castes, religions and regions where it had not previously been practised and for the steady inflation in amount of dowry needed to marry off daughters (Caldwell, Reddy and Caldwell 1983; Epstein 1973; Kapadia 1995; Srinivasan 2005). Dowry became the most widely cited factor in studies seeking to explain the spread and intensification of 'unwantedness' of daughters (John et al. 2008, p.72; Kaur 2007, p.240; Srinivasan 2005, p.608).

But, on its own, the growing importance of dowry is not sufficient to explain the divergence in sex ratios between India and Bangladesh since dowry had also spread to Muslim-majority Bangladesh and Pakistan, where it had not previously been practised (Anderson 2007). If, however, we analyse dowry as one aspect of the broader social organisation of marriage, family and kinship, other possible explanations come into view. In a country as large as India, we would not expect a uniform set of explanations to apply across its different contexts. What I would like to do here is to focus on two sets of explanations, each highlighting a different aspect of the processes of change. Each links the kinship practices associated with classic patriarchy to the growing adversity of sex ratios across India but traces the change through somewhat different processes. The first seeks to explain the intensification of son preference in the northern states, while the second focuses on the spread of son preference to the south.

The first set of explanations revolves around the social organisation of marriage, family and kinship within the classic patriarchy of the northern states of India (Agnihotri 2000; Das Gupta 1987; Das Gupta et al. 2003; John et al. 2008; Kaur 2007). What stands out in all these explanations is the prescriptive power and resilience of the rules, norms and values that spell out its patriarchal bargain, many of which had Brahminic and Shastric sanction and could be traced to the ancient lawgiver Manu (Basu 1999; Desai 1994).[8] These were most strictly enforced among the landed upper castes of the north-western states. The rigidity of these interlocking elements underpinned the prevailing culture of what Larsen (2009) describes as the *necessity* of sons. Only sons could continue the patrilineage, inherit land,[9] become the family breadwinner, look after parents in their old age and light the funeral pyre when they died. Daughters had to be married outside their village and lineage and were lost thereafter to their natal family; their labour and progeny would henceforth belong to their husband's family (Agarwal 1994). The rules of caste endogamy meant that marriage had to be within the same or allied *jati* groups but women had to be married 'upwards' into families of socially and ritually superior status within their caste hierarchy. As noted earlier, the inferiority of 'wife-givers' was signified by the payment of dowry, which has thus always been a visible symbol of the devalued status of daughters among these groups.

According to recent studies, changes in the wider economy had set off the reconfigurations in the patriarchal bargain, including its intergenerational dimension, but these had the effect of intensifying son preference. Whereas 'marrying up' had previously been defined in terms of marrying into a higher-status family, the changing structure of opportunities meant that marrying up now also included marrying more educated grooms, preferably in salaried employment. Consequently, the higher the position of men in the socioeconomic hierarchy, the more educated they were, the larger the dowries they could command – even those who were currently without jobs (John et al. 2008). Upwardly mobile families sought to consolidate their social status by marrying their daughters to men in good jobs in higher-status families and to signal their achievement with expensive weddings and lavish dowries. But this strategy required investment in the education of daughters as well, further increasing the costs of having daughters, for whom dowry would have to be paid but who were only ever 'transient' members of the natal family.

While studies noted that although parents expressed concerns about whether their sons would observe their obligations to ageing parents, as well as their belief that daughters were more caring and more dutiful[10] (though surprisingly rarely, according to John et al. 2008), they nevertheless implemented their desire for smaller families by 'avoiding' daughters and concentrating their resources on ensuring sons' future prospects (John et al. 2008; Kaur 2007; Larsen 2009). The reasons given for this apparently counterintuitive response were, according

to John et al., that 'there [was] some probability of a son earning and supporting his parents while the latter [could not] hope or desire this from a daughter'
(John et al. 2008, p.81). A similar logic was described by Kaur:

> Paradoxically, insecure economic circumstances for males may
> propel families to increase rather than decrease their investments
> in male children, hoping for their eventual success. Unchanged
> ideologies of males as the primary breadwinners contribute to this
> anxiety. (p.240)

In other words, quite aside from the decline in daughters' earning prospects,
cultural norms did not permit married women to provide any form of support to their parents or natal kin, even if they were in need (Das Gupta 1987,
p.92).[11] Any income she earnt after marriage had to go to her in-laws (Agarwal
1994; Das Gupta et al. 2003). Not surprisingly, as Kaur (2007) observed in the
course of her fieldwork: 'Old, widowed mothers said that they would rather lie
at an unwelcoming son's doorstep than ask for help from a daughter' (p.240).
    The second set of studies I want to touch on seeks to explain the rise of son
preference, and the accompanying rise in adverse sex ratios, in the southern states of India where they were previously unknown (Caldwell, Reddy
and Caldwell 1983; Kapadia 1995; Srinivasan 2012). As noted in Chapter 1,
southern states had been characterised by greater diversity in their kinship
practices, which encompassed patrilineal as well as matrilineal inheritance, a
preference for marriage within kin and hence within families of similar status, and the practice of bridewealth alongside the practice of dowry as well as
more equal forms of exchange. Daughters retained their natal ties after marriage and could continue to maintain mutually supportive relationships with
their parents (Das Gupta et al. 2003). This diversity began to diminish as, first,
Brahmins and then other upwardly mobile groups, who had been in a position
to take advantage of the Green Revolution technology and of new opportunities in the off-farm economy, now sought to signal their improved status. They
began adopting Brahminical practices associated with the north Indian patriarchal regime (Caldwell, Reddy and Caldwell 1983). When Epstein (1973)
first undertook fieldwork in rural Karnataka in the 1950s, bridewealth was a
taken-for-granted practice. When she returned in the 1970s, she found that it
had given way to dowry, led by wealthier farming families who had benefited
from the spread of irrigation and then spreading to the other castes who had
gained a foothold in the formal economy. Similar trends were reported from
other parts of south India (Kapadia 1995; Srinivasan 2012).
    While marrying upwards expressed aspirations to social mobility, the
increasing status asymmetry between wife-givers and wife-takers was signalled by the payment and size of dowry (Caldwell, Reddy and Caldwell 1983).
The search for grooms from higher-status families led the move towards non-
kin marriages and to marriage outside the village in order to increase the pool
of potential husbands but the relative scarcity of such husbands meant that

it increasingly became a 'seller's market'. Dowry demands became larger in magnitude, more insistent and lasted well into the years after marriage.

The fact that marital practices were changing across the southern states of India suggests that they had not been rigid, and they responded to changing material circumstances associated with the wider political economy of the region. But it was not coincidence that they were changing in the direction of practices long associated with the upper castes of *north* India. Rather, it reflected another important aspect of the caste system in India: the hegemonic status occupied by the Brahmin castes and their preponderance in the upper classes of the country. While their status had always been a central component of the caste system, it had been reinforced over time by various historical processes. It had been elevated in the course of the consultations carried out in relation to the codification of religious personal law by the colonial rulers where Hindu law had been codified as 'Shastric laws' as interpreted by Brahmin priests (Chapter 2). A similar process took place in independent India. Menon (1998) points to the homogenising intent of legislation passed by the government in relation to the Hindu religious code. The rejection of practices and lifestyles that did not conform to the north Indian upper-caste constructions of the family was legitimated on the grounds that these other practices were not 'Indian' (p.246). These processes of codification, as Menon points out, put an end to the diversity of Hindu laws as they were practised in different regions, in the process destroying the more liberal provisions that existed in many of these regions (p.245).

The tendency of lower and middle castes across India to signal their rise in the social hierarchy by adopting the customs, rites and beliefs of the Brahmins and adopting the Brahminic way of life commented on by Epstein in the 1970s had been documented in earlier anthropological studies. Srinivas (1956) describes this as a process of 'Sanskritisation', pointing out that caste created a stratified social framework within Hindu society within which the best way to stake a claim to a higher position was to adopt the custom and way of life of a higher caste (p.483). As this process was common to all castes except the highest, it meant that Brahmin customs and ways of life spread across the population, including to the lowest castes.

Later authors have argued that the language of 'Sanskritisation' was misleading (Basu 1999; Caldwell, Reddy and Caldwell 1983; Kapadia 1995; Srinivasan 2012). It was not Brahmin values per se that were being emulated but the values of the upper classes. Brahmins had long predominated in the highest ranks of the class hierarchy in India and had been the first to benefit from processes of education and modernisation in the colonial era. Upwardly mobile castes, drawn from the upper and middle castes, were attracted to Brahmanical values and practices because they were the values and practices of the dominant class (Fuller 1999, pp.36–37). Their concern was with becoming 'modernised' and 'urbanised', not with spiritual upliftment. The resilience of the practice of caste endogamy meant that they could not change their caste, but they could signal their increasing prosperity by adopting the practices of the most privileged class.

The influence of the norms and values of the dominant groups in a society in shaping its hegemonic values and practices can be found in many societies. What is striking about the Indian context, as Basu points out, is that its hegemonic values and practices are the values and practices of the groups in its social structure that are most conservative with regard to women: 'Sanskritization results in harshness towards women' (Srinivas 1962, p.61). This point was reiterated by Agnihotri (2000) in his analysis of the growing adversity of sex ratios across India and the 'negative prosperity effect'. He found that women in prosperous regions, groups and households experienced the greatest disadvantage. He concluded that the 'high' culture that accompanies and is emulated with prosperity was marked by a distinct ethos of female subordination (p.247). The critical element in the story of the growing adversity of sex ratios in India therefore is that core values of son preference – and the accompanying aversion to daughters – have been strengthened in the course of caste and gender stratified processes of growth and spread through processes of 'Sanskritisation', the dominant form taken by modernisation and class mobility in India.

The Bangladesh story

Bangladesh, as we have seen, shares several features in common with the classic patriarchy of north India but there are some important differences. Islamic law allows women to inherit land as both wives and daughters, although in both cases it is a fraction of male inheritance. Most studies noted that daughters tended to waive their rights to land in favour of their brothers, giving them a material basis for claims to brothers' support, but there was also evidence of daughters claiming their inheritance, under pressure of poverty or pressure from husbands (Kabeer 1989; Nath 1984). Such action had religious legitimacy even if it went against cultural norms. Both my study of Amarpur in 1979 and a more recent study by Arens (2011) suggest that many more women from landowning households claimed their share than the general literature suggested (Arens 2011; Kabeer 1986). Women from landowning households were thus not entirely assetless when they entered marriage; they were entitled to a valued form of capital, which they generally left with their natal family to stake a claim to their support but which they sometimes claimed for their conjugal one.

There are also important religious differences in the structural meaning of marriage. As various authors have noted, despite variations in the practice of Hinduism across India, marriage is regarded as a 'sacrament of transcendental importance', arranged by families but with an element of divine guidance (Aziz 1979; Caldwell, Reddy and Caldwell 1983, p.345; Borooah et al. 2009). By contrast, marriage among Muslims is seen as a civil contract, signed by the two parties, with the procreation of children as its main objective and the rights and duties of husband and wife spelt out in the *kabin nikah* (marriage contract). They include the husband's obligation to provide for his wife as long as the marriage lasted and provision for her maintenance (*mehr*) in the event of divorce. Both widows and divorced women could, and frequently did, remarry. Such an 'exit' clause does not feature among Hindu communities, although the law has made it easier than it used to be.

Many of the marriage practices that prevail in northern Indian states can also be found in Bangladesh but tend to express cultural 'preference' rather than religious 'prescription'.

Caste hierarchies never put down very deep roots in the East Bengal delta so caste endogamy was irrelevant among its Muslim population.[12] Discussions about desirable qualities in a spouse tended to mention the occupation, education and economic prospects of the groom and the beauty, age and education of the bride. It was, and still is, only among Hindu families in Bangladesh that caste is mentioned as an additional consideration.

While most marriages in Bangladesh tend to be outside the lineage, close-kin marriage is accepted and is widespread in some districts (Bleie 1990; Ellickson 1972; Joshi, Iyer and Do 2014).[13] There may be a growing preference for marrying daughters 'up' even if it means paying larger dowries, but earlier anthropological work by Aziz (1979) found that marriage tended to be between 'equals', in terms of social status and economic position, while other scholars found considerable mobility, with daughters being married 'sideways' into families of similar status and also married 'down' (Bertocci 1972; Lindenbaum 1981). Equally, there may be a preference for marrying daughters to someone from a different village to widen family networks and alliances, but there is no religious prescription to this effect. They can also be married within their natal village.

We see this flexibility in marital practices put to work in strategies to minimise dowry payments: marrying daughters off to close kin or within the natal village or to someone with lower status all reduced the size of dowry or eliminated the need to pay it (Amin and Huq 2008; Joshi, Iyer and Do 2014; Lindenbaum 1981). The rise in love marriages has also reduced the need to pay dowry. Other strategies included educating daughters since dowry was less likely to be demanded for educated brides. The exception was in the case of brides with higher-than-average education when higher-than-average dowries were demanded because it was harder to find equally or more educated husbands. However, the World Bank survey (2008) found that this problem was being partly circumvented across Bangladesh through the increasing practice of marrying off educated daughters to men with lower levels of education.

And, of course, one reason why this diversity of practices to get around dowry was possible was because dowry itself had no religious authorisation. It had only appeared among Muslims in Bangladesh sometime in the second half of the 20th century. The national survey figures cited by Amin and Das

(2013) confirm that its incidence was lower among Muslims than Hindus. Hindus had not only been paying dowry from earlier times but, even in the contemporary era, paid larger dowries than Muslims (Amin and Das 2013; Amin and Huq 2008).

In short, parents in both countries face particular challenges when it comes to ensuring 'good' marriages for their daughters in marriage markets whose rules systematically expand the pool of women that make suitable brides while restricting the pool of men that make suitable husbands. But parents in the Indian context have to deal with the prescriptive force of caste and lineage consideration over and above the concerns with occupation and social status that were likely to preoccupy parents in Bangladesh.

This difference between prescription and preference may also help to explain why parents in Bangladesh were more willing to look to their daughters for support in their old age as expectations of support from sons looked less certain. The patriarchal bargain may have placed responsibility for care of parents in their old age on sons – and there is still shame expressed by some parents about taking help from married daughters – but this has not prevented a shift in expectations when sons fail to live up to their obligations. In addition, the steady rise in women's paid activity rates in Bangladesh has meant that daughters are increasingly in a position to provide material as well as emotional support to their parents. Son preference has not disappeared, but daughters no longer face the same degree of discrimination from their birth onwards that they once did.

10.4 Is the Bangladesh paradox sustainable?

Returning to the question of the Bangladesh paradox, I have cited the considerable body of literature that has built up around attempts to explain it, but we are now beginning to see the emergence of studies asking whether the paradox is sustainable (Mahmud 2021; Raihan, Bourguignon and Salam 2023). While much of this book has focused on the positive aspects of Bangladesh's development story for reasons explained in the introduction, a shift in focus to its negative aspects suggests that, without radical reform, the answer is probably no. To explain why, I want to return to the issues that helped to frame Bangladesh's social achievements as a paradox in the first place: the dismal state of its economy, the poor quality of its governance and the steady rise of Islamic orthodoxy.

Starting with the question of economic performance, it is indeed the case that Bangladesh's social progress began at a time when the country was characterised by very low growth rates and high levels of absolute poverty. The early stages of progress were made possible through strategies which allowed the country to circumvent what would otherwise have constituted major obstacles to progress (Mahmud 2021). The adoption of low-cost vertical solutions to basic health problems meant fewer demands on the public budget and bypassed the need for investment in a broad-based system of public health. The reliance on NGOs in the delivery of social services helped to compensate for capacity deficits within government, including its financial and governance deficits.

However, there are limits to gains from low-cost solutions while the chequered history of the NGO sector and the growing diversity in their commitment and capacity suggests that it cannot compensate indefinitely for more systematic approaches to progress on the social front. The fact that some social indicators have been stagnating over the past decade raises question marks about the sustainability of the solutions that Bangladesh has relied on so far and directs attention once again to the possibility of income-led or policy-mediated pathways to social progress in the future (Mahmud 2021). Neither looks promising.

The country has been growing at a rapid pace, fuelled by garment exports, remittances and resilient agricultural growth, but, as in other parts of the world, it has been accompanied by an accelerating growth in inequality: the Gini coefficient, which measures income inequality, increased from 0.34 in the early 1990s to 0.48 in 2016 (Mahmud 2021). This does not bode well for the possibility of an income-led pathway to future social progress. Such progress would depend on private expenditures by households at a time when rising income inequality has meant that wealthy households are capturing an increasing share of the benefits of growth while the pace at which growth is trickling down to the poor has slowed down considerably (Sen, Mujeri and Shahabuddin 2007).

At the same time, continuing problems of governance curtail the likelihood of a policy-mediated pathway to social progress. Bangladesh has been ranked among the top 15 countries in the world in terms of per capita growth for more than a decade; it also outperforms many richer countries in terms of its human development indicators but it consistently ranks among the bottom 20% of countries in most international rankings of governance and institutional quality (Raihan and Bourguignon 2023). There is not much evidence that government is interested in embarking on a policy-mediated pathway. While domestic revenue will be needed to finance such a pathway, its tax policies continue to reflect the interests of the elite: Bangladesh has one of the lowest tax-to-GDP ratios in the world (Chapter 5, Note 12). The corruption, bribery, nepotism and 'deal-making' that characterise how things are done in the country are not confined to the political sphere or to the current regime but have become routinised practice in all spheres of public life (Raihan, Bourguignon and Salam 2023).

The final element of the paradox discussed in this book relates to the rising tide of Islamic orthodoxy. While progress on gender equality was achieved in spite of this, there is a question mark about whether this progress will be sustained in the future. This will depend on which of the competing national imaginaries currently at play will prevail in the coming years: one that can accommodate diversity and difference among the country's citizens or one that seeks to eliminate dissent and eradicate 'the other'.

There has been a proliferation of Islamic parties and organisations in recent decades. Some appear to be gaining a foothold in the political sphere; others have turned to terrorist tactics (Allchin 2019; Parvez 2019). While the Awami League continues to be regarded as more tolerant of religious diversity than the other main contenders for power, it has not only been willing to form alliances with Islamist parties when convenient, it has increasingly resorted to the repression of opposition politicians and independent critics in order to stay in power.

Its democratic backsliding has tended to erode trust in democracy itself. The voter turnout at the 2024 elections, which the Awami League won with an overwhelming majority since it was boycotted by the main opposition parties, varied from the initial estimate of 28% from the Election Commission to a hastily revised estimate of 40% but either way was considerably lower than the 80% in 2018.[14] Bangladesh has now been relegated to the lowest category in the international ranking of countries by the openness of civic space.[15]

At the community level, Islamist organisations and networks have increased their proselytising efforts while radical NGOs have either closed down or moved into the business of microfinance. The earlier efforts to build inclusive forms of citizenship through group-based deliberation and discussion have largely faded. In their place, a space has opened up at the grassroots level for *taleem* classes and Islamic welfare organisations that offer alternative forms of sociality as an effective means of 'domesticating women', reasserting the values of classic patriarchy and marginalising minorities.

At the same time, we have to keep in mind that that the progress reported in the paradox literature was due in no small measure to the agency and initiative that the ordinary men and women of Bangladesh demonstrated in their daily lives, an agency and initiative that drew on cultural traditions that have long accommodated religious difference, encouraged flexibility in the face of structural challenges and relied on pragmatism rather than dogma to adapt to changing circumstances.

The vision that inspired the founding of the new nation, and was inscribed into its first constitution, continues to be invoked by progressive forces around the country in their struggles for a better future. Their sense of nationalism has expanded beyond the ethno-linguistic identity of the majority to encompass the indigenous people of Bangladesh. While the early commitment to socialism has been replaced in the constitution by a commitment to economic and social justice, this is still a goal worth fighting for and likely to have more meaning for ordinary people than the earlier socialist ideal.[16] What has not changed is the importance given by progressive forces to a democratic and accountable state capable of carrying these commitments through for all citizens in the country. What has also not changed is the significance attached to secularism as the foundation of such a state. As religion is being turned once again turned into a politicised and divisive force in the country, secularism offers the promise of protection to religious minorities from persecution by the Muslim majority. But, just as importantly, it offers protection to men and women from the Muslim majority from the harsh orthodoxies of their own religion, leaving them free to practise their faith as they understand it and to carve out their own pathways to personhood.[17] The prognosis may be bleak but Bangladesh has managed to defy the prophets of doom in the past. It may do it again.

Notes

[1] Interestingly, in the light of some of the discussion in this book, Krause observes that the singular focus on the European experience of modernisation led to its theorisation as secularisation, a theorisation that might not have occurred if studies had included the US context and the significance of religiosity in American life.

[2] Rostow posited five stages of economic growth through which all countries had to pass to become developed: 1) traditional society, 2) preconditions to take-off, 3) take-off, 4) drive to maturity and 5) the age of mass consumption.

Modernisation was seen to entail the transition from 'traditional' to 'modern' forms of organisation, attitudes and values of the kind that characterised the West (Lerner 1958): 'the ideal of modernization without Westernization is self-contradictory' (Bauer 1981, p.205). Demographic transition models linked demographic behaviour with different stages of development (Davis 1945). The pre-industrial stage was characterised by high rates of birth and death so populations remained stable. This was followed by an urbanising/industrial stage that saw improvements in health care delivery and medicines, sanitation and infrastructure, which led to a sharp drop in death rates but little change in birth rates so populations began to grow. During the mature industrial stage, crude death rates continued to decline but economic development created incentives to reduce birth rates sufficiently to slow down the rates of population growth. Processes of modernisation underpinned demographic transition by breaking down traditional kinship domination of the reproductive behaviour of couples, changing sex roles, generating alternatives to early marriage and large families for women and stimulating new aspirations that encourage the move to smaller families.

[3] The frequent references in this book to the special efforts made by mothers to provide daughters with better chances in life than they themselves had appears to be supported by recent quantitative analysis of the 2007 and 2011 DHS data on ever-married women in Bangladesh by Heath and Tan (2018): they found that mothers of daughters were more likely than those of sons to take up waged work and that they did so in order to direct more resources to their daughters than did their fathers.

RESOLVING THE PARADOX   267

[4] The concept of 'daughter aversion' was added to this literature to emphasise that the existence of son preference in a society does not necessarily have to be accompanied by discrimination against daughters.

[5] Like Miller (Chapter 1, Note 14), Guilmoto also predicted rising sex ratios at birth in Bangladesh (p.523) but, a decade later, this had not happened. Recent evidence suggests that sex ratios at birth have started to decline in India, though, at 108 boys to every 100 girls, they remain higher than normal (Tong 2022). There is clearly important research to be done as to what brought about this positive turnaround but this is outside the scope of this book.

[6] In 2001, for instance, the child sex ratio among Muslims in the 0–6 age group was 105.2 boys:100 girls, compared to 107.8:100 for the overall population (Government of India, 2006).

[7] See Kabeer (1996) for an earlier attempt to explore the association between regional variations in kinship regimes, the 'quantity–quality' trade-off and the incidence of adverse sex ratios.

[8] In their analysis of the persistence of son preference in India, China and South Korea, Das Gupta et al. (2003) emphasise that it was not their patriarchal practices per se that distinguished them – after all, many other cultures share versions of these practices – but the *rigidity* which characterised the logic of their kinship systems and the limited scope for deviation that it permitted. It is a version of this explanation that I am putting forward here. Sopher (1980) notes that the present-day concentration of adverse sex ratios in the northern plains of India recalled 'an ancient geographic division of Indian cultural space', 'the Brahmanic land proper of antiquity' (p.149). Clearly India has been through enormous economic and social changes through the centuries and in the last decades but some aspects of caste-based social practices have shown astonishing resilience, particularly caste endogamy (see Reich 2019, pp.140–53). Estimates from 2011 suggest that inter-caste marriage in India was as low as 5.8% (Ray, Chaudhuri and Sahai 2017).

[9] Although the law had been reformed for Hindus to permit daughters to claim their share of family property, a daughter that sought to do so was likely to be alienated from her family or worse (John et al. 2008, p.72). In her study in rural Punjab, Das Gupta (1987) found that there was no question of a women owning land, despite the legislation: 'If she should try to insist on her right to inherit land equally under the civil law, she would stand a good chance of being murdered' (p.92).

[10] See for instance Da Costa (2008).

[11] For instance, Desai (1994) notes that the belief that a married daughter belongs to her husband's family, and that little economic support can be

expected from them was so strong in north India, 'that many parents, while visiting their married daughters, do not accept food or other hospitality from them' (p.45).

[12] Caste organisation does exist among Muslim groups in India (and can also be found in Pakistan; see Gazdar 2007) but is recognised by scholars to be 'looser, less rigid and more amenable to fairly rapid individual and social mobility than is the Hindu caste system' (Mines 1972, p.333).

[13] Some information on the prevalence of close-kin and within-village marriage comes Joshi, Iyer and Do (2014). Using 1996 survey data of around 4,000 women from the Matlab area, they found that around 18% had married a relative while 14% had married a non-relative within the same village. Dowry was less likely to be paid in marriages between kin but, more generally, 36% of women and 18% of men reported the payment of dowry at the time of marriage. The conflicting estimates may reflect differences in interpretation of what constituted dowry, but the low percentages are still worth noting.

[14] See: https://www.reuters.com/world/asia-pacific/pm-hasina-set-extend -tenure-main-bangladesh-opposition-boycotts-election-2024-01-06

[15] I should note here that the Awami League government was ousted by a popular movement in August 2024 as this book was going to print. The movement was fueled by outrage at the increasingly autocratic nature of the government. See: https://monitor.civicus.org/globalfindings_2023

[16] As Rahman noted in 1972, 'socialism was in the air but had yet to land on the ground' (Chapter 3).

[17] I draw here on Rajeev Bhargava's comments about the need for secularism in India: https://www.thehindu.com/news/national/secularism-is-also -to-protect-hindus-from-their-own-orthodoxies/article67353357.ece.

Appendices

Appendix 1. Description of the main research projects drawn on in this book

While a great deal of the book is drawn from published articles, books and reports, including many of my own books and articles, I have drawn more heavily on certain research projects than others. In particular, I have drawn on my PhD research carried out in 1979 and from my two most recent research projects. I therefore describe the approach to data collection taken in these projects. Tables 3 to 8 in Appendix 5 draw on these research projects, which are cited as sources for the different tables. Where I use quotations from our qualitative interviews that come from published articles, I cite the article in question. Where the quotations come from more recent interviews and have not been used in publications, I refer to the place and year of fieldwork.

1) My PhD research was carried out in Amarpur village in Faridpur district, where I lived from 1979 to early 1980. I carried out a census of all 437 households that made up Amarpur village at that time. This included separate questions to all ever-married women aged 15+ in these households – a total of 667 women (Table 4). A more detailed household survey was then carried out on 234 Muslim households randomly selected from the census. I carried out a separate survey of 528 ever-married women in these households (Table 5). The Coombs preference scales, which were estimated from responses to the survey of ever-married women, are described Appendix 2.

2) The second research I draw heavily on was carried out as part of the Research Partners Consortium on Pathways of Women's Empowerment (2006–10). It was funded by DFID and led by the Institute of Development Studies, Sussex (IDS), with partners from a number of countries in the global South including Bangladesh. I worked with BRAC Institute of Governance and Development in Dhaka to carry out research on women's paid work and empowerment. The IDS-BIGD team conducted a survey of 5,198 women randomly selected from village censuses that we carried out in eight districts of Bangladesh, including Amarpur. I refer to this as the IDS-BIGD 2008 survey (Tables 3, 4, 5, 7 and 8).

   I had become interested in the Bangladesh paradox by this time, particularly in evidence of declining son preference: a specific research component on this in Amarpur was funded by IDRC. In 2010, the research team returned to Amarpur to carry out qualitative interviews with 80 married women and 22 of their husbands to explore the question of son preference in greater detail. We were not able to interview more husbands because they either worked elsewhere in the country or outside it or else the women were widowed, divorced or separated.

3) The third research project was carried out after I joined LSE. It was titled 'Choice, constraints and the gender dynamics of labour markets in Bangladesh' and funded by the ESRC-FCDO Joint Fund for Poverty Alleviation (ES/L005484/1) between 2014 and 2017. I collaborated with the same research team at the BRAC Institute of Governance and Development. The LSE/BIGD team was able to follow up on 4,606 women out of the 5,198 women from eight districts that we had interviewed in 2008. We also surveyed 2,622 men randomly selected from our censuses of these districts. I refer to data from these as the 2015 LSE/BIGD surveys (Tables 6, 7 and part of 8). We carried out qualitative interviews in 2014 before the survey with 80 women from four of the study districts, including Amarpur, and so were able to revisit some of the women in Amarpur we had spoken to in 2010. A number of follow-up interviews were also carried out in 2017. Where I cite from women interviewed in the 2014/2016 round, I refer to the district where they are from to distinguish between urban and rural locations.

Appendix 2. Note on the Coombs preference scales

One way to measure desired number of children and their sex composition is through single-valued questions. What is the ideal number of children you would like? What is the ideal number of boys and girls you would like? The preference scaled developed by Coombs, Coombs and Mcclelland (1975) goes beyond this to allow respondents to rank their preferences beyond their initial preferences and offers independent measures of preferences for number and sex of children. Respondents are placed on a continuum ranging from 1 to 7. The information needed to locate individual position on the scales is obtained by asking respondents to order their preferences between different-sized families, given equal number of boys and girls and between different sex compositions, given a total family size of five. The IN scale, which measures preference for numbers of children, asks them to choose between two children, four children, six children and eight children – so each choice included equal numbers of boys and girls. The IS scale measures preferences for sex of children asks them to order their preferences about sex composition, when the number of children is held constant at five. The choices range from all girls (IS 1) to all boys (IS 7) to combinations with more boys or more girls. IS 4 indicates a preference for balanced sex composition.

Appendix 3. Note on sex ratios as indicators of gender discrimination

The use of gender differentials in births and deaths as indicators of gender inequality/gender discrimination has to take account of differentials that reflect biological differentials, and hence to be expected, and those that reflect social discrimination. In other words, the fairness or otherwise of *observed* gender differentials will depend on how they compared to *expected* differentials. Sex ratios at different stages of the life course are frequently used to capture possible gaps between observed and expected gender differentials.

The biological likelihood of survival for men and women differs across the life course so that sex ratios vary in different age groups and in the overall population. As a 'rule of nature', the sex ratios at birth (SRBs), the number of boys born for every hundred girls, is fairly constant at between 103 and 105 boys to every 100 girls. This is regarded as the 'biological norm', the benchmark for gender parity. Deviations in observed ratios from this norm suggests prenatal intervention. The higher-than-expected ratio of boys born to every 100 girls discussed in this book is generally accepted as evidence of female-selective abortion in line with strong son preference (Ritchie and Roser 2019). It can also reflect a differential 'stopping rule'; in other words, parents stop having children once they have had the desired number of sons.

Boys are more susceptible to birth complications and infectious diseases in the early years of life and hence more likely to die than girls in much of the world, regardless of wealth and income. The worldwide norm for gender differentials in under-five child mortality is 120 male deaths to 100 female deaths: girls are 20% more likely to survive in the under-five age group than boys. However, discrimination against girls increases their mortality rates and can reverse the differential so that girls are more likely to die than boys in some countries or among certain groups: this 'excess female mortality' is an indicator of gender discrimination. Gender differentials in mortality rates are often measured by child or juvenile sex ratios: the ratios of boys to girls early and childhood years. A female deficit in this age group indicates discrimination against daughters.

The other gender differential that features in the literature is life expectancy. In general, women can expect to have higher overall life expectancy than men. This differential reflects biological, environmental and behavioural factors that influence male and female mortality differently. Global estimates for life expectancy in 2019 were 74.2 years for women and 69.8 years for men (Thornton 2019). But the gender gap can vary across countries. It was smaller in lower-income countries in 2016 – 64 years for women and 60 years for men because of women's poorer access to healthcare relative to men. It was 83.4 and 78.2 in high-income countries. Extreme gender discrimination can lead to a reversal of the gap so that men have higher life expectancy than women. For instance, South Asian countries reported higher male life expectancy than female in the 1960s: it was 41.0 and 39.9 respectively for Bangladesh, 43.2 and 41.3 for India, and 47.8 and 45.9 for Pakistan. The sex ratio of the overall population can thus be used as a measure of gender discrimination. In the absence of marked gender discrimination, the expected ratio of women to every 100 men is around 105. Marked gender discrimination leads to lower sex ratios. However, the sex ratio of the overall population can be affected by various social phenomena such as migration. As a result, indicators of gender discrimination tend to use child or juvenile sex ratios as a more accurate measure.

One final point to note is that, while the international convention in reporting on sex ratios reports them as the ratio of males to every 100 females, the Indian literature tends to report on number of females to 1,000 boys. So, for instance, excess SRBs would be expressed according to international convention as more than 105 boys born to every 100 girls, but the Indian convention would report it as less than 950 girls born to every 1,000 boys. I have recalculated the Indian estimates in the text to reflect the international convention (see Tong 2022 for the conversion chart).

Appendix 4. Boxes: timelines and summary of key research on reproductive preferences

Box 1. Major disasters in Bangladesh between 1700 and 1975

Year	Event	Casualties
1769–76	Great Bengal Famine	'Eliminated almost a third of Bengal's population' (A. Ahmed 1962, p.140), although impact was less severe in East Bengal (N. Ahmad 1968, p.327)
1784–88	Floods and famine; radical shift in course of Brahmaputra River (1787)	Unknown (N. Ahmad 1968, pp.33, 101)
1873–74	Famine	Unknown (A. Ahmed 1962, p.141)
1876	Bakerganj cyclone and tidal wave	c.400,000 deaths (N. Ahmad 1968, p.51)
1884–85	Famine	Unknown (Bhatia 1967, p.164)
1897	Chittagong cyclone	c.175,000 deaths (N. Ahmad 1968, p.51)
1918–19	Influenza epidemic	c.400,000 deaths (M.R. Khan 1972b, p.384)
1943	Bengal Famine	2–2.5 million deaths (A. Ahmed 1962, p.141; M. R. Khan 1972b, p.384)
1947	Partition of India	Unknown; total deaths in partition c.1 million, but most were in west (Davis 1951, p.197)
1970	Cyclone and tidal wave	200,000–500,000 deaths (L.C. Chen 1973)
1971	War of Independence	c.500,000 deaths (Curlin, Chen and Hussain 1976, p.31)
1974	Famine	Officially c.30,000 deaths (Majlis 1977), although some estimates are much higher (e.g. 500,000 – Baldwin 1977; 80,000 in Rangpur district alone – Haque et al. 1977)

Source: Arthur and McNicoll (1978), Table 1, p.29. See source table for all citations above.

Box 2. Summary of findings from studies on reproductive preferences and behaviour (1970s to 2020s)

Author(s)	Source of data	Summary of findings
Stoeckel and Chaudhury (1973)	1968 survey – Matlab	Women with no living children wanted a total of four children, those with four children wanted seven children, while those with six or more children wanted between eight and nine children.
Ahmed (1981)	1975–76 survey – Matlab	Use of Coombs scales on sex and number preference suggested a strong preference for large numbers of children and an even stronger preference for a large number of sons. A third of the survey respondents expressed son preference so extreme that it excluded any desire for a daughter.
Nag (1991)	National surveys in 1969, 1975 and 1979	Women without sons were more likely than those with one or more sons to say they wanted additional children, regardless of how many children they had. For instance, among women with just one child, 13% of those who had a son were likely to say they did not want any more children, compared to just 8% of those who had a daughter. Among women with four children, 79% of those with at least one son, 85% of those with two sons and 89% of those with three sons said they did not want any more children, compared to just 43% of those with only daughters. However, among those with four sons, those wanting an additional child declined to 79%, suggesting the desire to try for at least one daughter.
Muhuri and Preston (1991)	Matlab DSS and 1982 census data	Mortality rates were considerably higher for higher-birth-order daughters than for the firstborn. Birth-order mortality effects were also evident for sons but were only evident after the second son and were weaker.
Rahman et al. (1992)	Matlab DSS and 1982 survey data	Son preference had significant effects on contraceptive use, suggesting parents' desire to have two or more sons and at least one daughter.
Razzaque (1999)	1984 survey and longitudinal data 1984–89	Among couples where wives who did not want any more children but husbands did, the likelihood of giving birth was 1.78 times higher than with couples where neither wanted any more. Among couples where wives wanted more children, but husbands did not, the likelihood was just 0.63 times higher.
Saha and Bairagi (2007)	1999–2000 Bangladesh Demographic and Health Survey and data from Matlab DSS 1978–2000	Fertility declined with parity, while, within each parity, fertility declined with increasing number of sons. So, among women with two children, 46% of those without a son at the start of the study period had an additional birth between 1999 and 2000, compared to just 30% of those with a son. Once again, there was evidence of son preference, but also the desire for at least one daughter: among women with two or more children. Those with at least one son and a daughter had the lowest fertility.

(Contd.)

Box 2. Contd.

Author(s)	Source of data	Summary of findings
Hossain, Phillips and Mozumder (2007)	Matlab DSS data and 1998 survey	Non-contracepting wives whose husbands desired additional children were 57% less likely to adopt a contraceptive method than women whose husbands did not desire additional children.
Gipson and Hindin (2008; 2009)	Cross section survey in 1998 in Jessore and longitudinal survey 1998–2003	Subsequent pregnancies were more likely in 2003 among couples who had both agreed in 1998 that they wanted more children (70%) and least likely among those who both agreed that they did not want any more (17%). Twenty-nine per cent of couples who had agreed in 1998 that they did not want any more children were likely to have terminated a pregnancy, compared to 2% of those where both had wanted more children. Where couples disagreed about wanting another child, around 6–7% reported a termination.
		Couples with only girls at the start of the period were 7–8% more likely to say they wanted another child than couples who had at least one of each. By contrast, couples with only boys at the start of the period were 3% more likely. The 'ideal' family size and composition appeared to be two sons and one daughter: 96% of couples in this group agreed that they did not want any more children. Much lower percentages were reported by all other groups. Among those with one son and no daughters, around 70% of couples agreed they wanted more children, compared to 80% of couples with one daughter and no sons. Among those with two daughters and one son, 24% wanted more children, compared to just 4% of those with two sons and one daughter. In other words, those with fewer boys than girls were generally more likely to try for another child than those with fewer girls than boys.
		While the incidence of pregnancy decreased over the study period for most couples, it increased among couples in which only the husband wanted more children. This suggested that wives who disagreed with their husbands about having more children were either less able to prevent pregnancy through consistent use of contraception or else acquiesced to their husbands' desire for more children.
		Finally couples who experienced a child death were over three times as likely to have a subsequent pregnancy than those who did not have a child death, reinforcing earlier evidence that the 'replacement' motive for having children was taking the place of the previous 'insurance' motive.

(Contd.)

Box 2. Contd.

Author(s)	Source of data	Summary of findings
Alam, Roy and Ahmed 2007	Matlab DSS and censuses in 1974, 1982 and 1996	Excess mortality of higher-order girls persisted in Matlab after 1974 in most birth orders but declined and then disappeared for children who were born after 1995. According to UNICEF (2011), excess female mortality in the under-five age group disappeared in 1997. Thereafter male mortality rates exceeded female.
Talukder et al. (2014)	Demographic and Health Surveys 1991 and 2011	Mean ideal family size declined from 4.5 to 2.2. This was accompanied by an increase in the proportion of women who wanted a two-child family – from 54% at the start of the period to 63% at the end. While there was still a moderate preference for sons, they found a decline in the desired sex ratio at birth (based on ideal number of boys and girls) from 124 boys to every 100 girls in the 1990s to 111 boys in 2011 – in other words, a nearly balanced composition. While 21% in the early 1990s had expressed a preference for two boys and a girl, this had declined to 8% in 2011. Only 1% expressed a preference for two girls and a boy.

Among those with one boy and one girl, 27% had wanted more children in 1993. This had declined to just 9% in 2011. Among women with two children, those with two girls were still more likely to want children in the future than those with two boys, but this had declined from 64% in 1993 to 36% in 2011. Thus a sizeable minority did not want any more children even if they had only girls. |
| Asadullah, Savoia, and Mahmud (2021) | 2014 nationally representative Women's Life Choices and Attitudes Survey. Women aged 20–39. | Sex composition of existing children continued to have an effect on women's desire for future children, but increasingly in the direction of a balanced composition. Women who had not yet had any children wanted an average of 1.54 children and expressed very similar desire for number of sons and daughters (mean values of 0.766 and 0.733). Among women with two children, the mean desire for additional sons was close to zero if they had at least one son. The mean desire for additional daughters was also close to zero if they had at least one daughter. On the other hand, the mean desire for children of a particular sex was significantly higher among couples who did not yet have a child of that sex than among couples who did. However, the study found that the preference for balanced gender composition was not reflected in fertility behaviour. A firstborn daughter was followed more rapidly by a pregnancy than a firstborn son. Among women with two children, the likelihood of a further pregnancy was much higher if neither was a son. Whether or not they had a daughter did not have this effect. They suggested that the gap between women's expressed preferences and actual behaviour was likely to reflect their deference to male preference for larger families as noted, for instance, in Gipson and Hindin. |

Appendix 5. Tables: demographic and socio-economic indicators

Table 1. A 'positive outlier': economic and social indicators in Bangladesh, India and Pakistan (1990s to 2011)

	Population (millions) 2011	Per capita GDP (1990)[a]	Per capita GDP (2011)	% below poverty line[b] 2010	Female labour force participation rate (age 15+)	Youth literacy rate (male) (2011)	Youth literacy rate (female) (2011)	Mean years of schooling (age 25+) 1990	Mean years of schooling (age 25+) 2011
Bangladesh	150	741	1569	76.5	57	75	78	2.9	4.8
India	1241	1193	3203	68.7	29	88	74	3.0	4.4
Pakistan	177	1624	2424	60.2	22	79	61	2.3	4.9

Source: Drèze and Sen (2013), Table A.1. Notes: [a]PPP: constant 2005 international $; [b]PPP $2/day.

Table 1. contd.

	Females per 1000 males in population (2011)	Life expectancy at birth: years (1990)	Life expectancy at birth: years (2011)	Life expectancy at birth: years (m) 2011	Life expectancy at birth: years (f) 2011	Total fertility rates (1990)	Total fertility rate (2011)	Infant mortality rates (2011)[a]	% low-birth weight babies (2010)
Bangladesh	976	59	69	68	70	4.5	2.2	37	22
India	937	58	65	64	67	3.9	2.6	47	28
Pakistan	968	61	65	64	66	6.0	3.4	59	32

Source: Drèze and Sen (2013), Table A.1. Note: [a]Mortality rate per 1,000 live births.

Table 1. contd.

	Life expectancy at birth years (m) 1970	Life expectancy at birth: years (f) 1970	SRB (m/f) 1970	SRB (m/f) 2010	SRB m/f 2020	Child sex ratio (m/f) 1950	Child sex ratio (m/f) 2021
Bangladesh	44.8	44.2	105	104	105	104	105
India	50.1	48.5	106	110	108	104	109
Pakistan	51.5	50.5	106	106	106	107	105

Source: Life expectancy data from www.worldlifeexpectancy (accessed 22 September 2023). Sex ratio at birth data from www.ourworldindata.org (accessed 22 September 2023). See also Hannah Ritchie and Max Roser (2019).

Table 2. India: demographic and socio-economic indicators by region and state (1970s to 1980s)

Region/state	TFR (1972)	Age at 1st marriage (1971)	Sex ratios (M: 100 F) 1981	Child mortality rates per 1,000 population (0–4) (1968–71)	Ratio of male to female infant/ child mortality rates (1968–71)	Percentage of couples using contraception 1979	Index of son preference	Percentage of couples using contraception 1979	FLFP rates (1971)	Percentage practising *purdah* (1974)	Percentage of female literate (1971)	Percentage of births medically attended (1975)
South												
Kerala	5.43	20.9	97	22.6	0.95	28.8	17.2	28.8	13	4.3	54.3	25.7
Tamil Nadu	4.97	19.6	102	46.6	0.95	28.4	11.5	28.4	15	4.9	26.9	21.9
Andhra Pradesh	4.88	16.4	103	43.9	0.90	26.5	8.9	26.5	24	9.4	15.7	12.2
Karnataka	5.68	17.9	104	42.2	0.93	22.4	11.2	22.4	14	5.4	20.9	15.9
Maharashtra	5.16	17.5	107	41.9	1.02	34.7	18.4	34.7	20	16.7	26.4	7.5
North												
Gujarat	6.19	18.3	106	67.5	1.10	20.1	20.8	20.1	10	41.8	24.7	9.7
Rajasthan	6.32	15.4	109	70.9	1.15	13.0	n.a.	13.0	8	62.2	8.5	4.1
Uttar Pradesh	6.85	15.6	113	81.2	1.36	11.5	25.0	11.5	7	46.4	10.7	2.5

(Contd.)

Table 2. contd.

Region/state	TFR (1972)	Age at 1st marriage (1971)	Sex ratios (M: 100 F) 1981	Child mortality rates per 1,000 population (0–4) (1968–71)	Ratio of male to female infant/child mortality rates (1968–71)	Percentage of couples using contraception 1979	Index of son preference	Percentage of couples using contraception 1979	FLFP rates (1971)	Percentage practising *purdah* (1974)	Percentage of female literate (1971)	Percentage of births medically attended (1975)
Madhya Pradesh	6.38	15.2	106	61.1	1.03	20.9	21.9	20.9	19	42.9	10.9	5.1
Punjab	6.32	20.1	113	35.6	1.38	25.0	31.3	25.0	1	44.6	25.9	11.3
Haryana	6.68	16.6	114	31.8	1.24	30.1	20.7	30.1	2	72.6	14.9	15.3
East												
Bihar	5.01	15.5	106	35.6	1.06	12.2	24.3	12.2	9	29.6	8.7	2.8
West Bengal	4.42	17.8	110	32.4	1.01	21.2	18.4	21.2	4	n.a.	22.4	n.a.
Orissa	5.65	17.2	102	57.8	0.87	24.4	15.7	24.4	7	27.7	13.9	6.8
All India	5.78	17.2	107	51.6	1.09	22.1	20.2	22.1	12	n.a.	18.7	n.a.

Source: Dyson and Moore (1983). Taken from Tables 1, 3, 4 and 5.

Table 3. Percentage distribution of women (aged 15–50+) by work status and own, family and community attitudes to their work (2008)

	Formal wage work	Informal wage work	Informal self-employment (outside)	Informal self-employment (home-based)	Unpaid economic activity	Economically inactive	Total
Number of cases	181	306	187	2456	909	1159	5198
% of total	3.5	5.9	3.6	47.3	17.5	22.3	100
Considers own productive contribution important	85.6	74.5	61.5	52.9	46.8	38.5	51.4
Family considers her productive contribution important	84.0	70.6	64.2	51.0	43.8	36.3	49.3
Standing in community improved because of paid contribution	25.7	21.6	21.1	14.5	8.9	—	15.9

Source: IDS/BIGD survey 2008.

Table 4. Mean parity by age group in Amarpur: 1979 and 2008

Age group	1979 (N)	Mean parity	2008 (N)	Mean parity
15–19	137	0.34	6	1.00
20–24	92	1.74	60	1.47
25–29	108	3.81	83	2.01
30–34	55	5.73	45	2.71
35–39	51	6.75	73	2.97
40–44	47	7.30	53	3.74
45–49	53	7.45	47	4.66
50+	124	7.00	128	5.76
Total	667		495	

Source: Kabeer (1986) and IDS/BIGD Survey 2008.

Table 5. Number and sex preference scales in Amarpur: 1979 and 2008

Number preference by age group

	1979	IN1	IN2	IN3	IN4	IN5	IN6	IN7
	N	%	%	%	%	%	%	%
<35 years	203	48	33	9	5	2	2	2
35+ years	142	32	31	12	11	1	3	10
Total	354	41	32	10	8	1	2	5
	2008	**IN1**	**IN2**	**IN3**	**IN4**	**IN5**	**IN6**	**IN7**
	N	%	%	%	%	%	%	%
<35 years	309	90	6	–	2	2	–	–
35+ years	298	73	12	–	9	5	–	–
Total	607	82	8	–	5	6	–	–

Sex preference by age group

	1979	IS1	IS2	IS3	IS4	IS5	IS6	IS7
	N	%	%	%	%	%	%	%
<35 years	201	13	10	13	19	14	14	16
35+	141	11	5	5	26	12	16	25
Total	341	12	8	10	22	13	15	20
	2008	**IS1**	**IS2**	**IS3**	**IS4**	**IS5**	**IS6**	**IS7**
	N	%	%	%	%	%	%	%
<35 years	315	26	23	3.2	17.8	13.3	12.1	4.8
35+ years	313	17	23	5.8	18.5	18.2	13.4	4.2
Total	628	21.5	22.9	4.5	18.2	15.8	12.7	4.5

Source: Kabeer (1986) and IDS/BIGD Survey 2008.

Table 6a. Desire for additional children by sex composition of surviving children: women aged 15–49 (2015 full sample)

Sex composition of surviving children	Total (N)	Wants more children (n)	Wants more children (%)
1 son, 1 daughter	602	37	6.15
0 sons, 1 daughter	252	195	77.38
0 sons, 2 daughters	219	81	36.99
0 sons, 3 or more daughters	100	11	11
0 daughters, 1 son	292	200	68.49
0 daughters, 2 sons	279	42	15.05
0 daughters, 3 or more sons	123	4	3.25
Those with more than one son and one daughter (3+ children)			
Daughters = sons	143	2	0.7
Daughters > sons	495	4	0.81
Sons > daughters	481	2	0.42
Total	2986	577	19.32
Missing values	249		

Source: LSE/BIGD Survey 2015.

Table 6b. Desire for additional children by sex composition of surviving children: women aged 15–49 (2015 Amarpur sample)

Sex composition of surviving children	Total (N)	Wants more children (n)	Wants more children (%)
1 son, 1 daughter	79	4	5.06
0 sons, 1 daughter	23	19	82.61
0 sons, 2 daughters	24	10	41.67
0 sons, 3 or more daughters	14	0	0
0 daughters, 1 son	34	26	76.47
0 daughters, 2 sons	32	4	12.5
0 daughters, 3 or more sons	12	0	0
Those with more than one son and one daughter (3+ children)			
Daughters = sons	13	0	0
Daughters > sons	55	1	1.82
Sons > daughters	50	0	0
Total	336	64	19.05
Missing values	47		

Source: LSE/BIGD Survey 2015.

Table 7a. Desire for additional children by sex composition of surviving children: men aged 15–49 (2015 full sample)

Sex composition of surviving children	Total (N)	Wants another child (n)	Wants another child (%)
1 son, 1 daughter	383	27	7.05
0 sons, 1 daughter	174	153	87.93
0 sons, 2 daughters	131	52	39.69
0 sons, 3 or more daughters	54	13	24.07
0 daughters, 1 son	179	151	84.36
0 daughters, 2 sons	123	22	17.89
0 daughters, 3 or more sons	48	7	14.58
Those with more than one son and one daughter (3+ children)			
Daughters = sons	64	1	1.56
Daughters > sons	181	6	3.31
Sons > daughters	170	5	2.94
Total	1507	437	29.00
Missing values	245		

Source: LSE/BIGD Survey 2015.

Table 7b. Desire for additional children by sex composition of surviving children: men aged 15–49 (2015 Amarpur sample)

Sex composition of surviving children	Total (N)	Wants another child (n)	Wants another child (%)
1 son, 1 daughter	48	6	12.5
0 sons, 1 daughter	19	16	84.2
0 sons, 2 daughters	20	8	40
0 sons, 3 or more daughters	7	1	14.29
0 daughters, 1 son	22	19	86.36
0 daughters, 2 sons	15	1	6.67
0 daughters, 3 or more sons	3	0	0
Those with more than one son and one daughter:			
Daughters = sons	6	0	0
Daughters > sons	20	0	0
Sons > daughters	19	0	0
Total	179	51	28.49
Missing values	33		

Source: LSE/BIGD survey 2015.

Table 8a. Descriptive statistics by age group for full survey (2008 unless otherwise stated)

	Age group 12–30	Age group 31–49	Age group 50+	Total
Number	2361	1814	1023	5198
Age first marriage (mean)	16	15	14	15
Consulted at marriage	66%	46%	25%	49%
Should have say in marriage	98%	96%	93%	96%
Mean number of children	2.04	4.03	6.06	3.8
Antenatal care	64%	36%	7%	39%
Post-natal care	40%	23%	5%	25%
Using family planning	64%	46%	3%	44%
Education				
None	18.2	56.4	75.7	42.8
Primary	31.0	26.0	18.9	26.8
Secondary	40.0	14.2	4.4	24.0
Higher (SSC+)	10.9	3.4	1.1	6.3
Taken loans	37	62	41	47%
Savings	42	57	28	44%
NGO membership	34%	49%	24%	37%
Paid work	57%	70%	50%	60%
Unpaid family labour	17%	18%	18%	18%
Inactive	26%	12%	32%	22%
2008				
Burqa/hijab: always	50%	48%	48%	49
Burqa/hijab: occasionally	7%	6%	4%	6
Burqa/hijab: never	44%	46%	48%	45
2015				
Burqa/hijab: always	66%	64%	53%	61
Burqa/hijab: occasionally	12%	10%	10%	11
Burqa/hijab: never	13%	16%	26%	18
2008				
Most important resource for women	Education: 85%	Education: 81%	Education: 78%	82%
Most important resource for self	Education: 38%	Credit: 39%	Credit: 35%	Credit: 32%
Sense of agency	70%	66%	54%	66%

Source: IDS/BIGD Survey 2008 and LSE/BIGD Survey 2015.

Table 8b. Descriptive statistics for Amarpur (2008 unless otherwise stated)

	Age group 12–30	Age group 31–49	Age group 50+	Total
Number	289	214	131	634
Age first marriage (mean)	17	16	15	16
Consulted at marriage	83%	64%	29%	62%
Should have say in marriage	100%	100%	100%	100%
Mean number of children	1.8	3.59	5.76	3.54
Antenatal care	75%	47%	7%	46%
Post-natal care	52%	30%	5%	31%
Using family planning	79%	49%	–	48%
Education				
None	13.8%	46.3%	61.1%	34.5
Primary	20.4%	22.9%	29.0%	23.0
Secondary	40.5%	24.8%	6.9%	28.2%
Higher (SSC+)	25.3%	6.1%	3.1%	14.2%
Taken loans	42%	74%	48%	54%
Savings	50%	74%	41%	56%
NGO	47%	70%	40%	53%
Paid work	51%	71%	45%	56%
Unpaid family labour	5%	4%	5%	5%
Inactive	44%	25%	50%	39%
2008				
Burqa – always	34%	35%	44%	36
Burqa – occasionally	5%	6%	5%	5
Burqa/hijab: never	62%	59%	51%	59
2015				
Burqa – always	53%	45%	39%	45%
Burqa – occasionally	19%	15%	16%	17%
Burqa/hijab: never	16%	27%	32%	25%
2008				
Most important resource for women	Education: 91%	Education: 90%	Education: 88%	
Most important resource for self	Education: 36%	Credit: 47.7%	Credit: 35%	Credit: 34%
Sense of agency	80.3%	76.2	54	66%

Source: IDS/BIGD Survey 2008 and LSE/BIGD Survey 2015.

References

Abdullah, Tahrunessa Ahmed and Zeidenstein, Sondra (1982) *Village Women of Bangladesh. Prospects for Change*, London: Pergamon Press.

Abu-Lughod, Lila (1990) 'The Romance of Resistance. Tracing Transformations of Power through Bedouin Women', *American Ethnologist*, vol. 17, no. 1, pp.41–55. https://doi.org/10.1525/ae.1990.17.1.02a00030

Abu-Lughod, Lila (2002) 'Do Muslim Women Really Need Saving? Anthropological Reflections on Cultural Relativism and Its Others', *American Anthropologist*, vol. 104, no. 3, pp.783–90. https://www.jstor.org/stable/3567256

Adams, Alayne, M; Rabbani, Atonu; Ahmed, Shamim; Mahmood, Shehrin Shaila; Al-Sabir, Ahmed; Rashid, Sabina F.; and Evans, Timothy G. (2013) 'Explaining Equity Gains in Child Survival in Bangladesh: Scale, Speed and Selectivity in Health and Development', *Lancet*, vol. 382, pp.2027–37. http://dx.doi.org/10.1016/S0140-6736(13)62060-7

Addy, Premen and Ibne Azad (1975) 'Politics and Society in Bangladesh', in Blackburn, Robin (ed.) *Explosion in a Sub-continent*, London: Penguin Books, pp.79–150.

Adnan, Shapan (1978) 'Class Structure and Fertility in Rural Bangladesh: Reflections of the Political Economy of Population Growth', Working Paper 11, Village Studies Group, University of Chittagong.

Adnan, Shapan (1990) *Annotation of Village Studies in Bangladesh and West Bengal: A Review of Socio-economic Trends over 1942–88*, Comilla: Bangladesh Academy for Rural Development.

Adnan, Shapan (1993) 'Birds in a Cage: Institutional Change and Women's Position in Bangladesh', in Frederici, Nora; Mason, Karen O.; and Sogner, Sølvi (eds) *Women's Position and Demographic Change*, Oxford: Oxford University Press, pp.285–319.

Adnan, Shapan (1998) 'Fertility Decline under Absolute Poverty: Paradoxical Aspects of Demographic Change in Bangladesh', *Economic and Political Weekly*, vol. 33, no. 22, pp.1337–48. http://www.jstor.org/stable/4406836

Adnan, Shapan and Rahman, Hussain Zillur (1978) 'Peasant Classes and Land Mobility: Structural Reproduction and Change in Rural Bangladesh', Working Paper 9, Village Study Group, University of Chittagong.

Agarwal, Bina (1994) *A Field of One's Own. Gender and Land Rights in South Asia*, Cambridge: Cambridge University Press.

Agarwal, B. (1997) '"Bargaining" and Gender Relations: Within and Beyond the Household', *Feminist Economics*, vol. 3, no. 1, pp.1–51. https://doi.org/10.1080/135457097338799

Agnihotri, Satish B. (2000) *Sex Ratio Patterns in the Indian Population. A Fresh Exploration*, New Delhi: Sage Publications.

Ahmed, Nilufer R. (1981) 'Family Size and Sex Preferences among Women in Rural Bangladesh', *Studies in Family Planning*, vol, 12, no. 3, pp.100–109. https://doi.org/10.2307/1966371

Ahmed, Rafiuddin (1981) *Bengali Muslims 1871–1906. A Quest for Identity*, Delhi and Oxford: Oxford University Press.

Ahmed, Rafiuddin (2001) 'The Emergence of the Bengali Muslims', in Ahmed, Rafiuddin (ed.) *Understanding the Bengali Muslims. Interpretive Essays*, New Delhi: Oxford University Press, pp.2–25.

Ahmed, Raisuddin (1999) 'Liberalisation of Agricultural Input Markets in Bangladesh', in Sidhu, S.S. and Mudahar, M.S. (eds) *Privatisation and Deregulation – Needed Policy Reforms for Agribusiness Development*, Dordrecht, Kluwer Academic Publishers, pp.175–90.

Ahmed, Raisuddin and Hossain, Mahbubur (1990) 'Developmental Impact of Rural Infrastructure in Bangladesh', Research Report 83, IFPRI, Washington.

Ahmed, Rehnuma (1985) 'Women's Movement in Bangladesh and the Left's Understanding of the Women Question', *Journal of Social Studies*, no. 30, pp.27–56.

Ahmed, Rehnuma and Naher, Milu Shamsun (1987) *Brides and the Demand System in Bangladesh*, Dhaka: Centre for Social Studies.

Ahmed, Sadiq (2023) 'Institutional Dimensions of Tax Reforms in Bangladesh', in Raihan, Selim; Bourguignon, François; and Salam, Umar (eds), *Is the Bangladesh Paradox Sustainable? The Institutional Diagnostic Project*, Cambridge: Cambridge University Press, pp.185–221.

Ahmed, Sania Sultan and Bould, Sally (2004) '"One Able Daughter is Worth 10 Illiterate Sons": Reframing the Patriarchal Family', *Journal of Marriage and Family*, vol. 66, no. 5, pp.1332–41. https://www.jstor.org/stable/3600343

Ahmed, Syed Masud (2005) 'Intimate Partner Violence against Women: Experiences from a Woman-Focused Development Programme in Matlab, Bangladesh', *Journal of Health, Population and Nutrition*, vol. 23, no. 1, pp.95–101. https://www.jstor.org/stable/23499189

Alam, Nurul and Bairagi, Radheshyam (1997) 'Does a Health Program Reduce Excess Female Child Mortality in a Son-Preferring Society?' in Khilat, M. (ed.) *Demographic Evaluation of Health Programmes*. Paris, CICRED, pp.205–21.

Alam, Nurul; Roy, Swapan K.; and Ahmed, Tahmeed (2010) 'Sexually Harassing Behaviour against Adolescent Girls in Rural Bangladesh', *Journal of Interpersonal Violence*, vol. 25, no. 3, pp.443–56. https://doi.org/10.1177/0886260509334281

Alam, Nurul; Van Ginneken, Jeroen; and Bosch, Alinda (2007) 'Decreases in Male and Female Mortality and Missing Women in Bangladesh', in Attanè, Isabelle and Guilmoto, Christophe Z. (eds) *Watering the Neighbour's Garden. The Growing Demographic Female Deficit in Asia*, Paris: Committee for International Cooperation in National Research in Demography, pp.161–82.

Alam, Sultana (1985) 'Women and Poverty in Bangladesh', *Women's Studies International Forum*, vol. 8, no. 4, pp.361–71. https://doi.org/10.1016/0277-5395(85)90017-2

Alamgir, Mohiuddin (1978) *Bangladesh: A Case of Below Poverty Level Equilibrium Trap*, Dhaka: Bangladesh Institute of Development Studies.

Alamgir, Mohiuddin (1980) *Famine in South Asia. Political Economy of Mass Starvation*, Cambridge, MA: Oelgeschlager, Gunn & Hain.

Ali, Jan A. (2023) 'Modernity, Its Crisis and Islamic Revivalism', *Religions*, vol. 14, no. 1, pp.1–25. https://doi.org/10.3390/rel14010015

Ali, Tariq (1983) *Can Pakistan Survive? The Death of a State*, Middlesex: Penguin Books.

Alkema, Leontine; Chao, Fengqing; You, Danzhen; Pedersen, Jon; and Sawyer, Cheryl S. (2014) 'National, Regional, and Global Sex Ratios of Infant, Child, and Under-5 Mortality and Identification of Countries with Outlying Ratios: A Systematic Assessment', *The Lancet Global Health*, vol. 2, no. 9, pp.E521–E530. https://doi.org/10.1016/S2214-109X(14)70280-3

Allchin, Joseph (2019) *Many Rivers, One Sea. Bangladesh and the Challenge of Islamist Militancy*, London: C. Hurst and Co.

Amin, Sajeda (2008) 'Reforming Marriage Practices in Bangladesh', Briefing No. 31, New York: Population Council.

Amin, Sajeda and Das, Maitreyi (2013) 'Marriage Continuity and Change in Bangladesh', in Kaur, Ravinder and Palriwala, Rajni (eds) *Marrying in South Asia. Shifting Concepts, Changing Practices in a Globalizing World*, Hyderabad: Orient Black Swan, pp.89–115.

Amin, Sajeda; Diamond Ian; Naved, Ruchira T.; and Newby, Margaret (1998) 'Transition to Adulthood of Female Factory Workers in Bangladesh',

Studies in Family Planning, vol. 29, no. 2, pp.85–200. https://doi.org/10.2307/172158

Amin, Sajeda and Huq, Lopita (2008) 'Marriage Considerations in Sending Girls to School in Bangladesh: Some Qualitative Evidence', Poverty, Gender, and Youth Working Paper no. 12, New York: Population Council.

Anderson, Siwan (2007) 'The Economics of Dowry and Brideprice', *Journal of Economic Perspectives*, vol. 21, no. 4, pp.151–74. https://doi.org/10.1257/jep.21.4.151

Anderson, Siwan and Mukesh Eswaran (2009) 'What Determines Female Autonomy? Evidence from Bangladesh', *Journal of Development Economics*, vol. 90, no. 2, pp.179–91. https://doi.org/10.1016/j.jdeveco.2008.10.004

Appadurai, Arjun (2004) 'The Capacity to Aspire: Culture and the Terms of Recognition', in Rao, Vijayendra and Walton, Michael (eds) *Culture and Public Action*, Palo Alto, CA: Stanford University Press, pp.59–84.

Arens, Jenneke (2011) *Women, Land and Power in Bangladesh. Jhagrapur revisited*, PhD dissertation, University of Amsterdam. https://dare.uva.nl/search?identifier=76976186-5e17-4921-b0c8-fba71965e991

Arens, Jenneke and Van Beurden, Jos (1977) *Jhagrapur: Poor Peasants and Women in a Village in Bangladesh*, Amsterdam: Paupers' Press Co-operative.

Arthur, Brian and McNicoll, Geoffrey (1978) 'An Analytical Survey of Population and Development in Bangladesh', *Population and Development Review*, vol. 4, no. 1, pp.23–80.

Asadullah, Md. Niaz and Chaudhury, Nazmul (2008) 'Holy Alliances: Public Subsidies, Islamic High Schools, and Female Schooling in Bangladesh', in Tembon, Mercy and Fort, Lucia (eds) *Girls' Education in the 21st Century. Gender Equality, Empowerment and Economic Growth*, Washington: World Bank. http://hdl.handle.net/10986/6554

Asadullah, M. Niaz; Amin, Sajeda; and Chaudhury, Nazmul (2019) 'Support for Gender Stereotypes: Does Madrasah Education Matter?', *Journal of Development Studies*, vol. 55, no. 1, pp.39–56. https://doi.org/10.1080/00220388.2017.1414190

Asadullah, Md. Niaz and Chaudhury, Nazmul (2010) 'Religious Schools, Social Values and Economic Attitudes: Evidence from Bangladesh', *World Development*, vol. 38, no. 2, pp.205–17. https://doi.org/10.1016/j.worlddev.2009.10.014

Asadullah, Md. Niaz and Chaudhury, Nazmul (2016) 'To Madrasahs or Not to Madrasahs: The Question and Correlates of Enrolment in Islamic

Schools in Bangladesh', *International Journal of Educational Development*, vol. 49, pp.55–69. http://dx.doi.org/10.1016/j.ijedudev.2016.01.005

Asadullah, Niaz, M.; Mansoor, Nazia; Randazzo, Teresa; and Wahhaj, Zaki (2021) 'Is Son Preference Disappearing from Bangladesh?', *World Development*, vol. 140, pp.1–16. https://doi.org/10.1016/j.worlddev.2020.105353

Asadullah, M. Niaz; Savoia, Antonio; and Mahmud, Wahiduddin (2014) 'Paths to Development: Is There a Bangladesh Surprise?', *World Development*, vol. 62, pp.138–54. http://dx.doi.org/10.1016/j.worlddev.2014.05.013

Asadullah, M. Niaz and Savoia, Antonio (2018) 'From MDGs to SDGs: Where Next for Bangladesh?', *The Asia Dialogue*. https://theasiadialogue .com/2018/09/04/from-mdgs-to-sdgs-where-next-for-bangladesh/

Ashwin, Sarah; Keenan, Katherina; and Kozina, Irina M. (2021) 'Pensioner Employment, Well-Being and Gender: Lessons from Russia', *American Journal of Sociology*, vol. 127, no. 1, pp.152–93. https://doi.org/10.1086/715150

Aziz, Ashraful K.M. (1979) *Kinship in Bangladesh*, Dhaka: International Centre for Diarrhoeal Diseases.

Aziz, Ashraful K.M. and Maloney, Clarence (1985) *Life Stages, Gender and Fertility in Bangladesh*, Dhaka: International Centre for Diarrhoeal Diseases.

Bairagi, Radheshyam (1980) 'Is Income the Only Constraint on Child Nutrition in Rural Bangladesh', *Bulletin of the World Health Organization*, vol. 58, no. 5, pp.767–72.

Bairagi, Radheshyam and Datta, Ashish K. (2001) 'Demographic Transition in Bangladesh: What Happened in the Twentieth Century and What Will Happen Next?', *Asia Pacific Population Journal*, vol. 16, no. 4, pp.3–16. https://doi.org/10.18356/f3000d63-en

Balk, Deborah (1997) 'Defying Gender Norms in Rural Bangladesh: A Social Demographic Analysis', *Population Studies*, vol. 51, no. 2, pp.153–72. https://www.jstor.org/stable/2174683

Bangladesh Garment Manufacturers and Exporters Association (2015) 'Trade Information', Dhaka: BGMEA. www.bgmea.com.bd/home/pages /tradeinformation#

Bano, Masooda (2008) 'Allowing for Diversity. State-Madrassa Relations in Bangladesh', Religions and Working Paper No. 13, University of Oxford.

Basu, Alaka Malwade (1999) 'Fertility Decline and Increasing Gender Imbalance in India, Including a Possible South Indian Turnaround', *Development and Change*, vol. 30, no. 2, pp.237–63. https://doi.org/10.1111/1467-7660.00116

Basu, Kaushik (2018) 'A Short History of India's Economy. A Chapter in the Asian Drama', WIDER Working Paper 2018/124.

Basu, Kaushik and Maertens, Annemie (2007) 'The Pattern and Causes of Economic Growth in India', *Oxford Review of Economic Policy*, vol. 23, no. 2, pp.143–67. https://doi.org/10.1093/oxrep/grm012

Bates, Lisa M.; Maselko, Joanna; and Schuler, Sidney Rith (2007) 'Women's Education and the Timing of Marriage and Childbearing in the Next Generation: Evidence from Rural Bangladesh', *Studies in Family Planning*, vol. 38, no. 2, pp.101–12. https://www.jstor.org/stable/20454394/

Bauer, Peter (1981) *Equality, the Third World and Economic Delusion*, London: Weidenfeld and Nicholson.

Bayram, Aydin (2014) 'The Rise of Wahhabi Sectarianism and Its Impact in Saudi Arabia', Atatük Üniversitesi İlahiyat Fakültesi Dergisi, Sayı: 42 Erzurum 2014.

Becker, Gary S. (1981) *A Treatise on the Family*, Cambridge, MA: Harvard University Press.

Begum, Najmir Nur (1988) *Pay or Purdah? Women and Income-Earning in Rural Bangladesh*, Winrock International Institute for Agricultural Development with Bangladesh Agricultural Research Council, Dhaka.

Begum, Saleha and Greeley, Martin (1979) 'Rural Women and the Rural Labour Market in Bangladesh: An Empirical Analysis', *Bangladesh Journal of Agricultural Economics*, vol. 11, no. 2, pp.35–55. https://doi.org/10.22004/ag.econ.225534

Begum, S. and Greeley, M. (1983) 'Women's Employment and Agriculture: Extracts from a Case Study', Seminar Papers, Women for Women: Dhaka.

Berg, Claudia; Emran, Shahe M.; and Shilpi, Forhad (2013) 'Microfinance and Moneylenders: Long-Run Effects of MFIs on Informal Credit Markets in Bangladesh', Policy Research Working Papers, The World Bank. https://doi.org/10.1596/1813-9450-6619

Bertocci, Peter J. (1972) 'Community Structure and Social Rank in Two Villages in Bangladesh', *Contributions to Indian Sociology New Series*, vol. 6, pp.28–52. https://doi.org/10.1177/006996677200600102

Bertocci, Peter J. (1982) 'Bangladesh in the Early 1980s: Praetorian Politics in an Intermediate Regime', *Asian Survey*, vol. 22, no. 10. pp.988–1008. https://www.jstor.org/stable/2643756

Bertocci, Peter J. (1976) 'Rural Development in Bangladesh. An Introduction', in Stevens, Robert D.; Alavi, Hamza; and Bertocci, Peter J. (eds) *Rural Development in Bangladesh and Pakistan*, Honolulu, HI: The University Press of Hawaii, pp.3–8.

Beverley, Henry (1872) *Census of Bengal 1871*, Calcutta: Bengal Secretariat Press.

Bhuiyan, Md. Nurul Momen (2010) *'Creating Good Muslims': Qawmi Madrasa Schooling in a Rural Town of Bangladesh*, PhD dissertation, Brunel University.

Biggs, Stephen and Justice, Scott (2017) 'Rural and Agricultural Mechanisation: A History of The Spread of Smaller Engines in Selected Asian Countries', in Mandal, Sattar, M.A.; Biggs, Stephen D.; and Justice, Scott E. (eds) *Rural Mechanisation. A Driver in Agriculture Change and Rural Development*, Dhaka: Institute for Inclusive Finance and Development, pp.23–76. http://inm.org.bd/inm-published-a-new-book-on-rural-mechanisation/

Blair, Harry (1978) 'Rural Development, Class Structure and Bureaucracy in Bangladesh', *World Development*, vol. 6, no. 1, pp.65–82.

Bleie, Tone (1990) 'Dowry and Bridewealth Presentations in Rural Bangladesh: Commodities, Gifts or Hybrid Forms?', DERAP Working Paper No. 10, Bergen: Chr. Michelsen Institute.

Bloom, David E.; Canning, David; and Rosenberg, Larry (2011) 'Demographic Change and Economic Growth in South Asia', Program on the Global Demography of Ageing Working Paper No. 67, Harvard School of Public Health.

Bora, Jayanta Kumar; Saikia, Nandita; Kebede, Endale Birhanu; and Lutz, Wolfgang (2023) 'Revisiting the Causes of Fertility Decline in Bangladesh: The Relative Importance of Female Education and Family Planning Programs', *Asian Population Studies*, vol. 19, no. 1, pp.81–104. https://doi.org/10.1080/17441730.2022.2028253

Borooah, Vani and Iyer, Sriya (2004) 'Religion and Fertility in India: The Role of Son Preference and Daughter Aversion', Cambridge Working Papers in Economics 436, Faculty of Economics, University of Cambridge.

Borooah, Vani; Quy-Toan, Do; Iyer, Sriya; and Joshi, Shareen (2009) 'Missing Women and India's Religious Demography', Policy Research Working Paper 5096, World Bank, Washington, DC.

Bose, Sugata and Jalal, Ayesha (1998) *Modern South Asia. History, Culture, Political Economy*, Routledge: New York and London.

Bose, Swadesh R. (1974) 'The Strategy of Agricultural Development of Bangladesh', in Robinson, E.A.G. and Griffin, Keith (eds) *The Economic Development of Bangladesh within a Socialist Framework*, London: Macmillan, pp.140–55.

Bourdieu, Pierre (1977) *Outline of a Theory of Practice*, Cambridge: Cambridge University Press.

Bourdieu, Pierre (1998) *Practical Reason: On the Theory of Action*, Cambridge: Polity Press

Boyce, James K. (1983) 'Winners and Losers. Peasant Mobility in Bangladesh', *Economic and Political Weekly*, vol. 18, no. 11, pp.385–90.

Boyce, James, K. (1987) *Agrarian Impasse in Bengal: Agricultural Growth in Bangladesh and West Bengal 1949–1980*, New York and Oxford: Oxford University Press.

BRAC (1983) 'The Net. Power Structure in Ten Villages', Research Monograph Series, Research and Evaluation Division, BRAC Dhaka. https://bigd.bracu.ac.bd/wp-content/uploads/2020/03/The-Net -Monograph_02.pdf

BRAC (1989) 'A Tale of Two Wings: Health and Family Planning Programmes in an Upazila in Northern Bangladesh', Research and Evaluation Division, BRAC, Dhaka.

Brown, Laurine V. and Zeitlin, Marian F. (1991) 'Evaluation of Nutrition Education Messages for Lactating Mothers and Weaning Age Infants: What Are the Food Costs?', Washington DC: Academy for Educational Development and US Agency for International Development.

Burki, Shahed Javed (1976) 'The Development of Pakistan's Agriculture. An Interdisciplinary Explanation', in Stevens, Robert D.; Alavi, Hamza; and Bertocci, Peter J. (eds) *Rural Development in Bangladesh and Pakistan*, Honolulu, HI: University of Hawaii Press, pp.290–316.

Cain, Mead T. (1978) 'The Household Life Cycle and Economic Mobility in Rural Bangladesh', in *Population and Development Review*, vol. 4, no. 3, pp.421–38. https://doi.org/10.2307/1972858

Cain, Mead (1984) 'Women's Status and Fertility in Developing Countries: Son Preference and Economic Security', World Bank Staff Working Papers No. 682. Washington, DC: World Bank.

Cain, Mead; Khanam, Syeda Rokeya; and Nahar, Shamsun (1979) 'Class, patriarchy and women's work in Bangladesh', *Population and Development Review*, vol. 5, no. 3, pp.405–38. https://doi.org/10.2307/1972079

Caldwell, Bruce and Khuda, Barkat-e- (2000) 'The First Generation to Control Family Size: A Microstudy of the Causes of Fertility Decline in a Rural Area of Bangladesh', *Studies in Family Planning*, vol. 31, no. 3, pp.239–51. https://www.jstor.org/stable/172265

Caldwell, John C. (1978) 'A Theory of Fertility: From High Plateau to Destabilization', *Population and Development Review*, vol. 4, no. 4, pp.553–77. http://www.jstor.org/stable/1971727

Caldwell, John C.; Reddy, P.H.; and Caldwell, Pat (1983) 'The Causes of Marriage Change in South India', *Population Studies*, vol. 37, no. 3, pp.343–61. https://doi.org/10.1080/00324728.1983.10408866

Caldwell, Pat (1996) 'Child Survival: Physical Vulnerability and Resilience in Adversity in the European Past and the Contemporary Third World', *Social Science and Medicine*, vol. 42, no. 5, pp.609–19. https://doi.org/10.1016/0277-9536(96)00109-8

Callan, Alyson (2008) 'Female Saints and the Practice of Islam in Sylhet', *American Ethnologist*, vol. 35, no. 3, pp.396–412. https://doi.org/10.1111/j.1548-1425.2008.00042.x

Chakma, Bhumitra (2010) 'The Post-colonial State and Minorities: Ethnocide in the Chittagong Hill Tracts', *Bangladesh, Commonwealth & Comparative Politics*, vol. 48, no. 3, pp.281–300. https://doi.org/10.1080/14662043.2010.489746

Chakrabarty, Dipesh S. (2000) *Provincializing Europe: Postcolonial Thought and Historical Difference*, Princeton, NJ: Princeton University Press.

Chakravarti, Uma (1993) 'Conceptualizing Brahmanical Patriarchy in Early India: Gender, Caste, Class and State', *Economic and Political Weekly*, vol. 28, no. 14, pp.579–85. https://www.jstor.org/stable/4399556

Chatterji, Joya (2023) *Shadows at Noon. The South Asian Twentieth Century*, London: Penguin Books.

Chaudhuri, Sudip (2020) 'Evolution of the Pharmaceutical Industry Bangladesh, 1982 to 2020', Centre for Development Studies Working Paper 495. http://dx.doi.org/10.2139/ssrn.3767822

Chaudhury, Rafiqul H. and Chowdhury, Zafrullah (2007) *Achieving the Millennium Development Goal on Maternal Mortality*, Dhaka: Gonoprokashani.

Choksy, Carol E.B. and Choksy, Jamsheed K. (2015) 'The Saudi Connection: Wahhabism and Global Jihad', *World Affairs*, vol. 178, no. 1, pp.23–34. https://www.jstor.org/stable/43555279

Chowdhury, A.M.R. (1990) 'Empowerment through Health Education: The Approach of an NGO in Bangladesh', in Streefland, Pieter and Chabot, Jarl (eds) *Implementing Primary Health. Experiences since Alma Ata*, Amsterdam: Kit Publishers, pp.113–93.

Chowdhury, AMR and Cash, Richard A. (1996) *A Simple Solution: Teaching Millions to Treat Diarrhoea at Home*, Dhaka: University Press.

Chowdhury, Mushtaque. R.; Bhuiya, Abbas; Chowdhury, Mahbub Elahi; Rasheed, Sabrina; Hussain, Zakir; and Chen, Lincoln C. (2013) 'The Bangladesh Paradox: Exceptional Health Achievement Despite Economic Poverty', *Lancet*, vol. 382, pp.1734–45. https://doi.org/10.1016/S0140-6736(13)62148-0

Chen, Lincoln C. (1982) 'Where Have the Women Gone? Insights from Bangladesh on Low Sex Ratio of India's Population', *Economic and Political Weekly*, vol. 17, no. 10, pp.364–72. https://www.jstor.org/stable/4370749

Chen, Martha Alter (1986) *A Quiet Revolution. Women in Transition in Rural Bangladesh*, Dhaka: BRAC Printers.

Cleland, John G. and Van Ginneken, Jerome K. (1988) 'Maternal Education and Child Survival in Developing Countries: The Search for Pathways of Influence', *Social Science and Medicine*, vol. 27, no. 12, pp.1357–68. https://doi.org/10.1016/0277-9536(88)90201-8

Cleland, John; Phillips, James F.; Amin, Sajeda; and Kamal, G.M. (1994) *The Determinants of Reproductive Change in Bangladesh. Success in a Challenging Environment*, Washington, DC: World Bank Regional and Sectoral Studies, World Bank.

Coombs, Clyde H.; Coombs, Lolagene C.; and Mcclelland, Gary H. (1975) 'Preferences Scales for Number and Sex of Children', *Population Studies*, vol. 29, no. 2, pp.273–98. https://doi.org/10.1080/00324728.1975.10410204

Da Costa, Dia (2008) '"Spoiled Sons" and "Sincere Daughters". Schooling, Security and Empowerment in Rural West Bengal, India', *Signs*, vol. 33, no. 2, pp.283–308. http://www.jstor.org/stable/10.1086/521053

Das Gupta, Monica (1987) 'Selective Discrimination against Female Children in Rural Punjab, India', *Population and Development Review*, vol. 13, no. 1, pp.77–100. https://doi.org/10.2307/1972121

Das Gupta, Monica and Bhatt, P.N. Mari (1997) 'Fertility Decline and Increased Manifestation of Sex Bias in India', *Population Studies*, vol. 51, no. 3, pp.307–15. https://doi.org/10.1080/0032472031000150076

Das Gupta, Monica; Zhenghua, Jiang; Bohua, Li; Zhenming, Xie; Chung, Woojin; and Hwa-Ok, Bae (2003) 'Why Is Son Preference So Persistent in East and South Asia? A Cross-Country Study of China, India and the Republic of Korea', *Journal of Development Studies*, vol. 40, no. 2, pp.153–87. https://doi.org/10.1080/00220380412331293807

Davis, Kingsley (1945) 'The World Demographic Transition', *The Annals of the American Academy of Political and Social Science*, vol. 237, no. 1, pp.1–11. https://doi.org/10.1177/000271624523700102

Deaton, Angus and Drèze, Jean (2002) 'Poverty and Inequality in India: A Re-examination', *Economic and Political Weekly*, vol. 37, no. 36, pp.3729–48. https://www.jstor.org/stable/4412578

Desai, Sonalde (1994) 'Gender Inequalities and Demographic Behaviour. India', The Population Council, New York. https://doi.org/10.31899/pgy1994.1003

Dev, Mahendra S. (2012) 'Small Farmers in India: Challenges and Opportunities', Working Paper-2012-014. Indira Gandhi Institute of Development Research, Mumbai. http://www.igidr.ac.in/pdf/publication/WP-2012-014.pdf

Devarajan, Shantayanan (2005) 'South Asian Surprises', *Economic and Political Weekly*, vol. 40, no. 37, pp.4013–15.

Devine, Joseph (2002) 'Ethnography of a Policy Process: A Case Study of Land Redistribution in Bangladesh', *Public Administration and Development*, vol. 22, pp.403–14. https://doi.org/10.1002/pad.245

Devine, Joseph (2003) 'The Paradox of Sustainability: Reflections on NGOs in Bangladesh', *The Annals of the American Academy of Political and Social Science*, vol. 590, no. 1, pp.227–42.

Drèze, Jean and Sen, Amartya (1995) *India: Economic Development and Social Opportunity*, Oxford: Oxford University Press.

Drèze, Jean and Sen, Amartya (2013) *An Uncertain Glory. India and Its Contradictions*, London: Allan Lane.

Dumont, Rene (1974a) 'Discussion of Papers by M. Anisur Rahman and Mohiuddin Alamgir', in Robinson, E.A.G. and Griffin, Keith (eds) *The Economic Development of Bangladesh within a Socialist Framework*, London: Macmillan, pp.59–66.

Duvendack, Maren and Palmer-Jones, Richard (2017) 'Microfinance, Women's Empowerment and Fertility Decline in Bangladesh: How Important Was Women's Agency', *Journal of Development Studies*, vol. 53, no. 5, pp.664–83. http://dx.doi.org/10.1080/00220388.2016.1205731

Duvvury, Nata (1989) 'Women in Agriculture: A Review of the Indian Literature', *Economic and Political Weekly*, vol. 24, no. 43, pp.WS96–WS112. https://www.jstor.org/stable/4395526

Dyson, Tim and Moore, Mick (1983) 'On Kinship Structure, Female Autonomy, and Demographic Behavior in India', *Population and Development Review*, vol. 9, no. 1, pp.35–60 https://www.jstor.org/stable/1972894

Eaton, Richard M. (1994) *The Rise of Islam and the Bengal Frontier, 1204–1760*, Delhi: Oxford University Press.

Elder-Vass, David (2007) 'Reconciling Archer and Bourdieu in an Emergentist Theory of Action', *Sociological Theory*, vol. 25, no. 4, pp.325–46. https://doi.org/10.1111/j.1467-9558.2007.00312.x

Elson, Diane and Pearson, Ruth (1981) 'The Subordination of Women and the Internationalization of Factory Production', in Young, Kate; McCullagh, Ros; and Wolkowitz, Carol (eds) *Of Marriage and the Market: Women's Subordination in International Perspective*, CSE Books: London, pp.144–66.

Ellickson, Jean (1972) 'Islamic Institutions: Perception and Practice in a Village in Bangladesh', *Contributions to Indian Sociology*, vol. 6, no. 1, pp.53–65. https://doi.org/10.1177/006996677200600103

Ellickson, Jean (1988) 'Never the Twain Shall Meet: Aging Men and Women in Bangladesh', *Journal of Cross-Cultural Gerontology*, vol. 3, pp.53–70.

Epstein, T. Scarlett (1973) *South India. Yesterday, Today and Tomorrow – Mysore Villages Revisited*, London: Macmillan.

Faaland, Just and Parkinson, J.R. (1976) *Bangladesh. The Test Case of Development*, London: C. Hurst and Company.

Farouk, Abdullah (1976) *The Vagrants of Dhaka City*, Dhaka: Bureau of Economic Research, Dhaka University.

Faruqee, Rashid and Khalily, M.A. Baqui (2011) 'Multiple Borrowing by MFI Clients. Current Status and Implications for Future of Microfinance', Policy Paper, Institute of Microfinance, Dhaka. http://inm.org.bd/wp-content/uploads/2016/01/policypaper_multiple_borrowing.pdf

Feldman, Shelley (1997) 'NGOs and Civil Society: Unstated Contradictions', *The Annals of the American Academy of Political and Social Science*, vol. 554, no. 1, pp.46–65. https://doi.org/10.1177/0002716297554001004

Feldman, Shelley (2009) 'Historicizing Garment Manufacturing in Bangladesh: Gender, Generation, and New Regulatory Regimes', *Journal of International Women's Studies*, vol. 11, no. 1, pp.268–88. http://vc.bridgew.edu/jiws/vol11/iss1/17/

Feldman, Shelley and McCarthy, Florence E. (1982) 'Conditions Influencing Rural and Town Women's Participation in the Labour Force', *International Journal of Intercultural Relations*, vol. 6, no. 2, pp.421–40. https://doi.org/10.1016/0147-1767(82)90022-0

Feldman, Shelley and McCarthy, Florence E. (1983) 'Purdah and Changing Patterns of Social Control among Rural Women in Bangladesh', *Journal of Marriage and Family*, vol. 45, no. 4, pp.949–59. https://doi.org/10.2307/351808

Freire, Paolo (1972) *Pedagogy of the Oppressed*, Harmondsworth: Penguin Books.

Fuller, Chris J. (1999) 'The Brahmins and Brahminical Values in Modern Tamil Nadu', in Guha, Ramachandra and Parry, Jonathan P. (eds) *Institutions and Inequalities: Essays in Honour of André Béteille*, New Delhi: Oxford University Press, pp.30–55.

Gardener, Katy (1998) 'Women and Islamic Revivalism in a Bangladeshi Community', in Basu, Amrita and Jeffery, Patricia (eds) *Appropriating Gender*, New York and London: Routledge, pp.203–43.

Gazdar, Haris (2007) 'Class, Caste or Race: Veils over Social Oppression in Pakistan', *Economic and Political Weekly*, vol. 42, no. 2, pp.86–88. https://www.jstor.org/stable/4419123

Geirbo, Hanne Cecilie and Imam, Nuzhat (2006) 'Dowry and the Transition to Marriage', Research Monograph Series, Paper 6. Research and Evaluation Division, BRAC, Dhaka.

Ghosh, Ambika (1974) 'Discussion of the Paper by Iftikhar Ahmed and Badrud Duza', in Robinson, E.A.G. and Griffin, Keith (eds) *The Economic Development of Bangladesh within a Socialist Framework*, London: Macmillan, pp.283–88.

Giddens, Anthony (1979) *Central Problems in Social Theory: Action, Structure and Contradiction in Social Analysis*, Berkeley and Los Angeles, CA: University of California Press.

Gipson, Jessica D. and Hindin, Michelle J. (2008) '"Having Another Child Would Be a Life or Death Situation for Her". Understanding Pregnancy Termination among Couples in Rural Bangladesh', *American Journal of Public Health*, vol. 98, no. 10, pp.1734–909. https://doi.org/10.2105/AJPH.2007.129262

Gipson, Jessica D. and Hindin, Michelle J. (2009) 'The Effect of Husbands' and Wives' Fertility Preferences on the Likelihood of a Subsequent Pregnancy, Bangladesh 1998–2003', *Population Studies*, vol. 63, no. 2, pp.135–46. https://doi.org/10.1080/00324720902859372

Goetz, Anne Marie (1992) 'Gender and Administration', *IDS Bulletin*, vol. 23, no. 4, pp.6–17.

Goetz, Anne Marie (1995) 'The Politics of Integrating Gender to State Development Processes: Trends, Opportunities and Constraints in Bangladesh, Chile, Jamaica, Mali, Morocco and Uganda', UNRISD Occasional Paper, No. 2, United Nations Research Institute for Social Development, Geneva.

Goetz, Anne Marie and Sen Gupta, Rina (1996) 'Who Takes the Credit? Gender, Power and Control over Loan Use in Rural Credit Programs in Bangladesh', *World Development*, vol. 24, no. 1, pp.45–63. https://doi.org/10.1016/0305-750X(95)00124-U

Goetz, Anne Marie (2001) *Women Development Workers. Implementing Rural Credit Programmes in Bangladesh*, Dhaka: University Press.

Government of Bangladesh (1972) Parliament Debates, 12 October 1972. Dhaka.

Government of India (2006) 'Social, Economic and Educational Status of the Muslim Community of India. A Report', Prime Minister's High Level Committee, Government of India.

Guhathakurta, Meghna (1985) 'Gender Violence in Bangladesh: The Role of the State', *Journal of Social Studies*, vol. 30, pp.77–90.

Guilmoto, Christophe Z. (2009) 'The Sex Ratio Transition in Asia', *Population and Development Review*, vol. 35, no. 3, pp.519–49. https://www.jstor.org/stable/25593663

Guilmoto, Christophe Z.; Saikia, Nandita; Tamrakar, Vandana; and Bora, Jayanta Kumar (2018) 'Excess Under-5 Female Mortality across India:

A Spatial Analysis using 2011 Census Data', *Lancet Global Health*, vol. 6, no. 6, pp.e650–e658. https://doi.org/10.1016/S2214-109X(18)30184-0

Hahn, Youjin; Islam, Asadul; and Nuzhat, Kanti (2018) 'Education, Marriage and Fertility: Long-Term Evidence from a Female Stipend Program in Bangladesh', *Economic Development and Cultural Change*, vol. 66, no. 2, pp.179–45.

Hall, Stuart (1996) 'Response to Saba Mahmood', *Cultural Studies*, vol. 10, no. 1, pp.12–15. https://doi.org/10.1080/09502389600490431

Haque, Enamul, A.K. and Bari, Eshtiaque (2021) 'A Survey Report on the Garment Workers of Bangladesh 2020', Asian Centre for Development, Dhaka.

Harris, Marvin (1976) 'History and Significance of the Emic/Etic Distinction', *Annual Review of Anthropology*, vol. 5, pp.329–50. https://www.jstor.org/stable/2949316

Hartmann, Betsy and Boyce, James (1983) *A Quiet Violence. View from a Bangladesh Village*, London: Zed Press.

Hartmann, Betsy and Standing, Hilary (1985) 'Food, Saris and Sterilization. Population Control in Bangladesh', Bangladesh International Action Group, London.

Hasan, Mubashar (2012) 'The Geopolitics of Political Islam in Bangladesh', *Harvard Asia Quarterly*, vol. 14, nos 1–2, pp.60–69. http://hdl.handle.net/10072/47246

Hashemi, Syed M.; Schuler, Ruth Sidney; and Riley, Ann P. (1996) 'Rural Credit Programs and Women's Empowerment in Bangladesh', *World Development*, vol. 24, no. 4, pp.635–53.

Hashmi, Taj I. (2000) *Women and Islam in Bangladesh: Beyond Subjection and Tyranny*, London: Macmillan.

Hasnath, Syed Abu (1987) 'The Practice and Effect of Development Planning in Bangladesh', *Public Administration and Development*, vol. 7, pp.59–75. https://doi.org/10.1002/pad.4230070105

Heath, Rachel and Mobarak, Mushfiq A. (2015) 'Manufacturing Growth and the Lives of Bangladeshi Women', *Journal of Development Economics*, vol. 115, pp.1–15. https://doi.org/10.1016/j.jdeveco.2015.01.006

Heath, Rachel and Tan, Xu (2018) 'Worth Fighting For: Daughters Improve Their Mothers' Autonomy in South Asia', *Journal of Development Economics*, vol. 135, pp.255–27. https://doi.org/10.1016/j.jdeveco.2018.07.003

Heintzman, James and Worden, Robert (1989) *Bangladesh: A Country Study*, Washington, DC: Library of Congress. http://countrystudies.us/bangladesh

Horvat, Branko (1974) 'Discussion of Papers by M. Anisur Rahman and Mohiuddin Alamgir', in Robinson, E.A.G. and Griffin, Keith (eds) *The Economic Development of Bangladesh within a Socialist Framework*, London: Macmillan, pp.59–66.

Hossain, Akhand Akhtar (2012) 'Islamic Resurgence in Bangladesh's Culture and Politics: Origins, Dynamics and Implications', *Journal of Islamic Studies*, vol. 23, no. 2, pp.165–98. https://doi.org/10.1093/jis/ets042

Hossain, Hameeda; Jahan, Roushan; and Sobhan, Salma (1990) *No Better Option. Industrial Women Workers in Bangladesh*, Dhaka: University Press.

Hossain, Mahabub (1988) 'Credit for Alleviation of Rural Poverty. The Grameen Bank in Bangladesh', Research Report 65, IFPRI in collaboration with BIDS.

Hossain, M.M. (1980) 'The Employment for Women', Proceedings from Conference on Thoughts on Islamic Economics, Islamic Economics Research Bureau, Dhaka.

Hossain, Mian B.; Phillips, James, F. and Mozumder, A.B.M. Khorshed (2007) 'The Effect of Husbands' Fertility Preferences on Couples' Reproductive Behaviour in Rural Bangladesh', *Journal of Biosocial Science*, vol. 39, no. 5, pp.745–57. https://doi.org/https://doi.org/10.1017/S0021932006001696

Hossain, Naomi (2008) 'Who Trusts Government? Understanding Political Trust among the Poor in Bangladesh', Asia Research Institute Working Paper No. 103. http://dx.doi.org/10.2139/ssrn.1316782

Hossain, Naomi (2017) *The Aid Lab. Understanding Bangladesh's Unexpected Success*, Oxford: Oxford University Press.

Hossain, Naomi and Kabeer, Naila (2004) 'Achieving Universal Primary Education and Eliminating Gender Disparity', *Economic and Political Weekly*, vol. 39, no. 36, pp.4093–100. http://www.jstor.org/stable/4415511

Huang, Julia Qermezi (2020) *To Be an Entrepreneur: Social Enterprise and Disruptive Development in Bangladesh*, Ithaca, NY: Cornell University Press.

Huntingdon, Samuel P. (1993) 'The Clash of Civilizations?' *Foreign Affairs*, vol. 72, no. 3, pp.22–49. https://www.jstor.org/stable/20045621

Husain, A.F.A. (1974) 'Social Infrastructure and Bangladesh Development', in Robinson, E.A.G. and Griffin, Keith (eds) *The Economic Development of Bangladesh within a Socialist Framework*, London: Macmillan, pp.309–21.

Hussain, Naseem Akhter (2010) 'Religion and Modernity: Gender and Identity Politics in Bangladesh', *Women's Studies International Forum*, vol. 33, no. 4, pp.325–33. https://doi.org/10.1016/j.wsif.2010.02.006

Huq, Maimuna (2008) 'Reading the Qur'an in Bangladesh: The Politics of "Belief" amongst Islamist Women', *Modern Asian Studies*, vol. 42, nos 2–3, pp.457–88. https://doi.org/10.1017/S0026749X07003149

Huq, Mujibul (1991) *Near Miracle in Bangladesh*, Dhaka: University Press.

Huq, Samia (2011) *Women's Religious Discussion Circles in Urban Bangladesh: Enacting, Negotiating and Contesting Piety*, PhD dissertation, Brandeis University, USA.

Huq, Samia and Khondaker, Sahida Islam (2011) 'Religion and Muslim Women: Trajectories of Empowerment', BDI Working Paper No. 2, BRAC Development Institute, Dhaka.

Inglehart, Ronald and Norris, Pippa (2003) 'The True Clash of Civilizations', *Foreign Policy*, vol. 135 (March–April), pp.62–70. https://www.jstor.org/stable/3183594

Islam, A. (2011) 'Medium and Long-Term Participation in Microcredit: Evaluation Using a New Panel Data Set from Bangladesh', *American Journal of Agricultural Economics*, vol. 93, no. 3, pp.847–66.

Islam, A.K.M. Aminul (1974) *A Bangladesh Village, Conflict and Cohesion: An Anthropological Study of Politics*, Cambridge, MA: Schenkman.

Islam, F. and Zeitlyn, Sushila (1989) 'Ethnographic Profile of Dhaka *bastees*', *Oriental Geographer*, vol. 31, pp.103–12.

Islam, Mahmuda (1979) 'Social Norms and Institutions', in Women for Women Research and Study Group (ed.) *The Situation of Women in Bangladesh*, Dhaka, pp.225–64.

Islam, Nurul (1974) 'The State and Prospects of the Bangladesh Economy', in Robinson, E.A.G. and Griffin, Keith (eds) *The Economic Development of Bangladesh within a Socialist Framework*, London: Macmillan, pp.1–15.

Islam, Nurul (1979) *Development Planning in Bangladesh: A Study in Political Economy*, Dhaka: University Press.

Jackson, Ben (1992) *Threadbare: How the Rich Stitch Up the World's Rag Trade*, World Development Movement, London.

Jackson, Cecile (2012) 'Speech, Gender and Power: Beyond Testimony', *Development and Change*, vol. 43, no. 5, pp.999–1023. https://doi.org/10.1111/j.1467-7660.2012.01791.x

Jackson, Cecile and Rao, Nitya (2004) 'Understanding Gender and Agrarian Change under Liberalisation: The Case of India', Background paper for UNRISD Report on Gender Equality: Striving for Justice in an Unequal World, Geneva: UNRISD.

Jahan, Rounaq (1972) *Pakistan. Failure in National Integration*, New York: Columbia University Press.

Jahan, Roushan (1979) 'Situation of Deviant Women', in Women for Women Research and Study Group (ed.) *The Situation of Women in Bangladesh*, Dhaka, pp.265–84.

Jansen, Eric G. (1987) *Rural Bangladesh. Competition for Scarce Resources*, Dhaka: University Press.

Januzzi, F.T. and Peach, J. (1980) *The Agrarian Structure of Bangladesh: An Impediment to Development*, Boulder, CO: Westview.

Jiggins, Janice (1987) 'Women in Bangladesh. An Economic Strategy Paper', Mimeo. World Bank, Dhaka.

Jinnah, Mohammed Ali (2004) *Quaid-e-Azam Mohammad Ali Jinnah Speeches: As Governor-General of Pakistan, 1947–1948*, Lahore: Sang-e-Meel Publications.

John, Mary E. (2011) 'Census 2011: Governing Populations and the Girl Child', *Economic and Political Weekly*, vol. 46, no. 16, pp.10–12. https://www.jstor.org/stable/41152095

John, Mary E.; Kaur, Ravinder; Palriwala, Rajni; Raju, Saraswati; and Sagar, Alpana (2008) *Planning Families, Planning Gender. The Adverse Child Sex Ratio in Selected Districts of Madhya Pradesh, Rajasthan, Himachal Pradesh, Haryana, and Punjab*, New Delhi: Action Aid and IDRC.

Joshi, Shareen; Iyer, Sriya; and Do, Quy Toan (2014) 'Why Marry a Cousin? Insights from Bangladesh', in Kaur, Ravinder and Rajni Palriwala (eds) *Marrying in South Asia: Shifting Concepts, Changing Practices in a Globalising World*, New Delhi: Orient Black Swan, pp.208–33.

Kabeer, Naila (1984) 'Minus Lives. Women of Bangladesh', Change International Reports: Women and Society, no. 10.

Kabeer, Naila (1985) 'Do Women Gain from High Fertility?' in Afshar, Haleh (ed) *Women, Work and Ideology in the Third World* London: Tavistock Publications. pp. 83–106.

Kabeer, Naila (1986) *The Functions of Children in the Household Economy and Levels of Fertility: A Case Study of a Village in Bangladesh*, PhD dissertation, London School of Economics.

Kabeer, Naila (1989) 'Monitoring Poverty as if Gender Mattered. A Methodology for Rural Bangladesh', IDS Discussion Paper 255, Brighton: Institute of Development Studies.

Kabeer, Naila (1991a) 'The Quest for National Identity: Women, Islam and the State', *Feminist Review*, no. 37, pp.38–58. http://www.jstor.org/stable/1395470

Kabeer, Naila (1991b) 'Cultural Dopes or Rational Fools? Women and Labour Supply in the Bangladesh Garment Industry', *The*

European Journal of Development Research, vol. 3, no. 1, pp.133–60. https://doi.org/10.1080/09578819108426544

Kabeer, Naila (1996) 'Gender, Demographic Transition and the Economics of Family Size: Population Policy for a Human-Centred Development', Occasional Paper 7, Geneva: UNRISD.

Kabeer, Naila (1997) 'Women, Wages and Intra-household Power Relations in Urban Bangladesh', *Development and Change*, vol. 28, no. 2, pp.261–302. https://doi.org/10.1111/1467-7660.00043

Kabeer, Naila (1998) '"Money Can't Buy Me Love?" Re-evaluating Gender, Credit and Empowerment in Rural Bangladesh', IDS Discussion Paper 363, Institute of Development Studies, Brighton. https://opendocs.ids.ac.uk/opendocs/handle/20.500.12413/13879

Kabeer, Naila (2000) *The Power to Choose. Bangladeshi Women and Labour Market Decisions in London and Dhaka*, London: Verso Press.

Kabeer, Naila (2001a) 'Ideas, Economics and the "Sociology of Supply": Explanations for Fertility Decline in Bangladesh', *Journal of Development Studies*, vol. 38, no. 1, pp.29–70. https://doi.org/10.1080/00220380412331322181

Kabeer, Naila (2001b) 'Conflicts over Credit. Re-evaluating the Empowerment Potential of Loans to Women in Rural Bangladesh', *World Development*, vol. 29, no. 1, pp.63–84. https://doi.org/10.1016/S0305-750X(00)00081-4

Kabeer, Naila (2011) 'Between Affiliation and Autonomy: Navigating Pathways of Women's Empowerment and Gender Justice in Rural Bangladesh', *Development and Change*, vol. 42, no. 2, pp.499–528. https://doi.org/10.1111/j.1467-7660.2011.01703.x

Kabeer, Naila (2016) 'Economic Pathways to Women's Empowerment and Active Citizenship. What Does the Evidence from Bangladesh Tell Us?', *Journal of Development Studies*, vol. 53, no. 5, pp.1–15. https://doi.org/10.1080/00220388.2016.1205730

Kabeer, Naila (2019) 'The Evolving Politics of Labour Standards in Bangladesh: Taking Stock and Looking Forward', in Sanchita Banerjee Saxena (ed.) *Labour, Global Supply Chains and the Garment Industry in South Asia*, London: Routledge, pp.231–60.

Kabeer, Naila with Assaad, Ragui; Darkwah, Akosua; Mahmud, Simeen; Sholkamy, Hania; Tasneem, Sakiba; Tsikata, Dzodzi; and Sulaiman, Munshi (2013) 'Paid Work, Women's Empowerment and Inclusive Growth: Transforming the Structures of Constraint', UN Women, New York.

Kabeer, Naila and Huq, Lopita (2014) 'The Power of Relationships: Money, Love and Solidarity in a Landless Women's Organization in Bangladesh', in Cornwall, Andrea and Edwards, Jenny (eds) *Feminisms, Empowerment and Development. Changing Women's Lives*, London: Zed Books, pp.250–76.

Kabeer, Naila; Huq, Lopita; and Mahmud, Simeen (2014) 'Diverging Stories of "Missing Women" in South Asia: Is Son Preference Weakening in Bangladesh?', *Feminist Economics,* vol. 20, no. 4, pp.138–63. https://doi.org/10.1080/13545701.2013.857423

Kabeer, Naila; Huq, Lopita; and Rahaman, Mahabur M. (2021) 'Material Barriers, Cultural Boundaries: A Mixed-Methods Analysis of Gender and Labour Market Segmentation in Bangladesh', WIDER Working Paper No. 2021/169, Helsinki: UNU-WIDER.

Kabeer, Naila; Huq, Lopita; and Sulaiman, Munshi (2020) 'Paradigm Shift or Business as Usual: Workers' Perspectives on Multi-stakeholder Initiatives in Bangladesh', *Development and Change,* vol. 51, no. 5, pp.1360–98. https://onlinelibrary.wiley.com/doi/full/10.1111/dech.12574

Kabeer, Naila and Kabir, Ariful Haq (2009) 'Citizenship Narratives in the Absence of Good Governance. Voices of the Working Poor in Bangladesh', IDS Working Paper, vol. 2009, no. 331, Institute of Development Studies, Sussex.

Kabeer, Naila; Mahmud, Simeen; and Tasneem, Sakiba (2018) 'The Contested Relationship between Paid Work and Women's Empowerment: Empirical Analysis from Bangladesh', *The European Journal of Development Research*, vol. 30, pp.235–51. https://doi.org/10.1057/s41287-017-0119-y

Kabeer, Naila and Matin, Imran (2005) 'The Wider Social Impacts of BRAC's Group-Based Lending in Rural Bangladesh: Group Dynamics and Participation in Public Life', Research Monograph Series No. 25, BRAC, Dhaka.

Kabeer, Naila; Simeen, Mahmud; and Castro, Jairo G. Isaza (2012) 'NGOs and the Political Empowerment of Poor People in Rural Bangladesh: Cultivating the Habits of Democracy?', *World Development*, vol. 40, no. 10, pp.2044–62. https://doi.org/10.1016/j.worlddev.2012.05.011

Kabeer, Naila and Sulaiman, Munshi (2015) 'Assessing the Impact of Social Mobilization: Nijera Kori and the Construction of Collective Capabilities in Rural Bangladesh', *Journal of Human Development and Capabilities*, vol. 16, no. 1, pp.47–68. https://doi.org/10.1080/19452829.2014.956707

Kabir, M.; Chowdhury, Rafiquel Islam; and Amin, Ruhul (1995) 'Infant and Child Mortality Levels and Trends in Bangladesh', *Journal of Biosocial Science*, vol. 27, no. 2, pp.179–92. https://doi.org/10.1017/S0021932000022689

Kabir, Sandra M. (1996) 'An Experience of Religious Extremism in Bangladesh', *Reproductive Health Matters*, vol. 4, no. 8, pp.104–09. https://doi.org/10.1016/S0968-8080(96)90307-9

Kandiyoti, Deniz (1988) 'Bargaining with Patriarchy', *Gender and Society*, vol. 2, no. 3, pp.274–90. https://doi.org/10.1177/089124388002003004

Kapadia, Karin (1995) *Siva and Her Sisters. Gender, Caste and Class in Rural South India*, Oxford and New Delhi: Oxford University Press.

Karim, Lamia (2004) 'Democratizing Bangladesh. State, NGOs and Militant Islam', *Cultural Dynamics*, vol. 16, nos 2–3, pp.291–318, https://doi.org/10.1177/0921374004047752

Karim, Lamia (2008) 'Demystifying Microcredit. The Grameen Bank, NGOs and Neoliberalism in Bangladesh', *Cultural Dynamics*, vol. 20, no. 1, pp.5–29. https://doi.org/10.1177/0921374007088053

Karim, Mahbubul (1995) 'NGOs in Bangladesh: Issues of Legitimacy and Accountability', in Edwards, M. and Hulme, D. (eds) *Beyond the Magic Bullet: Non-Governmental Organisations – Performance and Accountability*, West Hartford, CT: Kumarian Press, pp.132–41.

Karim, S. (2007) 'Gendered Violence in Education: Realities for Adolescent Girls in Bangladesh', ActionAid Bangladesh.

Kaur, Ravinder (2007) 'Declining Juvenile Sex Ratios: Economy, Society and Technology', *Margin: The Journal of Applied Economic Research*, vol. 1, no. 2, pp.231–45. https://doi.org/10.1177/097380100700100204

Kaur, Ravinder; Bhalla, Surjit S.; Agarwal, Manoj K.; and Ramakrishnan, Prasanthi (2016) 'Sex Ratios at Birth. The Role of Gender, Class and Education', UNFPA, India.

Khan, Akbar Ali (1996) *Discovery of Bangladesh. Explorations into the Dynamics of a Hidden Nation*, Dhaka: University Press.

Khan, Ayesha (2018) *The Women's Movement in Pakistan. Activism, Islam and Democracy*, London: I.B. Tauris.

Khan, Mushtaq H. (2000) 'The Political Economy of Religion and Secularism in Bangladesh', in Basu, Subho and Das, Suronjan (eds) *Electoral Politics in South Asia*, Calcutta: K.P. Bagchi and Co., pp.176–200.

Khan, Mushtaq H. (2013) 'Bangladesh. Economic Growth in a Vulnerable Limited Access Order', in North, Douglass; Wallis, John; Webb, Steven; and Weingast, Barry (eds) *In the Shadow of Violence: Politics, Economics and the Problems of Development*, Cambridge: Cambridge University Press, pp.24–69.

Khan, Mushtaq, H. (2014) 'Aid and Governance in Vulnerable States: Bangladesh and Pakistan since 1971', *The Annals of the American*

Academy of Political and Social Science, vol. 656, no. 1, pp.59–78. https://doi.org/10.1177/0002716214543900

Khandker, Shahidur R. (1987) 'Labor Market Participation of Married Women in Bangladesh', *The Review of Economics and Statistics*, vol. 69, no. 3, pp.536–41. http://www.jstor.org/stable/1925545

Khandker, Shahidur; Bakht, Zaid; and Koolwal, Gayatri B. (2009) 'The Poverty Impact of Rural Roads. Evidence from Bangladesh', *Economic Development and Cultural Change*, vol. 57, no. 4, pp.685–722. https://doi.org/10.1086/598765

Khandker, Shahidur K. and Samad, Hussain A. (2014) 'Dynamic Effects of Microcredit in Bangladesh', Policy Research Working Paper 6821, Washington, DC: World Bank.

Khuda, Barkat-e- (1985) *Rural Development and Change: A Case Study of a Bangladesh Village*, Dhaka: University Press.

Khuda, Barket-e- and Hossain, Mian B. (1996) 'Fertility Decline in Bangladesh: Towards an Understanding of Major Causes', *Health Transition Review*, vol. 6, Supplement, pp.157–67. https://www.jstor.org/stable/40652257

Kibria, Nazli (1995) 'Culture, Social Class and Income Control in the Lives of Women Garment Workers in Bangladesh', *Gender and Society*, vol. 9, no. 3, pp.289–309. https://doi.org/10.1177/089124395009003003

Kibria, Nazli (1998) 'Becoming a Garments Worker: The Mobilization of Women into the Garments Factories of Bangladesh', UNRISD Occasional Paper, No. 9, United Nations Research Institute for Social Development (UNRISD), Geneva.

Klasen, Stephan and Wink, Claudia (2003) '"Missing Women": Revisiting the Debate', *Feminist Economics*, vol. 9, nos 2–3, pp.263–99. https://doi.org/10.1080/1354570022000077999

Kramsjo, B. and Wood, Geoff D. (1992) *Breaking the Chains: Collective Action for Social Justice among the Rural Poor in Bangladesh*, London: Intermediate Technology Publications.

Krause, Monica (2021) *Model Cases. On Canonical Research Objects and Sites*, London and Chicago, IL: University of Chicago Press.

Kumar, Upendra (2017) 'Religion and Politics. A Study of Bangladesh Jamaat-e-Islami', *Asian Journal of Research in Social Sciences and Humanities*, vol. 7, no. 5, pp.146–65. https://doi.org/10.5958/2249-7315.2017.00304.5

Labowitz, Sarah and Baumann-Pauly, Dorothèe (2014) *Business as Usual Is Not an Option. Supply Chains and Sourcing after Rana Plaza*, Stern Centre for Business and Human Rights, New York University. https://www.stern.nyu.edu/sites/default/files/assets/documents/con_047408.pdf

Lahiri, Sajal and Self, Sharmistha (2005) 'Exogamy and Bias Against Daughters in Healthcare Provision: A Theory and Evidence from Two Northern States in India', Discussion Papers, Paper 39. http://opensiuc.lib.siu.edu/econ_dp/39

Lahoti, Rahul and Swaminathan, Hema (2016) 'Economic Development and Women's Labour Force Participation in India', Feminist Economics, vol. 22, no. 2, pp.168–95. http://dx.doi.org/10.1080/13545701.2015.1066022

Lakshman, Kanchan (2006) 'Islamic Radicalization and Developmental Aid in South Asia', DIIS Working Paper no. 2006/8, Danish Institute for International Studies, Copenhagen.

The Lancet (1978) 'Editorial: Water with Sugar and Salt', Lancet, vol. 312, pp.300–301.

Landell-Mills, Samuel (1992) An Anthropological Account of Islamic Holy-Men in Bangladesh, PhD dissertation, University of London.

Larsen, Mattias (2009) Vulnerable Daughters in Times of Change: Emerging Contexts of Discrimination in Himachal Pradesh, India, PhD dissertation, University of Gothenburg.

Larson, Ann and Mitra, S.N. (1992) 'Family Planning in Bangladesh. An Unlikely Success Story', International Family Planning Perspectives, vol. 18, no. 4, pp.123–29. https://www.jstor.org/stable/2133539

Lerner, Daniel (1958) The Passing of Traditional Society: Modernizing the Middle East, New York: The Free Press.

Lewis, David J. (1991) 'Technologies and Transactions: A Study of the Interaction between New Technology and Agrarian Structure in Bangladesh', Centre for Social Studies, Dhaka University, Bangladesh.

Lewis, David J. (1996) 'Understanding Rural Entrepreneurship in a Bangladesh Village: Individuals, Roles and Structures', Small Enterprise Development, vol. 7, no. 4, pp.22–31. https://doi.org/10.3362/0957-1329.1996.034

Lewis, David (2011) Bangladesh. Politics, Economy and Civil Society, Cambridge: Cambridge University Press.

Lewis, David (2017) 'Organizing and Representing the Poor in a Clientilistic Democracy: The Decline of Radical NGOs in Bangladesh', Journal of Development Studies, vol, 53, no. 10, pp.1545–67. https://doi.org/10.1080/00220388.2017.1279732

Lindenbaum, Shirley (1981) 'Implications for Women of Changing Marriage Transactions in Bangladesh', Studies in Family Planning, vol. 12, no. 11, pp.394–401. https://www.jstor.org/stable/1965996

Lindenbaum, Shirley; Chakraborty, Manisha; and Mohammed, Elias (1985) 'The Influence of Maternal Education on Infant and Child Mortality in Bangladesh', Special Publication no. 23, ICDDR, B. Dhaka.

Lintner, Bertil (2004) 'Religious Extremism and Nationalism in Bangladesh', in Limaye, Satu P.; Malik, Mohan; and Wirsing, Robert (eds) *Religious Radicalism and Security in South Asia*, Asia Pacific Centre for Security Studies, pp.413–36.

Lipton, Michael (1974) 'Discussion of the Paper by S.R. Bose', in Robinson, E.A.G. and Griffin, Keith (eds) *The Economic Development of Bangladesh within a Socialist Framework*, London: Macmillan, pp.156–63.

Maddison, Angus (1970) 'The Historical Origins of Indian Poverty', *Banca Nationale Del Lavoro Quarterly Review*, vol. 23, no. 92, pp.31–91.

Maddison, Angus (2006) 'The World Economy. A Millennial Perspective', Development Centre Studies, OECD Development Centre, Paris.

Mahmud, Simeen (2003) 'Female Secondary School Stipend Programme in Bangladesh', Background Paper prepared for Education for All Global Monitoring Report 2003/04, UNESCO Paris.

Mahmud, Simeen and Amin, Sajeda (2006) 'Girls' Schooling and Marriage in Rural Bangladesh', in Hannum, E. and Fuller, B. (eds) *Children's Lives and Schooling across Societies. Research in the Sociology of Education*, vol. 15, Leeds: Emerald, pp.71–99. https://doi.org/10.1016/S1479-3539(06)15004-1

Mahmud, Simeen and Sultan, Maheen (2016) 'Community Health Workers as Agents of Change: Negotiating Pathways of Empowerment', BIGD Working Paper no. 32, BRAC Institute of Governance and Development, Dhaka.

Mahmud, Simeen and Tasneem, Sakiba (2011) 'The Under-Reporting of Women's Economic Activity in Bangladesh: An Examination of Official Statistics', BDI Working Paper 1, Dhaka: BRAC Development Institute.

Mahmud, Wahiduddin (2008) 'Social Development in Bangladesh: Path-ways, Surprises and Challenges', *Indian Journal of Human Development*, vol. 2, no. 1, pp.79–92. https://doi.org/10.1177/0973703020080104

Mahmud, Wahiduddin (2021) 'Poverty Reduction and Social Progress in Bangladesh: Revisiting Some Development Ideas', in Arsel, Murat; Das Gupta, Anirban; and Storm, Servaas (eds) *Reclaiming Development Studies: Essays for Ashwani Saith*, London and New York: Anthem Press, pp.163–78.

Mahmud, Wahiduddin and Osmani, S.R. (2017) *The Theory and Practice of Microcredit*, London and New York: Routledge. https://doi.org/10.4324/9781315413174

Maloney, Clarence (1977) 'Bangladesh and Its People in Prehistory', *Journal of the Institute of Bangladesh Studies*, vol. 2, pp.17–20.

Maloney, Clarence; Aziz, Ashraful K.M.; and Sarker, Profulla C. (1981) *Beliefs and Fertility in Bangladesh*, Dhaka: International Centre for Diarrhoeal Diseases.

Mandal, Sattar M.A. (2017) 'Growth of Mechanization in Bangladesh Agriculture: Role of Policies and Missing Links', in in Mandal, Sattar, M.A.; Biggs, Stephen D.; and Justice, Scott E. (eds) *Rural Mechanisation. A Driver in Agriculture Change and Rural Development*, Dhaka: Institute for Inclusive Finance and Development, pp.77–95. http://inm.org.bd/inm-published-a-new-book-on-rural-mechanisation/

Mandelbaum, David G. (1970) *Society in India. 2 volumes*, Berkeley, CA: University of California Press.

Mannan, Qazi Abdul (1966) *The Emergence and Development of Dobhasi Literature in Bengal up to 1855*, Dacca: Dacca University Press

Martin, J.T. (1923) Census of India 1921. Calcutta: Government of India.

Mason, Karen O. (1986) 'The Status of Women: Conceptual and Methodological Issues in Demographic Studies', *Sociological Forum*, vol. 1, no. 2, pp.284–300.

Mason, Karen O. (1988) 'The Impact of Women's Position on Demographic Change during the Course of Development: What Do We Know?', Paper presented at the IUSSP Conference on the Position of Woman and Demographic Change in the Course of Development, Asker (Oslo), Norway.

Mason, Karen O. and Taj, Anju M. (1987) 'Differences between Women's and Men's Reproductive Goals in Developing Countries', *Population and Development Review*, vol. 13, no. 4, pp.611–38. https://www.jstor.org/stable/1973025

McCarthy, Florence E. (1967) *Bengali Village Women. Mediators Between Tradition and Development*, MA dissertation, Michigan State University.

McCarthy, Florence (1993) 'Development from Within: Forms of Resistance to Development Processes among Rural Bangladeshi Women', in Clark, Alice W. (ed.) *Gender and Political Economy. Explorations of South Asian Systems*, Delhi and Oxford: Oxford University Press, pp.322–53.

McCarthy, Florence E. and Feldman, Shelley (1983) 'Rural Women Discovered: New Sources of Capital and Labour in Rural Bangladesh', *Development and Change*, vol. 14, no. 2, pp.211–36. https://doi.org/10.1111/j.1467-7660.1983.tb00151.x

McCord, Colin (1976) 'What's the Use of a Demonstration Project?', Report no. 45, Dhaka: Ford Foundation.

McLeod, Julie (2005) 'Feminists Re-reading Bourdieu. Old Debates and New Questions about Gender Habitus and Gender Change', *Theory and Research in Education*, vol. 3, no. 1, pp.11–30. https://doi.org/10.1177/1477878505049832

McNay, Lois (1999) 'Gender, Habitus and the Field. Pierre Bourdieu and the Limits of Reflexivity', *Theory Culture Society*, vol. 16, no. 1, pp.95–117.

Menon, Nivedita (1998) 'Women and Citizenship', in Chatterji, Partha (ed.) *Wages of Freedom. Fifty Years of the Indian Nation State*, New Delhi: Oxford University Press, pp.241–66.

Miller, Barbara D. (1981) *The Endangered Sex. Neglect of Female Children in Rural North India*, Ithaca, NY, and London: Cornell University Press.

Miller, Barbara D. (1983) 'Son Preference, Daughter Neglect and Juvenile Sex Ratios. Pakistan and Bangladesh Compare', Women and International Development Working Paper 30, Michigan State University, East Lansing.

Mines, Mattison (1972) 'Muslim Social Stratification in India: The Basis for Variation', *Southwestern Journal of Anthropology*, vol. 28, no. 4, pp.333–49. https://www.jstor.org/stable/3629316

Mita, Rezina and Simmons, Ruth (1995) 'Diffusion of the Culture of Contraception: Program Effects on Young Women in Rural Bangladesh', *Studies in Family Planning*, vol. 26, no. 1, pp.1–13. https://www.jstor.org/stable/2138046

Momayezi, Nasser (1997) 'Islamic Revivalism and the Quest for Political Power', *Journal of Conflict Studies*, vol. 17, no. 2, pp.115–32. https://journals.lib.unb.ca/index.php/JCS/article/view/11753

Montgomery, Mark (1999) 'Mortality Decline and the Demographic Response: Towards a New Agenda', Policy Research Division Working Paper no. 122, Population Council, New York. https://doi.org/10.31899/pgy6.1023

Montgomery, Richard; Bhattacharya, Debopriya; and Hulme, David (1996) 'Credit for the Poor in Bangladesh: the BRAC Rural Development Programme and the Government Thana Resource Development and Employment Programme', in Hulme, David and Mosley, Paul (eds) *Finance against Poverty. Volume 2. Country Case studies*, London: Routledge, pp.94–176.

Muhuri, Pradip K. and Preston, Samuel H. (1991) 'Effects of Family Composition on Mortality Differentials by Sex among Children in Matlab, Bangladesh', *Population and Development Review*, vol. 17, no. 3, pp.415–34. https://www.jstor.org/stable/1971948

Murshid, K.A.S. (2022) *The Odds Revisited: Political Economy of the Development of Bangladesh*, Cambridge: Cambridge University Press.

Nag (1991) 'Sex Preference in Bangladesh, India and Pakistan, and Its Effect on Fertility', Working Paper 29, The Population Council, New York.

Naher, Ainoon (2006) *Gender, Religion and Development in Bangladesh*, PhD dissertation, Heidelberg University. https://doi.org/10.11588/heidok.00006546

Naher, Ainoon (2010) '"Defending Islam and Women's Honour against NGOs" in Bangladesh', *Women's Studies International Forum*, vol. 33, no. 4, pp.316–24. https://doi.org/10.1016/j.wsif.2010.02.005

Nath, Jharna N. (1984) *Dynamics of Socio-economic Change and the Role and Status of Women in Natunpur: Case Study of a Bangladesh Village*, PhD dissertation, University of Dhaka.

Nazneen, Sohela (2017a) *The Women's Movement in Bangladesh. A Short History and Current Debates*, Friedrich-Ebert-Stiftung, Bangladesh.

Nazneen, Sohela (2017b) 'Negotiating Gender Equity in a Clientelist State: The Role of Informal Networks in Bangladesh', in Waylen, Georgina (ed.) *Gender and Informal Institutions*, London: Rowman and Littlefield International, pp.161–81.

Nazneen, Sohela (2018) 'Binary Framings, Islam and Struggle for Women's Empowerment in Bangladesh', *Feminist Dissent*, vol. 3, pp.194–230.

Nazneen, Sohela and Masud, Rezwan (2017) 'The Politics of Negotiating Gender Equity in Bangladesh', ESID Working Paper no. 76, Effective States and Inclusive Development Research Centre, University of Manchester.

Nicholas, Ralph W. (1962) *Villages of the Bengal Delta. A Study of Ecology and Peasant Society*, PhD dissertation, University of Chicago.

Nicholas, Ralph, W. (1973) 'Elites, Classes and Factions in Indian Politics: A Review Article', *South Asian Review*, vol. 6, no. 2, pp.145–53.

Nicolini, Davide (2012) *Practice Theory, Work and Organisation. An Introduction*, Oxford: Oxford University Press.

Notestein, Frank W. (1945) 'Population-The Long View', in Schultz, Theodore W. (ed.) *Food for the World*, Chicago, IL: University of Chicago Press, pp.36–57.

Ortner, Sherry B. (1984) 'Theory in Anthropology since the Sixties', *Comparative Studies in Society and History*, vol. 26, no. 1, pp.126–66. https://www.jstor.org/stable/178524

Ortner, Sherry B. (1989) *High Religion: A Cultural and Political History of Sherpa Buddhism*, Princeton, NJ: Princeton University Press.

Ortner, Sherry B. (2005) 'Subjectivity and Cultural Critique', *Anthropological Theory*, vol. 5, no. 1, pp.31–52. https://doi.org/10.1177/1463499605050867

Ortner, Sherry B. (2006) *Anthropology and Social Theory. Culture, Power and the Acting Subject*, Durham, NC, and London: Duke University Press.

Osmani, S.R. (1990) 'Structural Change and Poverty in Bangladesh: The Case of a False Turning Point', *Bangladesh Development Studies*, vol. 18, no. 3, pp.55–74. https://www.jstor.org/stable/41968778

Osmani, S.R. (2015) 'The Impact of Microcredit on Rural Labour Market in Bangladesh', Working Paper no. 37, Institute of Microfinance, Dhaka.

Overseas Development Institute (2010) 'Bangladesh's Progress in Health. Healthy Partnerships and Effective Pro-Poor Targeting', Development Progress Stories, Overseas Development Institute, London.

Papanek, Hannah (1973) 'Purdah: Separate Worlds and Symbolic Shelter', *Comparative Studies in Society and History*, vol. 15, no. 3, pp.289–325. https://www.jstor.org/stable/178258

Paprocki, Kasia (2021) *Threatening Dystopias. The Global Politics of Climate Change Adaptation in Bangladesh*, Ithaca, NY, and London: Cornell University Press.

Parvez, Saimum (2019) '"The Khilafah's Soldiers in Bengal": Analysing the Islamic State Jihadists and Their Violence Justification Narratives in Bangladesh', *Perspectives on Terrorism*, vol. 13, no. 5, pp.22–38. https://www.jstor.org/stable/26798576

Patnaik, Utsa (1990) 'Some Economic and Political Consequences of the Green Revolution India', in Bernstein, Henry; Crow, Ben; Mckintosh Maureen; and Martin, Charlotte (eds) *The Food Question: Profits versus People*, New York: Monthly Review Press, pp.80–90.

Pattanaik, Smruti S. (2009) 'Ascendancy of the Religious Right in Bangladesh Politics: A Study of Jamaat Islami', *Strategic Analysis*, vol. 33 no. 2, pp.273–86. https://doi.org/10.1080/09700160802702668

Pattnaik, Itishree; Lahiri-Dutt, Kuntala; Lockie, Stewart; and Pritchard, Bill (2017) 'The Feminization of Agriculture or the Feminization of Agrarian Distress? Tracking the Trajectory of Women in Agriculture in India', *Journal of the Asia Pacific Economy*, vol. 23, no. 1, pp.138–55. https://doi.org/10.1080/13547860.2017.1394569

Paul-Majumder, Pratima and Begum, Anwara (2006) *Engendering Garment Industry. The Bangladesh Context*, Dhaka: University Press.

Pereira, Faustina; Shahnaz, Huda; and Hossain, Sara (2019) *Revisiting Personal Laws in Bangladesh. Proposals for Reform*, Leiden: Brill Nijhoff.

Phillips, James F.; Simmons, Ruth; Koenig, Michael A.; and Chakraborty, J. (1988) 'Determinants of Reproductive Change in a Traditional Society. Evidence from Matlab, Bangladesh', *Studies in Family Planning*, vol. 19, no. 6, pp.313–34. https://www.jstor.org/stable/1966627

Piechulek, Helga; Aldana, Jorge Mendoza; and Hasan, Md. Nazmul (1999) 'Feeding Practices and Malnutrition in Children in Rural Bangladesh', *Food and Nutrition Bulletin*, vol. 20, no. 4, pp.395–400.

Pitt, Mark, M. and Khandker, Shahidur R. (1998) 'The Impact of Group-Based Credit Programs on Poor Households in Bangladesh: Does the Gender of Participants Matter?', *Journal of Political Economy*, vol. 106, no. 5, pp.958–96. http://www.jstor.org/stable/10.1086/250037

Quine, Willard V. (1981) *Theories and Things*, Cambridge, MA: Harvard University Press.

Qureshi, Ishtiaq Hussain (1965) *The Struggle for Pakistan*, Karachi: Karachi University Press.

Rahman, Mizanur; Akbar, Jalaluddin; Phillips, James A.; and Becker, Stan (1992) 'Contraceptive Use in Matlab, Bangladesh: The Role of Gender Preference', *Studies in Family Planning*, vol. 23, no. 4, pp.229–42. https://www.jstor.org/stable/1966885

Rahman, Aminur (1999) *Women and Microcredit in Rural Bangladesh. An Anthropological Study of Grameen Bank Lending*, Boulder, CO: Westview Press.

Rahman, Hossain Zillur (2006) 'Bangladesh 2015. Crossing Miles…', PPRC Policy Paper. Power and Participation Research Centre, Dhaka.

Rahman, Hossain Zillur (2014) 'Urbanization in Bangladesh: Challenges and Priorities', Conference of the Bangladesh Economists' Forum, 21–22 June, Dhaka.

Rahman, Mizanur; Da Vanzo, Julie; and Razzaque, Abdur (2002) 'When Will Bangladesh Reach Replacement-Level Fertility? The Role of Education and Family Planning Services', *Population Bulletin of the United Nations. Completing the Fertility Transition*, Special Issues 48–49, pp.317–30. http://www.un.org/esa/population/publications/completingfertility /bulletin-english.pdf#page=330

Rahman, Md. Anisur (1974a) 'Discussion of Papers by M. Anisur Rahman and Mohiuddin Alamgir', in Robinson, E.A.G. and Griffin, Keith (eds) *The Economic Development of Bangladesh within a Socialist Framework*, London: Macmillan, pp.58–66.

Rahman, Md. Anisur (1974b) 'Priorities and Methods for Socialist Development of Bangladesh', in Robinson, E.A.G. and Griffin, Keith (eds) *The Economic Development of Bangladesh within a Socialist Framework*, London: Macmillan, pp.16–26.

Rahman, Rushidan, I. (1986a) 'The Wage Employment Market for Rural Women in Bangladesh', Bangladesh Institute of Development Studies, Dhaka.

Rahman, Rushidan, I. (1986b) 'Impact of the Grameen Bank on the Situation of Poor Rural Women', Bangladesh Institute of Development Studies, Dhaka.

Rahman, Rushidan, I. and Islam, Rizwanul (2013) 'Female Labour Force Participation in Bangladesh: Trends, Drivers and Barriers', ILO Asia-Pacific Working Paper Series.

Rahman, Tariq (2011) *From Hindi to Urdu: A Social and Political History*, New Delhi: Orient Black Swan.

Raihan, Selim and Bourguignon, François (2023) 'An Institutional Diagnostic of Bangladesh: An Introduction', in Raihan, Selim; Bourguignon, François; and Salam, Umar, *Is the Bangladesh Paradox Sustainable? The Institutional Diagnostic Project*, Cambridge: Cambridge University Press, pp.11–28.

Raihan, Selim; Bourguignon, François; and Salam, Umar (2023) *Is the Bangladesh Paradox Sustainable? The Institutional Diagnostic Project*, Cambridge: Cambridge University Press.

Ranis, Gustav (1974a) 'Discussion of Papers by M. Anisur Rahman and Mohiuddin Alamgir', in Robinson, E.A.G. and Griffin, Keith (eds) *The Economic Development of Bangladesh within a Socialist Framework*, London: Macmillan, pp.59–66.

Ranis, Gustav (1974b) 'Brief Reflections on the Central Issues of Policy in Bangladesh', *Bangladesh Development Studies*, vol, 2, no. 4, pp.839–56. https://www.jstor.org/stable/i40035827

Rashid, Haroun Er (1965) *East Pakistan. A Systematic Regional Geography and its Development Planning Aspects*, Lahore: Sh. Ghulam Ali and Sons.

Rashid, Sabina F. (2006) 'Small Powers, Little Choice: Contextualizing Reproductive and Sexual Rights in Slums in Bangladesh', *IDS Bulletin*, vol. 37, no. 5, pp.69–76.

Ray, Tridip; Chaudhuri, Arka Roy and Sahai, Komol (2017) 'Whose education matters? An analysis of inter caste marriage in India', Discussion Paper 17-05, Indian Statistical Institute, New Delhi. https://www.isid .ac.in/~epu/wp-content/uploads/2017/09/dp17-05.pdf

Razzaque, Abdur (1999) 'Preference for Children and Subsequent Fertility in Matlab: Does Wife-Husband Agreement Matter?', *Journal of Biosocial Science*, vol. 31, no. 1, pp.17–28. https://doi.org/10.1017/S0021932099000176

Razzaque, Abdur; Streatfield, Peter Kim; and Evans, Ann (2007) 'Family Size and Children's Education in Matlab, Bangladesh', *Journal of Biosocial Science*, vol. 39, pp.245–56. https://doi.org/10.1017/S0021932006001398

Razzaque, Mohammad A. (2010) 'Microfinance and Poverty Reduction: Evidence from a Longitudinal Household Panel Data Set', *Bangladesh Development Studies*, vol. 33, no. 3, pp.47–68. https://www.jstor.org /stable/23339852

Reay, Diane (2004) '"It's All Becoming a Habitus": Beyond the Habitual Use of Habitus in Educational Research', *British Journal of Sociology of Education*, vol. 25, no. 4, pp.431–44. https://www.jstor.org/stable/4128669

Redfield, Robert (1955) 'The Social Organization of Tradition', *The Far Eastern Quarterly*, vol. 15, no. 1, pp.13–21. https://www.jstor.org/stable/2942099

Reich, David (2019) *Who We Are and How We Got Here*, Oxford: Oxford University Press.

Riaz, Ali (2004) *God Willing. The Politics of Islamism in Bangladesh*, Oxford and New York: Rowman and Littlefield.

Riaz, Ali (2010) 'The Politics of Islamization in Bangladesh', in Riaz, Ali (ed.) *Religion and Politics in South Asia*, London and New York: Routledge, pp.45–70.

Ritchie, Hannah and Roser, Max (2019) 'Gender Ratio'. https://ourworldindata.org/gender-ratio

Robinson, E.A.G. (1974a) 'Discussion of Papers by M. Anisur Rahman and Mohiuddin Alamgir', in Robinson, E.A.G. and Griffin, Keith (eds) *The Economic Development of Bangladesh within a Socialist Framework*, London: Macmillan, pp.59–66.

Robinson, E.A.G. (1974b) 'Introduction', in Robinson, E.A.G. and Griffin, Keith (eds) *The Economic Development of Bangladesh within a Socialist Framework*, London: Macmillan, pp.xi–xxii.

Robinson, E.A.G. (1974c) 'Discussion of the Paper by A.F.A. Husain', in Robinson, E.A.G. and Griffin, Keith (eds) *The Economic Development of Bangladesh within a Socialist Framework*, London: Macmillan, 322–26.

Robinson, E.A.G. and Griffin, Keith (eds) (1974) *The Economic Development of Bangladesh within a Socialist Framework*, London: Macmillan.

Roser, Max (2024) 'Fertility Rate. How Does the Number of Children Vary across the World?' https://ourworldindata.org/fertility-rate

Rostow, Walt Whitman (1960) *The Stages of Economic Growth. A Non-Communist Manifesto*, Cambridge: Cambridge University Press.

Roy, Asim (1983) *The Islamic Syncretistic Tradition in Bengal*, Princeton, NJ: Princeton University Press.

Roy, Nihar Ranjan (1945) 'Medieval Bengali Culture – a Socio-Historical Interpretation', *Visva-Bharati Quarterly*, vol. 11.

Rozario, Shanti (2006) 'The New Burqa in Bangladesh; Empowerment or Violation of Women's Rights', *Women's Studies International Forum*, vol. 29, no. 4, pp.368–80. https://doi.org/10.1016/j.wsif.2006.05.006

Safilios-Rothschild, Constantina and Mahmud, Simeen (1989) 'Women's Roles in Agriculture. Present Trends and Potential for Growth', *Bangladesh Agricultural Sector Review*, UNDP and UNIFEM, Dhaka.

Saha, Unnati Rani and Bairagi, Radheshyam (2007) 'Inconsistencies in the Relationship between Contraceptive Use and Fertility in Bangladesh',

International Family Planning Perspectives, vol. 33, no. 1, pp.31–37. https://www.jstor.org/stable/30039190

Salway, Sarah; Jesmin, Sonia; and Rahman, Shahana (2005) 'Women's Employment in Urban Bangladesh: A Challenge to Gender Identity?', *Development and Change*, vol. 36, no. 2, pp.317–49. https://doi.org/10.1111/j.0012-155X.2005.00413.x

Sawada, Yasuyuki; Mahmud, Minhaj; and Kitano, Naohiro (2018) *Economic and Social Development of Bangladesh: Miracle and Challenges*, London: Palgrave Macmillan.

Schoen, Roslyn F. (2018) 'Shifting the Burden to Daughters: A Qualitative Examination of Population Policy, Labor Migration and Filial Responsibility in Rural Bangladesh', *Qualitative Sociology Review*, vol. 14, no. 3, pp.106–24. https://doi.org/10.18778/1733-8077.14.3.06

Schuler, Sidney Ruth (2007) 'Rural Bangladesh: Sound Policies, Evolving Gender Norms, and Family Strategies', in Lewis, Maureen A. and Lockheed, Marlaine E. (eds) *Exclusion, Gender and Education Case Studies from the Developing World*, Washington, DC: Centre for Global Development, pp.179–204.

Schuler, Sidney Ruth and Hashemi, Syed M. (1994) 'Credit Programs, Women's Empowerment and Contraceptive Use in Rural Bangladesh', *Studies in Family Planning*, vol. 25, no. 2, pp.65–76. https://www.jstor.org/stable/2138085

Schuler, Sidney Ruth; Hashemi, Syed M.; Cullum, Amy; and Hassan, Mirza (1996a) 'The Advent of Family Planning as a Social Norm in Bangladesh: Women's Experiences', *Reproductive Health Matters*, vol. 4, no. 7, pp.66–78. https://doi.org/10.1016/S0968-8080(96)90007-5

Schuler, Sidney Ruth; Hashemi, Syed, M.; Riley, Ann P.; and Akhter, Shireen (1996b) 'Credit Programs, Patriarchy and Men's Violence against Women in Rural Bangladesh', *Social Science and Medicine*, vol. 43, no. 12, pp.1729–42. https://doi.org/10.1016/S0277-9536(96)00068-8

Schuler, Sidney Ruth and Hossain, Zakir (1998) 'Family Planning Clinics through Women's Eyes and Voices. A Case Study from Rural Bangladesh', *International Family Planning Perspectives*, vol. 24, no. 4, pp.170–75.

Schuler, Sidney Ruth; Islam, Farzana; and Rottach, Elizabeth (2010) 'Women's Empowerment Revisited: A Case Study from Bangladesh', *Development in Practice*, vol. 20, no. 7, pp.840–54.

Scott, James C. (1990) *Domination and the Arts of Resistance: Hidden Transcripts*, New Haven, CT: Yale University Press.

Sen, Abhijit and Ghosh, Jayati (2017) 'Indian Agriculture after Liberalisation', *Bangladesh Development Studies*, vol. 40a, nos 1–2, pp.53–71. https://www.jstor.org/stable/26572744

Sen, Amartya (1990a) 'More than 100 Million Women Are Missing', *The New York Review of Books*, 20 December. https://www.nybooks.com /articles/1990/12/20/more-than-100-million-women-are-missing

Sen, Amartya (1990b) 'Gender and Co-operative Conflicts', in Tinker, Irene (ed.) *Persistent Inequalities. Women and World Development*, New York and Oxford: Oxford University Press.

Sen, Amartya (1999) *Development as Freedom*, New York: Knopf and Oxford: Oxford University Press.

Sen, Amartya (2013) 'What's Happening in Bangladesh?', *The Lancet*, vol. 382, no. 9909, pp.1966–68. https://doi.org/10.1016/S0140-6736(13)62162-5

Sen, Binayak (2019) 'Rural Transformation, Occupational Choice and Poverty Reduction in Bangladesh during 2010–2016', *Bangladesh Development Studies*, Vol. 42, nos 1–2, pp.263–87.

Sen, Binayak and Acharya, Shambhu (1997) 'Health and Poverty in Bangladesh', *World Health 50th Year*, no. 5, pp.28–29.

Sen, Binayak; Mujeri, Mustafa K.; and Shahabuddin, Quazi (2007) 'Explaining Pro-Poor Growth in Bangladesh: Puzzles, Evidence and Implications', in Besley, Tim and Cord, Louise J. (eds) *Delivering on the Promise of Pro-Poor Growth. Insights and Lessons from Country Experiences*, Basingstoke and Washington, DC: Palgrave Macmillan and World Bank, pp.79–113.

Sen, Binayak and Ali, Zulfiqar (2009) 'Spatial Inequality in Social Progress in Bangladesh', *Bangladesh Development Studies*, vol. 32, no. 2, pp.53–78. https://ideas.repec.org/a/ris/badest/0480.html

Sewell, William H. Jr. (1992) 'Theory of Structure: Duality, Agency and Transformation', *American Journal of Sociology*, vol. 98, no. 1, pp.1–29. https://www.jstor.org/stable/2781191

Shehabuddin, Elora (1992) 'Empowering Rural Women: The Impact of Grameen Bank in Bangladesh', Grameen Bank, Dhaka.

Shehabuddin, Elora (1999) 'Beware the Bed of Fire: Gender, Democracy, and the Jamaat-i-Islami in Bangladesh', *Journal of Women's History*, vol. 10, no. 4, pp.148–71. https://doi.org/10.1353/jowh.2010.0532

Shehabuddin, Elora (2008) *Reshaping the Holy. Democracy, Development and Muslim Women in Bangladesh*, New York: Columbia University Press.

Shove, Elizabeth; Pantzer, Mika; and Watson, Matt (2012) *The Dynamics of Social Practice. Everyday Life and How It Changes*, London: Sage.

Siddiqi, Dina Mahnaz (1996) *Women in Question. Gender and Labour in Bangladeshi Factories*, PhD dissertation, University of Michigan.

Siddhanta, Suddhasil; Agnihotri, Satish B; and Nandy, Debashish (2009) 'Sex Ratio Patterns among the Scheduled Castes in India 1981–2001'. https://doi.org/10.2139/ssrn.2733500

Simmons, Ruth (1996) 'Women's Lives in Transition: A Qualitative Analysis of the Fertility Decline in Bangladesh', *Studies in Family Planning*, vol. 27, no. 5, pp.252–68. https://www.jstor.org/stable/2137997

Simmons, Ruth; Baqee, Laila; Koenig, Michael A.; and Phillips, James F. (1988) 'Beyond Supply: The Importance of Family Planning Workers in Rural Bangladesh', *Studies in Family Planning*, vol. 19, no. 1, pp.29–38. http://www.jstor.org/stable/1966737

Simmons, Ruth; Mita, Rezina; and Koenig, Michael, A. (1992) 'Employment in Family Planning and Women's Status in Bangladesh', *Studies in Family Planning* vol. 23, no. 2, pp.97–109. https://www.jstor.org/stable/1966539

Skinner, Jonathan (1991) 'Prospects for Agricultural Land Taxation in Developing Countries', *The World Bank Economic Review*, vol. 5, no. 3, pp.493–511. https://www.jstor.org/stable/3990009

Sobhan, Rehman (1979) 'Politics of Food and Famine in Bangladesh', *Economic and Political Weekly*, vol. 14, no. 48, pp.1973–80. https://www.jstor.org/stable/4368187

Sobhan, Rehman (1991) 'Industrial Policies and State of Industrialization in Bangladesh', *Bangladesh Development Studies*, vol. 19, no. 1–2, pp.201–15. https://www.jstor.org/stable/40795402

Sobhan, Rehman (2000) 'The State of Governance in Bangladesh', in Sobhan, Rehman (ed.) *Changes and Challenges: A Review of Bangladesh's Development 2000*, Dhaka: Centre for Policy Dialogue.

Sobhan, Rehman and Ahmad, Muzaffer (1980) *Public Enterprise in an Intermediate Regime: A Study in the Political Economy of Bangladesh*, Dhaka: Bangladesh Institute of Development Studies.

Sopher, David E. (1980) 'The Geographic Patterning of Culture in India', in. Sopher, David E (ed.) *An Exploration of India. Geographical Perspectives on Society and Culture*, London: Longman, pp.289–326.

Srinivas, M.N. (1956) 'A Note on Sanskritization and Westernization', *The Far Eastern Quarterly*, vol. 15, no. 4, pp.481–96. https://www.jstor.org/stable/2941919

Srinivas, M.N. (1962) *Caste in India and Other Essays*, Bombay: Asia Publishing House.

Srinivasan, Sharada (2005) 'Daughters or Dowries? The Changing Nature of Dowry Practices in South India', *World Development*, vol. 33, no. 4, pp. 593–615. https://doi.org/10.1016/j.worlddev.2004.12.003

Srinivasan, Sharada (2012) *Daughter Deficit. Sex Selection in Tamil Nadu*, New Delhi: Women Unlimited.

Stevens, Robert D. (1976) 'Themes in Economic Growth and Social Change in Rural Pakistan: An Introduction', in Stevens, Robert D., Alavi, Hamza; and Bertocci, Peter J. (eds) *Rural Development in Bangladesh and Pakistan*, Honolulu, HI: University Press of Hawaii, pp.187–97.

Stoeckel, John and Choudhury, Moebul A. (1973) *Fertility, Infant Mortality and Family Planning in Bangladesh*, Dhaka: Oxford University Press.

Sukontamarn, Pataporn (2005) 'The Entry of NGO Schools and Girls' Educational Outcomes in Bangladesh', Political Economy and Public Policy Series no. 10, London School of Economics, UK.

Sukontamarn, Pataporn (2013) 'Bangladesh's Food for Education Program: The Effects on Two Groups of Targeted Households', *Education Economics*, vol. 21, no. 1, pp.79–91. https://doi.org/10.1080/09645292.2010.521659

Talukder, Md. Noorunnabi; Rob, Ubaidur; and Noor, Forhana Rahman (2014) *Assessment of Sex Selection in Bangladesh*, Dhaka: Population Council. https://doi.org/10.31899/rh10.1016

Talukder, Noorunnabi; Rob, Ubaidur; Hossain, Md. Irfanl; and Noor, Forhana Rahman (2015) 'Understanding Factors Influencing Adverse Sex Ratios at Birth in Bangladesh', Population Council, Dhaka.

Tharoor, Shashi (2018) *Inglorious Empire. What the British Did to India*, London: Penguin Books.

Thompson, W.J. (1921) *Census of Bengal, 1921*, Calcutta: Bengal Secretariat.

Thorner, Daniel (1974) 'Comments on Dr. Duza's Paper', in Robinson, E.A.G. and Griffin, Keith (eds) *The Economic Development of Bangladesh within a Socialist Framework*, London: Macmillan, pp.284–85.

Thornton, Paul; Devine, Joe; Houtzager, P. Peter; Wright, David; and Rozario, Santi (2000) *Partners in Development. A Review of Big NGOs in Bangladesh*, Dhaka: DFID.

Thornton, Jacqui (2019) 'WHO Report Shows that Women Outlive Men Worldwide', *British Medical Journal*, 365. https://www.bmj.com/content/365/bmj.l1631.full

Todd, Helen (1996) *Women at the Centre. Grameen Bank Borrowers after One Decade*, Boulder, CO: Westview Press.

Tong, Yumping (2022) 'India's Sex Ratio at Birth Begins to Normalize', Pew Research Centre. https://www.pewresearch.org/religion/2022/08/23 /indias-sex-ratio-at-birth-begins-to-normalize

Townsend, Janet and Momsen, Janet H. (1987) 'Towards a Geography of Gender in Developing Market Economies', in Momsen, Janet H. and Townsend, Janet (eds) *Geography of Gender in the Third World*, London: Hutchinson, pp.27–81.

Umar, Badruddin (1996) 'On the Subject of NGOs' (Bengali), *Ajker Kagoj*, 26 April.

UNDP (1989) 'Bangladesh Agricultural Sector Review, Main Report. Policies and Performance', UNDP, Dhaka.

UNDP (1996) 'A Pro-Poor Agenda. Poor People's Perspectives', UNDP, Dhaka.

UNICEF (2011) *A Perspective on Gender Equality in Bangladesh*, Dhaka: UNICEF.

UNICEF (2012) *Progress in Child Wellbeing*, Dhaka: UNICEF. http://www .unicef.org/bangladesh/Progress_on_Child_Wellbeing_2012.pdf

US Department of Commerce (1993) 'Population Trends Bangladesh', US Department of Commerce.

Vanek, Jaroslav (1974) 'Discussion of Papers by M. Anisur Rahman and Mohiuddin Alamgir', in Robinson, E.A.G. and Griffin, Keith (eds) *The Economic Development of Bangladesh within a Socialist Framework*, London: Macmillan, pp.59–66.

Van Schendel, Willem (2009) *A History of Bangladesh*, Cambridge: Cambridge University Press.

Varshney, Ashutosh (2017) 'Growth, Inequality and Nationalism', *Journal of Democracy*, vol. 28, no. 3, pp.41–51.

Villareal, Magdalena (1994) *Wielding and Yielding: Power, Subordination and Gender Identity in the Context of a Mexican Development Project*, PhD dissertation, University of Wageningen Holland.

Visaria, Abhijit (2015) 'Religion and Son Preference in India and Bangladesh: Three Essays on Comparing Hindus and Muslims on Son Preference and Sex Differentials in Child Health', Publicly Accessible Penn Dissertations. http://repository.upenn.edu/edissertations/2079

Visaria, Pravin M. (1961) 'The Sex Ratio of the Population of India', Monograph 10, Census of India 1961, New Delhi: Office of the Registrar General.

Visaria, Pravin M. (1967) 'The Sex Ratio of the Population of India and Pakistan and Regional Variations during 1901–1961', in Bose, A. (ed.)

Patterns of Population Change in India, 1951–61, Mumbai: Allied Publishers.

Vreede-de-Stuers, Cora (1968) *Parda: A Study of Muslim Women's Life in Northern India*, New York: Humanities Press.

Westergaard, Kirsten (1983) 'Pauperization and Rural Women in Bangladesh: A Case Study', Bangladesh Academy for Rural Development, Comilla.

Westergaard, Kirsten (1994) *People's Empowerment in Bangladesh. NGO Strategies*, CDR Working Paper no. 94.10.30, Centre For Development Research, Copenhagen.

White, Sarah C. (1992) *Arguing with the Crocodile. Gender and Class in Bangladesh*, London: Zed Books.

White, Sarah C. (2012) 'Beyond the Paradox: Religion, Family and Modernity in Contemporary Bangladesh', *Modern Asian Studies*, vol. 46, no. 5, pp.1429–58. https://www.jstor.org/stable/41683032

Wood, Geoffrey, D. (1999) 'From Farms to Services. Agricultural Reformation in Bangladesh', in Rogaly, Ben; Harriss-White, Barbara; and Bose, Sugata (eds) *Sonar Bangla? Agricultural Growth and Agrarian Change in West Bengal and Bangladesh*, New Delhi and London: Sage, pp.303–28.

World Bank (1972) 'Reconstructing the Economy of Bangladesh, vol. 1', Report SA-35a. https://documents1.worldbank.org/curated/en/240201468013773779/pdf/multi0page.pdf

World Bank (2003a) 'Bangladesh Development Policy Review: Impressive Achievements but Continuing Challenges', Report No. 26154-BD, Poverty Reduction and Economic Management Sector Unit, South Asia Region, World Bank, Washington, DC.

World Bank. (2003b). 'Bangladesh: Public Expenditure Review 2003', World Bank, Washington, DC.

World Bank (2006a) 'World Bank Annual Report 2006', World Bank, Washington, DC.

World Bank (2006b) 'Economics and Governance of Nongovernmental Organisations in Bangladesh', Development Series Paper no. 11, World Bank, Dhaka.

World Bank (2008) *Whispers to Voices. Gender and Social Transformation in Bangladesh*, Bangladesh Development Series Paper No. 22, World Bank, Washington, DC.

World Bank (2014) 'India: Women, Work and Employment', Report no: ACS7935, Washington DC.

Xu, Sijia; Shonchoy, Abu, S.; and Fujii, Tomoki (2019) 'Illusion of Gender Parity in Education: Intrahousehold Resource Allocation in Bangladesh', ADB Working Paper Series no. 1004, Asian Development Bank Institute, Manila.

Yan, Rani Yan and Roy, Raja Devasish (2019) 'Personal Laws of the Indigenous Peoples of the Chittagong Hill Tracts, Bangladesh: A Gender Perspective', in Pereira, Faustina; Huda Shahnaz; and Hossain, Sara (eds) *Revisiting Personal Laws in Bangladesh. Proposals for Reform*, Leiden: Brill Nijhoff, pp.212–45.

Zaidi, Batool and Morgan, Phillip S. (2016) 'In Pursuit of Sons: Additional Births or Sex-Selective Abortion in Pakistan', *Population and Development Review*, vol. 42, no. 4, pp.693–710. https://doi.org/10.1111/padr.12002

Index

www.ingramcontent.com/pod-product-compliance
Lightning Source LLC
Chambersburg PA
CBHW050332270326
41926CB00016B/3422